"This analysis of charities and th[...]
at any time but is especially use[...]
facing huge challenges as we e[...]"
**Baroness Jill Pitkeathley, President, NCVO
(National Council for Voluntary Organisations)**

"This timely book describes the interdependent web of
charities and civil society organisations and the public good
they bring and clearly illuminates a world that is too often
misunderstood... it will help those in charities, and those who
observe them, to navigate our increasingly uncertain future."
Dame Julia Unwin, Civil Society Futures

"Journalistic appeal and outstanding expertise combine
to provide an impartial, comprehensive understanding of
the sector. Perceptive insights into current opportunities
suggest even greater future roles for charities."
Charles Jardine, London South Bank University

"In an age when generalised cynicism extends to charities
and their donors, it is important to be reminded of the good
achieved by those who set up, run and voluntarily donate
their time and money to try and make things better. The
charity sector is underappreciated, often patronised and rarely
given sufficient credit. I hope this book helps to change that."
**Beth Breeze, Centre for Philanthropy,
University of Kent**

"Charities are needed, yet threatened right now, and
this engaging, exhaustive and passionately argued
book offers a corrective to simplistic accounts that
serve to marginalise charities' role in society."
James Rees, University of Wolverhampton

WHAT HAVE CHARITIES EVER DONE FOR US?

The Stories Behind the Headlines

Stephen Cook and Tania Mason

First published in Great Britain in 2021 by

Policy Press, an imprint of Bristol University Press
University of Bristol
1-9 Old Park Hill
Bristol
BS2 8BB
UK
t: +44 (0)117 954 5940
e: bup-info@bristol.ac.uk

Details of international sales and distribution partners are available at
policy.bristoluniversitypress.co.uk

British Library Cataloguing in Publication Data
A catalogue record for this book is available from the British Library.

ISBN 978-1-4473-5988-3 paperback
ISBN 978-1-4473-5989-0 ePub
ISBN 978-1-4473-5990-6 ePdf

Cover design: Latte Goldstein, River Design
Front cover image: Shutterstock 1447305383

Bristol University Press and Policy Press use
environmentally responsible print partners.

Printed and bound in Great Britain by TJ Books Limited,
Padstow

Charities are the eyes, ears and conscience of society. They mobilise, they provide, they inspire, they advocate and they unite. From small local organisations run entirely by volunteers to major global organisations with turnover in the hundreds of millions, their work touches almost every facet of British civic life.

(House of Lords Select Committee on Charities, *Stronger Charities for a Stronger Society*, March 2017)

Contents

List of abbreviations

Acevo	Association of Chief Executives of Voluntary Organisations
AMRC	Association of Medical Research Charities
ASH	Action on Smoking and Health
BAME	Black and minority ethnic
BHF	British Heart Foundation
BRAC	Building Resources Across Communities
CAF	Charities Aid Foundation
CAMI	Community Attitudes to Mental Illness
CASC	community amateur sports club
CEO	chief executive officer
CIC	community interest company
CIO	charitable incorporated organisation
CQC	Care Quality Commission
CRC	Community Rehabilitation Company
CRE	Commission for Racial Equality
CRUK	Cancer Research UK
CVS	Council for Voluntary Service
DCMS	Department for Digital, Culture, Media and Sport
DfID	Department for International Development
DHSC	Department of Health and Social Care
ESFA	Education and Skills Funding Agency
HHA	Hope Health Action
ICO	Information Commissioner's Office
IEA	Institute of Economic Affairs
IFAW	International Fund for Animal Welfare
IPS	industrial and provident society
IRW	Islamic Relief Worldwide
ISC	Independent Schools Council
JCWI	Joint Council for the Welfare of Immigrants
LGBT	lesbian, gay, bisexual and trans

NABB	National Association of Blood Bikes
NAO	National Audit Office
Navca	National Association for Voluntary and Community Action
NCVO	National Council for Voluntary Organisations
NGO	non-governmental organisation
NHS	National Health Service
NICE	National Institute for Health and Care Excellence
NSPCC	National Society for the Prevention of Cruelty to Children
OCS	Office for Civil Society
PAC	public accounts committee
PICC	peripherally inserted central catheter
PTSD	post-traumatic stress disorder
RNIB	Royal National Institute of Blind People
RNID	Royal National Institute for Deaf People
RNLI	Royal National Lifeboat Institution
RSPB	Royal Society for the Protection of Birds
RSPCA	Royal Society for the Prevention of Cruelty to Animals
SAS	Surfers Against Sewage
TfL	Transport for London
TR	Transforming Rehabilitation
Unicef	United Nations Children's Fund
VAT	Value Added Tax
VCS	voluntary and community sector
WHO	World Health Organization
WWF	World Wide Fund for Nature
XR	Extinction Rebellion

Acknowledgements

Our thanks go to scores, if not hundreds, of people who have helped us over the years to understand charities and voluntary organisations, including their successes, dilemmas and setbacks. We are particularly grateful to more than 80 people who agreed to be interviewed for this book, including ten users of charities' services who gave us their personal stories, and to a dozen charities we visited to gain a detailed impression of their work. Special thanks go to Joe Saxton, head of the research consultancy nfpSynergy, who conceived the idea of a book about the importance of charities, provided some initial funding, but stood back from deciding or approving the content. Several specialists kindly read and commented on parts of the book for us, which was invaluable, and we have drawn heavily on the knowledge and experience of colleagues at Third Sector and Civil Society Media: many thanks to them all, and to our editors at Policy Press who helped us improve the structure and the text. We would also like to pay special tribute to the late Daniel Phelan, who supported and celebrated the work of charities as founder of Civil Society Media and the Charity Awards.

Introduction

When the coronavirus pandemic took hold in the United Kingdom early in 2020, charities were among the first to draw attention to the resulting social distress and to take action. Foodbanks reported growing demand and did their best to meet it. Domestic abuse charities responded to a 50% increase in calls as successive lockdowns wore on. Calls to the National Society for the Prevention of Cruelty to Children (NSPCC) went up from an average of 600 a month to more than 900. The mental health charity Mind stepped up its advice and advocacy services, and 750,000 people joined a Royal Voluntary Service network of volunteers to support those who were self-isolating.

This was nothing new. It was, rather, a fresh illustration of the role charities play at times of national and international crisis. Many of them are experts in their field, close enough to people and communities to see where the need is, and flexible enough to respond swiftly. They were active in the two world wars; they joined the relief effort in the disastrous floods in eastern England in 1953; they played a leading role in tackling AIDS. During the war in Afghanistan, Help for Heroes was established and expanded rapidly to care for injured veterans. Charities respond continually to natural disasters abroad and at home.

They are also an integral part of society in normal times, best known for their work from day to day with those who are poor, sick, homeless or living with disability. But their role is not confined to the relief of individual need. They also play an essential part in education, medical research, the democratic process, the advancement of rights, the guardianship of culture and heritage, the stability and development of local communities, leisure, the protection of the environment and the delivery of public services. This complex proliferation of organisations and their role in promoting social and economic progress is not always well understood or recognised.

The purpose of this book is to make the breadth and depth of the work of charities more visible and better appreciated by categorising what they do and bringing it to life through case studies and interviews, including examples of their response to the coronavirus emergency. It also sets the historical context, examines recent scandals and criticisms and looks at the case for improvements in the governance, transparency and independence of charities.

Our starting point was almost two decades as journalists writing about the charity world. We went out to discover more about organisations we thought would provide vivid illustrations of particular causes. In some cases, these are large and well known; in others, not: we wanted to showcase charities of all shapes and sizes. We have tried to include the main areas where charities play a significant part, but in this wide and varied landscape there will inevitably be some omissions. We are presenting a sample rather than an inventory. Where we refer to the interviews we conducted for the book, these are distinguished from other sources by use of the present tense.

The demand for the services of charities in the coronavirus emergency increased by 42%, according to an early survey by the Charity Finance Group, while overall income was down by a third. Fundraising events such as the London Marathon were cancelled or scaled down, charity shops were closed for months and donations from individuals fell back. The government responded with a £750 million grant fund, but warned that this would not save every charity. The shape, size and profile of the charity world began to change as, for example, National Health Service (NHS) charities expanded and international development charities came under pressure. One survey by Pro Bono Economics indicated that one in ten charities expected to close by the end of 2020.

The record of charities indicates, however, that they will adapt to the huge economic and social disruptions and play a key role in the long-term recovery. Despite reduced resources and extra demand, they will continue to flag up important questions, raise money from the public and philanthropists, mobilise volunteers and community action, devise new ways of meeting social need, prop up state provision and confirm their essential role in what the welfare state pioneer Lord (William) Beveridge, writing about the future of voluntary action in 1948, called 'the good society'.

PART I

What are charities,
and why do we argue about them?

1

The many faces of charities

This looks like a big, prestigious organisation: its head office is a modern, eight-storey building opposite the entrance to Moorgate underground station in the City of London. It had an income of £243 million in 2018, which gives it roughly the same turnover as, for example, Caffè Nero, which in that year had nearly 650 coffee shops in the UK and Ireland. There are almost 4,000 staff in this concrete-and-glass building and in branches around the country. The chief executive has a team of seven directors who answer to him and in 2018 was paid a salary of £173,000.[1] Not a fat cat by City standards, but undoubtedly a high earner.

So is this a financial or professional services company, perhaps, or a large accountancy practice? No – it's actually a charity. It's the British Red Cross, founded in 1870, the work of which ranges from relief in UK disasters, such as flooding, campaigning against modern slavery and supporting refugees. In the COVID-19 epidemic its volunteers freed up hospital beds by helping patients go home after treatment and looking after them. It also helps with overseas disasters, working with the 190-strong International Federation of Red Cross and Red Crescent Societies and the International Committee of the Red Cross in Geneva.

The chief executive since 2014 is Mike Adamson, who has in the past also worked for a consultancy firm in the private sector and an NHS primary care trust in the public sector. He says the demands of leading a large organisation are similar across the sectors, including extensive travel and work in the evenings and at weekends:

"It eats up lots of time, and you have to be very disciplined in carving out time for other things that are important, including family and friends. But I've undoubtedly been happiest in the charity sector. There's the privilege of trying to make a difference in the world, combined with the freedom of manoeuvre that much of the public sector doesn't have, and with the independence that you find in the private sector."

At the other end of the scale from the British Red Cross is the Peak and Northern Footpaths Society, a small charity that was established in 1894 to make sure footpaths are kept open. Its first major success was in 1896, when it established a right of way from Snake to Hayfield, high on the Pennine hills in the north of England. Anyone out walking in Derbyshire, Cheshire and Lancashire is likely to come across the Society's trademark – the square, green metal signs indicating the paths.

The Society has about 1,200 members, who pay an annual subscription of £15. It owns a small building in Stockport, Cheshire and has no paid staff. Among the membership are about 100 volunteer 'inspectors', each of whom checks the footpaths in their local area at least every two years. The charity also has six 'courts and inquiries officers', also volunteers, who are familiar with footpath law and take up contentious cases, as when a public right of way is contested by landowners. Then there are about a dozen people who help with office work. "Most of our volunteers are hikers who as they get older want to put something back," says Dave Brown, secretary of the Society.

"I'd be surprised if any of our volunteers put in less than a day a week, and the inspectors are often walking the paths just for pleasure anyway. If paths are blocked or there are other problems, the volunteers report this to us and we take it up with the highway authorities. We're very much against having paid staff and prefer to remain entirely as volunteers. A while back, there was a proposal to pay someone, but there was an outraged reaction to that, even though we're quite well off."

These two snapshots prefigure the stories later in this book that illustrate in more detail the huge range of charitable activity and the extent to which it underpins many aspects of life in the UK. But the rest of this chapter and the two that follow paint the general picture and describe the context in which charities have to work: their structures, the rules they have to follow and the debates and disputes that surround them and constrain what they do.

How many registered charities?

Charities vary dramatically not only in size and income, but also in the balance between paid staff and volunteers. And there are a huge number of charities: at the start of 2020 there were 168,528 on the register of the Charity Commission for England and Wales.[2] Their total income was £80.5 billion – a bit less than the combined annual take of Tesco and Sainsbury's. In Scotland in 2020 there were another 25,000 registered charities with an income of £14 billion, according to the Office of the Scottish Charity Regulator, and in Northern Ireland, which also has a separate regulator, there were more than 6,000 registered charities in 2019, with a total income of £1.9 billion in 2017.

In England and Wales, 43% of charities on the register at the start of 2020 received less than 0.3% of that total income of more than £80 billion. The Peak and Northern Footpaths Society might be small, with an income (minus legacies) of £39,000 in 2019, but there were nearly 74,000 charities that are much smaller – so-called kitchen-table charities, all with annual incomes below £10,000.

At the other end of the scale, 2,356 charities registered in England and Wales at the start of 2020 – a mere 1.3% – have incomes above £5 million and together account for 72.5% of the total take of more than £80 billion. Some of the biggest are household names, such as the British Red Cross, Cancer Research UK (CRUK) – which had an income of £672 million in 2018/19 – and the National Trust (£595 million). The two biggest charities by income are perhaps less well known – the British Council, which had an income of £1.25 billion in

2018/19, and Nuffield Health, a chain of fee-charging hospitals and fitness clubs, which took in £993 million in 2019.

Charitable causes

It may come as a surprise that the British Council is a charity at all. It promotes British culture and language abroad, received a £184 million grant in 2018/19 from the Foreign and Commonwealth Office and looks very much like an arm of the state.[3] But the bulk of its income comes from teaching and running examinations in English in other countries – and the advancement of education is one of the main 'charitable purposes' that organisations have by law to pursue if they are to qualify as charities. Another such purpose is the advancement of health or saving lives, which is how private hospitals such as those run by Nuffield Health, or the prestigious London Clinic, come to be charities.

In England, Wales and Northern Ireland – the law in Scotland is slightly different – the legal definition of a charitable purpose includes a requirement to be for the public benefit.[4] That benefit can be to the public in general or 'a sufficient section of the public', such as people who live in a particular place or work in a certain profession. The remarkably wide range of charitable purposes means that all sorts of organisations, doing all kinds of things, can qualify to be charities.

The main starting point for charity law was the preamble to the Statute of Charitable Uses of 1601 in the reign of Elizabeth I. This preamble was retained when the statute was finally repealed in 1888, and was summarised shortly afterwards by the senior judge Lord Macnaghten as the four 'heads' of charity: relief of poverty, advancement of education, advancement of religion and other purposes beneficial to the community. These heads were revised and expanded in the Charities Act 2006 as 13 descriptions of charitable purposes covering a broad spectrum: as well as the familiar purposes of relief of poverty, health, education and religion, they include the advancement of citizenship, the arts, amateur sport, human rights, environmental protection and animal welfare. Other descriptions are conflict resolution; the relief of those in need by reason of youth, age, ill-health, disability, financial hardship or other disadvantage; the promotion of the efficiency of the armed forces or emergency services; and any other purpose 'analogous to or within the spirit of the existing charitable purposes'.

Yet more charities

So far we've referred to charities registered with the relevant charity regulators in the UK. But in England and Wales they are only part of the story. There are also about 180,000 charities that do not have to register, although they are subject to regulation by the Charity Commission.[5] In this category are charities with an income below £5,000 a year and so-called 'excepted' charities that include Christian churches, Scout and Guide groups and certain armed forces charities.

Adding registered and excepted charities together brings us to a total of nearly 350,000. But we're not finished yet. There is a third category known as 'exempt' charities – a mixed collection including more than 8,000 academy schools, further education colleges, many universities and most big national museums. Their total number is estimated by the Charity Commission to be nearly 15,000. They are exempt from registration with the Commission because they are considered to be adequately regulated by some other body, known as a 'principal regulator'.

Principal regulators are often government ministers, but universities and higher education institutions in England, for instance, have the Office for Students as principal regulator. However, all the principal regulators have an agreement with the Charity Commission designed to ensure that they follow the principles of charity law in the way they exercise their functions.

So we're now up to an impressive total of more than 360,000 charities in England and Wales with a combined estimated income as high as £160 billion. This is a complex sector, with many accretions and anomalies; over time, bits have been bolted on or sub-categories created to accommodate legal, social and political developments as they arose. In *Collins Concise Dictionary* the meanings of the word 'charity' are 'the giving of help, money, food etc. to those in need'; institutions set up to perform that giving; and 'a kindly attitude towards people'. In the world of charities as defined in law, that term 'etc.' stretches very widely; the phrase 'in need' is equally elastic; and kindliness is variable.

The result is that there are charities that do things that many people would not regard as charitable in the everyday sense, because they carry out quasi-governmental functions, such as state-funded academy schools or the British Council, or run controversial religious organisations such as the Jehovah's Witnesses or the Plymouth Brethren, or provide expensive private healthcare or education, such as the London Clinic or Eton College and other public schools.

The Institution of Mechanical Engineers is a charity. So is Send a Cow, which started by sending dairy cows to Uganda and now helps Africans get the most out of their land. Some housing associations are charities. The Hitchin Bridge Club in Hertfordshire is a charity. So is the British Boer Goat Society. Some think-tanks are charities, which can be controversial if they are associated with a political point of view. Some grant-making charities hold all their assets in investments and donate the income to good causes, mostly through other charities. Others rely on constant fundraising. Charities can be as big as private sector corporations or as small as a local reading group.

Legal structure of charities

Charities can also take a complex variety of legal forms, which determine their structure and the ways they can act.[6] Smaller charities that don't employ staff frequently take the form of the unincorporated association, which is essentially a contractual agreement between individuals to combine for a particular purpose. Such an association will have a governing document that sets out rules for matters such as membership, the appointment of office holders and the conduct of meetings, but it does not have a separate legal identity. This means it cannot borrow money, enter into contracts or take legal action in its own right, and officers can be held personally liable if the charity is sued or incurs debts.

Many charities, especially larger ones such as Oxfam or CRUK, restrict the personal liabilities of office holders by registering under company law as companies limited by guarantee. These are different from companies limited by shares, which distribute earnings to shareholders. Members of a company limited by guarantee hold no shares, but undertake to pay a nominal sum towards costs if the company goes out of business. Crucially, the company, and therefore the charity, has its own legal personality, which means it can enter into contracts, such as contracts of employment, in its own name rather than those of individuals. From 2013 a new legal form, the charitable incorporated organisation (CIO), was made available, which allows a charity to have the status of a limited company without having to register with Companies House as well as the Charity Commission.

Another legal form is the charitable trust, commonly used when someone donates assets or a sum of money to be used for charitable purposes. As in the case of an unincorporated association, a charitable trust does not have a legal personality of its own, which means that the trustees must act as individuals if they enter into contracts and are personally at risk if the charity is sued. Charitable trusts and so-called 'foundation CIOs' are run by trustees and do not have wider memberships, whereas unincorporated organisations and 'association CIOs' generally have a wider membership that has a role in some of the decision making. Charitable companies can choose whether or not to have wider membership.

A final twist to all this complexity is that a number of charities, some of them going back centuries, were originally established by Royal Charter, granted by the monarch. Before the development of modern company and charity law, one effect of a charter was to give an organisation its own legal personality, usually with the same limited liability as a company and the ability to enter into contracts, hold assets and borrow money. Historic charter bodies that are charities include many schools and universities. In more recent times, existing charities have been able to apply to the Privy Council for a Royal Charter: the British Red Cross, described at the start of this chapter, received one in 1908; the Institute of Fundraising received one in 2020.

This labyrinth of both function and form is defined by an accretion of statutes and court judgments going back a century and more; but the difficulty for the average citizen is that the legal test of a charity does not always coincide with popular interpretations of the word.

The benefits and burdens of charitable status

Leaving definitions aside, what are the advantages of being a charity? The main one in practice is tax relief. Charities were spared from tax on income when it was first introduced to finance the war against Napoleon in 1799. Nowadays charities are spared not only tax on most forms of income, but also corporation tax, capital gains tax and business or non-domestic rates on their buildings; they are also exempt from inheritance tax. In most circumstances they do have to pay value added tax (VAT), which remains a bone of contention between their representative bodies and HM Treasury.

Another significant advantage is Gift Aid, which was introduced by John Major when he was chancellor of the exchequer during the final months of Margaret Thatcher's premiership in 1990. This allows charities to claim back from HM Revenue and Customs the basic rate of income tax that has been paid by donors on the money they have donated; the scheme also gives an incentive for higher-rate taxpayers to give to charity, in that they can, in their annual tax return, claim back for themselves the difference between the basic rate and the higher rate of tax paid on any donations. In the year 2018/19 more than 70,000 charities received a total of more than £1.3 billion in Gift Aid, and all tax reliefs to charity totalled £3.8 billion.[7]

But tax breaks are not the only advantage: charities also share the reputational value of the word 'charity', with all its positive associations. For many people the word retains some of its religious resonance, deriving in part from the wording of the King James Bible, in which St Paul's letter to the people of Corinth talks of 'faith, hope and charity – but the greatest of these is charity'. A general aura of sanctity still surrounds the word 'charity'; this may have been damaged by recent scandals and controversies, described in the next chapter, but most charities still find that being able to describe themselves as such is a significant advantage when publicising themselves or raising funds.

The advantages do not come without burdens, however. The definition of charity for tax purposes is different from the definition for charity law purposes, and charities have to comply with both tax law and charity law. They also have to submit a report and accounts to the relevant charity regulator every year and demonstrate that they are following one of the defined charitable purposes for the public benefit. The trustees who govern them, who cannot be paid or benefit from them, except in unusual or strictly defined circumstances, have to manage carefully any conflict of interest and report any serious incidents to the regulator. They also owe numerous legal duties to the charity they serve, not to mention compliance with the law on employment, health and safety, data protection and so on.

Charities' income and contribution to the economy

So much for the advantages and burdens of charities: a key question is where charities actually get their money from. The popular conception is that it's all donated by the generous British public – ordinary citizens responding to the need of others for what *Collins Concise Dictionary* calls 'help, money, food etc'. But the picture is more complex than that, as evidenced by the *NCVO Almanac*, the annual volume of statistics produced by the National Council for Voluntary Organisations (NCVO).[8] Its analysis is based on what it calls 'general charities' – all charities registered in the UK, minus religious bodies, independent schools, government-controlled organisations and housing associations.

The 2020 analysis of the 166,592 general charities registered in the UK in 2017/18 shows that they had an income of £53.6 billion, of which more than £25.4 billion (47%) – the largest component – came from individuals. Only about half of that was in the form of donations or legacies, however – the rest came from things like membership subscriptions that confer benefits, such as a magazine; the rent paid by people in housing provided by a charity; and the income from charity shops, raffles and lotteries. So, less than a quarter of the income of general charities came from people donating freely and receiving nothing in return.

The second-largest component of the income of general charities in 2017/18 was £15.7 billion (29%) from national, local and foreign government sources, which was payment for providing public services, mostly paid under contract but sometimes by means of grants (this aspect of charity work is explored in Chapter 12). The remaining 24% of the income came, in descending size, from grant-making charities, investments, donations from the private sector and the National Lottery. More than 19 million people volunteered for charities at least once in 2018/19, according to the *Almanac*, and the most recent calculation by the Office for National Statistics in 2016 put the value of volunteering to the economy at £23.9 billion, had it been contributed as paid work.

Most of these figures are predicted to shrink significantly as a result of the coronavirus pandemic that began in 2020. In his introduction to the 2020 *Almanac*, Karl Wilding, then chief executive of the NCVO, said the pandemic had prompted a burst of giving to some causes, but had seriously hampered public fundraising:

> There is no doubt that the sector will be smaller in the immediate future. The questions are: how much smaller and for how long, and which organisations won't make it? The effects of the pandemic are felt differently by different sorts of organisations with different income profiles. But the urgent challenge is finding paths to recovery.

In June 2020 the charity Pro Bono Economics was predicting from its charity tracker survey that the sector faced a £10 billion funding gap in the second half of the year.[9]

Other not-for-profit organisations

The world of charity, taking the word in a wider sense, doesn't end with organisations that are legally constituted as charities. A key part of being a charity is that it is not for profit, in that it cannot benefit individuals other than defined beneficiaries. But there are thousands of organisations that are not set up as charities in the legal sense but are, to a greater or lesser extent, not for profit. They do work that many people would regard as charitable, in that they draw on philanthropic and altruistic motives and prioritise public or social good over private gain and profit. Their activities range from care and health services to leisure facilities and rehabilitation of ex-prisoners.

One category is community amateur sports clubs (CASCs). This legal form was set up by the government in 2002 and by 2020 there were more than 7,100 CASCs. They have to register with HM Revenue and Customs and follow strict rules in order to benefit from many of the same tax breaks as charities, including Gift Aid. Then there are community interest companies (CICs), a legal form introduced in 2005 to protect social purpose organisations that decide not to be charities, such as co-operatives, from being converted into for-profit companies. By 2019 there were 15,729 CICs, which are required to meet a community interest test and are permitted to be companies with shareholders, in which case 35% of profits can be distributed. But most CICs opt to be companies limited by guarantee.

Larger CICs are often organisations that were once part of the NHS; one example is Chime, which was spun out of the NHS in 2011 and provides hearing tests and other audiology services in Devon.[10] A successful smaller CIC is The Good Loaf in Northampton, which teaches about 100 vulnerable women each year how to bake, and runs a centre that helps them with problems such as drugs and alcohol, mental health, domestic or sexual abuse, parenting, debt and benefits.[11]

As well as CASCs and CICs, there are so-called mutuals, which cover a range of legal forms but all allow members, who can be staff, customers or suppliers, to control the business and either share in its profits or use them for a wider community purpose.[12] The department store John Lewis is a well-known mutual, where staff collectively own and profit from the business. Mutuals can be normal limited companies in which most of the shares are owned, directly or indirectly, by staff rather than investors. But they can also be what used to be called industrial and provident societies (IPSs), which had their roots in the self-help organisations that sprang up in cities in the north of England as industry expanded in the 19th century. The former IPS now has two legal forms: one is the co-operative society, where the owners can be the workers, independent producers, customers or a community of people with a common interest. In a co-op, profits not needed for reinvestment in the business are distributed to its members. The second form is the community benefit society, often known as a bencom, where any surpluses have to be devoted to community purposes – an example is examined in Chapter 8. Bencoms issue shares, which are not transferable and can be refunded only at their original value; and they can pay a low rate of interest, which is regarded as an operating cost rather than a distribution of profit.

CICs and mutuals are, in turn, part of the wider social enterprise movement that, according to Social Enterprise UK (SEUK), the membership body, consists of organisations that have a clear social or environmental mission, generate most of their income through trade, reinvest most of their profits, are independent of the state, are 'majority controlled in the interests of the social mission' and are accountable and transparent. In 2018 SEUK published research estimating that there were 100,000 social enterprises contributing £60 billion to the economy – 3% of gross domestic product – and employing two million people.[13]

One well-known social enterprise is Divine Chocolate, co-owned by the thousands of farmers in Ghana who supply the cocoa for the products and receive a share of the profits.[14] Another example is Community Dental Services, a business owned by its 286 staff which has 38 clinics in central England, working mainly under contract to the NHS and local councils with the aim of providing dental services to vulnerable people.[15]

The overall picture

So, where does all this leave us? We have registered charities, excepted charities and exempt charities; some charities are trusts, which means the trustees carry ultimate liability, while many have the protection for their trustees of limited liability company status, and many smaller ones are simply unincorporated associations. Then there are CASCs, CICs, mutuals of various kinds and social enterprises. All inhabit a world with rules and boundaries that have bulged and shifted over time in a complicated process of accretion and adjustment.

And what should we call it all? The charitable sector, the voluntary sector, the not-for-profit sector, the social sector, the third sector? Each title describes one or some parts, but none quite encompasses them all, although what they have in common is a social, philanthropic or charitable motivation in the widest sense. The term 'non-governmental organisation', commonly shortened to NGO, is perhaps the most accurate description, but in practice it has come to refer mainly to international development bodies. The term 'civil society', more familiar in other European countries, has increasingly been used in the UK, not least by the incoming Coalition government in 2010 when it wanted to replace Labour's term 'third sector' in the name for the relevant Whitehall unit. However, the term denotes all organisations that are independent of government and pursue the interests and collective will of citizens, including bodies such as political parties, many housing associations and trade unions, which are not readily seen as part of the world of voluntary action. Even the word 'charity' can be problematic, in that some charities have become so large and corporate that they conflict with a widely held conception that they should be unlike businesses and run by volunteers.

All this is perhaps why people sometimes give up trying to find a precise term to describe the sector and have instead resorted to the imprecise but evocative term 'a loose and baggy monster'. The term is borrowed from a description by the author Henry James of sprawling 19th-century novels such as *War and Peace* by Leo Tolstoy and *The Three Musketeers* by Alexandre Dumas.[16] The question also arises whether the monster should be rationalised. One experienced charity lawyer, David Alcock of Anthony Collins Solicitors in Birmingham, thinks improvements could be made to some of the legal forms, but there are good reasons for having them all: "The range on offer reflects the fact that people set up organisations to do a variety of things in a variety of ways, and the choice means there's a good chance they will get the structure that suits them."

As new legal forms have appeared and the social enterprise movement has expanded, charitable status has continued to be generally seen as the gold standard of the not-for-profit world. It enjoys the most advantages, both fiscal and reputational, albeit at the price of the strictest regulation and scrutiny. The National Audit Office (NAO), when reviewing the regulation of charities in 2012, raised the fear that scandal or misbehaviour by charity-like organisations might undermine vital public trust and confidence in charities proper.[17] Since then, ironically, it has been scandal and misbehaviour in charities themselves that has played a large part in shaking public trust in the sector and making it vulnerable to attack. This, along with a change in the political atmosphere around charities, is the subject of the next chapter.

2

What has gone wrong?

Charities frequently act as the canary in the mine, drawing early attention to social problems such as the extent of homelessness or poverty, and leading the way in providing relief. This was particularly evident at the start of the COVID-19 epidemic in 2020. Foodbanks were in the front line as unemployment and poverty increased; women's charities reported and responded to a growth in domestic violence during the lockdown periods, as detailed in Chapter 6; Shelter campaigned to prevent eviction of tenants falling into arrears with private-sector landlords; the Royal Society for the Prevention of Cruelty to Animals (RSPCA) publicised an increase in the abandonment of pets; and the Alzheimer's Society spelled out how restrictions on visiting care homes were increasing the confusion and suffering of people with dementia. Charities were also engaged in the policy debate on plans for national recovery from the coronavirus pandemic, particularly in relation to the environment. Wildlife and Countryside Link, for example, proposed the establishment of a Nature Service to take on rural projects and provide employment, and CPRE, the Countryside Charity (formerly the Campaign to Protect Rural England) launched a manifesto for a 'green recovery' that took issue with the government's plan to 'build, build, build'.

Generally, however, charities were in a gloomy place at the end of the second decade of the 21st century. For the best part of 20 years, until 2010, they had a reasonable relationship with government and were well protected by their general reputation and the positive associations of the word 'charity'. It was comparatively rare during that period for them to be criticised in the media or by politicians. Lately it seems as if they are under scrutiny all the time, and there have been periods when national newspapers and television current affairs programmes seemed to be competing with each other to come up with the next charity-knocking story.

Why has this remarkable change taken place? Charities, after all, are part of a tradition that began a millennium ago in Britain of doing good, serving others, defending the poor and weak, opposing injustice and pressing for change and progress in society. In today's world nearly everyone will be served or helped by a charity at some point in their lives: they might use a foodbank, benefit from advances in medical treatment from charity-funded research, be saved from drowning by the Royal National Lifeboat Institution (RNLI), enjoy subsidised tickets at the Royal Opera House – yes, it's a charity – or die in a hospice. Charities are a force for good, the conscience of the nation, part of its identity, part of its soul, even. What went wrong?

The answer lies in a combination of factors, of which one is the behaviour of charities themselves: the intensive fundraising methods of some big organisations, the level of salaries paid to some senior staff, some well-publicised cases of financial and managerial incompetence and the occasional failure of effective oversight by trustees. A new low was reached early in 2018 when the scandal broke about some Oxfam staff using the services of sex workers during the relief operation after the 2010 earthquake in Haiti – this is examined later in this book.

Another component was the shift in political attitudes to charities since the change of government in 2010, prompted in part by a different view of the role and purpose of charities that prevails among many Conservative politicians and some opinion formers in the media and think-tanks, and in part by recession and austerity after the global financial crisis of 2008. The politicians who took power were more likely than their Labour predecessors to argue that charities were getting above themselves and that their representative bodies should receive less subsidy in a time of financial austerity. A new regime at the Charity Commission for England and Wales reflected that change in political attitudes. Taken together, these various factors pitched charities into a more critical world.

High-pressure fundraising

Looking first at the conduct of charities, it is clear that some of the larger ones, in the drive for expansion and increased income, were seduced by the modern, database-driven methods of the marketing world. They fell into the habit of buying, selling and swapping lists of donors and potential donors, some of whom found themselves deluged by phone calls or mailshots that sometimes contained notelets or even coins – gifts intended to make people feel they had to give something back. Growing unease about fundraising was for years dismissed by some fundraisers as unworthy antagonism to good causes, but the suicide in May 2015 of Olive Cooke, 92 years old and a lifelong poppy seller for the Royal British Legion in Bristol, brought matters to a head. Although the inquest found that illness and depression lay behind her decision to end her life, the press focused on the pressure she had been under from charities. She had told her local paper that she had received nearly 270 mail appeals in a single month.

The Daily Mail went into overdrive. 'Shame of the charities that prey on the kind-hearted and drove Olive to her death', read a headline on 20 May. Chris Grayling MP, then leader of the House of Commons, spoke of "wholly inappropriate behaviour" and promised legislation. In July, under the headline 'Shamed: charity cold call sharks', the *Mail*'s reporters brought to light the callous attitudes to be found in some telephone fundraising agencies that worked for big charities, and gave details of the industrial-scale use of direct mail. The prevailing sense of anger prompted the government to set up a review, and it was perhaps fortunate for charities that this was led by an insider – Sir Stuart Etherington, then chief executive of the NCVO.

The review concluded that 'the balance between giving and asking has sometimes gone awry' and recommended replacing the Fundraising Standards Board with a new, self-regulatory body with enhanced powers, particularly on the use of personal data.[1] Despite political pressure for a statutory system, the government agreed to set up the Fundraising Regulator, financed by a levy on charities. Parliament also passed the Charities (Protection and Social Investment) Act 2016, which required charities to set tighter controls on the fundraising companies they employed and to explain their fundraising policies in their annual reports. This new fundraising environment was buttressed by closer scrutiny by the Information Commissioner and prefigured in many respects the European Union's (EU) General Data Protection Regulation of 2018, which gives citizens greater control of their personal data.

The whole episode forced a fundamental reassessment by charities of their fundraising practices and left many professional fundraisers, who had enjoyed considerable freedom for years, in a state of shock and confusion. It also caused tensions between big and small charities. The small mental health charity Sane was sure in 2016 that its income was suffering because of the unpopular fundraising methods of larger charities: "We're getting fewer and fewer donations because of the way they've behaved," its chief executive, Marjorie Wallace, said.[2] The small environmental charity Friends of the Lake District was not experiencing a fall in income, but its chief executive, Douglas Chalmers, was so concerned that he wrote to all its members in the same year to dissociate it from the 'inappropriate fundraising methods' of some big charities. 'The stories in the press represent a huge betrayal of trust by a minority of charities towards their donors,' he wrote. 'If I was a donor, I would be wondering if any charity I supported was behaving properly.'

The long-term effects of tighter regulation on the collective income of charities remain to be seen, but the outlook in 2019 was not encouraging. That year's *UK Giving* survey by the Charities Aid Foundation (CAF), based on 12,000 interviews with members of the public, found that 'the key measures of giving are on a downward path'.[3] Similarly, the data company Charity Financials found in its 2019 *Income Spotlight Report*, based on income figures in charity accounts rather than on interviews, that growth in fundraised income at the top 100 fundraising charities in the UK had fallen to 0.5% in 2017/18, compared to 2.8% the year before and between 4.5% and 6% between 2013 and 2016.[4] 'The challenge looming over the future,' it concluded, 'is to break through the apparent plateau in income growth, to regenerate public trust and the belief that giving to charities is a special, ethical and effective way of helping to address the social challenges which private and government sectors are not.' Any effect of tighter regulation on fundraising was, of course, compounded significantly by the income shortfall resulting from the coronavirus pandemic.

Large senior salaries

Before the Olive Cooke case and the resulting reforms of fundraising, the media was already focusing on the pay of charity chief executives. More than 90% of registered charities have no paid staff and fewer than 1% of them employ anyone earning £60,000 or more; many of the 909,000 people employed in the sector in June 2019 (about 3% of the UK workforce) work in low-paid jobs such as assistants in care homes; and, generally speaking, charities pay their staff less than the commercial sector.[5] But in 2013 *The Daily Telegraph*, which had been consistently sceptical about the government's commitment at the time to devoting 0.7% of the country's national income to overseas aid, published the fact that 30 executives in the 14 major charities that participate in the Disasters Emergency Committee – and dispense significant public funds when earthquakes, famines and other disasters happen around the world – were being paid more than £100,000 a year.[6] The story included a comment from the then chair of the Charity Commission, William Shawcross, about 'disproportionate salaries'. Senior charity pay began to be a matter for comment and dispute. The NCVO initiated its own inquiry which urged charities to publish their chief executives' pay within two clicks of the home page of their websites and explain how it is benchmarked against comparable jobs in other sectors. Some charities have followed this approach, but by 2020 it was not yet standard practice.

The payment of such salaries out of funds raised partly from the public on the grounds that they will be used for good causes in the UK or abroad clearly causes an unease that is not necessarily mitigated by the fact that the charities in question pay their senior staff significantly less than private or public sector organisations of similar size: Oxfam, for example, paid its chief executive £140,000 in 2018, well below the going rate for a private sector company with a similar turnover of more than £400 million. There tends to be less criticism of charities that do not rely on public fundraising but either earn their income from selling services or benefit from big endowments. Surveys show that the largest salaries are concentrated in the big healthcare foundations or providers such as Wellcome Trust, which paid the top member of its investment team £4.6 million in 2019, and the London Clinic (where the top salary was £1.27 million in 2018).[7] These two have not been the subject of hostile national media attention.

But some other charities that do not rely on public fundraising have attracted criticism over senior pay. The Consumers' Association, the charity that runs the *Which?* publications that earn the bulk of its income, came under fire from its own members in 2016 for a bonus scheme that meant its chief executive at the time received £462,000 in 2017; and in 2019 the birth control charity Marie Stopes International, which had received only £4 million of its £296 million income in 2018 from donations, was asked by the Charity Commission, following press attention from *The Daily Mail* and *The Sun on Sunday*, to explain why its chief executive was paid a package in 2018 of £434,500, half of it as a bonus.[8] (The charity was renamed MSI Reproductive Choices in 2020.)

Other scandals

As well as outcries about fundraising and high pay, there were also high-profile instances of financial or managerial incompetence, inadequate supervision by trustees or the abuse of charitable status. One of the most disturbing stories broke in 2012 about the Cup Trust, a cynical, sophisticated tax avoidance scheme set up as a charity to take advantage of Gift Aid, under which donations to charity are augmented by the amount of basic rate tax the donor has paid on the sum donated. Three years later, there was extensive media coverage of the collapse of Kids Company, a charity with a ground-breaking approach to helping marginalised children and teenagers, set up and led by the persuasive Camila Batmanghelidjh; she charmed David Cameron when he was prime minister and successfully solicited money from government departments. The running of the charity was strongly criticised by a committee of MPs in 2016,[9] but early in 2021 Mrs Justice Falk in the High Court refused an application by the Official Receiver to disqualify the trustees as company directors, calling them 'a group of highly impressive and dedicated individuals'. She added that it was 'more likely than not' that a planned restructuring of the charity would have succeeded were it not for a police investigation into allegations of sexual assault at the charity, which proved unfounded but prompted the collapse.[10] Media coverage of the case in 2015 and 2016 only reinforced the impression that some charities were profligate and incompetent, and the Oxfam scandal of 2018, mentioned at the start of this chapter, introduced the fear that some failed to protect vulnerable beneficiaries from exploitation. The spotlight swung onto the question of safeguarding by all charities, not just those involved in overseas aid and development. The Charity Commission updated its guidance on safeguarding soon after the Oxfam affair, and in 2020 published a report on a special school run by the Royal National Institute of Blind People (RNIB) which said there had been 'comprehensive failures in governance that placed the safety of young people in its care at risk and allowed harm or distress to be suffered by some'.[11]

The change in political attitudes

So much for the behaviour of charities: what about the other main element in the cloud that hangs over them – the shift in the attitude of government? In the first decade of the 21st century, under the Labour administrations led by Tony Blair and Gordon Brown, the sun shone on charities and the voluntary sector. Charity law was modernised, the Office of the Third Sector (later renamed the Office for Civil Society [OCS]) was set up in the Cabinet Office to smooth the path for charities and the sector was seen by the government as an important component in the drive to reform public services. Gift Aid was relaxed so that donations of any size – not just those above £250 – could bring a tax refund to charities. Many Labour MPs and ministers had worked in the sector when the party was in opposition and were sympathetic to it. In an ambitious document in July 2007, Brown pledged to invest an unprecedented half a billion pounds in the sector.[12] 'We set out ... a vision of how the state and the third sector, working together at all levels and as equal partners, can bring about real change in our country,' wrote the Prime Minister in the introduction.

All that was severely modified, however, after the global financial crisis and the formation of the Conservative-led Coalition government following the general election in 2010. Charities were not spared in the new era of austerity: the funding of capacity-building organisations set up by Labour came briskly to an end, and subsidies to umbrella bodies like the NCVO and the Association of Chief Executives of Voluntary Organisations (Acevo) were soon phased out. Responsibility for charities and voluntary organisations also slipped down the Whitehall hierarchy. The budget of the OCS fell from £227 million in 2009/10 to £56 million in 2014/15, a drop of about 70%.[13] When Theresa May became prime minister in July 2016, the OCS was moved from the Cabinet Office, seen as the policy centre of government, to the more peripheral Department for Culture, Media and Sport (later the Department for Digital, Culture, Media and Sport, DCMS); and after the general election of 2017, when the Conservatives lost their overall majority in Parliament, the sector lost a minister of its own and responsibility for it was added to the portfolio of the minister for sport. This prompted the shadow civil society minister at the time, Steve Reed MP, to remark that the government didn't quite know what to do with the OCS. "It should be at the centre of government rather than parked in a lay-by somewhere," he said.[14]

After 2010 there was also more overt criticism of charities from some parliamentarians, mainly on the right of the Conservative Party. Charlie Elphicke, MP for Dover and Deal until 2019 and a member of the public administration select committee, complained during a hearing of the committee that "Shelter doesn't provide any shelter" and that political lobbying by charities "subverts democracy and debases the concept of charity".[15] Elphicke, who was jailed for two years in 2020 for sexual assaults, went on: "If a member of the public puts a pound in a rattling tin, and that money is spent on press officers and Bell Pottinger to lobby a bunch of politicians, wouldn't that person feel a bit disgusted and a bit cheated?" His fellow committee member, Robert Halfon, Conservative MP for Harlow, said there were too many very large "Tesco-type charities" that spent millions of pounds lobbying in Whitehall and questioned whether such organisations should have charitable status. The fundraising scandal discussed above also prompted outspoken criticism from some MPs.

Trevor Morris, then visiting professor of public relations at the University of Westminster, told a Charity Finance Group conference in 2013 that charities were not seen as innocent any more, faced the prospect of more attacks and should prepare for a moral crisis. He said in a subsequent interview:[16]

> "The *Today* programme on BBC Radio 4 is a parade of heads of charities and NGOs making their case, often in a highly politicised way. The government is wrong, money must be spent, business must do something. It sounds like politics to me. It's not about helping poor old ladies or hedgehogs – there's a different feeling coming through. Some right-wing politicians have jumped on it because it's not risky any more – it's become acceptable to say not all charities are good ... The public has a sense that some charities are rather pleased with themselves – they pay themselves a lot of money, they hassle us in the street, they're not apologising. There's a sense that people are less deferential towards charities and more questioning of them."

The Charity Commission gets tough

The alteration in the political mood after the change of government in 2010 was mirrored by the general approach to the regulation of charities by the Charity Commission for England and Wales, a non-ministerial government department headed by a chair appointed by a government minister. The regime at the Commission had been relatively indulgent and charity friendly during the previous decade under two chairs appointed by Labour, Geraldine Peacock and Dame Suzi Leather. Things changed after the appointment as chair in 2012 of William Shawcross, a hawkish journalist, author on geopolitical subjects and biographer of Queen Elizabeth, the Queen Mother.

The new regime began in earnest after a report by the NAO in 2013 prompted by the Cup Trust scandal, mentioned above, stated that the Commission was failing to regulate charities effectively and 'does not do enough to identify and tackle abuse of charitable status'.[17] A drive began to improve internal efficiency, take a harder line with errant charities and generally toughen the rhetoric. Shawcross talked of the Commission as a 'policeman', albeit a friendly one. By 2015 he was able to report that the Commission had used its various statutory powers to tackle abuse and mismanagement in charities 1,200 times in 2014/15, compared to 216 times two years previously, and had opened 103 new statutory inquiries – the strongest intervention at its disposal – compared with 15 two years before.[18]

The new board that Shawcross appointed included one person with 25 years of experience working in social enterprise, but its composition was otherwise seen by some in the charity sector as indicating an emphasis on enforcement, with a particular focus on preventing charity funds being diverted to support terrorism.[19] One of the new board members was Peter Clarke, a former head of the Anti-Terrorist Branch at Scotland Yard, who said in an interview in 2013 that his role included helping to improve partnerships with the security services and other agencies.[20] In 2014, Shawcross told *The Sunday Times*: "The problem of Islamist extremism is not the most widespread problem we face in terms of abuse of charities, but is potentially the most deadly. And it is, alas, growing."[21] He said the Commission was currently running five inquiries and 43 'monitoring cases' into charities where there were suspicions related to terrorism, particularly in Syria.

In 2015 the Conservative Party cancelled a fringe event at its annual conference by the Muslim Charities Forum after an allegation in *The Daily Telegraph* that it had links with the Union of Good, which had funded Hamas, considered to be a terrorist organisation.[22] Two years later Baroness (Sayeeda) Warsi, co-chair of the Conservative Party from 2010 to 2012 and a former minister in the Coalition government, said in a lecture that the Commission had a "disproportionate" focus on Muslim charities that made them feel under scrutiny all the time.[23] This was unjustified, she said, referring to a reported statement by Tom Keatinge, director of the Royal United Services Institute's Centre for Financial Crime and Security Studies, that "the abuse of UK charities in support of terrorism is negligible. The standards are very high and awareness amongst the big charities of this issue is intense."[24]

The Commission's own annual reports, *Tackling Abuse and Mismanagement* – later renamed *Dealing with Wrongdoing and Harm* – show that in the five years from 2012/13 the number of statutory inquiries relating to terrorism that were opened or under way in each year ranged from 6 to 14, with an upward blip to 20 in 2014/15.[25] The number of terrorism-related 'serious incidents' reported to the Commission grew steadily from 1 to 27 over the same five years. The Commission's examples of terrorism-related incidents that charities should report include a member of staff being arrested under suspicion of terrorism offences, a charity's warehouse in a war zone being raided at gunpoint or a visiting speaker promoting extremist messages. The Commission maintained throughout that it was not targeting Muslim charities, but the subject was highly sensitive and some of the rhetoric soured its relations with Muslim charities.

Shawcross was succeeded as chair of the Commission in March 2018 by Baroness (Tina) Stowell, a Conservative peer who had been leader of the House of Lords from 2014 to 2016 and a member of the Cabinet for the second of those two years. On her appointment she resigned the Conservative whip to become an independent, or 'crossbench', peer; and after seven months she delivered a 'statement of strategic intent' which emphasised that charity was 'a vital force for good in society' and that the Commission shared responsibility to maximise its positive impact.[26]

But she was critical of the recent record of charities generally in an article in *The Times* after the Commission published its report on the Oxfam affair:[27]

> We've seen charities losing sight of what they stand for in pursuit of organisational advantage. We've seen charities engage in pressure-tactic fundraising, supposedly justified by the money that raises for the cause. We've seen charities that should be working together instead competing for scarce resources. And

we've seen charities putting their reputations before
their purposes in responding to failings.

This prompted Sir Stuart Etherington, then chief executive of
the NCVO, to complain in a letter to the Commission about
a lack of balance:[28]

> Charities have been far from complacent. I am
> concerned that the message coming from the
> commission is only a partial one. While claiming
> that it wants charity to thrive and inspire, it is only
> talking about how 'charity' has failed. Of course we
> want charities to learn from the mistakes of others,
> but these broad generalisations are far from helpful.
> Indeed, there is a real risk that they will achieve the
> opposite effect: they entrench public misconceptions
> and erode the public's trust.

Public opinion

All the factors outlined above – scandals in charities, harsher
political and media attitudes and a tougher approach by the
regulator – were significant in themselves. But collectively they
also influenced and chimed to some extent with the mood of
the public, which was perhaps the most significant effect of
all. There was a measureable change in the public's attitudes to
charities. One survey showed that people did not much like
being cold-called by charities, being stopped in the street by
'chuggers', being talked at by fundraisers on their doorstep in the
evening or receiving mailshots out of the blue from charities they
had no interest in.[29] Research on trust in charities, conducted
every two years for the Charity Commission, scored it in 2018
at 5.5 out of 10, compared to 5.7 in 2016 and 6.7 in 2012 and
2014.[30] Of the 45% of respondents who said in 2018 that their
trust in charities had decreased in the previous two years, 62%
cited negative news stories as a reason and 41% said they were
donating less because of their loss of trust. Regular surveys by
the research consultancy nfpSynergy showed that the proportion
of respondents who trust charities 'a great deal' or 'quite a lot'

dropped from 70% in 2010 to 54% in September 2018, with a low point of 47% in October 2015, soon after the fundraising scandal, and a relative recovery to 64% in February 2017.[31]

The historical perspective

The sobering and occasionally shocking stories that emerged in the 2010s are not entirely a new phenomenon. Ever since charities were first established in mediaeval times there has been a risk of abuse, often to do with trustees misapplying or appropriating charitable funds.

Criticism of charities by politicians is not new either. William Gladstone called charities "institutions of questionable value" when he was chancellor of the exchequer in 1863.[32] The government led by Margaret Thatcher was at loggerheads with the Church of England in 1985 over its report *Faith in the City*, which led to the Church – a charitable body – being labelled the unofficial opposition to the government: one cabinet minister was reported as dismissing the document as "pure Marxist theology" and another Conservative MP said it proved that the Church was governed by a "load of Communist clerics".[33] When Douglas, now Lord, Hurd was home secretary in 1986, he referred to organisations, including charities, that took issue with government policies as "strangling serpents".[34]

But anti-charity sentiment after 2010 was unusually intense, leaving charities collectively feeling bruised, demoralised and less sure of themselves. Occasional transgression by individuals made matters worse: charity staff or volunteers are convicted in the courts, from time to time, of helping themselves to charity funds. In 2018, for example, the former chief executive of Birmingham Dogs Home, Simon Price, was jailed for five years after defrauding the charity of around £900,000.[35] Five years earlier, five people were jailed in Southampton after they used fake identity documents and collecting tins with home-printed logos to collect money in pubs: they pocketed £26,000, while the cancer charity Marie Curie received £263.[36] Such cases, rather like the conviction of police officers, often attract enhanced publicity. Scandals and criminality are just as common, if not more so, in the private and public sectors, but charities are, in many ways, judged by higher standards than other parts of society.

The other side of the story

The harsh public narrative in recent years, compounded by a hesitant response from many charities, has caused a blurring and fading of the bigger picture. It has become easier for people to forget the size of the sector, its importance to the economy, the role that charities play in society and the contributions they have made and continue to make to a better quality of life in the UK. These aspects of the story have been receiving less airtime.

Despite media attention to large salaries there is also evidence that pay in charities is well below other sectors. In 2017, according to one authoritative survey, average pay in charities was 32% below other business sectors, and director and senior executive pay in London, where many big charities are based, was 50% below other sectors; in the country as a whole, the figure for charity chief executives was 31% below other sectors.[37]

The figures on the economy in the previous chapter also indicate that charities and the voluntary sector are not an optional extra or a luxury that is nice to have. One lawyer with extensive experience of working with not-for-profit organisations puts it like this in an interview with the authors:

> "Charities are not just a safety net for what other sectors can't deliver – they are a sector in their own right, employing large numbers, engaging volunteers and managing a lot of money. They deliver a huge amount of public good without which it is hard to see how society and the economy could manage."

A 2018 report by Civil Society Futures (of which more in Chapter 19), made a similar point:[38]

> Neither the public sector nor the market would be able to cope without the civil society action taking place across the country. It is the people informally helping their neighbours, getting involved

with schools, food banks, sports clubs and tenants associations, who power communities and make public services viable, from health to education, housing, policing and much more. It is the consumer organisations giving feedback to business, the workers and tenants associations asserting rights. It is the organisations of people with disabilities that have made the inadequacy of some services so clear.

Kate Mavor, chief executive of the charity English Heritage, who is interviewed in Chapter 15, has also become impatient with the negativity:

> "Charity is a massively important part of society and people should feel positive about it. These polls that say people don't trust charities make you feel like saying, for God's sake, someone get out there and tell the right story. We all know of the cases where they've done the wrong thing – they're accountable, they shouldn't have done it, and it's been a good alarm call to charities that you shouldn't get too eager about earning money and blurring the lines.
>
> "But we're held to a so much higher account than, say, Tesco. I can't write to someone with a Wikipedia entry that says they're interested in history because we're not allowed to cold-call people now, but Tesco can send you a leaflet or an e-mail promoting their products whenever they like. The standards are different and the story of all the real good that's done by charity needs to be heard, and policy makers need to understand it better."

Although surveys have shown a decline in trust in charities, they also indicate more positive aspects. For example, the Charity Commission's biennial trust survey, referred to above, showed in 2018 that 58% of respondents felt that charities played an 'essential' or 'very important' role in society and were more trusted than social services departments, companies, banks, MPs and newspapers.[39] A survey in 2017 by nfpSynergy found that 65% of respondents trusted information from charities 'a great deal' or 'quite a lot'; only a friend or family member was trusted more at 72%, while the figure for the BBC was 57%, the government 30% and politicians 15%.[40]

Despite the hardening of political attitudes, the government also still sees and encourages a role for charities in the delivery of overseas aid, the provision of some public services and action on social problems. The media and politicians also continue to rely on charities for analysis and information that underpins national debate on vital subjects. During the general elections of 2017 and 2019, for example, the Institute of Fiscal Studies, a charity, acted as a reliable and impartial information bank on the national economy. Wide publicity is given to charities' research and campaigning on subjects ranging from wildlife preservation to the shrinkage of services for vulnerable young people. The World Wide Fund for Nature's (WWF) *Living Planet Report 2018*, for example, which found that wildlife populations had fallen by 60% in the previous 40 years, was widely covered in the media; so was research by the children's charity Barnardo's, working with the all-party parliamentary group on school exclusion, which found that a third of local authorities had no more space in pupil-referral units for children excluded from school, putting them at risk of involvement in drugs and crime.[41,42]

★ ★ ★

By 2020, charities had been under the cosh in one way or another for the best part of a decade. The level of salaries, the Cup Trust, high-pressure fundraising, Kids Company, Oxfam and the RNIB have been directly in the spotlight. Campaigning by charities has been a notable focus of criticism, particularly by some Conservative MPs. For more than a century, charity campaigns have played a part in important changes in the law and improvements in social conditions that few people would now argue against. These range from the abolition of the slave trade to universal franchise and the proper protection of children or animals, some of which will be examined later in this book. But campaigning and change, by their very nature, involve controversy and dispute, and the next chapter takes a closer look at the arguments.

3

'Stick to your knitting': the curbs on campaigning

In 2013 Gwythian Prins, a member of the board of the Charity Commission for England and Wales, made a remark during an interview that became a catchphrase and a talking point in the voluntary sector.[1] Sitting in the impressive drawing room of the Athenaeum Club in London's Pall Mall, he argued that some charities were getting too deeply involved in campaigning. "The weather has changed on this front," said Prins, a historian and specialist in defence affairs. "The public expects charities to stick to their knitting, to use an old-fashioned phrase."

The remark signalled a renewed focus by the regulator, supported by some politicians, on the vexed question of whether charities should be allowed to campaign or get involved in politics – a question that has been controversial since Victorian times. Prins's clear implication was that charities should stay out of politics and confine themselves to the relief of distress. The contrasting view is that charities have always tried to eliminate the causes of distress – that William Wilberforce, for example, didn't achieve the abolition of slavery by providing soup kitchens for slaves. The late Stephen Lloyd, an influential charity lawyer, argued in 2014 that charities are 'necessarily and inevitably' caught up in politics:[2]

> If politics are not concerned with poverty, injustice, climate change, the distribution of wealth, human rights and education, what are they for? And since these, and many other issues, are the essence of charitable purposes, it is inevitable that charities

will engage with contentious political issues. It goes with the patch.

This chapter examines how the boundary between charities and politics has moved back and forth in modern times as political attitudes have fluctuated and the law has been developed and reinterpreted. In the second decade of the 21st century the pendulum swung towards a tighter regime, and many charities featured later in this book – especially those involved in the kinds of causes mentioned by Lloyd – have learned to tread carefully to stay out of trouble.

The history of charity campaigning

The simple relief of need was the principal function of charities in mediaeval times, when monasteries and the Church provided almshouses, hospitals and schools. These were financed by donations from a population that saw charitable works as a way of securing salvation in the next world. Charitable institutions became more secular after the dissolution of the monasteries by Henry VIII: the rising mercantile classes and the new gentry created by the redistribution of Church property discovered that 'they could create institutions of social change and reformation with their own wealth and charity'.[3] This flowering of charity lasted until after the Civil War of 1642–51 and included the establishment of many schools, four great London hospitals and charities for the poor and destitute that were often administered by parishes or guilds.

In the 18th century, however, there was a shift in the nature of charity because of concern that private bequests deprived families of their inheritance and were poorly administered.[4] In the middle years of the century, 'associational' charities flourished – charities that raised money from the public, using the tools of the emergent popular press, in order to tackle social problems such as abandoned children and prostitution. Examples were the Foundling Hospital, set up by the sea captain Thomas Coram in 1739 and still in existence as the children's charity Coram, and the Marine Society (now the Marine Society and Sea Cadets), founded in 1756 to train destitute boys as sailors. Nearly 1,400 charitable schools were founded in England and Wales between 1710 and 1800, many by the Society for the Promotion of Christian Knowledge and the Sunday school movement.[5]

Towards the end of that century, however, the Industrial Revolution was gathering pace and campaigning as we would recognise it today, directed mainly at the government and legislators, began to take shape. The gradual but momentous social changes resulting from the Revolution led in the 19th century to mass poverty and ill-health among workers in the mills and factories of the Midlands and north of England. Charitable organisations responded as well as they could, but better communications, developments in political thought and revolution in France and America also prompted more people to think it was possible and right to address the causes of social distress as well as the symptoms.

Social reformers and philanthropists, often motivated by religious feeling and supported by churches, led the way and succeeded in pushing through many of the social reforms that we now take for granted. These include the abolition of slavery, better conditions in factories and mines, the protection of children and animals, universal adult suffrage, penal reform, education for all, the abolition of the death penalty and the decriminalisation of abortion and homosexuality. The successful 21st-century campaigns to ban foxhunting and smoking in public places follow in this tradition and feature in later chapters.

In some cases the vehicle of the reformers was a charity; in others, the means were friendly societies, co-operatives or simply unincorporated associations. Bodies that were not charities did not benefit from the advantages – or suffer from the restrictions – of charitable status, including the exemption from most taxes, which became increasingly significant with the steady increase over time in types and levels of taxation. But they were all part of what would nowadays be called the voluntary sector – independent, non-governmental organisations set up and financed by concerned individuals to seek what they saw as the relief of need, the common good or the improvement of their society, and at times pursuing that cause by campaigning for political change.

Charity law on campaigning

But was it legitimate for charities to campaign for changes in the law? Some court decisions in the 19th century indicated that judges thought charities, while disbarred from supporting a specific political party, could have a political purpose. But a definitive change came in 1917, when relatives of the late Charles Bowman challenged the provision in his will that the National Secular Society should inherit his estate.[6] In this case one of the judges, Lord Parker, stated that the objects of the Society, such as the disestablishment of the Church and the provision of secular education, were 'purely political objects' and 'a trust for the attainment of a political object is not charitable since the court has no way of judging whether a proposed change in the law will or will not be for the public benefit'. Decisions on what was for the public benefit – a fundamental requirement for charities – were for Parliament, not the courts, it was argued.

The 'political rule' established in the Bowman case became, in effect, the law, and was confirmed and extended by decisions in subsequent landmark cases. One of these came in 1948 when the judicial committee of the House of Lords (the precursor to today's Supreme Court) confirmed the refusal of charitable status to the National Anti-Vivisection Society.[7] In this case, ironically, the Law Lords seemed to set aside the Bowman principle that the courts could not make decisions about public benefit, asserting that the benefit to laboratory animals would be outweighed by the detriment to medical research. The second case was in 1981, when the High Court upheld the Charity Commission's refusal to register Amnesty International, which campaigns on behalf of prisoners of conscience around the world.[8]

The judgment in the Amnesty case underpinned the guidance to charities, first issued by the Charity Commission in 1995, about restrictions on political activity. The guidance allowed political activity that was 'ancillary' to a charity's work, but ruled it out if it was 'dominant' – a distinction that required some arguable judgements. Since then, however, these guidelines have been revised and relaxed several times in the light of political and social developments, most notably after the election of the Labour government in 1997. The most significant revision came after an extensive critical analysis of the law by the Advisory Group on Campaigning and the Voluntary Sector in 2007, when its chair, Baroness Helena Kennedy QC, stated that most people working in charities thought the rules on campaigning were "a minefield of confusion".[9, 10]

The Group's report argued that politics and charity were not different things and never had been: 'The key areas that charities are involved in, such as health, education and environment, criss-cross into the political.' In the same year, the government policy document *The Future Role of the Third Sector in Social and Economic Regeneration* reaffirmed that an organisation with an overtly political purpose could not be a charity, but stated:[11]

> Provided that the ultimate purpose remains demonstrably a charitable one, the government can see no objection, legal or other, to a charity pursuing that purpose wholly or mainly through political activities.

The subsequent revision of the Charity Commission guidance in 2008 affirms that campaigning and political activity by charities can be 'legitimate and valuable':[12]

> However, political campaigning, or political activity, as defined in this guidance, must be undertaken by a charity only in the context of supporting the delivery of its charitable purposes. Unlike other forms of campaigning, it must not be the continuing and sole activity of the charity. There may be situations where carrying out political activity is the best way for trustees to support the charity's purposes. A charity may choose to focus most, or all, of its resources on political activity for a period. The key issue for charity trustees is the need to ensure that this activity is not, and does not become, the reason for the charity's existence. Charities can campaign for a change in the law, policy or decisions where

such change would support the charity's purposes. Charities can also campaign to ensure that existing laws are observed.

Controversial cases

This guidance comes into play especially during election campaigns, when the Commission monitors what charities are saying and considers complaints. In the run-up to the 2015 general election, for example, it censured four charities whose names appeared (by mistake, they later said) on a list of 5,000 organisations that signed a letter to *The Times* in support of the Conservative Party.[13] In the next general election campaign, two years later, the right-leaning Institute of Economic Affairs (IEA) was given 'formal regulatory advice' by the Commission about two publications, one of which proposed what should be in the Conservative Party manifesto, while the other criticised the Labour manifesto; Unity Group Wales, a charity supporting lesbian, gay, bisexual and transgender (LGBT) people, was told to take down Labour Party posters in Swansea; and the National Council of Hindu Temples, which e-mailed members suggesting they should support the Conservative Party, agreed to send a second e-mail asserting that the Council was politically neutral.[14]

Outside election periods, the Charity Commission concluded, in response to a complaint in 2010, that the Atlantic Bridge Research and Education Scheme was promoting the 'special relationship' between the UK and the US in a way that was not compatible with its charitable purpose of the advancement of education for the public benefit.[15] The charity had created a Margaret Thatcher Lecture and an award called the Margaret Thatcher Medal of Freedom, and the Commission said it was apparent from the lectures and the recipients of the medal that the charity's focus was on the late Baroness Thatcher's view when she was prime minister that the so-called special relationship should be strengthened and promoted. 'This suggests that the activities of the charity are promoting a political policy which is closely associated with the Conservative Party,' the report said. Atlantic Bridge, founded by the Conservative MP and former cabinet minister Liam Fox, was told to 'cease its current activities immediately' and carry out a governance review. Fourteen months later, it decided to close.

In 2014, the international development charity Oxfam put out a tweet, with a picture embedded in it, to publicise its forthcoming report entitled *Below the Breadline*. The tweet showed a raging sea with the caption 'A Perfect Storm, starring Zero Hours Contracts, High Prices, Benefits Cuts, Unemployment, Childcare Costs'. The Conservative MP Conor Burns replied to the tweet, saying that it amounted to 'highly political advertising' and he was going to complain to the Commission. The regulator accepted that the charity did not intend to act in a political way, but said it 'should have done more to avoid any misperception of political bias by providing greater clarity and ensuring that the link to the *Below the Breadline* report was more obvious'.[16]

Think-tanks such as the IEA and Atlantic Bridge are often involved in spats about their charitable status. Another case happened in 2008, when the Charity Commission found that the Smith Institute, named after the late former Labour Party leader John Smith, was vulnerable to the perception that it was involved in party politics because it had frequently held seminars at the 11 Downing Street residence of the chancellor of the exchequer.[17] A dispute ensued, and two years later the Institute decided to stop being a charity. In 2014, the Commission concluded that the left-leaning Institute for Public Policy Research, in its report *The Condition of Britain*, had exposed itself to the perception that it supported the development of Labour Party policy.[18]

Other restrictions on charity campaigning

The 2008 guidance has remained in force, despite periodic suggestions it should be tightened. Fresh restrictions on charity campaigning were, however, imposed by another route. These apply only in the 12 months before elections and are contained in the Transparency of Lobbying, Non-party Campaigning and Trade Union Administration Act of 2014, known as the Lobbying Act for short.[19] Its purpose is ostensibly to prevent wealthy individuals and corporations influencing the democratic process, but it affects all organisations that might campaign, including charities. It requires them to register with and report to the Electoral Commission as 'non-party campaigners' if they spend more than £20,000 in England, or £10,000 in other parts of the UK, on 'regulated activities' that can 'reasonably be regarded as intended to influence voters'. There are strict limits on how much registered campaigners can spend on regulated activities – canvassing, public events, transport costs and so on.

The law caused consternation and uncertainty among charities. Does spending include staff costs? What qualifies as communication with the public, as opposed to supporters? How should costs be calculated when working in coalition with other charities? The 300 pages of guidance produced by the Electoral Commission to answer these and other questions was pronounced 'incomprehensible' by Sir Stephen Bubb, at the time leader of Acevo.[20] For the 2015 general election, there were 12 charities among 68 non-party campaigners registered with the Electoral Commission, including the gay rights charity Stonewall, the RSPCA, the Woodland Trust and the Salvation Army, all of which were familiar with campaigning work and big enough to take the extra bureaucracy in their stride. But there was also evidence that the law was having a chilling effect. "Lots of my clients are downing tools," said Chris Priestley, a charity specialist at the law firm Withers. "They have taken the view that with the administrative burden of trying to track spend, and the fear of being on the wrong side of the law, the simplest thing is not to campaign."[21]

After the election, the Commission on Civil Society and Democratic Engagement, set up by a broad coalition of charities and NGOs to investigate concerns about the Act and chaired by the former Bishop of Oxford, Lord Harries, concluded:[22]

> It had a negative impact on charities and campaign groups speaking out on crucial and legitimate issues ahead of the election … Charities and campaign groups reported to us that they found it difficult to know what was and was not regulated activity, and as a result many activities aimed at raising awareness and generating discussion ahead of the election have not taken place.

The government asked the Conservative peer Lord (Robin) Hodgson to review the workings of the Act, but cited lack of parliamentary time when it declined to act on his proposals.[23] The Labour Party pledged to repeal the Act, which remains a source of grievance for many charities and infrastructure organisations, including the NCVO, Acevo and CAF.

The government followed up the Lobbying Act with further initiatives on campaigning which charities found even more worrying. Shortly before the 2015 election, the then secretary of state for communities and local government, Eric Pickles, told Parliament that the IEA, one of the think-tanks mentioned above, had "undertaken extensive research on so-called 'sock puppets'":[24]

> "They have exposed the extensive practice of taxpayers' money being given to pressure groups and supposed charities, in turn being used to lobby the government and parliament for more money and more regulation. This is an issue which needs to be addressed. My department has set an example to the rest of Whitehall by amending our standard grant agreements to impose a new anti-lobbying, anti-sock puppet clause."

After the election returned the Conservatives with a small majority, the junior Cabinet Office minister at the time, Matt Hancock MP, emulated Pickles by announcing that all government departments would be required to insert a clause in all grant agreements, spelling out that the funding could not be used for activity intended to influence Parliament, government or political parties.[25] His statement again referenced the IEA research 'exposing the practice of taxpayers' money given to pressure groups being diverted to fund lobbying rather than good causes or public services'. It went on: 'Taxpayers' money must be spent on improving people's lives and spreading opportunities, not wasted on the farce of government lobbying government.'

When it was pointed out in Parliament by the then shadow charities minister, Anna Turley, that Hancock had recently received a donation of £4,000 from Neil Record, founder of a currency management company and chair of the IEA, Hancock replied that he had had no discussions with the IEA about the announcement and "it is right that taxpayers' money should be spent on the things for which it was intended, not on ensuring that lobbyists can take politicians out for lunch".[26] The Cabinet Office also issued a statement asserting that the decision 'to end the farce of government lobbying government' had been taken 'entirely on the advice of civil service officials'.[27]

Hancock's proposal raised the hackles of the voluntary sector as rarely seen before. Sir Stuart Etherington, then chief executive of the NCVO, said it amounted to charities being required to "take a vow of silence". It was potentially more damaging than the Lobbying Act, he said, because it was a matter of policy rather than legislation, and therefore more difficult to challenge.[28] "That's why you have to draw a line in the sand, because otherwise it might become more problematic – these guys aren't going to stop on this issue," he told a conference.

The fear among charities was that the proposal would prevent organisations in receipt of government funding from taking part in what they regarded as normal activities beneficial to all concerned, such as raising policy questions, hosting visits by MPs, presenting research findings to Parliament or contributing to the general policy debate.[29] An intensive backroom struggle with the Cabinet Office went on for several months and culminated with a threat by the NCVO to initiate a judicial review of the policy.

This prompted the government to back down, to the extent that the proposal was revised and more carefully worded.[30] The new guidance still prohibited paid-for lobbying and 'undue' attempts to influence policy using government funding, and some sector bodies, such as the National Association for Voluntary and Community Action (Navca), remained suspicious of it. Crucially, however, it allowed for what the sector regarded as 'legitimate influencing activity' and the change was regarded by Etherington as a victory:[31]

> Our principal concern with the original clause was
> that it was counterproductive and would have meant

grant-funded charities were unable to provide policy-makers with crucial insight that improves legislation, regulation and public services. This fundamental flaw has been recognised by government and the new guidance is crystal clear in saying that activities such as raising issues with ministers and civil servants, responding to consultations and contributing to the general policy debate are not only permitted but actively welcomed.

Successes despite restrictions

In summary, then, campaigning has been, and seems likely to continue to be, something of a minefield for charities. But relatively few charities choose to get deeply involved in sustained campaigning, especially on the national political stage; in the words of Gwythian Prins quoted at the start of this chapter, most of them more or less stick to their knitting, in the sense that they are involved exclusively in uncontroversial community, philanthropic or relief work in the UK and abroad. But the minority that do campaign persistently, or are involved in a mixture of relief work and campaigning, depending on current circumstances in their area of concern, are constantly under scrutiny, susceptible to challenge by politicians, censure by the regulator or legal restrictions. Governments since 2010 have, when pressed, acknowledged the importance of the campaigning role of charities in principle, but the record suggests that they were simultaneously inclined to restrict it. Some campaigning organisations, including Greenpeace, Friends of the Earth and Amnesty International, have chosen over time not to be charities in order to avoid the restrictions, or have been denied charitable status by the Charity Commission. Some of them have set up subsidiary charitable arms to provide education and research, follow other permitted charitable purposes or raise funds.

Whatever the recent arguments about charity campaigning, however, the fact remains that many beneficial changes in the law in the late 20th and early 21st centuries were the result of charity campaigns – some lasting for years – in alliance with sympathetic parliamentarians. The Royal Society for the Prevention of Accidents (RoSPA) and the Consumers' Association, for example, both campaigned successfully to make it compulsory for people to wear seatbelts in cars from 1983; RoSPA and the road safety charity Brake were also involved in the campaign to ban drivers from using mobile phones from 2003. Kidney Care UK was involved in the introduction of the kidney donor card, the precursor to modern donor cards, in 1971; a coalition of charities including the Child Accident Prevention Trust and the Children's Burns Trust were behind the change to building regulations in 2010 that made it compulsory to fit thermostatic mixer taps in new bathrooms; and a coalition of charities including the Campaign to Protect Rural England, Keep Britain Tidy, the Marine Conservation Society and Surfers Against Sewage helped to bring in the tax on plastic bags in England in 2015.

Whether they are charities or not, campaigning organisations are the part of the wider voluntary sector that forms the awkward squad – dissenting, protesting and fighting for their beliefs by political and other means. Sir Stephen Bubb, former chief executive of Acevo and founder of the think-tank Charity Futures, argued in a lecture in 2017 that campaigning has been an essential function of charities and other voluntary organisations in the modern era:[32]

> "The last 50 years have confirmed the role of charity and civil society in driving change and campaigning against injustice. We can all point to the campaigns that we like, or indeed don't. The diversity of the sector is demonstrated in such crusading. The Countryside Alliance wants foxhunting back while the RSPCA and many others do not. Looking at many of the major social advances of later years, it's been relentless and effective charity action that has delivered, from clean beaches and protected woodland, to mandatory seat belts and no smoking in public buildings, access to abortion, gay rights, disability … On a plethora of issues, charity lobbying has driven public sentiment and government reaction."

The next four parts of this book illustrate and analyse the work of charities under four headings, including 'Improving lives and communities', 'A junior partner in the welfare state?' and 'Preserving the past, preparing for the future'. But the first of them – 'Changing the world' – uses detailed case studies to amplify the subject of this chapter: campaigning.

PART II

Changing the world

4

The health of the nation

One of the incidental effects of the coronavirus crisis was to lift obesity high up the public health agenda. Charities and medical royal colleges in the UK had been campaigning for years for measures to reduce consumption of salt, sugar and fat, especially by children, but had achieved only limited results. The biggest breakthrough had come in 2016, when the government introduced the Soft Drinks Industry Levy, which taxed producers of drinks that contained more than 5 grams of sugar per 100 millilitres. When it came into effect two years later, a minister – making use of a calculation by CRUK – acknowledged that teenagers consume 'nearly a bathtub of sugary drinks each year'.[1] The campaign had been led by Sustain, a charity that runs a variety of projects to improve food and farming, backed by the chef and food writer Jamie Oliver. Once the tax came in, however, campaigners felt that any further measures were being kicked into the long grass by the government.

All that changed after the Prime Minister, Boris Johnson, emerged in April 2020 from intensive care after a battle with COVID-19. Doctors were already becoming aware that obesity was a factor in the disease, and on 25 July Public Health England issued a report saying 'people with Covid-19 who are living with overweight or obesity, compared with those of a healthy weight, are at increased risk of serious Covid-19 complications and death'.[2] Two days later the government announced new measures to combat obesity, including a ban on TV and online advertising before 9 pm of foods high in fat, sugar and salt.[3] The announcement was accompanied by an interview with Johnson saying he had been "way overweight … I was too fat".

The episode was an example of how the personal experiences of people in power can suddenly give momentum to long-standing, but struggling, charity campaigns. As part of its Children's Food Campaign, Sustain had been pressing for more than ten years for the TV ban, which its deputy chief executive, Ben Reynolds, welcomed as 'real game-changer'.[4] He pointed out that obesity was not just about personal willpower: 'You just have to look at the environment that we live in – the torrent of unhealthy food that bombards us – dominating advertising, our high streets, through to in-store promotions – it's everywhere.'

The difficulties of making headway against the opposition of the food industry and some politicians prompted the formation in 2015 of the Obesity Health Alliance, which has more than 40 members including health charities such as Diabetes UK, the British Heart Foundation (BHF) and CRUK, and medical royal colleges. It has agreed ten policy proposals, of which the main ones are restricting the promotion and marketing of unhealthy food and drinks, and reformulating food products to reduce calories and sugar. Caroline Cerny, Alliance lead, says that charities played a vital role in the Alliance:

> "The medical royal colleges are useful for their clinical voice, and they can put up some knowledgeable experts who can give real insight into how obesity is affecting their clinical practice. When you're trying to meet ministers, charities can open doors – they carry weight because they are seen as having credibility with the public. They also have a big reach and can get their supporters involved. The big charities can also get meetings with a broader focus – with the DCMS about advertising, for example."

Cerny says the proposed ban on advertising before 9 pm was a breakthrough because it was "a population-wide measure", as opposed to policies focused on individual choice and responsibility, which tend to be favoured by a government sceptical about 'the nanny state'. But she says there is still a long way to go – the measure needs primary legislation, and the food industry is fighting back.

The charity campaign against tobacco

While progress on obesity remained piecemeal, the campaign on smoking had already scored a big hit. By 2020 it seemed inconceivable that people should ever have eaten meals in restaurants full of cigarette smoke. As recently as the year 2000, smokers could still light up pretty much anywhere, except on aeroplanes and the London Underground. But within a few years that seemed plain wrong – the thought of a pub or sports clubroom thick with tobacco haze became repellent to most people.

Even the power of the tobacco lobby, and the substantial revenues from taxes on tobacco – an estimated £9.1bn in 2019/20, according to the Office for Budget Responsibility – could not prevent the enactment of the law against smoking in public places.[5] Public opinion shifted dramatically: when a ban was first mooted in 2003, people were either indifferent or firmly opposed, depending, usually, on whether they smoked or not. But public support for a ban doubled between 2003 and 2005.[6] And by the time the Health Act was passed two years later, making it a criminal offence to smoke in premises that are open to the public or constitute someone's place of work, there was overwhelming support for the change.[7] So what happened in a mere four years to turn the issue on its head?

The answer, in short, is a highly effective campaign spearheaded by a tiny charity called Action on Smoking and Health (ASH). It was set up in 1971 by the Royal College of Physicians after the UK government refused to act on the College's demands for policies to cut smoking. ASH gets nearly all its funding – about £765,000 in 2019 – from two other health charities, the BHF and CRUK, and uses it to influence public policy on tobacco. It coordinates the Smokefree Action Coalition, the umbrella group formed in 2003 to campaign for the ban on smoking in public that eventually comprised more than 60 organisations. When the Coalition started lobbying for smoke-free legislation, the debate was framed very much around what were called the 'rights' and 'freedoms' of smokers. But ASH opposed this by promoting the rights of employees not to be subjected to potentially lethal second-hand smoke at work.

This health message changed the debate. The former Labour MP Kevin Barron, an ardent anti-smoking campaigner who chaired the health select committee of MPs at the time, says that it was science that won in the end by proving that breathing in secondary smoke was damaging, and that it was ASH and other charities that brought this science to the attention of the public and policy makers. "At the time there were more than 120,000 people dying a premature death each year in the UK because of smoking," says Barron. "If that was road traffic accidents or war, we'd try and stop it."

The campaign employed tactics including public opinion polls, briefings of MPs, proactive and reactive media work, direct contact with local authorities, employers and legal experts, and profile-raising events. In a review of the campaign, ASH staff wrote that building the evidence base for their messages was of key importance, as was making it public at the right time.[8] 'For example,' they wrote, 'when health minister John Reid said he feared that banning smoking in public places would lead to more smoking in the home, so harming children, a paper was put together for a Royal College of Physicians' report collating the domestic and international evidence against this.'

ASH was also aware that in other countries the hospitality trade and the tobacco industry had successfully collaborated to resist anti-smoking legislation and support a voluntary approach instead; so another key strand to the campaign was to drive a wedge between these two powerful vested interests. Campaigners discovered that if a voluntary approach to smoke-free regulation was no longer on offer, the second-best options of each industry were different. The hospitality sector preferred nationally applicable legislation, as this would give a level playing field to geographically dispersed hotel and restaurant chains, and better protection against litigation. The tobacco lobby, by contrast, would rather have legislation that would permit local variation, which would be easier to fight location by location. The Labour government, meanwhile, had made clear that if a voluntary approach was off the cards, it would prefer locally applicable legislation. This prompted the hospitality trade to fight harder for its approach and made it easier for ASH to foment a split between it and the tobacco industry. Further pressure was put on employers by the threat of staff making claims under health and safety law. More than 50 such cases were begun, and although none made it to court before the smoking ban was passed, they had the desired effect on the debate.

There were still obstacles, not least opposition from the secretary of state for health at the time, former MP John (later Lord) Reid, who was an ex-smoker. Reid did not want legislation, and even when he accepted that a ban was inevitable he proposed exempting pubs and clubs that did not serve food. This proposal was in Labour's general election manifesto in 2005.[9] But the ASH campaign was given a shot in the arm by an extraordinary comment from Reid at a public meeting:[10]

> "I just do not think that the worst problem on our sink estates by any means is smoking but that it is an obsession of the middle classes. What enjoyment does a 21-year-old mother of three living in a council sink estate get? The only enjoyment sometimes they have is to have a cigarette."

The resulting media furore over Reid's clumsy assertion, combined with declarations about the risks to health by, among others, Sir Liam Donaldson, the government's chief medical officer at the time, helped to split the Parliamentary Labour Party and shore up support for the anti-smoking lobby.[11] The charity coalition led by ASH convinced the Conservatives to allow a free vote on the issue by their MPs, and on St Valentine's Day in February 2006, Parliament voted by a majority of 200 to pass the Health Bill.[12] The smoking ban came into effect on 1 July 2007. When ASH analysed the government's own impact assessment and concluded that more than 600,000 people would quit smoking as a result of the new law, it declared it to be 'the single biggest public health gain since the introduction of the National Health Service'.[13]

Deborah Arnott, chief executive of ASH, wrote about the charity's tactics in *The Guardian* newspaper after the law was changed:[14]

Campaigning of this kind is literally a confidence trick. The appearance of confidence both creates confidence and demoralises the opposition. The week before the free vote, we made sure the government got the message that we knew we were going to win and it would be better for them to be on the winning side.

In the event, an overwhelming 91% of Labour MPs who voted came out against the position on which the party had fought the election two years earlier.[15] Barron says the contribution from ASH and other charities was crucial to getting the legislation passed:

"The story that was not told at the time was that the charities were rallying their supporters and sending them to their MPs' constituency surgeries to ask them if they would vote in favour of a comprehensive ban. This was vital information, as we knew what was likely to happen when the actual vote came along in Parliament – we knew we would probably win the first vote. That in the end was what got us the numbers and got us the ban."

ASH also acted as the secretariat to the all-party parliamentary group on smoking and health and organised a visit by the health select committee of MPs to Dublin to see how the ban already enacted in the Irish Republic was working in practice. Arnott said the campaign went from nowhere to victory in a very short time. 'Some ideas reach a point at which their time has come,' she wrote. 'But some will also often need a vigorous campaign before politicians notice the obvious.'

But ASH wasn't finished yet. In 2008 the charity published a report reviewing the progress of controls on tobacco and calling for a new law prohibiting retailers from displaying tobacco products, and outlawing the sale of cigarettes and tobacco from vending machines.[16] The report also called for the removal of all colours, corporate logos, branding and positive images from tobacco packaging. Within a year, the Health Act 2009 brought in the ban on vending machines, effective from October 2011, and on the display of tobacco products in shops in England, Wales and Northern Ireland. ASH and its coalition partners also campaigned for standardised packaging, which was made compulsory by the Children and Families Act 2014.[17] This not only forced tobacco companies to sell their products in packets showing alarming images such as diseased lungs or children wearing oxygen masks, but also outlawed the sale of tobacco in small quantities. After May 2017, smokers were permitted to buy cigarettes only in packs of 20 or larger, and tobacco in 30-gram pouches. Menthol-flavoured cigarettes were banned from May 2020.

These new laws, promoted so effectively by one small charity, have been accompanied by a substantial fall in smoking, which is generally acknowledged to be one of the biggest causes of ill-health. An analysis of hospital admissions published in the *British Medical Journal* in 2010 showed that in the first year after the ban, emergency admissions for heart attacks in England fell by 1,200, saving the NHS more than £8 million.[18] According to Public Health England, 14.7% of adults in England were smokers in 2018, down from 19.8% in 2011.[19] In 2000, 26.8% of adults aged 16 and over had been smokers.[20]

Another campaign that played a part in changing public opinion in the build-up to the ban on smoking in public places was an unmissable TV and poster campaign by the BHF in 2003. It showed repulsive images of fat dripping from the end of a cigarette and fatty deposits being squeezed out of a human artery. It received extensive media coverage, and traffic to the BHF website spiked by 78%.[21] Another BHF advert featured two young men in a pub looking at a smiling woman smoking a cigarette. "Ugh," remarks one. "Like kissing an old ashtray."

Alcohol campaigns

When the first national coronavirus lockdown began in March 2020, the volume of sales in alcohol shops shot up by a third, according to the Office for National Statistics.[22] By September, however, it was clear that the increase in retail sales did not outweigh the loss of sales in pubs and restaurants: a total of

1.3 billion litres were sold in the four months to 11 July, compared with 2 billion litres in the same period the previous year.[23] But the charity Alcohol Change UK published a survey in April showing that 20% – an estimated 8.6 million adults – of drinkers were drinking more frequently and 15% of them were drinking more in each session.[24] Three months later the charity repeated the research and found that heavier drinking by a minority was continuing even though the first lockdown was easing.[25]

At the same time the charity also reported a fourfold increase in visits to its website, which has advice and information about how to keep drinking under control and where to find help and support. It also referred to research showing a link between increases in alcohol-related hospital admissions and decreases in spending on alcohol services since 2012. "By properly funding alcohol treatment services the government can save the NHS money, aid the national recovery effort and save lives," said Dr Richard Piper, chief executive of the charity.

Like many charities, Alcohol Change UK thus led the way during a national emergency in analysing the situation in its area of expertise, coordinating help and support for citizens and arguing for policy change by the government. In doing so it was building on nearly a decade of campaigns by both Alcohol Concern (which combined with Alcohol Research UK in 2017 to form Alcohol Change UK) and CRUK. Dryathlon, which involved giving up alcohol for January, was launched by CRUK in 2013; it was primarily a fundraising campaign, but it also reduced supporters' consumption of alcohol, which is a known cause of some cancers. In its first three years 170,000 'Dryathletes' raised more than £17 million.[26] Dry January, by contrast, was devised by Alcohol Concern as a public health campaign intended to counteract Christmas and new year binge drinking and the growing consumption of alcohol by the British. One study of global drug use suggested that Britons got drunk more often than the inhabitants of any other country in the world.[27]

The idea for Dry January came from one woman, Emily Robinson, who decided to run a half-marathon in February 2011.[28] She found the training hard and decided to see if giving up drinking would help. She noticed not only that she slept better, lost weight and had more energy, but also that everyone wanted to talk to her about what it was like to give up drinking for a while. One year later, Robinson joined the staff at Alcohol Concern and the idea for Dry January 2013 was born.

In that year, 4,350 people signed up. The following year more than 17,000 reported that they had stopped drinking for the month.[29] A study by the University of Sussex six months later found that of 900 abstainers surveyed, 72% had kept harmful drinking down afterwards and 4% were still not drinking.[30] Alcohol Concern struck up a partnership with Public Health England, and the government contributed £500,000 to Dry January in 2015, funding the campaign's first radio advertisements.[31] That year, 50,000 people gave up alcohol for the month, and in 2017 a YouGov survey found that four million had taken part.[32] Although Dry January did not start out as a fundraising event, several other charities joined the campaign as fundraising partners, encouraging supporters to take part and raise sponsorship. The success of Dry January and Dryathlon prompted Macmillan Cancer Support to create its own alcohol-abstinence fundraising event, Go Sober for October, in 2014.

Care of the mentally ill

Charities also led the way during the coronavirus pandemic in identifying its damaging effects on mental health, providing help and support and arguing for improved services. Two months after the first lockdown in March 2020, the Centre for Mental Health – a charity focused on research and policy – published a study estimating that 500,000 more people in the UK would suffer from depression and other mental health problems as a result of isolation, fear, grief, boredom and job insecurity in the expected recession.[33] It called for a continued financial safety net, government advice to businesses and institutions and targeted support for former COVID-19 hospital patients and health workers. Mind – the new name for the charity formed when three pioneering organisations merged in 1946 to become the National Association for Mental Health – published a survey showing that 65% of people with experience of mental health problems said their mental health was getting worse, and created a section of its website with comprehensive practical advice on improving mental well-being.[34]

The attention given to mental health during the pandemic owes much to increased public awareness and sensitivity about the subject in the 21st century. This was partly the result of Time to Change, a 15-year campaign by Mind and Rethink Mental Illness, another charity, to change attitudes. The treatment of those with mental illness had improved enormously since the 18th century, when people could pay to watch the disturbed behaviour of the patients in 'bedlam'– the Bethlem Royal Hospital, located until 1936 in the grand, colonnaded building which is now the Imperial War Museum in London. In Victorian times the attitude to mental illness was more humane, but treatment was based in large asylums with strict regimes which remained the norm well into the 20th century.

In the 1970s, however, the government was persuaded to adopt a policy of 'care in the community'. This involved closing many of the big asylums and arranging for people to live independently, with psychiatric supervision if necessary, or to be cared for in smaller units and hostels. But care in the community had its failures. In one notorious case in 1992 a newly married man, Jonathan Zito, died after being stabbed in the face on a train platform in London by Christopher Clunis, a young man with a history of mental illness who had been deemed suitable for independent living despite repeated episodes of violent behaviour.[35] This and other incidents led to a backlash in the tabloid press, which contended that community-based mental health services were failing to protect the public from what it called 'schizos' or 'psychos'.[36]

The regular Community Attitudes to Mental Illness (CAMI) surveys, funded by the Department of Health and Social Care (DHSC), revealed fear and discriminatory attitudes.[37] When the survey began in 1994, only 42% of a representative sample of the population believed that 'mental hospitals are an outdated means of treating people with mental illness'. The proportion agreeing that 'it is frightening to think of people with mental problems living in residential neighbourhoods' rose from 15%

in 1994 to 26% in 1997. In that year 33% also believed that 'anyone with a history of mental problems should be excluded from public office'.

Mind decided to try to help bring public attitudes into line with public policy. Sue Baker, hired in 1996 to set up the charity's media department, recalls one memorable double-page tabloid spread featuring pictures of machetes dripping with gore, accompanied by accusations that the government had blood on its hands because of its care in the community policies. She also remembers Mind's head of policy returning from a visit to the regions and relating how someone had thrown a brick through a young woman's window when her neighbours discovered she had recently been discharged from a psychiatric hospital: "We were hearing these sorts of things all the time, but for me that was the final straw."

She organised a project called 'Not just sticks and stones', based on interviews with nearly 2,000 people with mental health difficulties who told story after story about being refused jobs, education or housing, losing friends or relationships or being verbally or physically abused.[38] The media launch of the results was a great success, securing "wall-to-wall coverage on all the TV stations for 24 hours", according to Baker, and from then on there was a discernible shift in the tone of press coverage. Subsequent CAMI surveys revealed a softening of public attitudes, albeit marginal, and Baker and her colleagues became convinced that a high-profile, multifaceted campaign to reduce the stigma of mental illness could have a real impact.

After two years in New Zealand working for the Mental Health Foundation there, Baker was rehired in 2007 to lead Time to Change, the joint campaign between Mind and Rethink, financed for four years with a grant of £20 million from Comic Relief and the Big Lottery Fund. The project ran programmes with employers and schools and helped people with experience of mental illness to tell their stories and set up campaign groups; from 2011 the DHSC also contributed funding. The evaluation of Time to Change from 2008 to 2014, based partly on an analysis by the Institute of Psychiatry, Psychology and Neuroscience (IoPPN) at King's College, London, had encouraging results.[39] This analysis drew on a survey in which 1,000 people who had used mental health services in the last 12 months were interviewed about their experiences. It said:

> Comparing 2014 with 2008, there were significantly fewer experiences of discrimination with respect to friends, family, social life, dating, mental health staff, finding a job, keeping a job, police, education, religious activities, privacy, starting a family, or being shunned. The evaluation also notes a direct correlation between these findings and the Time to Change campaign. When the data from all time points are aggregated, a significant relationship between awareness of Time to Change and each of the outcomes is apparent.

In 2017, Time to Change and the IoPPN also released research showing that reporting of mental health by the print media was more balanced and responsible than before.[40] This study was based on an analysis of articles on mental illness in 27 local and national newspapers on two randomly selected days of each month during 2016. For the first time since the study had begun in 2008, there were more articles promoting mental health or portraying mental illness in a sympathetic way (50%) than stories that portrayed people with mental illness as a danger or problem to others or as hopeless victims (35%). The remainder were mixed or neutral.

Professor Sir Graham Thornicroft, who leads the team at the IoPPN, credits Time to Change with making a definitive impact on attitudes to mental illness:

> "There is no doubt that stigma and discrimination are slowly but steadily decreasing in England. This is against a backdrop where, before Time to Change, they were actually increasing. The team at King's College has published over 100 scientific papers about stigma since Time to Change began, looking in detail at many aspects of the impact, and we've seen how it has improved knowledge, attitudes and behaviours. I

do not think that all the stigma reduction in England is due to Time to Change, but I do think it has been the leader in this field and made the major contribution to these forms of social progress."

The biggest lesson from ten years of Time to Change, says Baker, who went on to become the campaign's global director, was that it demonstrated the effectiveness of leadership by people with direct personal experience:

"It's those of us with mental health problems leading change in our communities, workplaces, schools, at a national level – using our mental health issues as an asset, not a deficit. It was because so many people stayed silent for so long that you didn't realise you sat beside or were managed by or managed someone who had a mental health problem. All of that was hidden because people were so afraid of the consequences of being up-front about it."

Steve Loft was one such individual. In 2011 he was signed off from his job at Transport for London (TfL) for eight months while being treated for stress and depression. But going back to work was a trial. "It was like there was a big exclusion zone around me – nobody knew what to say to me," he recalls. "Although I had a good line manager, he did not have a clue about how to deal with someone with a mental health problem." Loft discovered that TfL had in fact signed the Time to Change pledge two years earlier, and he persuaded the company to set up an intranet site and a peer-support group that by 2019 had nearly 300 members. Time to Change supplied resources and speakers, and Loft became a 'workplace champion':

"This is really powerful as it gives people confidence to share their own experiences. I've seen a sea-change in attitudes to mental health in the last six years. I go out now and train other champions, and if I had a pound for every time someone said attitudes are changing, I'd be a rich man. I think there is going to come a tipping point. I'm old enough to remember all the things that used to happen with race, but then at some stage people just weren't prepared any longer to listen to other people talking and acting in a discriminatory way. I still think mental health has got a way to go, but it's certainly shifted a hell of a lot in those few years, and that's got a lot to do with those charitable organisations that have worked really hard to change things. Now, when people come back to work at TfL after being off for stress, I've noticed that others go and talk to them – they're not frightened any more. When I was off work, a lot of my problems stemmed from the fact that, as a middle-aged bloke, you just weren't conditioned to talk about your mental health. But it's very different now."

Unfortunately, however, in October 2020 the DHSC declared that it could not continue to fund Time to Change, and the charities that had run it for 15 years reluctantly announced its closure, with a warning that the gains made as a result of the campaign were at risk of sliding backwards.[41] Time to Change ended on 31 March 2021, very likely a direct casualty of the pressures on public spending created by the coronavirus pandemic.

Cervical screening

Other health campaigns by charities may be less high profile than those on smoking or mental health, but they appear regularly. They often form part of the controversies, debates and stories in the media that lead to improvements in official policy or changes in funding decisions. Early in 2018, for example, BBC News reported on a survey of more than 2,000 women which showed that one in four of them did not take up regular invitations to have a smear test, and that the figure was one in three for the 25–35 age group, in which cervical cancer is the most common form of cancer.[42] The reason women most commonly cited for not booking a test was embarrassment about a stranger examining their bodies. The research had clear implications for social policy and clinical practice, however, and Steve Brine MP, then the junior health minister responsible for cancer, pledged to support a campaign to reassure women and improve the level of response to invitations to smear tests, which are offered every three years to women aged between 25 and 49 and every five years to those between 50 and 64.

Who carried out and publicised the survey in question? It was a small charity called Jo's Cervical Cancer Trust, founded in 2000 by a London businessman, James Maxwell, after the death from cervical cancer at the age of 40 of his wife, Jo. She had wanted other women to have what she had missed: better screening and diagnosis, more medical information, the confidence to challenge doctors, and communication with others suffering from the disease.

In the following 20 years the Trust expanded and made a significant contribution to advances in the prevention and treatment of cervical cancer, including the introduction in 2008 of a programme of vaccination for girls in school against human papilloma virus, the cause of nearly all cases of the disease. In 2020 the Trust was employing about 25 people, running a comprehensive website, campaigning for better prevention and treatment, providing detailed medical information and offering emotional and practical support to women. Its annual income in 2019 of £1.6 million was a mixture of voluntary donations, grants from the DHSC and the Scottish Government, and gifts in kind such as advertising on Google.

★ ★ ★

Changing people's behaviour is rarely easy, especially when it involves asking them to re-examine deep-seated attitudes or to stop doing something they find pleasurable or convenient. The examples in this chapter show that it can be done through a combination of information, persuasion and legislation, and that charities have played a key part in both large- and smaller-scale measures to produce change affecting people's physical and mental health. The next chapter examines the involvement of charities in campaigns about something just as fundamental and often more controversial – human rights and equality.

5

Equality, slavery and human rights

When George Floyd, an unarmed Black[1] man, died after a White police officer knelt on his neck for nearly nine minutes in the US city of Minneapolis in June 2020, there was an upsurge of protest around the world, especially in the UK. There were marches and demonstrations all around the country throughout June, even in provincial centres such as Bournemouth and Cheltenham; protestors dumped the statue of the 18th-century slave trader Edward Colston into Bristol harbour and daubed the words 'was a racist' on the statute of Sir Winston Churchill in Parliament Square in London.

The protests took place under the banner of the Black Lives Matter movement, which started when Trayvon Martin was shot dead by a vigilante in Florida in 2013. The movement gathered strength from a shocking series of police shootings of Black people in US cities in the following years, and a UK version of Black Lives Matter was set up in 2016 for a demonstration on the fifth anniversary of the fatal shooting by the Metropolitan Police of Mark Duggan in north London. But the protests of June 2020, some of which resulted in clashes with police and a number of arrests, created a dilemma for the estimated 200 registered charities in England that are Black led or work in the area of race relations.[2]

"Most of them are involved in service delivery and are not campaigning organisations," says Elizabeth Balgobin, a charity governance consultant specialising in equality and diversity:

> "A lot of them have council grants that restrict what they do or might have a reputation clause, and there would be a fear of being criticised as political. Some

staff might be involved, but that would be privately, below the radar. A lot of the activists are young people who aren't working through charities."

Nevertheless, some charities published statements of support, including the Bristol-based Stand Against Racism and Inequality (SARI), which said it would not be joining in demonstrations because of coronavirus social distancing rules, but 'stands in absolute solidarity with the mission and belief of Black Lives Matter, "imagining and creating a world free of anti-Blackness, where every Black person has the social, economic, and political power to thrive"'.[3] Irvin Campbell, the charity's chair, added that SARI could not condone any criminal acts in relation to the Colston statue, but believed it ought to be in a museum rather than a public space.[4]

Meanwhile two different UK organisations, neither of them charities, were using Black Lives Matter in their titles and raising funds for their activities. In their public statements, they seemed caught in a debate between revolutionary and evolutionary approaches. The one founded in 2016, Black Lives Matter UK, was raising funds in 2020 on the GoFundMe website, where it states that it aims to 'dismantle imperialism, capitalism, white supremacy, patriarchy and the state structures that disproportionately and systematically harm Black people in Britain and around the world'.[5] An earlier update on this site adds that 'a charity structure would not allow us the freedom and flexibility to do our political work in the ways we wish to do them'. The other organisation has a website, blacklivesmatter.uk, which states it is a 'non-political, non-partisan, non-violence Black Lives Matter platform', and dissociates itself from the other organisation.

It's clear that informal bodies and pressure groups, which often communicate and organise through social media, play a greater part in demonstrations and protests than organisations constituted as charities. But charities in the UK have played a leading part in researching the nature of racism and discrimination and in campaigning for changes in policy and attitudes, and are likely to continue to do so. Their work began after the Second World War when immigrants from the British Commonwealth came to the UK, partly to help rebuild the economy and partly to escape unemployment and poverty.

From Enoch Powell to Black Lives Matter

The start of post-war immigration is popularly seen as the arrival in Southampton in 1949 of the *Empire Windrush*, bringing nearly 500 Jamaican men to join the UK labour market. Immigration from the Caribbean grew through the 1950s, but the government did not consider that immigration control or race relations legislation was necessary until 1958, when the effects of discrimination and disadvantage boiled over onto the streets. First in Nottingham and then in Notting Hill in west London, White gangs roamed the streets attacking Black people; nine White 'teddy boys' were eventually jailed. From the early 1960s, immigration from Pakistan and India also began to grow significantly, particularly to Bradford, Leicester and Southall in west London.

There followed two decades when governments of both main parties progressively tightened immigration control and, in parallel, gradually strengthened measures to outlaw discrimination. By the end of the process the British Nationality Act of 1971 had put Commonwealth citizens on virtually the same footing as citizens of other countries if they wanted to enter Britain; and the Commission for Racial Equality (CRE), set up in 1976 to replace previous, weaker arrangements, had been given the power to investigate and prosecute acts of both direct and indirect discrimination. In 2007, the CRE was subsumed into the Equality and Human Rights Commission under legislation that also imposed a duty of promoting racial equality on many public authorities.

Despite both the restrictions on immigration and the measures to prevent discrimination, British society was marred by conflict and controversy over race. In 1968 the Conservative MP Enoch Powell made the notorious speech in which he said, "like the Roman, I see the Tiber flowing with much blood".[6] In 1981, riots sparked by harsh police action against Black people broke out, first in Brixton in south London and then in the Liverpool district of Toxteth. In 1986, PC Keith Blakelock was killed during a riot on the Broadwater Farm housing estate in Tottenham, north London, where a Black woman had died of heart failure during a police raid. In 1993 the Black teenager Stephen Lawrence was murdered in south London by a gang of White racists; the subsequent inquiry report declared that the Metropolitan Police was 'institutionally racist' and led to the establishment of enhanced procedures for complaints against the police.[7] The behaviour of the police towards Black people has continued to produce flashpoints, such as the shooting of Mark Duggan by officers in north London that led to disturbances on the streets in 2011.

Over the years there has been some reduction in racial discrimination and disadvantage, resulting in increased proportions of people from Black and minority ethnic backgrounds in Parliament, the arts, the media, other professions and sport. But discrimination and disadvantage continue to come to light in British society in areas ranging from education to employment and the criminal justice system. Black Caribbean pupils were around three times more likely to be permanently excluded from school in 2015/16 than White British pupils, for example, and one in ten adults who were Black or of Pakistani, Bangladeshi or mixed origin were unemployed, as compared to one in twenty-five White people.[8] Black people were more than three times as likely to be arrested as White people and more than six times as likely to be stopped and searched by police; 12% of the prison population was Black, compared to 3% of the population as a whole.[9,10] All this helps to explain why the Black Lives Matter movement found such fertile ground in the UK.

The role of charities in race relations

During the second half of the 20th century, charities and voluntary organisations were closely involved, at several levels, in attempts to create a society free from racial discrimination and conflict. At the local level in the 1950s, many community relations organisations – some of them paternalistic in style – were set up, such as the Bristol Committee for the Welfare of Colonial Workers or the Nottingham Commonwealth Citizens Consultative Committee. Many churches became involved in local initiatives. Immigrant groups set up organisations with local branches to oppose discrimination in employment, such as the Indian Workers Association and the Black Workers Movement.

At a national level, some existing organisations became involved in race relations. Political and Economic Planning (PEP), a think-tank that had been founded in 1931 and influenced many social reforms of the post-war period, produced several studies on race in the 1960s. These are credited with prompting the extension of race relations legislation in 1968 to cover discrimination in housing and employment as well as in access to public places. A further series of PEP studies in the 1970s, jointly financed by the Home Office and the Calouste Gulbenkian Foundation, a grant-making charity, formed the backdrop to the Race Relations Act 1976, which outlawed indirect discrimination and created the CRE.

The Institute of Race Relations, a think-tank with charitable status, was set up in 1958 to study the relations between races everywhere, and between 1963 and 1969 – financed by the Nuffield Foundation, a grant-making charity – produced *Colour and Citizenship*, a massive, ground-breaking 800-page study of British race relations.[11]

Two of the most influential and effective charities on immigration and race relations were the Joint Council for the Welfare of Immigrants (JCWI) and the Runnymede Trust, both of which were still active in 2020. The JCWI was set up in 1967 and since then has campaigned against the perceived injustices of the increasingly complex web of immigration laws and regulations. It has used the courts, the media and its political influence both to challenge policy and to pursue individual cases. Early in 2019, the JCWI successfully challenged the so-called 'right to rent' rule, part of the 'hostile environment' for illegal immigration brought in by the former prime minister, Theresa May, when she was home secretary in 2016. The rule, which required landlords to check the immigration status of prospective tenants, was declared by the High Court to be a breach of human rights law.[12] The Court of Appeal overturned this decision the following year, but the charity pledged to take the case to the Supreme Court.[13] In August 2020 the Home Office scrapped an algorithm it had been using to assess visa applications after the JCWI and the tech-justice organisation

Foxglove threatened it with judicial review. The two groups claimed the algorithm entrenched racial bias and discrimination in the visa-processing system, but before the case made it to court, the Home Secretary, Priti Patel MP, agreed to suspend the use of the tool pending a redesign of the process.[14]

The Runnymede Trust was named after the island in the Thames where in 1215 King John and his barons signed the Magna Carta, which was seen (erroneously, according to some historians) as a guarantee of individual rights and freedoms as well as a brake on the powers of the Crown. The charity was founded in 1968, partly in response to Enoch Powell's 'rivers of blood' speech, to contribute to public education on race relations by conducting research and engaging with policy questions. Its co-founder, Anthony (later Lord) Lester, who died in 2020, had been involved in the drafting of earlier legislation on race relations, and in the 1970s was special advisor to Roy Jenkins, the home secretary in the Labour government when, as mentioned above, the most far-reaching piece of race relations legislation was passed.

Usha (now Baroness) Prashar became assistant director of the Runnymede Trust in 1975 and helped to steer through the new Race Relations Act 1976. She says the charity was influential because it established itself as authoritative:

> "Its credibility was based on the fact that it was not sensational, gave accurate information and analysis, and influenced government departments on what good race relations policies might be. We had highlighted how the 1968 Race Relations Act was limited because it didn't deal with indirect discrimination. And the 1976 Act did finally deal with it. It was a recognition that discrimination could be systemic and therefore you had to look at institutionalised discrimination and racism. The concept of indirect discrimination was, in my view, the most innovative aspect of that law. As the law went through, Runnymede was in the background playing a role and setting a climate with the broader work it was doing, and was also involved in specific

things such as drafting amendments at the committee stage of the Bill and providing briefings to MPs."

The Runnymede Trust also played a part in persuading health authorities to put more resources into treating sickle cell anaemia, which mainly affects Black people. An influential Runnymede publication in 1976 was *Publish and Be Damned*, which led to a code of practice for the media about handling stories concerning race. *Real Trouble* analysed the treatment of Asian youths arrested during the march in 1979 by the National Front through Southall, west London, during which a young anti-fascist demonstrator, Blair Peach, died. The training of magistrates was subsequently improved.

But there were other milestones of progress towards racial equality that were, according to Prashar, erected partly by the efforts of smaller, informal, mainly Black-led voluntary and community groups. One was the abolition of the 'sus' law – the power in the Vagrancy Act 1824 that allowed police to stop and search anyone they considered to be acting suspiciously. The power had been used extensively by the police in Black communities and was considered to have contributed to the riots in British cities. Mavis Best, for example, led a group of Black mothers in south London in the Scrap Sus Campaign, which held demonstrations, lobbied politicians and played a part in the abolition of the power, as recommended by the Royal Commission on Criminal Procedure in 1981. Prashar says:

"I think minority communities did see bodies like Runnymede as agents for change, but at that time in the 1960s and '70s many of them established their own self-help groups, almost as an alternative, because they did not feel part of the existing charitable sector. I think there was a certain amount of racism in the local white voluntary sector at the time. It has changed to some extent in that you do now have people from minority communities running mainstream charities, and charities themselves have realised they have got to involve and engage with minority communities. It's patchy, but it's beginning to change."

Despite continuing disputes about the nature of, and remedies for, racism in British society, it is clear that a number of respected charities made the running in improving race relations and outlawing racial discrimination in the second half of the 20th century, and continue to advocate for the rights of minorities. Other influential charities in the field of race relations have sprung up more recently, including two focused on challenging racism in football and sport – Kick It Out, and Show Racism the Red Card. The work of the Stephen Lawrence Charitable Trust, founded after the murder of the Black teenager in 1993, includes support for community organisations, and career guidance and bursaries for young people to study architecture, as Stephen had wanted to do.

Race equality within charities

As Prashar indicates, charities were in some cases slow to assess whether they were reaching beneficiaries in minority communities, or reaching them in an appropriate way. It was not until the first decade of the 21st century, for example, that the BHF improved its services to people of South Asian origin, who are at particular risk of heart attacks: it began to fund grassroots community organisations, produce information leaflets and DVDs in various languages and set up stalls at summer melas (community fairs).[15] Similarly, Macmillan Cancer Support began employing ethnic minority community liaison officers and interpreters and Prostate Cancer UK produced targeted information for Afro-Caribbean men, who are more likely to suffer from the condition, and features them prominently in its publicity.

Progress on racial equality has also been slow in both charity governance, which is dealt with in Chapter 20, and the sector's workforce more generally. Official figures in 2019 showed that the proportion of non-White staff in the public and private sectors was 12%, but in the voluntary sector it was 9% (14% of the UK population is non-White).[16] In 2018 Thomas Lawson, then chief executive at Leap Confronting Conflict, a charity that supports young people, called on charity leaders to recognise and tackle what he called 'the ingrained racial prejudices that permeate organisations in the sector'.[17]

The issue was urgent enough for Acevo to commission and publish research in 2020 that showed that 68% of Black and minority ethnic (BAME) people working in charities had 'experienced, witnessed or heard of' examples of racism at work; it called for charities to adopt explicit race equity goals in both their own organisations and the work they do.[18] The NCVO, the biggest and most influential of the sector umbrella bodies, was also shaken by the issue. A report on equity, diversity and inclusion in the 105-strong workforce by an external consultant in 2020 was not published externally, but the chief executive, Karl Wilding, who had succeeded the long-serving Sir Stuart Etherington in 2019, said in a blog: 'That we are a structurally racist organisation is now clearer than ever.'[19] Wilding resigned in January 2021 after 23 years at the organisation. In the following month details of the consultant's report appeared in the press: it said bullying and harassment on the grounds of race, gender, sexual orientation and disability were common and there was an 'in-crowd' of 'white, abled people'.[20] In response, the interim chief executive, Sarah Vibert, said there was a 'toxic culture': 'We were shocked and ashamed that an organisation with such a long and proud history as NCVO has enabled such a culture to persist and we are absolutely determined that this should change and fast.'[21]

These reports from Acevo and the consultant for NCVO came in the wake of the launch online of #CharitySoWhite (CSW), which followed the publication of a slide from training material by the charity Citizens Advice that was deemed to be racist. Under the heading 'Barriers we find in BME communities', the slide contained bullet points such as 'an intrinsically cash-centric culture', 'very close-knit extended families', 'evidence of gender bias and discrimination' and 'a cultural focus on honour and shame'.[22] Martha Awojobi, then a fundraiser for the domestic abuse charity Refuge and a CSW committee member, told a conference:

> "Something that's really struck me in the last few months since I joined the campaign is our utter unwillingness as a sector to say the word 'racism'. This is the very beginning of the conversation that

needs to be had. Structural racism is at the forefront of the reason why there is no diversity in our sector – and the reason why BAME people keep leaving."

In August 2020, the 4F Group, which called itself 'a multicultural team of various faiths and beliefs', published a report which criticised CSW for calling the training material racist and said Citizens Advice was wrong to admit that the material was 'unacceptable' and promoted racial stereotypes.[23] The content was part of efforts to understand and help minorities, it argued, and could be seen as racist only if taken out of context.

Am I not a man and brother?

Charities had their biggest success in the field of race and human rights more than two centuries before the emergence of Black Lives Matter. One of the most memorable images of the campaign in question showed a Black slave, on his knees and half naked, holding up his manacled hands above the inscription: 'Am I Not a Man and Brother?' This was first produced in the form of a medallion by the famous English pottery company Wedgwood and became the badge of the Society for Effecting the Abolition of the Slave Trade, founded by a group of Quakers and evangelical Protestants in 1787. Josiah Wedgwood, founder of the Stoke-on-Trent pottery company, was an ardent supporter of abolition. The image was used on fashionable items including crockery, necklaces, brooches, hairpins and snuff boxes – the forerunners, in effect, of the pin badges, T-shirts, car stickers and wristbands issued by modern charities and campaigners.

Many people disapprove of the image today because it shows the subject as a humble supplicant and fails to reflect both the suffering of slaves and their attempts to free themselves through their own efforts, including rebellion. But in its day it was highly effective, and the inscription became a catchphrase. Wedgwood sent a packet of the medallions to Benjamin Franklin, president of the Pennsylvania Abolition Society in the US, who replied that its power was 'equal to that of the best written Pamphlet, in procuring favour to those oppressed People'.[24]

The drive to abolish slavery is widely regarded as the prototype of campaigns for human rights and equality. Over two decades, it built up support through pamphlets, lecture tours and petitions to Parliament, and William Wilberforce's Bill abolishing the trade in slaves by British ships was passed into law in 1807 with only 16 votes against it in Parliament: it was reported that MPs were carried away by the success, rising to their feet and cheering. The movement was renamed the Anti-Slavery Society in 1823 and eventually achieved the abolition of the practice of slavery itself in the British Empire in 1833 – three days before Wilberforce died. The campaign against slavery in its modern forms also continues in the work of Anti-Slavery International, founded in 1839.

This humanitarian campaign was described in a lecture by Andrew Purkis, a historian and charity expert, as "the first great national, organised voluntary sector political agitation. It established the model for countless other agitations in the rest of the 19th century and beyond, in tandem with progressive extensions of the political franchise."[25] Many of these 'agitations' were not legally set up as charities, but were charitable in the sense that they were conducted by like-minded social reformers voluntarily forming and financing an organisation dedicated to procuring a specific benefit in people's lives.

Penal reform and working conditions

One campaign that got under way at about the same time as the drive against slavery was led by John Howard, who was appointed lord lieutenant of Bedfordshire in 1773. He was shocked by conditions in the county jail and other prisons he visited, and went on to promote new laws to end the system in which jailers were not salaried and made their living by charging prisoners for food and bedding. He also went on journeys through Europe in search of a humane model for English prisons, publishing his findings in two substantial volumes. When he died of typhus in 1790, he was busy inspecting Russian military hospitals.

Howard's work led to the separation of men and women in jails, a better diet for prisoners and a reduction in the range of crimes that carried the death penalty. But by the middle of the 19th century concern was growing in the government that prisons were getting too soft, and new legislation led to a harsher system based on what the assistant director of prisons, Sir Edmund du Cane, called 'hard labour, hard fare and hard board'. A new charity named after John Howard, the Howard Association, was formed in 1865 to try to soften the regime.

The Association campaigned for better independent inspection of prisons, more effective management and staffing, improved diet, the end of capital and corporal punishment, and useful employment in place of the punitive but unproductive time prisoners were made to spend on the treadmill. In 1921 the Association merged with the Penal Reform League to become the Howard League for Penal Reform and, as such, it has remained active and vocal, although the Prison Reform Trust was also formed in 1981 by people who wanted to emphasise different concerns. The League played a significant role in the abolition of the death penalty in 1965, and its most successful campaigns have included improvements in the treatment of young people in custody, the removal of restrictions on the books prisoners are allowed to have and the abolition of the fee that people convicted of offences formerly had to pay to the court.

The humanitarian concerns that came to the fore in the 19th century went far beyond slavery and the treatment of prisoners. Growing industrialisation entailed punishingly long shifts for factory workers, which gave rise to the campaign to restrict working hours. The Factories Act of 1833 laid down that children between 9 and 13 years of age should not work longer than 8 hours a day in the cotton mills, and those between 14 and 18 no longer than 12 hours. But pressure was growing to restrict the working day to 10 hours for everyone in factories of all kinds. The campaign was a collaboration involving 'short time committees' formed by millworkers themselves, members of the Church of England, a few mill owners such as John Fielden, and Lord Shaftesbury, leader of the Factory Reform Movement in Parliament.

This movement was given impetus by the fiery pamphleteering and oratory of Richard Oastler, who wrote of 'Yorkshire slavery' in the textile mills of the industrial North, and of streets 'wet by the tears of innocent victims at the accursed shrine of avarice, who are compelled (not by the cart-whip of the negro slave-driver) but by the dread of the equally appalling thong or strap of the over-looker'.[26]

Success for the campaign came in the form of the Factories Act 1847, which was perceived by some MPs as revenge by landowners in Parliament for the repeal of the corn laws earlier that year: the relaxation of restrictions on importing corn was going to hit their profits, and the shortened working day would hit the profits of the mercantile class in turn.[27]

Shaftesbury, an evangelical Christian who had had an unhappy childhood, was an inveterate reformer whose campaigns earned him the nickname of 'The Poor Man's Earl'. Among other things, he led campaigns to improve care of the insane, spare women and children from working underground in mines and prevent 'climbing boys' being employed as chimney sweeps. In 1885, shortly before his death, he also founded the London Society for the Prevention of Cruelty to Children ('London' was in due course changed to 'National'), which succeeded five years later in persuading Parliament to pass a law to protect children from abuse and neglect. The National Society for the Prevention of Cruelty to Children (NSPCC) is now part of the social fabric in the UK; it has statutory powers under the Children Act 1989 to apply for care and supervision orders for children at risk. The charity also incorporates ChildLine, which children can phone for help if they are frightened or being mistreated. The Howard League and the NSPCC are examples of how some campaigns of the 19th century have lived on, with changing emphases, into the 20th and 21st centuries; and Shaftesbury's concerns about the condition of asylums and people with mental illness are also still being pursued by charities, as discussed in the previous chapter.

Other rights campaigns

Other examples of charities succeeding in changing the law are happening all the time, although their role is not always widely noticed. In December 2017, for example, the High Court ruled that the government's changes to a benefit called the Personal

Independence Payment were 'blatantly discriminatory' against people with mental health problems.[28] The case was brought on behalf of a single complainant by the Public Law Project, a legal charity, using evidence supplied by the National Autistic Society, Disability Rights UK, Revolving Doors and Inclusion London – all of them charities. Mind, as the country's best-known mental health charity, also took part in the case, on the grounds that the rights of people not directly involved could also be affected. Early in 2018, the government decided not to challenge the court ruling and said it would pay some people the allowances that had been denied them.

★ ★ ★

Human rights and equality have clearly been high on the agenda for voluntary organisations and charities. There is little doubt that they have played a crucial part, by conducting research and campaigning, in changing the law, changing social attitudes and improving life for disadvantaged groups in society, including racial and other minorities. 'Moments' in history, such as the killing of George Floyd, will give a fresh focus and impetus to long-standing campaigns, but charities were there before and will still be there afterwards, for the long haul. Charities have also been deeply involved in the liberation of women, who, until relatively recently, were treated as the property of their husbands, excluded from education and most professions and denied the right to vote: this is the first subject of the next chapter.

6

Rights for women and gay liberation

The value of charities that support victims of violence against women and girls quickly became apparent during the first coronavirus lockdown in the UK early in 2020. In the first few weeks, calls to the National Domestic Abuse Helpline, run by the charity Refuge, increased by 66% and visits to its website increased tenfold.[1] And at the end of April another domestic abuse charity, Women's Aid, doubled the hours that its live-chat service was available, after demand rose by 41% in one week.[2]

Charities were not surprised by this, as similar spikes in domestic violence had also happened in other countries, such as China, which had locked down earlier than the UK. They immediately asked the government for emergency funding and remodelled their services to comply with lockdown rules by working at home, online or by telephone.[3] The government responded with a £76 million fund, including £10 million for refuges, which was distributed by Whitehall departments to charities they already worked with.[4]

One such charity was Hestia, which runs refuges in London and the south-east of England. Its chief executive, Patrick Ryan, recalls that in the first week of May, it managed within a few days to open a new 12-bed refuge in a building previously used by foreign students. A month later, it received funding to open a second 12-bed crisis refuge. Hestia also resurrected a pre-existing relationship with the Royal Pharmaceutical Society for a new initiative at Boots stores, which put up posters and added details to its till receipts about the charity's Bright Sky app, which provides a UK-wide directory of domestic abuse services. Ryan says:

"We knew we needed to reach victims who were trapped at home with their abusers under lockdown. At that time the only places people could go were to the shops or to the pharmacy. So we developed Safe Spaces, which gave victims of domestic abuse the opportunity to ask for help in their Boots. They get to use the safe space of the consultancy room and access to information about local domestic abuse services. We know that over 100 victims across the UK used the pharmacy Safe Space in the first three weeks. Lives have been changed and saved."

Turning the tide on domestic violence

When the pandemic started, charities providing refuge for women had been going for nearly half a century. The first domestic violence shelter in Europe was set up in Chiswick in west London in 1971 by Erin Pizzey, the social activist and writer, whose parents had both been violent when she was growing up. In an interview in 2016, Pizzey recalled that if women wanted to leave a violent relationship before the 1970s, the social services department would probably take their children into care; the police wouldn't get involved because it was "just a domestic"; and victims would be cast out of their homes with no money and nowhere to go. "What was so shocking was that the government knew what was going on," said Pizzey. "They knew these were women who were in the most terrible situations and yet they did not lift a hand to help."

Pizzey's answer was to convert a two-up, two-down terraced house, which she had opened as a community hub for housewives, into Chiswick Women's Aid, a refuge for abused women. Mattresses were donated by the Salvation Army and local shops contributed food. The charity expanded, rebranded as Refuge in 1993, and attracted the support of the late Diana, Princess of Wales. In 2019 it was running a national network of refuges, an advisory service and a telephone helpline and was campaigning for a fully funded national strategy on domestic violence, including stronger action from the police and courts. One week after the second lockdown began in England in

November 2020, Refuge issued a warning that calls to its helpline were rising sharply again, and published a dossier with recommendations about actions that needed to be taken to prevent recurrence of the spike in domestic abuse that occurred during the first lockdown.[5]

The growth of charities to support abused women, and their increasing influence on government and society, has been witnessed over three decades by Vivienne Hayes, chief executive of the Women's Resource Centre, an umbrella body that provides training, information and support for women's organisations, mainly small ones. She says setting up the first refuges was the beginning of the shift in public attitudes:

> "I last ran a refuge in 2005, and even then the women who came in still thought, 'oh, it's just me, it's my fault, it must be something I've done wrong'. But if the women in the refuge are able to discuss with each other, and with the workers, the fact that violence against women and girls is not an individual act – that it's systemic and institutionalised and is not the fault of the woman – that's a huge thing for them. But that process can only happen in women-only safe spaces, which is what those early refuges provided. From those refuges grew the seeds of the movement of women who wanted to challenge the acceptance of domestic violence and the wider system of male violence against women."

The campaign against domestic violence ran in conjunction with the burgeoning women's liberation movement, and in the years immediately after the first refuges opened other measures helped to empower women: contraception became available on the NHS in 1974, for example, and the Sex Discrimination Act 1975 outlawed discrimination at work and in the provision of goods and services. As more women gained the confidence to become activists, new organisations sprang up, tackling fresh issues, providing services and lobbying for change.

In 1991, after 15 years of sustained campaigning by women's groups, the appellate committee of the House of Lords – the equivalent at the time of the Supreme Court – finally overturned the long-held principle in English law that a man who had sex with his wife against her will could not be convicted of rape. Another key moment came in 1992 when Kiranjit Ahluwalia, a woman jailed for murdering her husband three years earlier, had her conviction overturned. Ahluwahlia had endured ten years of physical and sexual violence before finally retaliating and setting him on fire. The women's rights group Southall Black Sisters took up her case and campaigned for her murder conviction to be commuted to manslaughter.[6] Says Hayes: "That set a legal precedent that if women retaliate or use violence against a perpetrator, their own experience of abuse will be taken into account. That was another massive step forward."

Charities in the women's sector have also had some success in challenging the most restrictive aspects of the Legal Aid, Sentencing and Punishment of Offenders Act 2012, which governs legal aid to people affected by domestic violence. "It's still not OK, but as a result of campaigning by the charity Rights of Women and others, amendments were accepted that took the sharp edges off a very damaging bill," says Hayes. Women's organisations were also instrumental in overturning the Parole Board's decision in 2018 to release John Worboys, who had been convicted for raping women in his London taxi, and they argued that victims of serious sexual and violent crimes should be able to use the Human Rights Act if they felt police had failed in their duty to investigate properly.[7] The Supreme Court agreed.[8] Hayes concludes:

> "The women's charity sector and women's organisations are at the centre of all the gains for women in this country, all the rights for women. Appropriate remedies don't happen without women's organisations and activists working to force the government to give those remedies. All the gains to date are as a direct result of campaigning."

This view appears to be endorsed in the government's own consultation in March 2018 on the proposed new law on domestic abuse:[9]

We listened when professionals told us that this abuse was not just characterised by physical violence, and that victims of domestic abuse are often subjected to wider abuse through control and coercion which permeate all aspects of their life. We have rolled out Clare's Law [the Domestic Violence Disclosure scheme] which allows anyone to ask if their partner has a violent history. We also introduced Domestic Violence Protection Orders to give the police and courts better options for controlling the harmful behaviour of dangerous perpetrators. There has been great progress in the response to domestic abuse and the way we treat victims and survivors.

Hayes says there is still some way to go in how domestic abuse is officially reported because it is often not categorised as such, but she agrees that nowadays women "no longer think it's OK for a man to hit them". Attitudes to rape have shifted too, she says – the idea that it's something perpetrated by a stranger in a dark alley is outdated now, and most people are aware that the majority of rapes are committed by men already known to the victim.

'The victim is not at fault'

Sheila Coates is director of the South Essex Rape and Incest Crisis Centre, a small charity that provides counselling, emotional support and practical information for women. She has worked with victims of sexual violence since 1983 and says that until the early 2000s nobody knew very much about sexual abuse:

> "People knew the word rape and understood what rape meant, to a degree, but there were still lots of myths, such as that the victim must have asked for it, it was her own fault, she shouldn't have been out on her own so late, her skirt was too short. And no one knew anything at all, really, about child sexual abuse."

But the murders of ten-year-old Holly Wells and Jessica Chapman by Ian Huntley at Soham in Cambridgeshire in 2002 thrust child sexual abuse into the spotlight, and the media started taking a much greater interest in sexual violence and violence in relationships. Coates says things have changed dramatically since then:

> "As well as more coverage, pressure from the women's sector was relentless. For 30 years we just repeated the same things, over and over, in all the forums where they needed repeating: the Home Office, the Ministry of Justice, local authorities, the health services, the social services. We have loads of campaigning and activist groups, who go out and push the message that the victim is not at fault and that there is help out there. If you think about domestic violence, it's very rare now that men will sit in pubs or clubs and openly tell other men about beating their wife up. Women just aren't prepared to put up with abuse any more, because it's not the hidden issue it used to be."

Coates says that one result that has had an impact is the Victims Code, which sets out the minimum service that victims should receive from the criminal justice system:[10] "We still don't get the right level of convictions, and we still don't have a system where victims can always access the support they want, but it's moving in the right direction and at least we are talking about it."

The long-term trend is a decline in abuse and an increase in successful prosecution. In 2005, 8.7% of the female population of England and Wales experienced some form of abuse by a partner; by 2020 the figure was 6.2%.[11] The number of convictions for domestic abuse-related crimes increased by 61% to 70,853 a year between 2008 and 2017.[12] Pressure to prosecute abusers has been increased by the Convention on the Elimination of all Forms of Discrimination Against Women, an international treaty adopted in 1979 by the United Nations General Assembly.[13] The UK has also ratified the Istanbul Convention, brought into force in 2014 by the Council of

Europe (the continent's human rights body, distinct from the EU); this commits governments to take action against violence against women and domestic violence.

This is a world away from the time when women were still treated as little more than the property of men. Until 1895 the City of London had a byelaw that 'wife beating is prohibited between the hours of 10 pm and 7 am, because the noise keeps the neighbours awake'. In 1905, a stipendiary magistrate hearing an assault charge against a Salford man told the defendant's wife: "This is the way with you women. You chatter, chatter, chatter until you irritate. You get the man mad, then you get struck and you come here. Try to keep your mouth shut and you will get on better."[14] As recently as 1984, the Commissioner of the Metropolitan Police described domestic violence, along with dealing with stray dogs, as "rubbish work for police officers".[15] Charities have been at the heart of changing attitudes and achieving reform.

Votes for women

It's now taken for granted that all adults, male and female, can vote in local and national elections, but this was not the case until 1928. From Tudor times until the 19th century, only people who owned property of significant value could vote. The Reform Act of 1832 codified the system, extending suffrage to men who rented property of a specified value, but still only one man in seven was entitled to vote. Further changes to the property qualification meant that by 1884 some 60% of men were enfranchised.

The story was very different for women.[16] Until the 1832 Act specified that only men could vote, women who owned significant property – which was rare – did have the right to vote in parliamentary elections. But even before the 1832 Act, agitation had begun for votes for all women, and in 1869 single women who owned property and paid rates to the local authority were permitted to vote in municipal elections – the principle invoked was 'no taxation without representation'. This limited local franchise was extended to some married women in 1894, and by the turn of the century it was estimated that one million women had the right to vote in local elections.

But the real battle was over parliamentary voting, and it was voluntary action that promoted the cause and produced the change. In the middle of the 19th century a number of societies were founded to press for votes for women: the philosopher and political economist John Stuart Mill was the first MP to call for female suffrage, in 1866, and three years later published his essay *The Subjection of Women*. It argued that the legal subordination of one gender to another was wrong in itself, formed an obstacle to human improvement and 'ought to be replaced by a principle of perfect equality that doesn't allow any power or privilege on one side or disability on the other'.

Little progress was made until 1897, however, when Millicent Fawcett founded the National Union of Women's Suffrage Societies. This organisation, supported by 'suffragists', pursued constitutional methods, such as putting pressure on reluctant MPs. Six years later, however, Emmeline Pankhurst and her daughters, Christabel and Sylvia, founded the Women's Social and Political Union; this was supported by 'suffragettes', whose motto was 'deeds, not words'. They adopted noisy and violent tactics, including large parades, the heckling of speakers who opposed them, stone throwing, arson and hunger strikes. Thousands were arrested, many were imprisoned, and some were force-fed when they went on hunger strike. Most famously, Emily Davison died after walking in front of the King's racehorse at the Epsom Derby in 1913 and was portrayed as a martyr to the cause.

At the start of the 20th century a majority of MPs were known to be in favour of women's suffrage, but the Liberal government led by Herbert Asquith before the First World War refused to allow a vote on the question. The Pankhursts suspended their campaign when the war broke out in 1914, but the cause was strengthened as more women started working in key parts of the economy to make up for men who were serving in the armed forces. When David Lloyd George, a supporter of votes for women, became prime minister in 1915, the door began to open: a law passed at the end of the war in 1918 gave parliamentary voting rights to all men, and to women over 30 who were on the electoral roll for local government elections (or married to a man who was); for the first time, it also allowed women to stand for Parliament. Ten years later, all women gained the vote. It was a great victory for voluntary action and campaigning.

Contraception, forced marriage and equal pay

After votes for women had been won, the focus for women's charities and campaigners shifted to other forms of equality and emancipation for women, including freedom from domestic violence, examined at the start of this chapter. Two other examples are control of fertility and forced marriage. The charity MSI Reproductive Choices is now the largest provider of abortion and contraception services, with 600 clinics around the world. (In 2020 the charity deliberately distanced itself from its original namesake, birth control pioneer Marie Stopes, after deciding that her views on eugenics were at odds with the charity's purpose and values.) Karma Nirvana supports victims of honour-based abuse and forced marriage by providing training, running a national helpline and lobbying for policy change. The charity's small team deals with between 700 and 800 calls each month, around 300 of which are from professionals seeking advice for their clients.[17] The Leeds-based charity was set up in 1993 by Jasvinder Sanghera, who had escaped a forced marriage by running away from home at the age of 16. In 2014, after ten years of campaigning, forced marriage finally became a criminal offence in the UK; five years later, however, there had been only four convictions.[18]

Another burning issue has been, and remains, equality in the workplace. The Equal Pay Act of 1970, consolidated in the Equality Act 2010, means women have to be paid the same as men doing the same work. But it has not eliminated the gender pay gap, where women are employed disproportionately in lower-paid jobs and are still often paid less in equivalent jobs. The Fawcett Society, which evolved from Millicent Fawcett's campaign for women to be given the vote, continues to campaign for gender equality and human rights, and in January 2018 published a review of sex discrimination law that made a wide range of recommendations on equal pay and pensions, maternity and paternity rights, workplace harassment and violence against women and girls.[19] By chance, it was published just before the *Financial Times* printed an article about The Presidents Club, a charity that had recently held a fundraising dinner after which young women, hired as hostesses and instructed to wear revealing black outfits, reported being groped and propositioned by guests.[20]

The Fawcett Society called the episode 'completely outrageous' and pointed out that, under its proposed reforms, women would be protected from sexual harassment of this kind by customers or clients of their employer. The Presidents Club, which had become increasingly seedy after 33 years as a fundraising charity, was quickly shut down.[21] Early in 2018, the 100th anniversary of votes for women, a poll of listeners of BBC Radio 4 chose Millicent Fawcett as the most influential woman of the 20th century; a statue of her was unveiled in Parliament Square later in the year. In November 2020, the Fawcett Society announced it had opened talks about a possible merger with the Young Women's Trust; while both charities claimed to be financially stable, they said they recognised the challenges that lay ahead.[22]

Charities and gay rights

The playwright and wit Oscar Wilde, and the mathematician and wartime code-breaker Alan Turing, are among the best-known examples of thousands of men whose lives were wrecked by criminal sanctions imposed on homosexuals in the UK. Wilde was convicted of 'gross indecency', spent two years in jail with hard labour and died in self-imposed exile in Paris in 1900; Turing was convicted of the same offence in 1952, accepted chemical castration with female hormones in order to avoid prison and committed suicide two years later.

But it was the trial and imprisonment of Lord Montagu of Beaulieu and two other men in 1954 that finally put the country on the road to reform. The Buggery Act of 1533 had carried the death penalty, and two men were hanged as late as 1835. In 1861 the death penalty had been removed for the offence, replaced in 1885 by the offence of 'gross indecency', covering any sexual activity between men (sexual activity between women was never criminalised). The Montagu case caused such a public and political sensation that the Conservative government set up a committee under Sir John Wolfenden, an educationalist and former headmaster of two public schools, to re-examine the law.

The Wolfenden Report of 1957 recommended the legalisation of homosexual acts in private between two consenting adults over the age of 21, but the government refused to consider legislation.[23] The lord chancellor at the time, Viscount Kilmuir, was quoted in *The Times* as saying: "I am not going to go down in history as the man who made sodomy legal."[24] This stalemate prompted the formation of the first voluntary organisations to campaign publicly for reform, including the Homosexual Law Reform Society and its related charity, the Albany Trust. The Society produced briefings for MPs, organised public meetings and was instrumental in the eventual passage of the Sexual Offences Act 1967, which implemented Wolfenden's main recommendations.

However, this was only the start of the drive for full equality. The Campaign for Homosexual Equality made much of the running in the 1970s by recruiting members, organising conferences and holding demonstrations. A UK version of the Gay Liberation Front (GLF), which had been active in the US for ten years, undertook direct action, including disrupting the Festival of Light, a movement organised by the Christian morality campaigner Mary Whitehouse. The GLF eventually split into various organisations including Gay News, Gay Switchboard and Outrage.

A significant setback for campaigners came in 1988 when Section 28 of the Local Government Act of that year outlawed the 'intentional promotion' of homosexuality in schools and the teaching 'of the acceptability of homosexuality as a pretended family relationship'.[25] One response to this was the establishment of Stonewall, a new campaigning and lobbying organisation named after the Stonewall Inn in New York, where repeated police raids had culminated in a riot in 1969 that gave fresh impetus to the gay rights movement in the US. Stonewall was eventually registered by the Charity Commission in 2003, which signified official confirmation that it has an approved charitable purpose – the promotion of equality and diversity – which is carried out for the benefit of the public.

Stonewall said that research it conducted in its early years revealed that more than half of the estimated 1.7 million gay people in the UK workforce did not feel they could be open about their sexuality at work; of those who were 'out', two-thirds had experienced discrimination at work, more than one-third had considered resigning because of it and a fifth of harassed employees had considered suicide.

Stonewall considered that the answer to this problem was to ask employers to proclaim publicly their support for gay staff: if a whole organisation was responsible for creating a more accepting environment, it believed, pressure on individual gay employees would be reduced. But a consultation with 65 major UK employers revealed resistance – the issue was perceived to be too difficult and private.

The success of Diversity Champions

Stonewall forged ahead nonetheless and launched its Diversity Champions programme in January 2005, offering employers a clear framework for progress. Recommended action included appointing a senior manager as sponsor of lesbian and gay diversity, creating an employee network group and promoting practices and policies inclusive of lesbian and gay staff. The programme was targeted at certain sectors, including the UK's 100 largest companies and the armed forces; the strapline, 'People perform better when they can be themselves', summarised the business case.

The charity managed to convince all 65 of the employers it had consulted to take part in Diversity Champions when it was launched. By the end of 2005, 143 organisations had signed up, and by 2017 the figure was 750; members included household names such as British Airways, Nike, Tesco, the Metropolitan Police, Barnardo's, Goldman Sachs, the Conservative and Labour parties, Liverpool Football Club, the Royal Air Force and even the Royal Navy, which until 2000 had been expelling people for being gay. Stonewall sends staff to talk to member organisations and provides them with resources such as model workplace policies on diversity and inclusivity, and leaflets to which they can add their own branding. Equality organisations in other countries have consulted Stonewall about following the model of Diversity Champions.

British Land (BL), a commercial property business in the UK, joined Diversity Champions in 2014 and launched its BL Pride Alliance, a network of LGBT staff and other employees willing to stand up against homophobia, biphobia and transphobia: by 2018, around 170 of BL's 250 staff were Alliance members. Paul Macey, the company's property finance director in that year and co-chair of the alliance, says Diversity Champions helps organisations to become more inclusive:

> "Every organisation that's a Diversity Champion gets a relationship manager at Stonewall. They also do an annual workplace conference which is a great resource, because you can go to the various seminars and it allows you to align your attendance with wherever your organisation is on the journey. Last year I went to the one on how to implement monitoring, which was really helpful when we came to introduce monitoring ourselves."

Stonewall has become probably the best-known gay rights organisation in the UK and has helped to bring about most of the crucial developments of the two decades since 2000. These include lowering the age of consent to 16 for men, as for women, the repeal of Section 28, the end of the ban on gay people in the armed forces, the adoption of children by gay couples, civil partnerships, equal access to goods and services and, finally, in 2014, gay marriage.

Indications of progress are that 45 'out' LGBT MPs were elected in 2019, and that a 2018 story line in *The Archers*, the time-honoured soap opera on BBC Radio 4, concerned a gay couple seeking a surrogate mother to bear a child for them.[26] Without Stonewall and a raft of other charities and voluntary groups promoting LGBT rights, it seems unlikely that these extensive advances in the law and social attitudes would have happened as soon as they did.

7

Protecting animals and the natural world

When children returned to school after several months at home because of the first wave of the coronavirus pandemic, one of them was the 17-year-old Swedish climate activist Greta Thunberg. She had taken a gap year to spread her message about runaway global warming, and in August 2020 posted a photo of herself on Instagram with her satchel, commenting that 'it feels so great to finally be back in school again'.[1]

Thunberg, who has a form of autism called Asperger Syndrome, rose to fame in 2017 for leaving school every Friday to protest outside the Swedish Parliament about political inaction on the climate crisis. Over three years her #FridaysforFuture demonstrations mobilised hundreds of thousands of students to take similar action, and Thunberg has addressed several international climate summits and meetings of world leaders. The school strikes coincided with the rise of Extinction Rebellion (XR), a UK-based movement that shares her determination on climate change: from October 2018, thousands of protestors blocked traffic, occupied landmarks, stripped off in Parliament and generally made a nuisance of themselves. Copycat groups sprang up in other countries.

Thunberg and XR have contributed to driving the climate crisis up the public and political agenda. In May 2019 the UK Parliament became the first national legislative body to declare a climate emergency – with no binding policy commitments attached – and a month later a YouGov poll showed public concern about the environment at record levels.[2,3] In December 2019, *New Scientist* summarised the impact of Thunberg and

XR under the headline: 'The year the world started to wake up to climate change'.

Have Thunberg and XR succeeded where traditional environmental charities and NGOs have failed? After all, scientists and experts have been aware of the dangers of climate change for decades. In 1972 the Club of Rome published *The Limits to Growth*, predicting ecological collapse, and 20 years later the Union of Concerned Scientists issued a warning of 'vast human misery' if the world didn't change its ways.[4] Greenpeace, probably the world's most famous environmental body, has campaigned fiercely against powerful fossil fuel interests, while WWF has been tracking the decline of biodiversity since 1970 with its Living Planet Index. Since 2015, a coalition of civil society groups have been calculating how the global burden should be fairly shared among nation-states, publishing a series of landmark reports outlining their findings.[5]

But these more established NGOs failed to ignite the same sense of urgency as Thunberg and XR. After XR occupied the Greenpeace headquarters in London in October 2018, complaining that 'the NGOs have failed us',[6] Rex Weyler, co-founder of Greenpeace International in 1979, conceded the point:[7]

> In the 1970s, in the early years of Greenpeace and other new ecology movements, we thought that the ecological change would be simple, that once people understood the threats, they would demand change … We may have underestimated the status quo – corporate elite, bankers, politicians, and even common citizens dependent upon the economic system – attachment to the old patterns of consumption and growth. The new social movements are blowing up these social logjams.

Harjeet Singh, global lead on climate change at ActionAid International, admits that the sector should have been warning about a climate 'emergency' right from the start, but argues that charities laid the foundations for Thunberg to stand on:

"I accept that critique – we, as civil society organisations, did not invest enough into turning it into a real people's movement. We kept seeing climate change as an environmental issue, instead of trying to turn it into a political ask. That said, if Greta had been around in the 1990s, I'm not sure she would have been the same phenomenon. She is the right person at the right time. By the time she appeared, we were already seeing major climate impacts and patience was running thin with heads of state – we could all see that rich countries were talking big but doing little. So when Greta came along, with her personality, her demeanour, her credibility, she really struck a chord with people. But she came at a moment when all the building blocks were in place, thanks to the work by civil society that had gone before. The basic awareness was there, the architecture was there."

Singh adds that the restrictions on legally constituted civil society organisations inhibit their ability to foment civil disobedience of the kind that XR encourages:

"As organisations, we rely on fundraising, we are registered with regulators, we have to comply with various laws, we have to hire and pay staff to carry out professional research and analysis, and we need an organisational structure in order to operate. That's what makes us viable, and makes us effective, to whatever extent. But that in itself becomes our enemy – it means we can't become a movement, because being a movement carries too many risks. I'm very cognisant that I can only protest to an extent – I can wear a T-shirt, but I can't do anything that could harm my organisation's image or put it at any risk legally or politically. But in an ecosystem of change, you need everybody. You need a movement that has no limits, you need a Greta who can speak out and be a figurehead, but you also need organisations who are embedded in communities on the ground and can do deep analysis and lobbying."

XR, which has no official constitution and is a decentralised network that welcomes anyone as long as they adhere to its ten core principles, appears to recognise that conventional charities can be useful allies.[8] One e-mail it sent to ActionAid UK said:

> We recognise that as NGOs you have years of experience, resources and professionalism in campaigns and movement-building, where XR may not. You have a passionate and active membership and you help to guide mainstream opinions. We want to hear your feedback and see if and how we can amplify each other's work and if there are areas of collaboration.

Thunberg also appears to have accepted this point by donating her prize money to more conventional humanitarian and charitable organisations: her US$100,000 Human Act Award from the Human Act Foundation was donated to the United Nations Children's Fund (Unicef), for example, and €1 million from the inaugural Gulbenkian Prize for Humanity was split between charitable projects, among them ActionAid India and Bangladesh, the Bangladeshi-based global NGO Building Resources Across Communities (BRAC), and the Stop Ecocide Foundation.[9, 10, 11, 12] Thunberg has also set up the Greta Thunberg Foundation in Sweden to distribute the income she receives from book royalties, donations and prize money.

Although Greenpeace has been criticised by XR, it has been involved in non-violent direct action ever since its inception in 1971, when its three founders sailed to Alaska to disrupt a nuclear test by the US on one of the Aleutian Islands. Their contest with the Pentagon sowed the seeds that eventually led to the Comprehensive Nuclear Test Ban Treaty. Subsequent Greenpeace campaigns have involved harassing whaling ships, destroying a test crop of genetically modified wheat and occupying nuclear power stations. Such activities meant that it could not maintain its charitable status in the UK, with the accompanying tax breaks, says Lisa Cave from Greenpeace UK:

> "Greenpeace in the UK began as a registered charity – the Greenpeace Environmental Trust – but the Charity Commission rules changed in 1991 and our active campaigning, peaceful actions that sometimes led to arrests, and the political lobbying work that we were doing, no longer fitted in. So we split in two – the Trust kept going and Greenpeace Ltd was formed to carry on our campaigning work. Our supporters were mostly moved over to Greenpeace Ltd and the Trust was reduced in scale, restricting its activities to research, educational work, and other activities that fall inside charity regulations."

Most environmental charities continue to rely on campaigning that centres on collaboration, persuasion and consensus. At the start of the coronavirus epidemic in 2020, for example, The Climate Coalition, a charity with 100 member organisations ranging from the Women's Institute to the British Mountaineering Council, drew up a seven-point plan for a 'green recovery' and presented it to MPs and the Prime Minister. Its recommendations included creating jobs in home insulation, accelerating the introduction of electric vehicles and creating and protecting more healthy green spaces. It remains to be seen to what extent this will bear fruit.

Environmental charities are not the best funded: those in the 'conservation, environmental and heritage' category took only 4% of public donations in 2018, according to the annual report on giving published by CAF, based on a monthly survey of 1,000 people.[13] In 2019, 11 of the UK's leading scientists wrote an open letter to the 100 richest foundations and 100 wealthiest families, calling for more support for environmental causes. They said the current allocation of just 2% of all philanthropic funding to climate-related causes was far too low in the light of the ecological collapse taking place.[14] But environmental issues are beginning to attract more support; in February 2020 Jeff Bezos, founder of Amazon and then the world's richest man, promised US$10 billion to support groups and individuals working to combat climate change.[15]

Animal charities

Charities for the protection of animals have always fared better than their environmental counterparts: they remain one of the three most popular charitable causes in the UK, along with medical research and children. The CAF giving report mentioned above found that 26% of adults had donated to an animal charity in the previous four weeks and that animal welfare organisations attracted 8% of all donations. In 2020, nearly 1,200 charities registered with the Charity Commission for England and Wales listed the welfare of animals among their objects; their titles ranged from A Dog's Tale to Bunny Burrows and the British Hen Welfare Trust.

Campaigns to protect animals came earlier in the UK than many of the campaigns to protect humans, including children. Towards the end of the 18th century there was growing concern about bull-baiting, cock-fighting, foxhunting, the condition of pit ponies and the maltreatment of working and agricultural animals generally. In 1822 a law was passed to prevent cruelty to cattle, and two years later the Reverend Arthur Broome convened a meeting in Old Slaughter's Coffee House in London that resulted in the foundation of the RSPCA.

This charity, like the NSPCC, has become an essential part of national life in the UK. The treatment of animals is always a highly emotional subject, however, and the tension between animal welfare and animal rights involves the charity in continual controversy, not least over its legal power to initiate prosecutions for animal cruelty.

The WWF was set up in Switzerland in 1961 as an international fundraising organisation to work in collaboration with existing groups. It has learned over time that strident public criticism of opponents is not the only way to achieve its goals, and that working in partnership can sometimes bring the best results. For example, it has a project with the Chinese government to establish nature reserves for pandas. Its global partnership with Coca-Cola since 2007 has helped to conserve endangered rivers and wetlands around the world, and has supported farmers in East Anglia, where the company has manufacturing and distribution plants, to improve land management and reduce agricultural pollution.[16]

One of the WWF partnerships is with the Royal Society for the Protection of Birds (RSPB), which has more than a million members, including 195,000 youth members. The RSPB was founded in Manchester in 1889 by Emily Williamson, who was outraged by the trade in feathers for women's hats and formed the Society for the Protection of Birds, which was awarded a Royal Charter in 1904.[17] It quickly gained popularity and joined forces with the quaintly named Fur, Fin and Feather Folk in one of the sector's earliest mergers. Over time, persistent lobbying has produced results: a law banning the importation of feathers was passed in 1921 and 86 years later, in 2007, the RSPB and its campaigning partner Birdlife were behind a ban on importing live wild birds into the EU.[18]

An end to foxhunting

Hunting with dogs was a familiar part of British country life for hundreds of years. It was variously seen by the aristocracy as an important social activity, by squires and farmers as a method of pest control and by children on ponies as a way to develop their riding skills. Enthusiasts considered it an exciting day out, galloping through the landscape behind a pack of dogs in pursuit of a fox.

Not everyone liked it, however: the poet and playwright Oscar Wilde famously referred to foxhunting as 'the unspeakable in pursuit of the uneatable'. Nineteenth- and early 20th-century legislation on animal cruelty related mainly to controlling experiments on live creatures and protecting domestic and captive animals, and the RSPCA was unwilling at the time to oppose foxhunting. As a result, the League Against Cruel Sports, a charity, was founded in 1924 with the aim of ending the hunting of foxes, stags, otters and hares.

Two private member's bills to outlaw hunting with dogs failed in Parliament in 1949, as did three more in 1992, 1993 and 1995. But opposition to foxhunting was rising in the country and Parliament, and the Labour Party's manifesto when it won the 1997 general election promised a free vote in Parliament. The first success came north of the border, in 2002, where the recently established Scottish Parliament outlawed foxhunting with dogs and hare coursing – the chasing and killing of hares by greyhounds. The League then concentrated on obtaining similar legislation for England and Wales, working in collaboration with two other charities, the International Fund for Animal Welfare (IFAW) and the RSPCA, the latter of which had opposed a ban as recently as 1960 but was now in favour.

In 2004, by 356 votes to 166, the House of Commons finally passed the Hunting Act, one of the most contentious pieces of legislation of the new century. There were massive protest rallies by the Countryside Alliance, and the House of Commons was invaded by shouting opponents. James Gray, the Conservative MP for North Wiltshire, railed against a "disgraceful, prejudiced and ignorant little bill".[19] The House of Lords refused to pass the measure, but the government used the rarely invoked Parliament Act to overrule the upper chamber, and in March 2005 the law came into force.

Mike Hobday, who led the League's campaign to change the law, says the greatest factor in turning public opinion against foxhunting was probably the invention of the hand-held video camera. In the 1980s and 1990s this had enabled activists to record and publicise the often gruesome detail of the kill, which usually had few witnesses. The image of a fox being torn apart began to displace more romantic visions of the pack of hounds casting about for a scent and streaming across the fields to the sound of the hunting horn. When he was hired in 2001, Hobday says, the job was no longer to persuade MPs and the public that foxhunting was cruel – it was to get MPs to put pressure on the government:

> "This was done by a three-way coalition of charities whose role was to convene and coordinate MPs of all parties who thought hunting was wrong. The League provided activism, the RSPCA provided reputation, IFAW provided money, and all three

contributed with staff and resources. I'm confident the change in the law wouldn't have come about without charities, for several reasons. The League and IFAW brought to public attention the more extreme scenes of suffering and brought the issue out of the shadows. Secondly, MPs were reporting that they had bigger postbags on foxhunting than on the first invasion of Iraq in 1990, and that was because members of welfare organisations were writing to their MPs. And thirdly, the reason the prime minister, Tony Blair, finally bowed to pressure from MPs was because they were united and coherent in their view, which owed much to the support they got from the charities – during debates they could draw on case studies, information and arguments against the pro-hunting movement."

From sewage to plastic

Another small environmental charity that has achieved significant results is Cornwall-based Surfers Against Sewage (SAS), which in 2019 had an income of £2.3 million, 21 staff and 90,000 volunteers. It was founded in 1990, when there was still so much sewage getting into the sea that surfers frequently fell ill. "There were long outfall pipes, so sometimes sewage did go one or two kilometres out," says Dom Ferris, the charity's head of community and engagement until the end of 2019. "But it washed and blew back in with the tides and the winds. You still stood a one in seven chance of contracting gastroenteritis."

When the water companies were privatised in the 1980s, the conditions imposed on them included improving sewage treatment. But this was very expensive, and SAS suspected the companies would do the minimum. Wearing wetsuits and gas masks, its supporters protested at Parliament and water company offices. But it also pushed for tougher EU regulation, which culminated in the revised EU Bathing Water Directive of 2006.[20] In 1990, only 27% of UK beaches met the minimum bathing water standards.[21] By 2018, it was 97.9%.[22] The willingness of the water industry and its regulators to listen to SAS also led to a change in the charity's methods: instead of protesting outside they went inside, wearing suits and ties, to meet water company directors, regulators and MPs.

Meanwhile plastic pollution was becoming one of the worst of modern environmental disasters. In July 2017 an international team of researchers found that since 1950, when large-scale plastic production and use began, around 4,900 million metric tons, or 60% of all plastics ever produced, were accumulating in landfills or the environment.[23] Their report said that by 2050 this figure would, on current trends, more than double to 12,000 million metric tons. Other studies show that bags, bottles, six-pack rings and discarded fishing nets collect in gigantic swirls in the oceans.[24,25] Many plastic items also break down into minuscule fragments, known as microplastics, that are ingested by sea creatures, contaminate sea salt and tap water and even end up buried in the Arctic ice. According to a 2017 United Nations Environment Programme report, some 100,000 marine mammals and turtles and one million sea birds are killed by marine plastic pollution annually.[26]

SAS realised that plastic was the new sewage, and by 2018 had increased the number of its annual 'beach cleans' to 1,750: in that year, 35,500 volunteers removed more than 63 metric tons of marine plastic litter from 571 UK beaches in one week.[27] But it also started to mobilise at the grassroots by setting up 'Plastic Free Communities' and putting pressure on the government. One objective of such communities, which can be just a village or a whole city, is to get businesses to reduce the amount of single-use plastic items they use or sell; another is to encourage the local authority to adopt policies to limit plastic waste.

The project set out in 2017 to establish 125 Plastic Free Communities by 2020.[28] Truro in Cornwall was the first town to gain plastic-free status; Plymouth Waterfront became England's first plastic-free city district. Bayfield, a community on Lake Huron in Canada, is the first Surfers Against Sewage International Plastic Free Community.[29]

Along with Greenpeace, SAS also launched a petition to persuade the UK government to introduce a deposit return scheme for plastic bottles and aluminium cans. The UK uses 38.5 million single-use plastic bottles every day, and fewer than half are recycled.[30] Such schemes are already in place in several other European countries; Norway, for example, manages to recycle 97% of its single-use plastic bottles.[31] In October 2017, SAS delivered 257,000 signatures in support of the campaign to 10 Downing Street, and the following year the government announced it would introduce such a scheme in England and Wales by 2023, subject to another consultation.[32] SAS also submitted Freedom of Information requests about Parliament's own use of plastic and used the results to lobby for it to be plastic free.[33]

Ferris admits that when the plastics campaign was launched, SAS wasn't too sure how it would be received, but says "it's gone absolutely bananas". This success can be partly attributed to the Attenborough effect – in late 2017, the BBC broadcast Sir David Attenborough's *Blue Planet II*, with shocking footage of plastic waste clogging up the oceans and albatrosses unwittingly feeding plastic particles to their chicks. But Ferris says that SAS was "part of the movement that forced the BBC's hand on it, so rather than us benefiting from it, it was actually the environmental sector that led the way".

SAS was also part of a coalition of charities in a successful campaign called Break the Bag Habit. This was led by the Campaign to Protect Rural England, and also included Keep Britain Tidy, the Marine Conservation Society, Thames21 and Greener Upon Thames.[34] For three years they ran a coordinated campaign for a charge of five pence on plastic carrier bags in England, which was finally introduced in 2015.[35] Between the date when the charge was introduced and 2019, the number of bags given out in supermarkets fell by 86%, and plastic pollution in general climbed up the national agenda.[36]

Charities and green shareholder power

Campaigning and harnessing public opinion to sway corporate behaviour is one way of protecting the environment; another is to use financial muscle. Most charities are small and short of money, but a few have enormous sums invested in global stock markets and other assets. These are mainly charitable foundations that invest their endowments and give the annual income as grants to other charities. Most have now woken up to the power that they can wield as shareholders.

An example is the Church Commissioners for England, established as a charity in 1948 to manage the extensive property and investments of the Church of England and provide, among other things, for pensions for the clergy. After 30 years of achieving an average return of 8.5% per annum, its portfolio was worth £8.7 billion by 2019, making it one of the wealthiest UK charities.[37]

The Commissioners have always tried to align their investments with the values of the Church by excluding certain assets. The list has changed over time in line with developments in wider society; for instance, a tobacco exclusion was added in the 1960s when evidence of the harmful effects of smoking became impossible to ignore. More recently, companies that derive significant revenues from coal mining or oil sands extraction have been excluded. The list now includes armaments, gambling, tobacco, pornography, high-cost lending, civilian firearms, human embryonic cloning and various contributors to climate change.[38]

The Commissioners' approach went awry in 2014 when it was revealed they had a stake in Wonga, the now-defunct payday lender that charged interest upwards of 1,000%.[39] The story broke two days after the Archbishop of Canterbury, the Most Reverend Justin Welby, had criticised the company for pushing vulnerable borrowers into debt.[40] The Church had not realised that it owned the holding because it was in a pooled investment fund, and it was almost a year before the link was finally severed.

A better example of the Commissioners' efforts has been their engagement with major oil companies on climate change and their progress on the international policy goal of limiting global warming to a rise of below two degrees Celsius. The pressure produced mixed responses from the oil giants, according to the Commissioners' former head of responsible investment, Edward Mason. BP and Shell, he says, were broadly positive; BP developed a new 'two-degrees scenario' against which it can assess the resilience of its business, while Shell launched a subsidiary called New Energies to explore opportunities in the low-carbon economy. ExxonMobil, on the other hand, was not so responsive, and in 2016 the Commissioners collaborated with a major US pension fund and some of Europe's largest asset managers to file a shareholder resolution to put pressure on the company in the wake of the Paris Agreement on climate change.[41] Between them, the group owned more than $1 billion in Exxon shares.

The resolution asked the company to publish an assessment of how its business would be affected if global warming was to be restricted to two degrees. ExxonMobil's directors recommended that shareholders should vote down the resolution, and in 2016 only 38% of shareholders voted in favour. But a year later the same resolution was proposed, and on that occasion 62% voted for it. Mason says: "This was really quite unprecedented in the area of climate change and sent a very strong signal to Exxon that investors want them to engage better and disclose better."[42] ExxonMobil wrote to shareholders in December 2017, seven months after the vote, pledging to publish information on the implications of two degrees Celsius scenarios.[43]

★ ★ ★

A key message from many of the stories in this chapter is that successful campaigning on the environment and animal welfare is often a subtle double act: street-level activism by Thunberg and XR would probably not have had such an impact if environment charities and NGOs had not, over decades, played a big part in gradually raising public and political awareness of climate change. Thunberg provided a 'moment' – as did the killing of George Floyd in the battle against racism – that was based on a firm foundation laid by charities over time. To bring about the transformation needed to avert the worst effects of climate change, a whole mosaic of actors will be needed, as described above by Harjeet Singh of ActionAid. Similarly, the League Against Cruel Sports might not have been able to mount its successful campaign against foxhunting without hunt saboteurs filming the kills, getting horse-whipped by hunt followers and falling foul of the law. This interconnectedness poses a delicate problem for charities, which have to tread a careful line to maintain their respectability, their support and funding from a wider public and their valuable charitable status.

PART III

Improving lives and communities

8

Local action and self-help

When the first coronavirus lockdown began in the UK in March 2020, the charity Shift recruited 50 observers to examine what was going on in their communities. Shift aims to 'help prevent and reduce social problems through positive behaviour change', and this initiative was part of its project to build a better society through better relationships.

After 100 days, the enquiries and interviews of the observers were presented in a report that said local government bodies had tried to help vulnerable citizens during the emergency, but much of the immediate response came from informal mutual aid. Combining its findings with a range of other research, it concluded:[1]

> Ten million people, 19 per cent of the adult population, have been giving at least three hours a week to care for others outside of their family since the lockdown began. Forty per cent of us now feel a stronger sense of community. Two million have joined local support groups on Facebook alone and 4,300 mutual aid groups are now connecting more than three million people. Nimble, new groups have been more effective in many areas than established organisations who have been worrying about losing income, furloughing staff and medium-term survival.

This upsurge in local, often informal, community activity was confirmed by the formation of Covid-19 Mutual Aid UK, which runs a website that lists and supports hundreds of autonomous groups formed by people wanting to help their neighbours.[2] The charity Royal Voluntary Service, in partnership with the health service, also recruited 750,000 'NHS Volunteer Responders' in only four days: they use a mobile phone app to connect them with people who need medical supplies, transport to hospital or someone to 'check in and chat' with them.[3]

Some of the COVID-19 mutual aid groups sought help and advice from established local voluntary sector support and development charities, often called councils for voluntary service (CVS), according to Navca, the umbrella body for CVSs. "Our members have good relations with mutual aid groups," says Clare Mills, head of communications at Navca. "Some groups are very ad hoc – just two or three streets coming together to meet a need. Some will be more long-lasting, and our members can help them form legally constituted groups." However, Navca members were facing a perilous future in 2020 because of threats to their income, including to grants from local councils.

The local voluntary response to the coronavirus epidemic follows a pattern established in previous crises such as the 1918/19 influenza pandemic, the economic depression of the 1930s and the floods on the east coast of England in 1953.[4] Each response was a varying mixture of spontaneous action and organisation by government bodies and charities such as the British Red Cross or the Salvation Army.

About 600 well-established local organisations are members of Locality, a charity that fosters organisations that are 'place-based and community-centred'. Locality was formed by a merger in 2011 of the Development Trusts Association and the British Association of Settlements and Social Action Centres. Many members of Locality have acquired significant assets and developed ways of supporting themselves through selling services and trading. Between them in 2016 they owned £779 million of assets producing income of £372 million – roughly the same as the sum the city of Derby, with a population of 250,000, spent on its public services.[5] Of this amount, £261 million was earned from trading and contracts with the public sector. Steve Wyler, the former chief executive of Locality, says:

"There are many things going on all over the country – different strands of philanthropy and self-help, producing all sorts of social action. It goes on for many reasons, but mainly because of people themselves. The charities that do the best work acknowledge that change comes from the people they work with rather than the charities themselves, and it can be dishonest for the charities to claim the credit. Their important role is as a catalyst, and at their best they create the conditions for people to flourish."

Some members of Locality have become what are known as 'community anchors' – larger organisations with multiple roles, including the provision of services and encouraging collaborative ventures with government and businesses. As examples, Wyler singles out Coin Street Community Builders, which fought off developers and created locally focused facilities on London's South Bank; the Sunlight Development Trust, which runs community activities alongside local health services in the Medway area of Kent (one project is called Medway Men in Sheds); and the Alt Valley Trust in a deprived area of Liverpool, which runs an apprentice programme and business support services as well as sports and health improvement centres. One of the most successful community anchors is in the port city of Hull.

The story of the Goodwin Development Trust

Close to the centre of the city lies a patch of open ground surrounded by unlovely 1960s housing erected after the German bombing in the Second World War. It's just some grass, a few trees, a couple of benches. But it provoked a social movement that has had a far-reaching effect.

In 1994 a retired nurse, Irene Andrews, was unhappy about the Labour-controlled city council's proposal to build on this patch, visible from her tower-block window, which was one of the few public spaces on the Thornton Estate. Andrews decided to fight the proposal, and local tenants' associations supported her: when the council eventually backed down, the tenants began to consider what else they might do for the quality of life of the 5,000 people on the estate. Hull was a run-down city, struggling to recover from the loss of its fishing industry, and the Thornton Estate had a lot of social problems. Most of the shops on nearby Goodwin Parade had closed down, so the local people persuaded the owners to let them use one: this was the birth of the Goodwin Development Trust, a charity which by 2018 had a turnover of £5 million and employed 180 people.

The Trust began by giving housing advice and posting job vacancies, and went on to run nurseries, a youth centre, community wardens, a theatre, a radio station, a refugee advice service and some allotments. It built The Octagon, a purpose-designed community centre, and put up well-insulated, low-cost housing that contrasts sharply with the drabness around it. Most recently it took over a redundant Anglican church and converted it for leisure use, calling it Thornton Village Hall. Peter McGurn is chief executive of the Trust:

> "We want to challenge the assumption that we're just a crap council estate. This is still a poor community in a northern wasteland, but we've stopped it getting worse. In fact, the Goodwin Trust has become an essential part of public sector infrastructure – without us things would fall apart round here. We were actually given a cheque – I think we've still got it somewhere – which was made out to 'Goodwin City Council'."

The success of the Trust has resulted partly from bidding for development funds and taking advantage of government initiatives. Early on, for example, it persuaded the council to give it a disused old people's home, then secured £1.5 million of funding from the EU and English Partnerships – a former government agency – to turn it into a nursery and other community facilities. And when the Labour government started the Sure Start programme in 1999, Goodwin succeeded in becoming the 'accountable body' for its area and setting up children's centres.

Another success factor, says McGurn, was following the principle that community bodies benefit most by acquiring buildings which can both bring in revenue and be used as security for loans to finance more projects.[6] This was given a boost by the Localism Act 2011, which sets out ways community organisations can acquire public assets.

A prime example was building The Octagon after a local audit showing the need for a doctors' surgery and more council offices on the estate. A total of £5 million was raised, half from the NHS and the council, and the rest from the EU Regional Development Fund, and within three years the building was up and earning revenue. When the offices ceased to do well in 2018, the space was leased to the Hull and District Table Tennis Association.

A fundamental strength of the Trust, says McGurn, has been its initial decision that its trustees must be residents of the estate:

> "Right from the start, it was written into our articles of association that you could not be a director of the Trust unless you lived here. I think it's the single most powerful thing we have ever done, because it says that the expertise doesn't lie with lawyers, accountants, bank managers or even politicians. It doesn't lie with anyone except the people who live in this community. And the way to make those people expert in what they do has been to let them do it."

When austerity set in after the 2010 election, the Trust went through a bad patch and for seven years ran loss-making budgets, made possible by the assets it owned. But it succeeded in winning £2.3 million from a government programme in 2012 to buy and refurbish 60 disused houses. By 2018 it had become a housing association, and built 41 more well-insulated homes, with colourful exteriors, and was planning homes for the elderly near Hull Royal Infirmary.

The multiple initiatives of the Goodwin Trust make it an unusually strong example of local action: people organising themselves to improve facilities in their community, doing battle with government and other agencies where necessary, building up their assets, developing their trading and other income, and defending their independence. But why did it take off so successfully?

McGurn says luck was involved – being in the right place at the right time. But another key element was that the people who started Goodwin were local, had years of experience of community activity and were in it for the long term rather than three-year projects.

> "They took a decision early on not to just go out with a begging bowl, because he who pays the piper calls the tune: they were determined to do what they wanted to do, not what someone else wanted. It was also important that we had a Labour government under Tony Blair that thought community-based social enterprise was a good thing that they were prepared to put money into. We were smart enough to spot that opportunity, and Locality was also hugely important to us. We can't influence macro-economics, but we can do something about the micro-economics and get money to stick in the community. And organisations like ours are increasingly filling the spaces being vacated by the state."

The legacy of Sir Horace Plunkett

A charity with an unusually eccentric founder is the Plunkett Foundation: Sir Horace Plunkett was an Irishman who built a house in Dublin with a revolving open-air bedroom to promote his health, and learned to fly at the age of 70.[7] He was an advocate of co-operative agriculture, which his foundation promoted for decades in British Commonwealth countries. When the closure of village post offices and shops was accelerating in the UK after 2005, it began helping them to stay open and was a partner in a programme between 2007 and 2012 which saved some 200 community shops.

James Alcock, executive director of the Plunkett Foundation, acknowledged in 2019 that setting up community shops and pubs will not reverse the general tide of closures. "The statistics from Camra [the Campaign for Real Ale] show that 18 pubs are closing every week," he says. "In the whole of 2017, only 25 community pubs opened, so the battle is being lost spectacularly." It was also becoming harder to raise money for community ventures, he says, since nearly all funders had ceased to include a grant element with loans, partly because they saw how successfully many community shops managed to sell shares: "The market is awash with organisations offering loans, but raising finance entirely from loans is a challenge for small community businesses – they don't generate enough profit to service them, although pubs have a bit more potential than shops to take on debt." Of every seven enquiries the charity receives about community shops, only one comes to fruition; for pubs, the figure is one in eighteen.

Nonetheless, it is clear that charities like the Plunkett Foundation and Locality, working in partnership with charitable and other funders, play a significant role in assisting some local communities in preserving and building the assets, services and networks that improve life for their inhabitants. Most community shops and pubs are set up as community benefit societies, known as bencoms (a legal form described in Chapter 1), which in most cases cannot – because they are allowed to pay interest to private shareholders – also register as charities in order to claim the advantages this brings. But that doesn't inhibit the success of those that do manage to get off the ground: the Foundation says that community shops have a 95% success rate, compared with 46% for small businesses generally.

The Foundation also found that community pubs were more active during the first coronavirus lockdown than commercial pubs: it surveyed all 116 community pubs in June 2020, and nearly 70% of the 66 that responded said they were continuing to operate in some way, including through takeaway and delivery services. A UK-wide survey of members of the British Institute of Innkeeping in the same month found that only 28% of respondents were continuing to offer takeaway, collection and delivery services.[8] The difference was likely to have been the greater reliance of community pubs on volunteers rather than paid staff, as in the case of The Duke of Marlborough in the Suffolk village of Somersham.

Bringing The Duke back to life

Somersham's local pub is named after the victor of the Battle of Blenheim in 1704. There are tubs of petunias in the car park of the timber-framed, listed building, and a huge walnut tree overhangs the garden. For years, it was owned and run by Roger and Hazel Mason, but by 2014 they were nearly 70 and wanted to retire. The market for pubs was weak, however, not least because more people were drinking at home: the number of pubs in the UK fell from 50,000 in 2008 to 39,000 in 2018, according to the Office for National Statistics.[9] It seemed likely that The Duke would be converted into a private house.

As on the Thornton Estate in Hull, this was averted by the initiative of one woman, Sarah Caston. A local doctor who comes from a nearby farming family, she called a meeting attended by 150 of the village's 700 inhabitants, and it was clear there were plenty of people who wanted to save The Duke. Steve Wright, a local hop farmer, says: "I've lived in Suffolk villages all my life, and I know that villages that haven't got a pub start to die." He and 11 others joined a committee to work out the options, and asked for advice from the Plunkett Foundation and Pub is the Hub, founded by the Prince of Wales in 2001, which fosters community initiatives in rural areas.

Somersham Community Pub Ltd was set up early in 2015 as a bencom. The committee estimated that more than £438,000 would be needed, and an appeal was launched for investors to buy £50 shares, which were spared taxation on 30% of the sum put in. The amount raised rose swiftly to £120,000, stalled, then revived with fundraising events in barns, coverage on television and radio, and leafleting at Liverpool Street station in London. HM Revenue and Customs agreed that loans to the pub would qualify for Social Investment Tax Relief, but the clinching contribution was £90,000 – half grant, half loan – from the Plunkett Foundation and Co-operative and Community Finance, a £4 million fund that supports co-ops and social enterprises. Others were interested in buying The Duke, but the committee had taken advantage of the Localism Act 2011, placing it on the local council's list of 'assets of community value': this meant that a community group had six months' grace before other contenders were considered.

By Easter The Duke was open again. At first it was run by volunteers for three days a week, and the only food was from a pizza van and nearby Chinese and Indian takeaway restaurants. But by the autumn a manager and chef had been recruited, and soon the pub was open five days a week and serving its own food. By 2018 income was beginning to exceed running costs, and part-time kitchen and waiting staff were employed. The pub survived the first coronavirus lockdown of 2020, and by August was open again with one-way ordering systems and staff behind screens and visors. Subsequent lockdowns reduced it to selling takeaway beer through a 'collection window', but the committee remained optimistic. Frances Brace, in charge of public relations, says there is a real sense of community ownership:

> "Around a hundred people have contributed with skills including management, accountancy, building renovation and maintenance, gardening, interior design, tree surgery and catering. When 40 tons of stone were donated for the car park, six people turned up to help barrow it round. The material for the curtains was donated by a local silk weaving company, and Sarah Caston made them up. These are acts of kindness from people who value the existence of a social and economic hub in the form of a historic rural pub. Above all, saving the pub has brought people together and helped them to get to know each other."

Community organisers

The cases mentioned so far in this chapter – the COVID-19 support groups, the Goodwin Development Trust and The Duke of Marlborough – are all examples of local people acting on their own initiative, taking advantage in the last two instances of measures introduced by the Coalition government of 2010–15, including the Localism Act 2011, to stimulate community projects. But spontaneous initiatives and established community organisations can be lacking: as the Relationships Observatory report by Shift, cited at the start of this chapter, says of the first coronavirus lockdown: 'The community responses in some areas have been non-existent or largely ineffective.'[10]

An attempt to reach into such areas and kick-start community action was made by the Coalition government as part of the Big Society idea espoused by the prime minister at the time, David Cameron. This was the programme to train 5,000 community organisers, which recognised the importance of local action, especially in deprived areas. The concept of community organising has its origins in the work of Saul Alinsky in Chicago in the middle of the 20th century, and of the Brazilian writer Paolo Freire, who died in 1997.[11]

The programme started with funding of £15 million and was later given an extra £7.5 million. The first 500 organisers were paid a salary of £20,000 for a year and attached to existing organisations, such as development trusts; their brief was to listen to local people about their concerns and help them come up with remedies. Lawrence Hill in Bristol was one area that received four trainee organisers, but after 15 months only two of them remained, partly because of the difficulty of funding the salaries of the other two after the first year.[12] The successes of the two remaining organisers included helping a resident persuade the council to extend a sports programme for teenagers, working with a shop owner to set up a 'town team' to smarten up the high street, helping residents of a tower block to make greater use of their community room and organising a welfare reform advice session. "A lot of what we're doing is building a web of relationships," said Steve Crozier, one of the organisers. "We're bringing people together who might live close together, but don't know each other."

When the programme ended, an assessment by the Ipsos MORI social research institute found that 'the programme approach was successful in mobilising large numbers of people around specific issues and areas of mutual self-interest', but 'creating a broader movement for change in communities, which was an ambition at the outset of the programme, is considerably more challenging'.[13] In 2015, however, Locality, which had run the programme on behalf of the government, set up an independently financed Company of Community Organisers, which then won a further £4.2 million of government funding to run the Community Organisers Expansion programme. It registered as a charity, aiming to bring the number of trained organisers up to 10,000 by 2020 and to establish a national academy for community organising. Nick Gardham, chief executive of Community Organisers, says the first programme "dropped a pebble in the pond" but lacked something to hold it all together:

> "Locality had employed the organisers, and local organisations were the hosts, but the organisers weren't allowed to promote the agendas of the hosts, some of which had been established for ages. Our approach is to work with the local organisations rather than through them, building the capacity of local residents rather than holding all the skills in one individual. The previous programme was about organisers, but we're thinking more about organising. There are lots of people doing stuff already at community level and we look at where community organising skills can be best applied."

How does this work in practice? Take the Wirral, the promontory on the other side of the Mersey from Liverpool, where wealthy residential areas such as West Kirby alternate with pockets of deprivation such as Leasowe. Stephanie Hughes, a young local woman, took part in the expansion programme and ran a campaign known as 'Save our 106'.

The number refers to a bus that served part of the Leasowe housing estate, where many vulnerable and disabled people live, linking it directly with the nearby shops and the hospital about two miles away. When Merseytravel rerouted the 106 in September 2017 so that it no longer served the estate, Hughes and a colleague picked up messages from concerned residents, began knocking on doors, called a series of public meetings and enlisted the help of a councillor and the local Labour MP, Angela Eagle. Hughes says that 100 people came to the second meeting and a petition attracted 800 signatures:

"We also collected some case studies – one man was spending £100 a month on taxis to get to his hospital appointments. The bus company was saying no one had to walk more than 400 metres to get to an alternative bus stop, but we measured it and it was more than twice that distance. One man had a fall on the way to the bus stop and lay in the snow for an hour before he was rescued."

In August 2018, 12 local people, accompanied by Eagle, travelled to the headquarters of Merseytravel in Liverpool to mount a protest and hand in the petition. But the company refused to reinstate the service and continued to argue that residents could use a combination of other buses to reach the shops and hospital. Hughes says the campaign will continue:

"There's more to it than just the bus. It has created a network of local people by breaking down barriers between them. It's connected the young and the old and reduced social isolation. More people are coming to the afternoon tea event we organise. OK, so only 12 people turned up at the Merseytravel protest, but that's 12 people who were mobilised to get on the train and walk through Liverpool with their heads held high, and they will take that forward."

Hughes has also trained more than 50 local people in the principles of community organising, one of which is that organisers shouldn't do for people what they can do for themselves:

"Everyone has something to contribute, and in the end these things have to be community led. I can't be in charge. A lot of the people just take the training back into the life of their communities, although some want to volunteer to do more. We need to spread the skills as widely as possible – it needs to be grassroots and raw."

Successes of community organising include a campaign to persuade the Nationwide Building Society to open a branch in Glastonbury, Somerset, after all other banks in the town had closed, and the establishment of an 'organisation workshop' on the Marsh Farm estate in Luton which enabled more than 40 unemployed or marginalised people to develop their skills and confidence by creating a community farm from a derelict field.

One of the debates about community organising is whether its central purpose is to prompt people to do for themselves the things that public bodies cannot or will not do, or to help them to persuade those public bodies to do things, or do things differently. Gardham says the two things are not mutually exclusive and it can often work better if communities do things for themselves, such as running playgroups and parks and removing litter, rather than relying on the local council:

> "That can be much more powerful. It delegitimises the role of the state. Everyone linked the Big Society to the decline in public spending, making it look like an attempt to get government off the hook and get people to do things for themselves. But when David Cameron launched it in 2010, he said it was all about transferring power to the local level, and community organising is part of that. His advisor Lord [Nat] Wei was involved at the time, and he said if nothing came of it other than people getting to know their neighbours, it would be a success."

9

Supporting other people

One of the quickest and most effective responses by a charity to the coronavirus emergency in the UK came from FareShare, which distributes surplus food to people who need it. Before the pandemic it was handling about 20,000 tonnes of food a year, supplying about 930,000 people a week; by the middle of June 2020 that number had more than trebled to 3.2 million. But it was still not meeting all the demand, which was expected to grow as economic pressures increased in the wake of the crisis. "We're really terrified about the next couple of years," says FareShare's chief executive, Lindsay Boswell, a former army officer who also ran the Institute of Fundraising for many years.

FareShare was established in 1993 as a partnership between the homelessness charity Crisis and the supermarket giant Sainsbury's, but became an independent charity ten years later in order to extend its help beyond homeless people. It now works on two levels: its core business is taking large quantities of surplus food from the industry supply chain, sorting and repacking it and allocating it to member charities that pay a nominal subscription and distribute the food to their beneficiaries. But in 2017 it also launched FareShare Go, in which more than 7,000 local charities collect and distribute surplus food directly from nearby supermarkets at the end of each day: all 3,000-plus Tesco stores and some Waitrose and Asda ones take part.

FareShare Go hit problems in the first coronavirus lockdown, when panic buying cleared many supermarket shelves, leaving nothing spare at the end of the day. But the opposite was the case for the charity's core service as the hospitality industry ground to a halt: food producers and suppliers found themselves with mountains of stock they couldn't sell to restaurants and cafes. Boswell says:

> "It was an extraordinary spike – the highest peak in our 25 years. I remember one supplier who wanted us to take 24 pallets of lemons. That's a lot of lemons, but how many gin and tonics weren't being drunk in pubs? So we went from famine to feast in a matter of days."

But the boost in supply continued to be outstripped by demand as the number of front-line charities and community groups seeking food from FareShare more than trebled. Other food charities said the same: the Trussell Trust, which supports a network of 1,200 foodbanks in the UK, reported an 89% rise in foodbank use during April 2020, compared with the same month in 2019, and the Independent Food Aid Network, which works with 346 foodbanks, saw demand soar by 175%.[1]

FareShare's ability to respond rapidly to the crisis was partly a matter of luck: it had just completed a £12 million lottery-funded investment in its management team and its operational capacity – bigger warehouses, bigger chillers, more vans and forklifts. This turned out to be crucial, according to Boswell:

> "I shudder to think what would have happened if we hadn't just done all this. We wouldn't have been able to cope. But because we had all this additional capacity, we were able to click our fingers and go, 'OK, we now need to operate at three times the normal level in order to maximise the food we get out to front-line organisations – what do we need to do differently in order to achieve this?'"

FareShare also struck lucky with volunteers. Boswell had heard that foodbanks in Asia had lost volunteers at the start of the emergency because many were elderly people who had to go into isolation. To forestall the problem in the UK, he contacted the British Red Cross to spread the word, and in one week in April 2020 FareShare received more applications from people offering to sort, pack and deliver food than it had had in the whole of 2019.

FareShare also suspended membership fees for its charity partners and embarked on persuading the food industry to donate their surplus food along with money to buy more of it. This was very successful; Tesco, for example, purchased £16 million worth of food that was split between FareShare and the Trussell Trust. FareShare borrowed two warehouses outside Coventry and Oxford – one from Asda and one from the toyshop chain The Entertainer – in order to receive and repackage the extra stock. Other companies contributed too, Boswell says:

> "If you've got a Hovis lorry and a tinned meat lorry, obviously you need to mix those pallets up before they go on to a foodbank. Sainsbury's came up with a £3 million donation for logistics costs, so we were able to employ commercial staff to repackage that food and get it out as mixed pallets. Then we had British Gas vans coming and picking it up for individual foodbanks, because lorries that take 24 pallets can't normally get down roads that foodbanks are on. So British Gas did all the last-mile delivery for the Trussell Trust."

FareShare's work was given another huge boost during the pandemic by the high-profile support of footballer-turned-campaigner Marcus Rashford, who persuaded the government to reverse its decision not to fund free meal vouchers for disadvantaged children during the 2020 summer holidays. Rashford encouraged the public to donate to FareShare during the pandemic and was photographed volunteering at the charity's Greater Manchester warehouse in October, the day after Parliament had voted to back the government's decision not to extend the free meals scheme for school holidays until Easter 2021. During the day immediately after the parliamentary vote, FareShare recorded its highest ever figure for individual donations in a 24-hour period and recorded almost 6,000 new donors over the week.[2] After Rashford spoke to the Prime Minister on the phone, the government again changed its mind and pledged to extend provision over the winter.

FareShare's essential mission as a charity is to link two endemic problems – food waste and hunger – so they both become less of a problem. Producers can end up with too much stock because of over-ordering, oversupply, regulatory glitches or weather conditions that produce bumper crops. FareShare once took dozens of crates of olive oil because there were only nine months before its sell-by date, but regulations said there must be a year. It also took multiple pallets of a well-known soft drink because the labels had been printed in the wrong shade of grey. Before FareShare, such produce would most probably have been thrown away. By 2019 the charity had 21 regional warehouses and hundreds of volunteers repacking and delivering the goods to nearly 11,000 charities in 1,960 villages, towns and cities.[3]

One volunteer taking part in FareShare Go was Rosemarie Ramsay, who would visit the local Tesco Express in Catford, south London, every Tuesday evening to collect leftover bread, fruit and vegetables, eggs, meat, ready meals, pet food, sometimes even flowers. She was the volunteer manager at Mount Zion United Church in Lewisham, which helps disadvantaged and vulnerable people in one of London's most deprived boroughs with a range of services relating to health, state benefits, consumer rights and housing. She would take the food to a Mount Zion group meeting where most of it was sorted into bags to be distributed to about 110 beneficiaries a week. Ramsay says:

> "Some people from the meetings take the food home and cook it themselves. We also ask about people's neighbours, because at the end of the day we're trying to build up communities. So people will tell us about the man down the road or on the floor above, and we'll give them a bag of food to take to him as well. Other times we will cook the food and freeze it, and then take people meals or soups already prepared."

Helping people back to work

It's a Thursday morning in north Peckham, another gritty, multiracial area of south London, and Leroy Lodge is one of 12 people – nine Black, three White, and three of them women – taking part in a course that will qualify them to work in the security industry. The trainer, Jonathan Pettit, is telling them all they need to know about drugs if they take a job as door staff in clubs and bars. "Amphetamines, crack cocaine, mephedrone, crystal meth are all stimulants, as opposed to depressants," says Pettit. "You're entitled to search people for illegal drugs – if they say you can't look in their bag, you don't let them in." During a break in the session Lodge, who's previously been a cleaner and hotel porter, says he'd prefer to work in building security rather than on the doors: "I'm 61 now and looking for something a bit quieter. I'm finding the course very helpful, but I find it hard to retain all the information. So far, so good, though – I do feel confident it will lead to a job."

The course is taking place at Pecan, a building on a corner of Peckham High Street with colourful, graffiti-style decorations along its side wall. Its name is the acronym for Peckham Evangelical Churches Action Network, a charity that was set up in 1989 as a response to street disturbances in the area in preceding years. There are something like 40 churches on Peckham High Street alone, most of them Black-led Pentecostal churches: an academic study in 2013 found more than 240 Black-majority churches in the London borough of Southwark as a whole.[4] But the charity does not emphasise its Christian basis or try to convert people, and some time ago it dropped the requirement for staff to be practising Christians and now employs some Muslims: Lodge, who is not a churchgoer himself, is surprised to hear of Pecan's religious origins. Chris Price, Pecan's chief executive, says eight churches combined to found Pecan, and the 20 that are now members select the charity's trustees:

> "The founders decided something needed to be done
> in the wake of the riots, and began to knock on doors
> on the North Peckham Estate and ask what should

happen. What came back was that people didn't have work and didn't know how to get into work, so we started off running our first employment programmes – what's needed to hold down a job, how to develop your skills and interests, and so on. At first, they were run by a few volunteers, but after more than 20 years we now also do computer training, English for speakers of other languages, maths, first aid, health and safety. We have a furniture reuse social enterprise as well, and we run the foodbank for Peckham."

Pecan's income comes partly from government funding of its employment work and partly from fundraising, including grants from charitable trusts. At its peak before the 2008 financial crash, it had an income of £4 million and 120 staff. Then the cuts and the Coalition government's redirection of employment training work to big, private sector contractors brought the income down to £250,000 and the staff to nine. Price says that Pecan survived only because it retained a few key contracts and was able to sell one building it owned in order to pay off the mortgage on the other. By 2019 it had climbed back to an income of £1 million and 28 staff, helped by between 30 and 40 volunteers; but it lives, like many charities, with constant uncertainty about the future.

What seems clear, however, is that Pecan is liked and respected by local people – unlike some neighbouring high street shops, it was spared from damage in the disturbances of 2011 sparked by the death of Mark Duggan (mentioned in Chapter 5). It also has a creditable track record: of 1,100 people who went through its employment programmes in 2019, about a third succeeded in getting jobs or going into further education, according to Price. One of the four programmes it runs is general, but the other three are aimed at ex-prisoners, workers aged over 40 and people from troubled families. In the latter programme, called Family Works, two out of seven people who went through it in 2017 were in employment a year later. Pecan also runs a women's service that started among people leaving prison and has helped participants to gain places at university and retrieve their children from the care of the local authority.

Price, who has spent 25 years working in the voluntary sector, including at an HIV/AIDS charity, is a Methodist. He has led Pecan since 2011 and has a relaxed style that includes jeans and a red floral shirt:

> "The role of religion in Pecan is that we are a Christian organisation doing what we see God would want in the world. We're not about persuading people to become Christians and we don't mention religion unless they ask. When a potential funder of our women's group at All Saints Church was asking whether people of other faiths could take part, the door opened and a woman in a hijab came in, which sort of provided the answer. I hope that through contact with Pecan people do come closer to God, whether they recognise it or not – our aim is to transform lives through the three themes of kindness, belief and hope.
>
> It's vital for us that we are a registered charity. People's trust in charities – especially smaller, local charities – is high, and they see us as part of the community. And of course there are some valuable tax advantages, including the fact that we don't have to pay business rates on our building."

The role of religion in supporting people

Pecan is a vivid modern example of community action that originates in religious faith. For centuries churches were the main dispensers of charity, and religious belief was the principal inspiration for individual charitable activity. From the start of the industrial age, secular philanthropy became more common and grew in parallel. But the Church of England, the Roman Catholic Church, the Methodists and other, smaller churches have continued to be the sources or facilitators of charitable work, particularly at a local level. The same is now true of mosques, Jewish synagogues, Sikh gurdwaras and Hindu temples. Much of the work of religious groups is focused on supporting individuals in need.

There was also a strong religious element in the 'settlement' movement between 1880 and 1930, when so-called settlement houses were established in poor urban areas where university graduates and middle-class volunteers would live and try to improve the lives of the people around them. The first and best-known settlement in the UK, Toynbee Hall in the East End of London, was founded in 1884 by a Church of England vicar, Samuel Barnett, and his wife, Henrietta, who wanted to attract future leaders of society as volunteers so they would learn about how the poor lived. Among those who spent time at Toynbee Hall were Lord Beveridge, whose work provided the blueprint for the welfare state after the Second World War, and Clement Attlee, prime minister between 1945 and 1951. Over time, Toynbee Hall and other settlements in London and elsewhere shed much of their overt association with religion and became part of the British Association of Settlements and Social Action Centres, abbreviated to Bassac, which merged with the Development Trusts Association in 2010 to form Locality, mentioned in the previous chapter in the context of the Goodwin Development Trust in Hull.

One of the advantages of the ancient parish system, and of the wealth the churches enjoyed in past centuries, is that each parish often has not only its own church but a church hall or other buildings which are often used for community purposes such as playgroups, youth clubs, social activities for the elderly, advice centres or even theatre groups. These established networks were a principal reason why the Trussell Trust was able to expand its foodbanks so rapidly in the years of austerity that followed the financial crash of 2008: they could use church premises.[5]

When fire engulfed the Grenfell Tower in inner west London in June 2017, killing 72 people, the parish priest of nearby St Clement's church, the Reverend Alan Everett, was woken at 3 am by the pandemonium in the streets. "I came down to the church, opened the doors and turned the lights on," he told *The Guardian* newspaper.[6] The result was that people who wanted to help started to arrive, and the church became a relief centre, providing food, drink and a place for survivors to rest and talk. Within days it was like a refugee facility, piled high with donations of food and clothes. On most Sundays the church attracts a congregation of between only 30 and 60 people, according to Everett, but it was a natural centre of the entire community when disaster struck: local people knew that, in a sense, the doors were always open and the lights on. The ClementJames Centre – the community development charity associated with the church, which specialises in education, adult learning and employment support and has a staff of more than 20 – also became a key part of the relief effort that followed the fire.

Another example of the role of the church in local communities came at the start of 2014, when England was hit by widespread flooding and many charities played their part in the relief work alongside state services. In Chertsey in Surrey, where the Thames had burst its banks, the emergency services and the local council were helped by – among others – the British Red Cross, the Royal Voluntary Service and even the RSPCA.[7] What became the base for their activities? The natural choice was the Anglican church of St Peter, where the work of volunteers was coordinated and, among other things, people helped to fill the sandbags that were used to protect nearby homes from the rising water.

In some deprived communities the church plays a pivotal role all the time. One example is All Saints church in Chatham, one of the Medway towns in Kent that has suffered from the closure of the Royal Dockyard, which was once the main employer in the area. The church is near Luton Road, a dilapidated area of bedsits and cheap takeaway food shops where addiction and prostitution are common. Next to the church is the Magpie Centre, a former pub, which runs a cafe, a lunch club, a gardening group, computer classes, craft sessions and an after-school club. In 2017 the All Saints Community Project had about 40 active volunteers and employed 11 people, but was struggling constantly for funding to supplement its meagre earned income, according to the manager, Louise Shrubsole:

"The project is unique because it has emerged from the local community. It's valued in the local area because it comes from within. For example, we've got a group that helps people with depression and anxiety, and the idea for that came from someone who was taking part in the craft sessions."

In an increasingly secular society, the involvement of the Church in community action alienates some people. But religion has been a powerful motivator in charitable activity down the centuries and clearly continues to play a strong role. Organisations that support people in need or provide community facilities are often started and run by religious organisations, with varying degrees of emphasis on adherence to religion. Community initiatives supported by public funds, however, are usually entirely secular.

Work for former prisoners: Blue Sky

England, Wales and Scotland have the highest per capita prison population in Western Europe.[8] Prisons in these parts of the UK release around 80,000 people annually, but nearly half of them commit another crime within a year, and reoffending costs society an estimated £16 billion each year.[9,10,11,12] Studies show that having a job reduces the propensity to reoffend by around 10%, but fewer than a fifth of prisoners have a job to go to after their release.[13,14]

Steve Finn, a former bank robber, wanted to stay away from crime after he came out of prison, but whenever he tried to get a job, he found that the door was slammed in his face as soon as he admitted to a criminal record.[15] He was surviving by doing odd jobs for friends and family, but many people he had known in prison were being lured back into a life of crime and winding up inside again.

Then he met Mick May, a former banker, and together they decided to create an agency to provide employment for ex-prisoners and help them to find a home and deal with other problems. The charity Blue Sky Development & Regeneration was born, later described by former prime minister David Cameron as "the only company in the country where you need a criminal record to work there".[16] The charity operates in the south and east of England, employs former prisoners and seeks contracts on the basis that it is cheaper than most competitors and provides social value. People are employed for six months while also being trained and helped to find a permanent job elsewhere. Training is tailored to people's circumstances and job aspirations, such as forklift driving or obtaining a chainsaw licence: the charity sticks to the model of 'employ, then train', so that recruits can earn immediately.

Blue Sky won its first contract with Slough Borough Council in Berkshire for maintaining parks and gardens, and its model proved attractive to other local authorities that recognised the social benefits as well as the cost savings. After three years, it had helped 130 ex-prisoners to find work. As austerity began to bite after 2010 the charity also started contracting with private sector providers of public services, such as Veolia, Amey and Sodexo. This was highly successful, and between 2012 and 2015 Blue Sky employed more people than in all the previous seven years.

It also created a new, more flexible employment model called Agency★, in which Blue Sky employees are integrated into the staff of client organisations. Two of the best-known UK companies, Virgin and the consultancy and financial services company Deloitte, were early clients, and Agency★ has worked with more than 30 companies.

In its first ten years Blue Sky passed the milestone of finding jobs for 1,000 ex-prisoners – equal to the population of a large prison – and by 2018 was employing around 200 a year.[17] In 2017 it merged with another charity, the Rehabilitation of Addicted Prisoners Trust, to become the Forward Trust, but the well-known Blue Sky name was still used to describe the employment model. Carwyn Gravell, the charity's director of business development, says the merger was driven by the potential to grow and reach more people:

> "If you take addiction as the biggest cause of crime, and employment as one of the single biggest determinants in helping people to stop offending, then put those two things together and you've got an effective service. Forward Trust delivers services to support people with addiction, drug and alcohol recovery. We work in 18 prisons to deliver that work, we support offenders' family relationships, and we do some work on mental health and well-being as well."

Data submitted by Blue Sky to the Justice Data Lab – a service run by the Ministry of Justice to help organisations demonstrate their impact on reoffending – showed that Blue Sky employees were up to 23% less likely to reoffend than the general prison population in the first six months after their release.[18] "That is still one of the highest-performing interventions on record," says Gravell. In 2016 Deloitte did some work free of charge for the charity, looking at the benefit to the state from its unique employment model.[19] Gravell says this showed that for every ex-prisoner who completed the Blue Sky programme, £18,600 of net benefit was generated – income to the state from tax and National Insurance, and savings in the cost of prison and crime.

Charities that help prisoners

There are around 1,700 organisations that help people and families cope with a prison sentence by providing advice and support, ranging from housing to mentoring, arts classes and help with addiction.[20,21] In 2019 five UK prisons boasted a Clink Restaurant, where prisoners gain skills by preparing, cooking and serving haute cuisine to prison visitors.[22] Prisoners who work in the restaurants study for City & Guilds qualifications in food preparation, food service and customer service, improving their chances of securing jobs in the hospitality industry on their release.

Another criminal justice charity is Storybook Dads (and Mums), which helps to maintain the vital emotional bond between imprisoned parents and their children by recording bedtime stories that can be played to children at home. Every year in the UK around 230,000 children endure having a parent in prison, and they are twice as likely as others to suffer from mental health or behaviour problems.[23] Maintaining family links is known to be highly important in reducing the risk of recidivism, but research shows that more than 40% of prisoners do lose contact.[24,25]

Storybook Dads arranges for prisoners in 107 prisons to record a story or song on a CD, which is then sent to the editing suite at the charity's headquarters in HM Prison Channings Wood in Devon, where mistakes are edited out and music and sound effects are added. More than 830 prisoners have been trained to use audio- and video-editing software, which gives them a better chance of employment upon release.[26] In 2018, Storybook Dads produced 5,505 CDs and DVDs, taking the total since the charity was launched in 2002 to more than 65,000. Ninety-seven per cent of the prisoners taking part in the project told the charity it had improved their relationship with their children.[27]

Charities that work in the prison system were among those most disrupted by the outbreak of COVID-19 in early 2020. Modelling by Public Health England projected that, without containment measures, between 2,500 and 3,000 inmates and staff could die from the virus in the UK's jails. Charities were forced to suspend visits and adapt their services as thousands of prisoners were confined to their cells for 23 hours a day. Pact, the Prison Advice and Care Trust, lobbied the government to help prisoners to maintain contact with their families by supplying more mobile phones. The charity also sent tens of thousands of activity packs into jails to help keep prisoners occupied.

Anne Fox, chief executive of Clinks, the umbrella network for more than 500 of the charities and voluntary organisations working in the criminal justice system, said it was possible that access to prison by charities would be restricted for months, and that this would compound mental health problems among prisoners.[28] She was also worried about the impact the pandemic would have on the sustainability of member charities, especially those that rely on trusts and foundations for their funding. In July 2020 she said: "I've already got members telling me that they're expecting to be out of business in two years' time because in criminal justice we have a smaller group of funders anyway, and the pipelines are drying up."

As Fox indicates, charities that help prisoners find it less easy to attract funding and donations than more popular causes such as medical research, animals or children. The same goes for charities that help substance abusers to beat addiction, rescue people from modern slavery and trafficking, support young people in or leaving care or find employment for people with disabilities. The Nelson Trust supports sex workers to leave the sex industry; Circles UK supports and rehabilitates sex offenders by convening small groups of volunteers to provide a 'circle of support' around a convicted offender. Those on the margins of society have a harsh life, and without the work of such charities it would be harsher still.

10

The wider world

International development charities were among the first to suffer from the effects of the coronavirus pandemic. Stephanie Draper, chief executive of the aid charities umbrella group Bond, predicted that the sector could lose up to 40% of its total annual revenue.[1] A survey of Bond members in April 2020 revealed that more than 40% of them thought they would have to close within six months, with smaller bodies most at risk. Among the first to cut jobs was Oxfam, the giant of the sector: it announced that its international division would shed 1,450 of almost 5,000 jobs and withdraw from 18 countries.[2] A tenth of the 2,000 staff at Oxfam GB were at risk.[3]

The fall in income came as personal donations were hit by economic hardship, fundraising activities fell back, charity shops closed for months and income from the state began to shrink. In July, the government cut £2.9 billion from overall aid spending, a 19% reduction on the previous year's figure of £15.2 billion: more than 70% of aid spending goes through the Department for International Development (DfID), from which some large charities get up to 20% of their income.[4,5] Matters were made worse, according to Draper, by the government decision to merge DfID with the Foreign and Commonwealth Office from September 2020, raising fears that money would be diverted from the most needy countries to strategic and political priorities. Draper said the merger "marked the beginning of the UK turning its back on the world's poorest people", and called it a "tragic blow" when the government also reduced its commitment to international aid from 0.7% of gross national income – enshrined in law since 2013 – to 0.5% for 2021.[6]

Despite opposition from hundreds of charities, MPs from seven parties and the Archbishop of Canterbury, Chancellor Rishi Sunak confirmed the intention in his one-year spending review in November 2020, breaking a 2019 manifesto pledge and, in effect, cutting the aid budget by a third to £10 billion in 2020–21. However, the move required a change in the law and the government looked likely to endure a bruising battle to get it through Parliament. The move was criticised by former prime ministers including David Cameron, and some senior Conservative backbenchers. A junior minister in the Foreign and Commonwealth Office, Baroness (Liz) Sugg, who had worked with Cameron, resigned in protest.

The UK has a strong record in development work and is recognised internationally as a leader in the field. The 0.7% of national income target was adopted by several United Nations member countries in 1970, but only five nations consistently met it in the five years to 2018.[7] The growth in aid spending was mirrored in the income of the UK's aid charities: research by Bond showed that their collective income grew by 59% over the ten years to April 2016, to more than £3.8 billion.[8] This far outstripped the percentage growth in the income of charities as a whole, which increased by only 10% over the same period. The research also showed that a third of the entire international development sector's income was received by only eight charities, all with incomes of more than £100 million a year.

The role of charities in international aid

International aid has its origins in the European Recovery Programme – also known as the Marshall Plan – that funded reconstruction in Europe and Asia after the Second World War. Since then, foreign aid and development has become a huge, complex and contentious activity, with total official aid flows estimated at US$297 billion (£224 billion) a year in 2019.[9] Aid can include infrastructure projects such as roads and ports, education and welfare programmes, healthcare, technical assistance, humanitarian work and disaster relief. Sometimes donor governments attach political strings, such as stipulating that the money is used for programmes to wipe out the production of drugs, or 'structural adjustment measures' – jargon for paying off a country's debt on condition that changes are made in its domestic policies. Multilateral aid is funded by more than one state, through programmes run by the World Bank or the United Nations, while bilateral aid is given directly from one country to another.

But governments do not deliver development by themselves, and the growth in aid budgets has boosted the rise of a whole industry of NGOs that raise money for, and awareness of, the plight of poor countries, and spend it on building capacity or delivering services in those countries. The world's largest non-governmental donor is the Bill and Melinda Gates Foundation, set up by the Microsoft founder and his wife in 2000, which has given away more than $50 billion (£38 billion).[10] The biggest development charity in the world is BRAC, a Bangladesh-based NGO that focuses on helping girls, women and the ultra-poor through microfinance and a range of social justice programmes. BRAC employs 110,000 people in 11 countries and has an annual expenditure of around £750 million.[11]

In the UK, a search for 'overseas aid/famine relief' on the Charity Commission for England and Wales website returns 10,566 results; 112 of these charities have incomes of more than £10 million. After the British Council, the biggest UK players are Oxfam and Save the Children, followed by the Royal Commonwealth Society for the Blind, known as Sightsavers. One of the most familiar UK aid charities is Comic Relief which, through its biennial Red Nose Day and Sport Relief fundraising events, has raised more than £1 billion since 1984, helping, among other things, to educate more than a million children in Africa and to buy anti-mosquito bed nets for one million people.[12]

The successes of aid programmes

There is little doubt that increasing levels of international aid have played a part in the fall in the numbers of people living below the threshold for extreme poverty, defined by the World Bank in 2015 as $1.90 per day. In that year, the latest for which world poverty figures are available, 736 million people lived in abject poverty, or 10% of the planet's population.[13] But this proportion is actually a cause for celebration when you consider that it was nearly 36% in 1990 and 42.2% in 1981.[14,15] According to the US-based non-profit public policy organisation the Brookings Institution, the world reached a tipping point in September 2018:[16]

> For the first time since agriculture-based civilisation began 10,000 years ago, the majority of humankind is no longer poor or vulnerable to falling into poverty. By our calculations, as of this month, just over 50 per cent of the world's population, or some 3.8 billion people, live in households with enough discretionary expenditure to be considered 'middle class' or 'rich'. About the same number of people are living in households that are poor or vulnerable to poverty ... Barring some unfortunate global economic setback, this marks the start of a new era of a middle-class majority.

There are many examples of the effectiveness of aid, starting with the battle against malaria. Death rates plummeted by 60% from 2000 to 2015, saving more than seven million lives and preventing more than a billion cases, largely thanks to the RMB Partnership to End Malaria.[17] This is a global programme launched in 1998 that involved more than 500 partner organisations, including many drug companies and charities, in providing insecticide-treated mosquito nets, diagnostic testing, spraying and other activities. As recently as 2017 there were still 219 million cases of malaria and 435,000 deaths annually, according to the World Health Organization (WHO).[18] But the proportion of children in sub-Saharan Africa who sleep beneath a bed net has increased from 5% to nearly 50% in a decade and WHO believes that global mortality rates can be cut by 90% by 2030.[19,20]

Another example is trachoma, the biggest infectious cause of blindness in the world. In 2000, 15% of the population of the West African country of Ghana – more than 2.8 million people

– were infected with or at risk of contracting trachoma, despite the fact that the disease is entirely preventable and treatable. But in 2018 WHO announced that Ghana was the first country in sub-Saharan Africa to eliminate trachoma.[21] This had been achieved by a collaborative cross-sector, international effort by more than 20 NGOs, including the UK charity Sightsavers. Ten countries have now eliminated trachoma completely.[22]

On other fronts, Unicef reported in 2018 that the global rate of mortality for children under five had been cut by 58% since 1990.[23] Bangladesh has had particular success, reducing its child mortality rate by almost 80% over the period.[24] In Afghanistan, nearly 80% of the country's minefields have been cleared of mines over three decades: Herat province, the most dangerous, was finally declared free of mines in 2018 after a ten-year clearance effort led by the UK charity the HALO Trust.[25]

As well as raising money and public awareness of poverty and disease in the world, charities have been at the forefront of lobbying governments. At the G8 Summit in Gleneagles, Scotland, in 2005, the charity coalition Make Poverty History mobilised supporters to press the world's richest nations to write off an extra £30 billion of debt owed by poor countries and to reaffirm their commitment to the Millennium Development Goals (MDGs).[26] The MDGs in 2000 were a significant step forward for international development because they were the first common and transparent framework agreed by multiple states at the United Nations.

Progress over the next 15 years was mixed: the first target of halving world poverty was achieved five years ahead of the deadline, but this was largely because a significant proportion of the Chinese population were lifted out of poverty by the country's rapid economic growth.[27] In most countries progress fell short, and in the very poorest of them the data does not exist to assess achievements. But the MDGs paved the way for an even greater international commitment to world development in September 2015 – a new set of 17 ambitious Sustainable Development Goals, agreed at the largest-ever gathering of heads of state in New York. The 17 goals and 169 targets cover a broad range of issues, among them poverty and hunger, climate change, health and education, sustainable urban planning and protecting natural habitats. The deadline for achieving each goal and target is 2030.

The economist Ian Goldin is professor of globalisation and development at the University of Oxford and a former economic advisor to President Mandela. In his 2018 book, *Development: A Very Short Introduction*, he wrote:[28]

Aid flows have never been more effective in encouraging growth and reducing poverty. The reasons are simple. First, developing countries on average have never been better governed, and their economies have never been more effectively managed. Second, although there is a real danger of this being reversed, aid has increasingly been flowing to those countries that are able to use it effectively. Third, the aid community and academia have evolved over the past 70 years. There is a better understanding of what works and what does not, and of the need for coherence between aid, macroeconomics, trade and other policies. Common processes and goalposts have been established, such as the Millennium Development Goals and Sustainable Development Goals, which have greatly improved the effectiveness of aid and reduced tied aid, vanity projects and corruption. We live in an era when for the first time in history we can realistically imagine and achieve in our lifetimes a world free of poverty and many of the diseases that have afflicted humanity for millennia.

The development landscape, and the work of agencies, is multifaceted and complicated, as this extract points out. The difficulty and complexity of the work is such that some NGOs have distanced themselves from the word 'charity', believing it does not adequately describe their activities and impact. Simon O'Connell, executive director of Mercy Corps Europe, has publicly argued that the charity label is unsuitable for development organisations because they do so much more than simply raising money or giving voluntary help. Instead, he said, they are "complicated agents of social change" and must work harder to ensure they are portrayed as such by the media.[29]

This complexity also means it is not easy to discern the impact that individual aid or development organisations have on a particular cause or community. Most development successes cannot be attributed to any one initiative or player; they are the result of a variety of inputs from a multitude of actors and of partnerships between donors and providers. But that is not to say that we cannot build some picture of the impact that individual organisations make, whether large, established players or tiny newcomers.

The case of Islamic Relief

Among the larger aid charities, one of the most high-profile is Islamic Relief Worldwide (IRW), which was founded in 1984 in response to famine in Ethiopia and by 2018 had an income of £127 million.[30] It is based in Birmingham, has offices or partner organisations in 49 countries and in 2019 was running programmes in 33 of them. About 20% of donations are made in the UK, 17% in the US and 10% in both Canada and Sweden. Although IRW raises money mainly from Muslims and operates chiefly in Muslim-majority countries in the Middle East, Asia and Africa, its beneficiaries include people of all faiths and it does not proselytise, according to Naser Haghamed, the charity's chief executive until February 2021. In 2005 IRW became a member of the Disasters Emergency Committee, which coordinates the efforts of the 13 biggest UK aid agencies when major disasters strike around the world. More than half of its spending in 2020 was on humanitarian aid, and 37% was on longer-term development projects.

The successes, however, have been tarnished by an episode that reflects the passions aroused by conflicts in the Middle East and the role of Israel. In July 2020, Heshmat Khalifa resigned as a trustee after *The Times* newspaper uncovered Facebook posts by him before he became a trustee calling Israelis 'the grandchildren of monkeys and pigs' and Egypt's President al-Sisi a 'pimp son of the Jews'. His place on the board was taken by the chair of Islamic Relief Germany, Almoutaz Tayara, whose

Facebook posts from 2014 and 2015 – again, before he became a trustee – were also revealed by *The Times* the following month, calling the Palestinian militant organisation Hamas 'great men' who were 'responding to the divine and holy call of the Muslim brotherhood'.

Immediately, all members of the five-strong IRW board were replaced, the charity released a statement that all forms of discrimination, including anti-Semitism, were unacceptable and the new board was summoned to meet the Charity Commission about its governance.[31] In an astute move, the charity also recruited Dominic Grieve, the former Conservative MP and attorney general, to chair a commission on vetting trustees and senior staff and on redefining expectations of conduct. Soon after the commission started work, anti-Semitic social media posts dating back to 2014 from Tayeb Abdoun, the charity's network and resource development director, also came to light and he too had to resign.[32] Just days later, Naser Haghamed, the charity's chief executive, announced that he would be stepping down for health reasons, topping off a calamitous period for the organisation.[33] Matters improved, however, when the Charity Commission said in January 2021 that it was satisfied that IRW was making the necessary improvements to the vetting of trustees and oversight of their social media. Grieve's commission also concluded that 'there is no evidence whatever that the reputational issues that have arisen over the conduct of trustees have had any link to the way IRW carries out its charitable work'.[34, 35] Two other large aid charities, Oxfam and Save the Children, have been involved in scandals concerning, in their cases, failures of safeguarding and sexual harassment, which are described in Chapter 21.

The controversy over IRW came at a time when it was particularly active in the crises caused by the civil war in Syria and the war in Yemen between the government, supported by Saudi Arabia, and the Houthi rebels, backed by Iran. By 2020 IRW's biggest programme was in Yemen, where it was the main partner of the United Nations World Food Programme and was employing 2,800 staff to distribute food to 2.2 million people every month. To ensure the aid went to individual civilians, the charity was also employing 300 monitors who made sure it was not handed out to men who bring a large number of identity cards to a collection point, claiming to be representing the holders. Haghamed says there is always the danger of aid diversion in war zones:

> "In the mountainous areas it's difficult for people to reach the collection points and we are planning to deliver house to house by motorbike. One of our advantages is that we have access to countries where other NGOs do not – we have been working in Yemen for 17 years now and have a reputation and a lot of credibility there. One reason for that is that nearly all of our staff are local, so there are hardly any expats with high salaries and expenses."

The coronavirus pandemic had a drastic effect on the operations of IRW, as on those of other aid charities, as it adapted to frequently changing information and guidance on best practice. In Yemen, for example, it had to set up more food distribution centres to avoid overcrowding, and to spend more on protective equipment for staff. Operational costs were cut by £2.4 million, and the charity said it expected 'further hurdles and uncertainty in late 2020 and 2021', including disruption to development programmes such as schooling, and increasing need among small farmers and businesses.

Fundraising, however, held up strongly. Although hundreds of community fundraising events in the UK and other countries were cancelled, some went ahead in the form of Zoom meetings, and more resources were put into direct marketing and online fundraising, which the charity had been developing for the last decade. It set up a 'virtual mosque', and income during the holy month of Ramadan, when the charity normally receives between 30% and 40% of its income, was a third higher than in the previous year. A peer-to-peer fundraising drive, in which supporters ask for contributions from friends, family and colleagues, raised £465,000 through the donation website JustGiving, and by August the charity was 'cautiously optimistic' that income for 2020 would compare favourably with 2019, while warning that recession and rising unemployment would affect disposable income and, potentially, charitable giving.

The fundraising position at IRW appeared to contrast with the general picture at aid charities during the pandemic that was given at the start of this chapter, and suggested that research among more than 4,000 UK residents in 2013 still held good. A study by the polling company ICM on behalf of JustGiving found that Muslims gave an average of £371 to charity in 2012, followed by Jewish donors (£270), Protestants (£202), Catholics (£178) and Hindus (£171).[36]

Meanwhile, Islamic aid agencies in the UK face difficulties that others do not, according to Haghamed:

> "Islamophobia has an impact and we are not seen in the same way. The most common question I get is, do you only help Muslims? Is that question asked of Christian or Jewish agencies? We help everybody. We don't discriminate, we are neutral, and we categorically deny any links with designated organisations or political groups."

Another disadvantage is that some banks won't deal with Muslim charities for fear of sanctions from governments, particularly the US, that suspect some charitable funds are reaching groups designated as terrorist. HSBC stopped servicing IRW, which now works mainly through Barclays and money transfer companies such as Western Union. "It's a daily issue for us, and it won't end soon," says Haghamed. "We now use euros rather than US dollars, and we are able to get funds into countries including Somalia and Afghanistan."

Hope Health Action

A much smaller UK faith-based charity in the development world is Hope Health Action (HHA), which began by building a hospital in northern Haiti in 2007 and later supported refugees in Uganda, which in 2019 had the biggest refugee crisis in Africa because of people fleeing conflict in the neighbouring Democratic Republic of Congo and South Sudan.[37] HHA was set up by Carwyn Hill in 2005 after he read a message on a noticeboard at a Christian conference from someone from Haiti who needed accommodation. Hill invited him to stay at his house; his guest turned out to be the president of the Baptist Convention in Haiti, and the pair struck up a friendship. The pastor invited Hill to visit him in Haiti and told him about his vision for a health facility for the local community, where rates of infant mortality were among the worst in the world. Hill says he was astounded by the poverty and lack of basic medical equipment and resolved to help. He raised funds for the project, and before long was devoting himself to it full time.

The facility opened in 2007 as a small general practice clinic and soon began providing respite care for children with disabilities. Then, on 12 January 2010, Haiti was hit by a massive earthquake: because HHA was already established there and appeared high up on internet searches for charities supporting those affected by the quake, it raised more money in three months than in the previous three years combined. There was a huge demand for spinal injury treatments for victims of the earthquake, prompting HHA to set up one of Haiti's first spinal units. HHA also partnered with Médecins Sans Frontières and other charities to set up a cholera treatment centre in the north of the country, with 250 beds that were full for months.

Over the next few years HHA's clinic developed into a proper hospital, named Hospital HCBH, and eventually employed around 280 Haitian doctors, nurses and administrators. Alongside the spinal and neurological rehabilitation unit and a respite centre for disabled children, the hospital has an emergency department and a maternity, neonatal and paediatric unit that can perform Caesarean sections around the clock. Overall, around 20,000 patients are treated each year, with many returning multiple times.[38] Income reached a peak of around £900,000 in 2010 but by 2018 had fallen to about half that.[39]

The hospital's response to the coronavirus epidemic was to turn the sports centre into a COVID-19 isolation ward, which was accredited by the WHO as one of Haiti's national centres for treating the disease. But HHA's income, like that of most aid charities, came under pressure and the charity appealed to its supporters for extra donations.

As well as employing Haitian staff at the hospital, HHA relies on volunteers from the UK to fundraise and to help on the ground. But this kind of international volunteering facilitated by charities is not without its controversies. Critics say that by providing free labour – or even paying for the privilege of being there – 'voluntourists' are taking work away from local people desperate for jobs.[40] Public amenities and infrastructure tend to work better and last longer when local people build them, it is argued. And no matter how well intentioned volunteers are, they cannot achieve sustainable change. Campaigns such as #nowhitesaviors have attracted thousands of followers on Twitter, posting advice to would-be volunteers such as: 'It's very possible to come and visit developing countries for the beauty and adventure rather than coming to try and save us or do something you aren't qualified for.'

Art in aid: Flying Seagull Project

Not all aid charities provide primary assistance such as food, healthcare or education. Ash Perrin is founder and 'ringmaster' of the Flying Seagull Project, which puts on entertainment for refugee children such as circus workshops and performance art. Perrin was an aspiring actor, supporting himself by clowning at children's parties, when he had the idea for the Seagulls after visiting an orphanage in Cambodia and being astonished by the impact he made just by playing his guitar for the children. He cut short his planned six-month trip abroad and flew home the next week, spending the rest of his travel fund on a van which he painted with colourful seagulls and packed with juggling balls, spinning plates, wigs and stilts.

He and a friend then set out for Romania, where they spent the next three months dressing up as clowns and entertaining children in institutions and impoverished communities with music and art workshops and circus and magic shows. "That was 2008, and from the very first day in Romania I never looked back," Perrin says. "The purest connection you can have with a kid is play – that energy exchange and comedic interaction, meeting on the level of what's funny and what's fun."

The Flying Seagull Project was registered as a charity in 2010, and the small team of part-time staff and volunteers spent their summers raising funds by performing at UK festivals, then travelling abroad to entertain children from the autumn. For the first seven years the small troupe of entertainers focused mainly on Romania, but also visited Albania, Cambodia, Ghana and India, which were chosen mainly because members of the troupe had personal connections or had identified a need there.

After the refugee crisis in Europe began in 2015, the Flying Seagull Project spent most of the next three years working with refugee children on the borders of Greece, where there were about 15,000 refugees. The Seagulls did eight to ten shows a day for seven weeks continually, then bought two large circus tents, put them up in two camps in northern Greece, and performed in them alternately. Perrin says they spent much of 2018 on the Greek island of Lesbos, entertaining refugees in the notorious Moria camp, which was later destroyed by fire in 2020:

> "There were 8,000 people imprisoned in a camp built for 1,000. They called it Europe's Guantanamo. It's horrific, there were teenagers locked up without trial and without any representation. When all this gets unravelled, they'll study it in schools and wonder how a civilised continent allowed this to happen."

In late 2018 the Seagulls embarked on a Nonstop Big Top Tour, putting up one of the tents for a week or two in one place, then moving on to another. For five days a week they would run three sessions a day in the tent – various combinations of games, workshops and shows. Perrin says play is so powerful that children change:

> "Play puts you in the exact present moment. Whether that's in Moria camp or a slum in Ghana, the opportunity to play a game is so alluring and attractive and natural that they instantly let go of everything else that's going on, and they're just little kids playing duck duck goose, even if they're surrounded by

tanks. I got the kids all singing one day when the adults were shouting and arguing, and you know, it's impossible to keep fighting when you've got a load of kids beside you singing 'you're happy and you know it'. It reframes reality. It's very powerful."

The charity's work in refugee camps came to a sudden halt in the coronavirus pandemic, and £150,000 it expected to raise at summer festivals in the UK in 2020 evaporated (its total income the previous year was about £400,000). Perrin says the impact was "fairly catastrophic", but the Seagulls adapted immediately by closing their office, keeping only a skeleton staff and producing videos in both English and Romanian that could substitute for live shows. They also began doing socially distanced events for fostered and asylum-seeking children in the UK and Holland, and explored how they might set up a big top to do future shows near Athens. "Our job remains cheering up those in need, and there's never been such need," says Perrin. "The situation is pretty horrible, but people look to us to be positive."

Perrin wasn't surprised by the safeguarding scandals at Oxfam and Save the Children, described later in this book, and worries that the bigger an agency gets, the harder it is to keep everybody accountable and prevent "bad eggs" taking advantage of situations.

> "I personally feel that if you work in a charity you should be flawless. I expect the highest standards from my team. We have a no-alcohol policy on nights before we work, and zero drugs. We don't even have desserts, because little Polly who did a bake sale at her school and raised me £20 didn't do it so that we can eat a trifle."

How does Perrin deal with the emotions involved in working in chaotic and highly charged environments with traumatised children and young people? His searingly honest reply offers a glimpse into the motivation of those who forgo a 'normal' lifestyle to devote themselves to a charitable cause:

"I don't, frankly. I numb it and box it and force it down, and that's worked for me until recently. But I cried my eyes out about a week ago when I was working with some teenagers in Moria camp. It was raining so we were doing tightrope walking inside. It was so funny watching all these 14-year-olds who looked like 30-year-olds, giggling like eight-year-olds as they tried to walk a wire. Then one lad came in, pretending to be tough and macho, and eventually I managed to get him to walk the wire. Then suddenly I noticed the self-harm cuts all the way up both arms. He was riddled with them, some a year old, some a month old, some yesterday's. And then I noticed most of the lads in the room had cut their arms to shreds. But this lad in particular looked like an injured dog. He was cowering and I could see in his eyes deep fear and loneliness, and complete disempowerment. I left that day and I just wept. He's 15 maybe, just a baby. For now, I'm turning it into motivation. I am deeply furious. People ask me if it's love that powers me, but it's not, it's that I'm so pissed off and disgusted and appalled by the things that are happening and I don't know whose fault it is and I don't know what I'm meant to do about it. But I know I can't do nothing."

11

Community arts

Theatres and concert halls, many of which are charities, were brought to a halt almost overnight by the first coronavirus lockdown in March 2020. Flagship venues including the Royal Opera House, the Royal Albert Hall, the National Theatre, the Royal Festival Hall, the Birmingham Symphony Hall and the Bridgewater Hall in Manchester closed their doors for months. The orchestras and theatre groups that would have performed in them – many of them also charities – were suddenly deprived of most of their work. It was a desperate time for both institutions and individual artists and performers: they were the first to be shut down and feared they would be the last to restart normal activities.

In July the DCMS announced a £1.5 billion fund to support culture, heritage and the arts, of which £500 million in grants and £270 million in loans were distributed to arts organisations by the Arts Council. A five-stage 'roadmap' was drawn up for a gradual return to live performance, but this was halted at stage two during the second lockdown in November: rehearsals and training were allowed, as were performances for broadcast and recording purposes, but no live audiences were permitted. Many charitable venues found alternative ways of reaching audiences: the National Theatre broadcast videos of past productions and asked for donations from people who watched them, and the Royal Albert Hall arranged a two-week programme of Promenade concerts without an audience and made them available on BBC television. Glyndebourne Opera performed in the open air in the summer. But it was going to be a long time before normal levels of activity and income were restored.

Arts charities divide into three rough groups. The first is the kind of organisation mentioned above: national or regional arts charities, often with some public funding, that provide art for art's sake and fulfil their main charitable purpose of 'the advancement of arts, culture, heritage and science' by providing high-quality cultural events to audiences from far and wide. Below this, a second layer consists of local arts charities that usually have additional purposes, including education, community development and the advancement of health. Most are big enough to own buildings and employ staff and are often involved in regenerating disadvantaged and troubled areas by building social cohesion: their social goals often take precedence over the quality of the art. The third layer, which is very extensive and almost completely amateur, offers people opportunities to develop their creativity and improve their well-being through participation in activities that range from taking part in amateur theatres, choirs and orchestras to learning to play an instrument, making tapestry or bell ringing. Such organisations bring people together and provide some of the glue that binds communities. The second and third layers of arts organisations are the focus of this chapter, starting with one in the middle layer.

Nucleus Arts in Chatham

Tanya Outen was a hairdresser for 20 years but started to paint while recovering from illness. She painted at home for a while, then saw an advert for artists' studios at the charity Nucleus Arts, near her home in Chatham, Kent. She applied, and in 2018 installed herself in one of the studios, working on pictures that feature her trademark technique of abstract designs in bright acrylic paint and glitter, surfaced with hard-wearing resin. One of her best-selling creations is sets of small table mats.

"It's been a lifeline to me, and to a lot of other people, I think," says Outen, showing off her small studio where the shelves are stacked with artist's materials and the walls are hung with her work:

> "I'm busy here for seven or eight hours a day – if I could sleep here I probably would. Part of the

beauty of it is that it's very affordable. It's not just the workshop and the painting that matter, though – it's nice to be around other creative people. There's the social interaction, having a reason to get up in the morning, and not being on your own. And it's given me confidence – I never thought I could stand up in front of people and run a workshop, but I have. You're encouraged to do that sort of thing here."

Outen's studio is one of 16 run by Nucleus Arts. The other occupants include jewellers, photographers, a milliner and a crochet artist. Some have other jobs, but all use their studios for at least 20 hours a month. Each studio tenant undertakes to volunteer for five hours a month for Nucleus: some help in the garden, one hand-paints the signboard for every exhibition that Nucleus puts on, another researched the history of a local building the charity had bought. Most complete their volunteering hours, but if they don't, they have to reimburse the charity at the hourly rate of the national minimum wage.

The tenants are also encouraged to use their skills to give something to the local community. The crochet artist, for example, ran a project to produce 5,000 poppies to mark the centenary of the end of the First World War: people of all ages in the local area joined in to make flowers, which were hung in red clusters in the nave of nearby Rochester cathedral for a memorial service in November 2018.

Nucleus Arts is located just off the pedestrianised but somewhat bleak High Street, which has more than its fair share of pound shops, betting shops, charity shops, empty shops and hard-up people asking you for change: Chatham is still struggling to recover from the closure in 1984 of the dockyards in the river Medway that were its mainstay for centuries. Nucleus has a busy, art-filled cafe fronted by an area with covered outdoor seating and clusters of tall, green potted plants. Next door to the cafe is a large exhibition space that hosts up to 30 shows every year, all with free admission; artists can hire it for prices starting at £350. The adjoining building houses the studios and a large conference room available for hire. The charity has another property with six more studios half a mile away, and a Grade II listed building in nearby Rochester for a pottery kiln, a darkroom and a second exhibition space. So it's a substantial organisation that turns over more than a quarter of a million pounds a year.

Like most arts venues, Nucleus had to close its doors during the coronavirus lockdowns. But it devoted itself to alternative activities, such as making storage space available to a project supplying food to vulnerable people, distributing packs of craft materials for children and working with the charity Age UK on a magazine about mental health for elderly people. In the summer of 2020, before the second lockdown, the galleries had reopened with social distancing.

The credentials of Nucleus as a community arts centre are most evident in the courses and festivals it runs and planned to restart as soon as possible. Social Art is a free weekly session billed as 'creative activities and conversation in a relaxing, calm environment'; Young at Art is a free, twice-monthly creative workshop for people over 55; the Lego Club for children runs once a month on Saturdays, with a small entry charge; Art Inclusive is a programme that tries to use creative activity to help isolated people and groups. Once a year there is an arts festival and a Fun Palace, where many of the artists who use the studios exhibit their work and organise street activities, which in 2018 included alternative street theatre, book and poetry readings and a group of Bollywood dancers from India. 'Championing creativity to enhance people's lives' is the charity's slogan.

Dalia Halpern-Matthews is a trustee of the Halpern Charitable Foundation, which runs Nucleus. The charity was set up in 2002 by her parents: her father was an architect who wanted to be a sculptor when he retired, found there were few facilities for artists in his home town of Chatham and set up the foundation to provide some. Halpern-Matthews says the area has very diverse communities and is close to some of the highest deprivation in the country:

> "There are people with real need, and if the cycle is not broken, it will carry on. Art Inclusive is about social exclusion, which might be for reasons of ethnicity, age, mental health or being an ex-offender – there can be endless reasons for being isolated, and

the programme uses creativity to help people feel part of the world around them. Social Art has been used by 500 people over two years, some as young as 18 and some in their 90s, some with no disabilities, some with significant ones. Some people in these programmes are referred to us by social services departments or their doctors – social prescribing, which is increasing. I participate in various social isolation and health networks, which helps make us visible. But our overall aim is to be affordable, approachable, accessible and excellent in the arts. What we do is not therapy, but it is therapeutic – that's an important distinction."

As well as running Nucleus Arts, the foundation has two other charitable activities, one of which is to the benefit of the 40 or so Jewish families in the area – the upkeep of the Chatham Memorial Synagogue, a listed building of 1869 which is one of only five synagogues designed by the ecclesiastical architect Hyman Collins.

The other charitable purpose concerns the care of people with physical or mental health problems or disabilities: Halpern-Matthews' brother Adam had mental health problems from the age of 12, and when a local hospital closed its interim care unit where he and others lived, the foundation bought a building to provide similar accommodation. It is now leased to a mental health charity that provides 11 units for people who can live independently, but with help on hand.

The foundation is not dependent on subsidy, although it benefits from relief from 80% of local council business rates on its buildings, which is one of the tax advantages charities enjoy. It normally gets about 75% of its income from the cafe and from renting the studios and mental health accommodation, and 25% from investments. "We have a charitable heart but a commercial head," says Halpern-Matthews, using a phrase that crops up frequently in the charity sector.

Even if the finances are right, the governance of a small charity like Nucleus Arts is far from simple. Oversight by the trustee board of Kids Company, the charity for deprived inner-city children that was heavily subsidised by the government, was a matter of controversy after its widely publicised collapse in 2015.[1] That caused charities such as Nucleus to stop and think carefully, according to Halpern-Matthews:

> "For smaller charities, governance is barely on the radar, but it requires a rigorous approach and the utmost integrity. Trustees have absolute responsibility, and you need people on the board who can ask the right questions and understand the difference between the operational and strategic aspects of the organisation. A new governance code was issued a few years ago, and we adapted that to our needs, overhauled all our policies and procedures and made sure we had everything in place. It takes time, but you can't ignore it. One thing we did was change how long a trustee can serve, to three years before re-election and a maximum of six years, so it's not an appointment for life. I had served two terms as chair and had to stand down when our new code came in."

The wider scope of community arts

The third layer of arts organisations consists of 63,000 groups involving ten million people in the UK and Ireland who, according to estimates based on government figures, take part regularly in choirs, amateur theatre groups, morris dancing troupes, pottery or painting classes, ukulele festivals and more.[2] They are supported by Voluntary Arts, which is funded by the four Arts Councils in the UK and the Republic of Ireland and aims to promote and increase participation in creative cultural activities.

Many of these arts groups are members of some 200 other national associations formed as long ago as the Victorian era to link participants in activities that ranged from lacemaking to playing in brass bands. But these associations tended to exist in isolation, and when the Charities Act 1991 set in motion a drive for voluntary arts bodies to register as charities, the need arose for an organisation to represent, help and advise them, no matter what their individual activities might be. That was when Voluntary Arts was born.

But the word 'voluntary' is something of a euphemism, according to Robin Simpson, chief executive of Voluntary Arts: essentially, he says, it means 'amateur'. Most of the groups are registered charities and consist of people who know each other and simply want to follow whatever their interest is. The motive of participants is relatively selfish in the context of most charitable activity, in that they do not explicitly set out to help others or make the world a better place. But their existence, Simpson argues, makes all sorts of wider social benefits possible:

"The typical pattern is that they meet weekly and work towards a concert, an exhibition or an event, so there is always a public performance or opportunity. If you ask them, they will say that is their purpose, but I would say it's also the weekly meeting, the social side, the skills development. They have a lot in common with adult education classes. What they do also benefits the local community, even though that is not their stated purpose.

Does the choir rehearsal reduce knife crime? No, but it does mean that things are happening locally, the lights are on somewhere, and all that helps. These groups offer benefits to individuals such as a sense of well-being, creativity that exercises the brain, physical benefits from singing and dancing – but there is also the element of social cohesion, fostering diversity by bringing people together, a sense of identity, place and civic pride. They contribute a massive amount to society even though they're not set up with the specific intention of doing that."

The activities of such arts organisations were also brought to an abrupt halt by the coronavirus lockdowns, which Simpson describes as "a weird but fascinating time" that exposed and clarified the difference between voluntary and professional arts. Professional bodies immediately lost the bulk of their income, and Simpson thinks that many will prove unviable once the government's £1.5 billion aid package ends. Voluntary arts groups, by contrast, support themselves through members' subscriptions and local fundraising, supplemented by the sale of tickets for events and occasionally by a grant from the National Lottery Community Fund or another charitable funder. Few have buildings or staff and most were able to remain dormant for the duration of restrictions, according to Simpson:

> "But a lot of groups have continued to keep in touch online or with Zoom calls, and have also mobilised to help each other or neighbours in ways that had nothing to do with the arts. It was as if the social grouping formed for arts activities took on a wider purpose of supporting each other and local communities."

Some groups also became more creative by mixing together separate recordings of their music, for example, and developing their skills in using information technology. Voluntary Arts also started holding daily open Zoom conferences as soon as lockdown was declared, and these developed into sessions with themes such as 'arts and well-being'. They acted as "a sounding board and a creative think-tank", according to Simpson:

> "There was also a thirst to get back together and start playing, because doing things remotely is just not the same. But voluntary arts groups are a bit like cockroaches surviving a nuclear winter, although people don't always like me saying that. They will find a way to make it work, because they exist in more subtle circumstances than the major arts organisations."

More generally, the resilience of voluntary arts bodies has been tested by austerity, recession and reduced public funding. In particular, Simpson says that the owners of public buildings are finding it harder to give subsidised rates to arts groups. There has also been increased regulation in the form of health and safety rules, child protection, insurance requirements and the cost of public performance of works in copyright:

> "We live in a more regulated state. Child protection has made a lot of groups duck out of work with young people; sometimes they're just scared off. And what if someone comes to your concert and falls over and breaks a leg – does your insurance cover you properly for that? It's very worrying for some groups and we give them a lot of help with that sort of thing."

Other pressing questions are diversity and good governance. Organisations that receive Arts Council funding are required to show that they are attracting participants and audiences from diverse communities. This can raise questions for some groups that Voluntary Arts helps and advises. The bell ringers in the village church, the gospel choir in south London or the members of the steel band in Birmingham tend to come from single ethnic groups, even though they may want to spread their net more widely. "When they need more members and audiences to be viable, the drive to be more inclusive can pay dividends," says Simpson:

> "But a lot of our advice and guidance is about good governance – best practice, things to check and be on top of. This means we have to do a lot of work on our own governance, so if people ask about an equal opportunities policy, for example, we can show them ours. Often people don't realise they have to do risk assessments and so on. A bigger issue, though, is that in the majority of cases the trustees are also the participants, so there is very little distance between the two groups. A lot of organisations have been run by the same individual for 20 or 30 years and he or she has become irreplaceable. The problem is not bad practice but a lack of understanding; after all, they didn't get together to be a charity – they got together to have a sing-song. We argue that regulation is for

a good reason; people say 'we used not to have all this red tape', and we say 'yes, but you used to have Jimmy Savile'."

Drama Express: 'the buzz of team spirit'

One morning in August 2020 an unusual arts event took place in Victoria Gardens in the centre of Truro in Cornwall. After months of meeting online only, 12 young performers and eight supporters from the theatre group Drama Express came together in real life to take part in a workshop. It started with some socially distanced, virtual hugging and continued with an outdoor recreation of a Zoom session, a skit on Prime Minister's Question Time featuring a gifted Boris Johnson mimic and a scene from the group's pantomime that had been touring village halls when the first lockdown put a stop to live performances. The open-air entertainment was watched by passers-by and filmed by local television.

Drama Express is a group of young people who need additional support: some are autistic, some are deaf, some are blind and some are wheelchair users, but all of them love to take part in performing arts. The day in the park was a great success, according to the group's founder and leader, Simon Allison. "I was worried the young people were going to be anxious, but it was amazing how focused and relaxed they were," he says. "We'd been meeting online during lockdown and doing some different activities like creative writing, but it was good to start performing again."

Drama Express is an example of the thousands of local arts groups supported by Voluntary Arts. Allison works for Sense, the charity that supports people who have combined sight and hearing impairments, and has always been involved in drama and script writing. He started the group in 2014 because he felt that a lot of young people he worked with had real interest in and talent for performance arts but couldn't cope with the pressure and competition of mainstream organisations: "We did three or four workshops, there was a lot of interest, we got some Arts Council funding, which makes you feel recognised, and went on from there."

The group's performances so far include shows about Helen Keller, the deaf-blind American woman who learned to communicate in sign language and Braille, and Richard Lander, the Truro-born explorer who died in Nigeria in 1834. Interviews with parents and volunteers who give their time and expertise to the group indicate that the main benefits for its members include gaining confidence and social skills.

Drama Express began as a CIC but decided to convert to being a charity because Allison, who spends one day a week running the group with the help of voice coaches and dance teachers, found that charitable status made funders more confident about supporting it. In 2020 it had an income of about £18,000 from organisations including Comic Relief, Tesco, Cornwall Community Foundation and more than 40 local charities and businesses. Its supporters include the actors Morwenna Banks and June Brown, who played Dot Cotton in *EastEnders* on BBC TV.

Allison was planning to hold more outdoor workshops in the summer of 2020 and then assess when to go back into theatres: "Performance is important, but just being together is important as well. There's no better buzz than when the team spirit gets going." But he says fundraising is always at the back of his mind, particularly since the coronavirus pandemic put an end to events such as pub quizzes: "We had to rethink how to do it, and so far we've been doing OK with funding bids."

The funding of voluntary arts

Sally Taylor has 30 years' experience of arts charities and is now chief executive of the Koestler Trust, a charity that holds an annual exhibition of art made by people in prison. She says an increasing number of arts organisations such as Drama Express are putting participants at the heart of what they do – "art being done with people rather than at them", as she puts it. Her favourite example is West Acre theatre in Norfolk, which was started by a theatre director and his actor wife who began by putting on plays in a tent in the summer. Then they got money from the Heritage Lottery Fund to build a permanent theatre in a disused former school, which is also used for reading groups, art exhibitions and films. All the money they make goes towards bursaries for young people in the area to go to drama school, says Taylor:

> "So what was possibly a slightly selfish enterprise to begin with has actually grown and contributed a huge amount to the community. I love the fact that the money is going into bursaries for young people and they come back in the summer and are part of the show. It's a really nice, circular model."

But Taylor says funding for arts charities is becoming more difficult, not least because local councils rarely give grants any more. The funds available from charitable trusts and foundations are mostly shrinking or not growing, and wealthy individuals such as Mark Zuckerberg, Bill Gates and Warren Buffett are mostly concentrating on single issues chosen by them rather than setting up foundations to which other charities can apply: "They have gone instead for things like making sure every child in Africa has a malaria net, which is absolutely fine, but it does mean that the grant-giving pot is unlikely to get bigger because foundations are picking their causes rather than forming a generalist fund." At the same time, says Taylor, the minimal amount of tax paid in the UK by the companies of some billionaires means less money for the state that could be spent on social services.

She says she welcomes tighter compliance but is concerned that some funders also require charities to report too often and too extensively about how they are using the money. Is it really necessary, she asks, to fill in a long form twice a year to account for how a grant of less than £10,000 is being used? "This has got to be proportionate," she says.

PART IV

A junior partner in the welfare state?

12

Public service contracts

Charities have always delivered services, ranging from support for the poor and destitute to education or hospitals. The crucial questions have been: who decides what the services should be, and who finances them? In mediaeval times the decisions were mostly made by religious institutions and the services delivered by monks or church officials. The resources came either from the Church's extensive property income or from donations; when the wealthy made large donations these were often earmarked for a specific purpose.

But these services were patchy, and eventually the need for greater consistency and wider access prompted the state – if only to head off social unrest – to make decisions about what the services should be and to finance them out of taxation. At first, state provision of services was minimal and charities remained the principal providers of social services. But over several centuries the balance changed – slowly at first, but then more rapidly when the Industrial Revolution gave rise to increasing social problems in the expanding cities.

The process culminated in the establishment of the welfare state in the 20th century, which in turn led to the modern phenomenon of charities being contracted by the state to provide some of the services that the state requires by law or deems desirable. Such provision of public services is one of the most controversial aspects of the work of charities in modern times and forms the focus of this chapter. There are two main controversies, both of which are essentially political. The first is about funding: the pressure on public authorities to control public spending pushes charities to put in the lowest possible bids in order to win work, which can lead to a lowering of standards of service or prompt them to subsidise public contracts from voluntary income. The second is about independence – whether charities that accept work under contract from government should refrain from speaking freely about it and challenging politicians and their policies.

The financial crisis caused by the coronavirus pandemic added dramatically to these familiar concerns. Roughly half of charities' contracts from the public sector come from central government, which even after the relaxing of the first lockdown restrictions was facing the worst recession in modern times, foreshadowed by a 20.4% shrinkage of the economy between April and June 2020. The other half come from local authorities, which were facing 'a perfect storm, simultaneously increasing spending and reducing incomes', according to the Institute of Fiscal Studies in the summer of 2020.[1]

The history of public service delivery

An early example of services ordained by the state came in 1563 in the reign of Elizabeth I, when the first of several 'poor laws' empowered each parish to tax its inhabitants and set up workhouses, where the destitute lived and did menial tasks. In practice, however, many workhouses were still financed mainly by donations, according to the historian W.K. Jordan.[2]

Jordan also pointed out that the Tudors 'saw charity as a necessary aspect of public policy rather than a requirement of Christian morality'.[3] This was epitomised by the Statute of Charitable Uses of 1601, often called the Statute of Elizabeth, which first codified what the state expected charities to do. This ranged from poor relief to education, the 'marriage of poor maids' and the upkeep of bridges and sea defences. The Canadian academic Blake Bromley has argued that this was 'a remarkable and troubling example of the state seeking to co-opt the agenda and resources of the charitable sector. It is disturbing to realise that the enumerated objects are almost solely a reflection of Elizabeth I's political and economic policies and programs.'[4]

After the Tudors came two centuries when charities, financed by wealthy individuals, philanthropists and reformers, continued to be the main providers of services, setting up many schools, hospitals and asylums. But the social problems caused by the Industrial Revolution proved to be beyond the scope of private charity. As the charity historian David Owen put it: 'Henceforth, indeed, it became only a matter of time until the state would move, cautiously or decisively, into areas previously occupied by the voluntary agencies.'[5]

At first, the provision of state services was indeed cautious. It was not until 1870, for example, that local authorities were empowered to finance schools out of local taxation; to a great extent, charitable and state provision remained separate. But the two started to mingle as government began to give more public money to charities to provide services it considered socially desirable. By 1900, for example, more than 200 charities had received government assistance to look after poor children.[6] National and local government began to fund charitable hospitals, benevolent societies and homes for the elderly: by 1929, charities in Liverpool received 13% of their income, and those in Manchester 17%, from public authorities.[7,8] In the Great Depression of the 1930s the National Council of Social Service (which later became the NCVO) received more than £1.5 million from the government to run 'occupational clubs' for the unemployed to take part in activities such as boot mending, drama groups and tending allotments.[9]

But statutory services required by law were a different matter. When compulsory health insurance was introduced shortly before the First World War, the friendly societies – voluntary self-help organisations that had proliferated in Victorian times – were commissioned by the government to administer it because of their extensive experience.[10] But the general position was that publicly funded public services that the state had decided to provide were delivered mostly by public authorities, staffed by their own employees.

The establishment of the NHS and the welfare state raised the question of whether there was still a role for charities in delivering services. Lord Beveridge, whose 1942 report *Social Insurance and Allied Services* has formed the blueprint for the welfare state, argued six years later that charities were far from redundant, not least because many forms of social need remained and 'the state cannot see to the rendering of all the services that are needed to make a good society'.[11]

The delivery of state services by state organisations and employees remained the norm until 1979, when the Conservative government led by Margaret Thatcher began 'outsourcing' services – mainly to private companies, and eventually to charities and voluntary organisations. From 1981, local authorities were required to submit a growing range of their activities to compulsory competitive tendering, starting with functional matters such as building and the maintenance of parks. This was gradually extended to include welfare and cultural services, where charities had the track record and expertise to put in successful bids.

The Labour government between 1997 and 2010 tried to modify the resulting so-called 'contract culture' by allowing councils to consider factors other than cost. It also sought to increase the provision of public services by charities and other not-for-profit organisations generally, arguing that the 'third sector' was often more innovative, less bureaucratic and better attuned to the needs of beneficiaries.[12]

Between 2000 and its peak in 2009, voluntary sector income from government increased by 58%, from £10.5 billion (32% of the sector's income) to £16.6 billion (37%).[13] After 2010, that figure fell back under the Coalition government's austerity policies to £15.7 billion (29%) in 2017/18.[14] This was 5.5% of total public spending on procurement of services of £284 billion in that year.[15]

The role of charities thus moved from direct provision in the Victorian era to a complementary role to the state in the early 20th century, to a supplementary role when the welfare state was created and to more of a partnership with the state in the 21st century.[16] They now provide publicly funded social housing, care of the elderly and disabled, education, healthcare, children's services, nurseries, gyms, swimming pools, museums, advice services and more.

Success story: the Shaw Trust

The Shaw Trust is a large charity with an annual income of just over £208 million (in 2019) that comes mainly from contracts with the government and local councils to provide support and training for disabled and unemployed people and former prisoners. At the start of every board meeting someone who has benefited from the charity's work stands up to tell their story: this is intended to remind the trustees of what the charity is there for. Sir Kenneth Olisa, the businessman and philanthropist who chairs the charity's trustees, says this wouldn't happen at private sector service providers like Capita:

> "They're too busy producing their key performance indicators. When public services are outsourced, I think it should be to organisations that care about the beneficiary, and that by definition is a charity, not a business. Charities care about the person. We obviously care about the invoice as well, but that comes second. We don't pay dividends to shareholders. We only exist for our beneficiaries. Every pound we make goes back into the Shaw Trust: it doesn't go into inflated salaries and bonuses, it goes into making better services. That's the whole point of charity."

One beneficiary who told his story at a Shaw Trust board meeting was Joseph Law, who had struggled to find work after leaving the Navy. "It was impossible," he says. "I applied for 223 jobs and I got five replies. That's soul-destroying." He went to see a money lender, who turned out to be a drug dealer. "He asked me to sell some stuff. I kept putting it off until I was a week away from losing my flat, and I took something off him. Next thing I knew, I was in court and got sent to prison."

During his three-year sentence, Joseph was contacted by Anthony Dandera, a senior case worker employed by the Shaw Trust under a contract with HM Prison and Probation Service to help people in prison to learn new skills and gain qualifications. When Joseph was released, Dandera found temporary accommodation for him and helped him get a job building crab pots in the Devon seaside town of Paignton. Joseph kept the job and was soon able to move into his own flat. "The Shaw Trust was instrumental in getting me out of prison early," he says. "They're excellent – they help so many people."

The charity was founded in 1982 in the village of Shaw in Wiltshire, delivering government contracts to help disabled people to find employment. It also launched small businesses to employ disabled people: a horticulture enterprise, a book recycling business and a website accessibility-testing company. By 2010 its income had topped £80 million.

Over the next decade that figure more than tripled. It merged with another employment charity, took over the Disabled Living Foundation (another charity), launched the Shaw Education Trust to run academy schools for young people with special educational needs and worked with the largest charity in the criminal justice sector to bid successfully for seven of eighteen HM Prison and Probation Service contracts in the programme that supported Joseph Law. It also acquired the Prospects Group, a commercial education company, and the not-for-profit training enterprise Ixion Holdings (Contracts) Ltd. But Olisa says the charity's core activity remains helping people to rebuild their self-esteem and improve their lives:

> "One way we do this is through skills and employment, and that's the core of the old Shaw Trust. But these days we also do lots of other things. Thanks to Prospects, for example, we teach kids in Feltham Young Offenders Institution life skills; Ixion does skills training all over the place; at the Jobcentres we teach people how to set up and run their own business. We've also still got a laundry in Scotland that employs disabled people and ex-offenders, and horticultural activities that educate people with mental impairments. And we have our charity shops that employ people and raise income. So we're definitely heterogeneous."

Cautionary tales: the Work Programme and Transforming Rehabilitation

One government programme that the Shaw Trust took part in successfully was the Work Programme, the Coalition government's main welfare-to-work scheme. Other charities found it harder, however. One criticism of the programme was of its payment-by-results model, where contractors received a small fee when clients joined the scheme but were paid the rest only once the clients had been placed in work and managed to stay employed for up to two years. Another criticism was 'creaming and parking', where it was said that the prime, mostly private sector, providers took people with the best prospects of re-entering the job market, found them work and were therefore paid quickly – hence the term 'creaming'; and at the same time more problematic cases were referred to, or 'parked' with, voluntary sector subcontractors that inevitably took longer to place people in work and therefore to get paid.[17] While the Shaw Trust was resilient enough to cope with this system, it created severe cash-flow problems for other charities.

For example, the charity Tomorrow's People, one of the subcontractors, closed in 2018 after an unexpected fall in income from the programme, owing £1.63 million to creditors and making most of the staff redundant.[18] The charity's chief executive, Baroness (Deborah) Stedman-Scott, had complained that it was probably carrying more risks than its private sector prime contractor.[19] Another cautionary tale about public service delivery by charities was Transforming Rehabilitation (TR), a programme launched in 2013 by Chris Grayling MP, who had also been in charge of the Work Programme but was now the secretary of state for justice. He and the then prime minister, David Cameron, had been impressed by the work of a charity, the St Giles Trust, that helps former prisoners break the cycle of reoffending, and they wanted to offer similar help to everyone leaving prison.

This was an ambitious project with huge potential dividends for society in that it extended statutory supervision and rehabilitation to a group that had not previously received it – those sentenced to less than a year in prison. But it was also daunting, because this group consists of some 40,000 prolific, low-level offenders, many of them with multiple problems, chaotic lifestyles and addiction to alcohol or other drugs.[20] They are usually more difficult to rehabilitate than more serious criminals with longer sentences, and measures that might stop them committing crime need significant expertise and extra resources.

Rather than work through the country's 35 existing self-governing probation trusts, which were part of the public sector, Grayling chose privatisation. To supervise the most dangerous offenders, a National Probation Service was set up, which remained part of the public sector. But for the bigger job of rehabilitating those sentenced to less than a year, England and Wales were divided into 21 new areas and tenders were invited that were worth £2.25 billion over five years. The government emphasised, as it had with the Work Programme, that it wanted charities as well as the private sector to be involved in the work, and charities were cautiously enthusiastic.

Each area contract involved a prime contractor and a range of subcontractors. Most of the successful primes were partnerships that altogether included 16, mostly large, voluntary organisations. Only one, however, was not led by the private sector: most were consortia headed by big companies, such as Sodexo Justice Services and Interserve.

But these so-called Community Rehabilitation Companies (CRCs) hit trouble from the start, as was spelled out in a series of reports in subsequent years by two select committees of MPs and the NAO, which scrutinises public spending on behalf of Parliament. The public accounts committee (PAC) reported in March 2018 that the new system had been rushed into existence without adequate piloting, the CRCs had received up to a third less work than expected and 14 of them were forecasting a loss.[21] The chair of the PAC, Meg Hillier MP, commented that TR was "showing worrying signs of becoming a contracting catastrophe". The following year Working Links, which called itself 'a public, private and voluntary company' and was running three CRCs, went into administration.

The PAC also considered that the involvement of charities and voluntary organisations in TR was 'woeful', and this was echoed a few months later in a report by the justice committee of MPs, which said it was 'deeply regrettable' that voluntary organisations, especially smaller ones, were less involved in probation work than they had been before TR.[22] In October 2018, according to the NAO, only 159, or 11%, of the 1,433 voluntary organisations working in the criminal justice sector at the time were providing services directly to CRCs.[23]

Clinks, the umbrella body for voluntary organisations working in criminal justice, found that only 44 of the 132 member organisations that responded to a survey had been involved with CRCs, and that half of those that were engaged thought their contribution unsustainable, even though a third of them were subsidising it from charitable reserves or other funding.[24] The Clinks report concluded: 'Many of the organisations we heard from do not believe that their ethos and values align with that of CRCs. Voluntary organisations blame the erosion of their relationship on unhelpful targets that are focused on volume and a lack of meaningful, outcome-driven targets.'

In July 2018 the then justice secretary, David Gauke, accepted that TR wasn't working and announced that the contracts with CRCs would be terminated 14 months early. As the Ministry of Justice set about designing a second generation of probation contracts, the NAO noted that they would no longer include payment by results, which had been such a problem for some of the charities with the best credentials for rehabilitating former prisoners.[25]

Problems with local authority contracts

The Work Programme and TR were big national programmes, administered in Whitehall. But about half of the voluntary sector's income from government comes from contracts (and a few grants) from local authorities. This proportion slipped from 52% in 2004/05 to 46% in 2016/17, which reflects the tight squeeze on local council spending during the years of austerity that followed the global financial crisis.[26] Many charities have managed their relationships with local authorities successfully, but some have got into difficulties.

One example of this was 4Children, a charity set up in 1983 that by the late 1990s was successfully supporting more than 2,000 after-school clubs. It came to grief principally because of its involvement with Sure Start, a flagship programme of the Labour government, launched in 1998 with the aim of improving childcare, early education and family support. The programme's goal was setting up 3,500 Sure Start centres, which were funded centrally at first and then through local councils.

By 2010, 4Children had won contracts to run 40 centres, and this momentum continued even after the financial crash and the formation of the Coalition government in 2010.[27] The charity was appointed as the new government's Early Years strategic partner, providing policy advice to ministers as well as training and support to other organisations, and embarked on an ambitious expansion plan.[28] By 2014 it had doubled its income to nearly £30 million and taken out a loan of £1.7 million to support the expansion.[29]

But the decade of generous resources for Sure Start was over: in real terms, its budget in 2016 was 47% lower than in 2011.[30] 4Children found that it couldn't cover its loan repayments, even with wages reduced to a minimum and many workers on zero-hours contracts. In the year to March 2015 it made a £3 million loss and exhausted its reserves. Anne Longfield, the chief executive for more than 20 years, left to become the government's new children's commissioner for England, and the trustees decided to wind up the organisation and transfer its services to Action for Children, a much larger charity. There was time for a relatively smooth handover: only three services had to close, and more than 1,000 of its 1,068 employees were taken on by Action for Children.[31] But the episode was a vivid example of how changes in the external environment, such as funding decisions and government priorities, can mean that contract dependence and the complexities of commissioning are a strategic risk for charities.

The case of Newcastle upon Tyne

One local authority with a strong relationship with local charities is Newcastle upon Tyne, which in the year 2017/18 awarded £48 million, nearly all in the form of contracts rather than grants, to more than 300 organisations in the voluntary and community sector (VCS).[32] This was 16% of what the council calls 'influenceable spend' – the £312 million of its total expenditure of £998 million in that year that was susceptible to council decision making, unlike wages, housing benefit and central government grants for specific purposes, such as schools.

This level of spending is partly the result of using provisions in the Social Value Act 2012 that allow councils to consider issues other than cost and relevant experience when awarding contracts; such issues include the provision of local employment, the feedback from service users in previous contracts and opportunities for small and medium-sized organisations. Councillor Joyce McCarty, deputy leader of the city council and co-chair of the voluntary sector liaison group, says charitable organisations have helped the council to support the most vulnerable in times of austerity: "Put simply, we are a better and more resilient city because of the dedicated voluntary and community sector."

About 80% of Newcastle's £48 million spending in 2017/18 on the VCS was for adult social care and children's services, including care homes, home help and special schools – services in which charities have strong expertise.[33] The Coquet Trust, for example, received nearly £3.5 million for contracts to provide live-in, day and respite care for adults with learning disabilities, and Percy Hedley – a charity named after the philanthropist whose will trust helped to found it in 1953 – received nearly £5 million to educate children with cerebral palsy. Smaller amounts also went to arts and culture, community groups, crisis services, environmental organisations and public health projects, including £11,000 to the North East Music Cooperative and £61,000 to Tyneside Rape Crisis. Nearly £1 million was ring-fenced as the Newcastle Fund, which gives grants of less than £50,000 to organisations in the most deprived areas of the city: one recipient was PROPS, a charity that aims to help young people affected by the drug addiction or alcohol abuse of a family member.[34]

But charities in Newcastle have not been immune from tensions with the council over service delivery. These include the constant pressure to drive down costs; demands for highly detailed bidding and frequent, lengthy accounting for how the money is spent, both of which consume scarce staff resources; and pressure for contracting charities to stay silent about problems. A report in 2018 by Newcastle CVS warned that voluntary organisations that prioritise public sector delivery risked losing their roots and becoming part of an 'ersatz public sector', especially if contracts included clauses preventing them from criticising the public sector:[35]

> The effects of procurement bureaucracy on the one hand, and on the other a pursuit of growth through public sector contracts, threaten to lift certain voluntary organisations effectively out of the voluntary sector, leaving them as little more than contract delivery agents with few or no ties to the social causes and impacts that the voluntary sector exists to achieve … For some organisations, this has provided opportunities for growth and expansion; for others it has been a path to reduced capacity and in some cases closure.

Sally Young, chief executive of Newcastle CVS until 2019, says the city has managed to direct a higher proportion of its spending to the voluntary sector than most local authorities. It has also responded positively to the sector's calls for more proportionate reporting and complained less than it used to when funded voluntary organisations took a different line to that of the council on controversial questions such as drugs policy or homelessness. But the continuing pressure on costs means that "at some point nobody will be able to afford to provide these services", she says. The city council, she adds, guarantees its own staff the local living wage, with holidays and pensions, but does not allow for voluntary sector service providers to do the same: "It's a two-tier situation, and the surveys we do of our members show that it's getting worse."

The pitfalls of contracting

Clearly, public service delivery by charities is fraught with practical and ideological difficulties. The practical difficulties start with bureaucratic hurdles and competition for contracts against both the private sector and other charities. According to a report by the NCVO, barriers that voluntary organisations face when bidding for contracts include disproportionate pre-qualifying questionnaires (PQQs) and invitation to tender (ITT) documents, such as a 49-page PQQ and 99-page ITT relating to the government's Troubled Families initiative, which ran between 2011 and 2016.[36] Contracts are seldom longer than five years, and are more likely to be three, while charities' liabilities are usually more long term than that. The Newcastle CVS report cited above found in 2018 that several charities in neighbouring Gateshead, in contravention of the principles of the local agreement between charities and the council, were being given extensions to public sector contracts lasting no longer than three months at a time, with the result that they were unable to plan effectively and staff were constantly uncertain about their jobs.

Another trend cited by the NCVO is for local authorities to issue a smaller number of bigger contracts, which can exclude smaller charities with important local experience and give the advantage to big national charities, whose contract-winning machines sometimes overwhelm, and are resented by, local organisations. Charities often find that margins on contracts are too small to produce a surplus for reinvestment. As public authorities cut costs, charities are often tempted to put in low bids, planning to make up any shortfall through fundraising. A survey of 400 charity leaders in 2017 by the sector think-tank NPC, which does research and helps charities improve their impact, found that many charities were subsidising their public sector contracts.[37] 'Of those who deliver public sector contracts, 64% say they use other sources of income to deliver these contracts,' the report said. 'Fifty-seven per cent report having to turn down contracts because the operational risk is too high.' When the Charity Commission for England and Wales published a report in 2016 on 94 charities that were in financial difficulty, it found that the cause in 22 cases was dependence on public sector funding.[38]

The difficulties are further illustrated by a survey in 2018 by Hft, a large learning disability charity, of the chief executives of 56 private sector and charitable providers of publicly funded social care for people with learning disabilities.[39] Fifty-nine per cent said they had handed contracts back to local authorities in the previous year, and 68% said they would have to do so in the coming year. They said contracts were being made unviable by rising wage bills, particularly for agency workers needed to plug gaps in permanent staffing. Four in five said recruitment was hampered by low pay that could not be increased because of the small margins on contracts.

Threats to independence and matters of principle

These practical and financial problems can also threaten the independence that is one of the hallmarks of charities. The guidance from the Charity Commission for England and Wales on delivering public services points out that trustees must always exercise independent judgement: 'This is particularly important for charities that deliver public services, where public authorities may seek to influence or direct the charity's decision-making. There is also a risk that the general public may perceive the charity to be compromising its independence if it receives funding from a public authority.'[40]

One threat to independence is the periodic attempts by the government to restrict public discussion by charities of any concerns they have about the suitability or standards of the services they are contracted to provide. The salient example of this, examined in Chapter 3, came in 2016 when the then junior Cabinet Office minister, Matt Hancock MP, announced that all government grants and contracts were going to include a clause specifically preventing recipients from using any of the money to attempt to influence politicians or lobby for change. The government, evidently realising it was vulnerable to a challenge in the courts, eventually backed off and watered down its proposal.[41] But the threat reappears in different forms from time to time, as when *The Times* newspaper revealed in 2018 that charities with government contracts to help benefit claimants were being told they must not do anything that would attract negative publicity to the secretary of state for work and pensions at the time, Esther McVey MP, and should 'pay the utmost regard to the standing and reputation' of the minister.[42]

For some people, objections to the provision of public services by charities are less a matter of practical difficulty or independence and more a simple matter of principle: when the author and journalist William Shawcross became chair of the Charity Commission for England and Wales in 2012, for example, he warned against charities becoming 'a junior partner' in the welfare state:[43]

> My personal view is that some charities have become dependent on the state and I think that most members of the public, when asked, would say a charity is an organisation funded from private donations, not public funds.

A similar objection came from Frances Crook, chief executive of the Howard League for Penal Reform, who told a fringe event at the Conservative Party conference in 2015 that organisations that exist mainly to deliver services on behalf of the government ought not to be called charities: a public service contractor was a completely different animal to a voluntary organisation, she argued.[44]

Many of the controversies about service delivery were analysed in 2018 in a report by the consultant John Tizard and the journalist David Walker for the Smith Institute, a Labour-leaning think-tank (no longer a charity, as related in Chapter 3).[45] Their report concluded that the state had come to regard charities and social enterprises as not very different from businesses, and expected them to use charitable income and voluntary labour to subsidise contracts. They commented in a blog:[46]

> The evidence is that a competitive contracting approach and outsourcing have transformed the role and nature of many charities and the social sector. It has sometimes driven a wedge between some large, commercially-minded charities and smaller community groups. Many charities have adopted the language and sometimes the behaviours of outsourcing businesses, or new public management and neo-liberalism, which is far from their origins, values and missions.

The outlook for service delivery

Political developments and the state of the economy will no doubt play a major part in how service delivery by charities will change and develop in the future. The recession expected in the aftermath of the coronavirus pandemic was bound to put increasing pressure on charity contracts with both central government and local authorities. The main political parties acknowledge the importance of charities and the expertise and ethical standards they bring to their work in society. But this plays out in different ways at different times: under Labour between 1997 and 2010, the economy was strong, the government was sympathetic and service-delivery charities were focusing on receiving 'full cost recovery' in their contracts; the period of austerity that began under the Coalition government and the Conservatives in 2010 obliged charities to learn to live with shrinking budgets and to subsidise public sector contracts from charitable sources.[47]

Many charities involved in public service delivery no doubt feel trapped. On the one hand, the financial and bureaucratic pressures of contracting can push them towards lowering their standards, and lead in some cases to closure, especially if service delivery is their main or only source of income. On the other hand, contracts may be an important way – or the only way – for them to fulfil the charitable objectives for which they were founded, and may offer the only route to survival: declining to bid for contracts, or walking away from them, often goes against the grain because it may involve abandoning beneficiaries, possibly to a provider with lower standards, and letting down members of staff.

But the bottom line is that charities will in most cases do their best to cling on to a source of income that has provided getting on for half of their collective revenues. Some will do their best to win more work: the 2017 NPC survey quoted above found that around a third of those currently delivering contracts expected to be delivering more in three years' time, and only 15% thought they would be delivering fewer.[48] The fact is that some charities derive nearly all their income from public contracts and would simply cease to exist without them.

The prospect therefore is a continuing struggle to strike a deal that allows them both to survive and to maintain their independence and ethical standards.

13

Reducing the burden on the state

There are 238 lifeboat stations around the 13,000-mile-long combined coastlines of Great Britain and Ireland, and many might think that saving lives at sea is an essential public service that should be financed by the state from taxation. But ever since its foundation in 1824, the Royal National Lifeboat Institution (RNLI) has been a charity, funded entirely by public donations that in 2019 totalled about £200 million, and continues to serve both the UK and the Republic of Ireland. The money comes from legacies, fundraising events such as open days or rowing races, and contributions dropped into boxes on the bars of pubs. It is spent on new boats, equipment and buildings, and on paying more than 2,000 technical, administrative and support staff. The 4,700 crew members and 20,000 community fundraisers are all unpaid volunteers, and over nearly two centuries the charity has saved more than 140,000 lives.

The lifeboats are not the only vital public service provided by a charity. Hospices and air ambulances are charities as well, although a proportion of their costs are financed by the state. Hospices receive an average of about 30% of their income from the NHS; air ambulance aircraft and crew are financed almost entirely by donations, while the medical staff they carry are employed and paid by local ambulance services.

All three services were badly affected by the coronavirus pandemic, mainly because their charity shops were closed for several months and most of their usual fundraising activities in 2020 were cancelled. The RNLI, expecting to lose a significant portion of its usual income for the year, brought in economies including a 50% salary cut for its chief executive. To prevent some hospices going out of business as a result of the collapse in fundraising, the government gave them £200 million of the £750 million it made available to charities at the start of the coronavirus emergency. The air ambulances received £6 million from the same fund and in many cases launched emergency appeals.

This chapter looks at the origins and current role of these three vital charitable services, hears from some of their leaders, volunteers and beneficiaries and considers how they coped with the pandemic and planned to recover from its effects.

Lifeboat volunteers

The lifeboat *Lester* clatters rapidly down the slipway at the end of Cromer pier and hits the sea with a massive splash. For a moment the windows of the cockpit are obscured by a cascade of water; then the wipers clear it, the cox eases forward the twin throttles and the boat surges away from the Norfolk coast into the grey-brown waves of the North Sea.

It's a mild but breezy Sunday morning in January and the crew of eight volunteers are out on a practice launch, making sure everything will be working properly when the next 'shout' comes. They are in a nine-year-old Tamar class vessel that can carry more than 40 survivors and is self-righting, which means it can roll over completely in the worst weather and emerge the right way up.

Suddenly an alarm begins to sound, but turns out to be nothing more serious than a loose sea-cock. It's soon tightened up, the pumps clear the water from the bilges and the test run continues: the boat twists, turns, accelerates, slows down: the engines, the trim tabs, the bow thrusters are all working perfectly. The boat is brought up the slipway and relaunched several times so everyone gets some practice, and afterwards there is a debrief of the team, a varied group that includes a worker in a crab-processing factory, an information technology specialist, a chef, a school caretaker, a crew member of a fishing boat, an estate agent and a furniture restorer.

Surveys indicate that about 13% of the UK population volunteer for charities each year, and the stories of the crew give an insight into their motives and experience.[1] Chris Key did a lot of surfing when he was younger, joined the crew to put his knowledge of the sea to good use and is now fully trained in radar, navigation and first aid. One shout he took part in came when a coaster caught fire at sea near the Bacton gas terminal, a few miles along the coast:

> "There's plenty of adrenaline in what we do – it's a great feeling. There are 28 volunteers altogether, and we're like a big family. There are squabbles sometimes, but the most important thing is that we know what we're doing, we've got the same heart and we watch each other's backs."

Wes Stokes, an estate agent, says he has a notice on his office desk warning clients that he could be called away at any time:

> "It's a lot of fun, and everyone makes an effort to get on a shout – that's a big driver. It might sound a bit perverse, but you're actually longing for your pager to go off. There can be a bit of ear-bending at home – it's not always welcome when you're out on the boat. But it's probably more difficult for young families than for me."

Ady Woods, the cox, is a local handyman and window cleaner who's been part of the crew for 30 years. The incidents that stick in his mind include the ball to celebrate 200 years of the lifeboat station when a shout came in near the end of the evening. "At first we thought it was a wind-up, but it was a yacht in trouble a fair few miles off," he says. "We just went out in our dickie bows with our yellow overalls on top – that one made the national papers." Less amusing was pounding over high waves for 70 miles at more than 20 knots to bring in a man with a broken leg from a yacht, and recovering a body after two men got into difficulties in a small boat one Christmas Eve.

Modern navigation aids and better safety equipment mean big shipwrecks and major loss of life are now rare on this coast, once called 'the devil's throat' because of its dangerous sandbanks and tides. Much of the lifeboat's work nowadays concerns bringing in ill or injured crew from passing vessels or oil and gas rigs, towing yachts because they've run out of fuel or got a rope wrapped round their propeller, and saving windsurfers and kayakers.

But inscribed in the paving at the entrance to the pier are reminders of dramatic past incidents. 'Lifeboat Louisa Hearwell, Fernebo of Gothenburg, 9/10 January 1917, 11 lives saved,' reads one. This rescue was achieved in a gale in an open lifeboat powered only by oars and a crew whose average age was more than 50. They were led by one of the most famous lifeboat men in the RNLI's history: Henry Blogg, who was in the crew for 53 years until he retired in 1947 at the age of 71. His most-admired exploit was in 1933, when the wind and tide prevented the lifeboat getting alongside the 65-ton barge *Sepoy* to rescue two injured crew members; eventually Blogg twice ran the front of the boat onto the deck of the barge, each time snatching off one of the casualties.

Early in the coronavirus pandemic nearly all RNLI fundraising events were cancelled, a third of paid staff were put on the government's Job Retention Scheme and in May 2020 the chief executive, Mark Dowie, was predicting a £45 million shortfall in the year's income (by the end of the year, the figure was looking more like £30 million, about 15% of usual income).[2] Economies were introduced, such as pausing the replacement of equipment and buildings, and alternative fundraising was put in place, including online quizzes, online shops and asking people to donate every time their chosen lifeboat was called out or to pay £30 to have their name painted on a boat's hull. By August some RNLI shops were reopening, the regular summer appeal to supporters was producing results and the predicted shortfall was shrinking. Although the future remained uncertain after subsequent lockdowns, it seemed likely the RNLI – one of the country's best-supported and most popular charities – would weather the storm. The fact that the RNLI was not eligible to apply for the £750 million fund for charities suggested that the government thought so too.

The hospices and their history

In normal times more than 200 hospices in the UK – charities that specialise in the care of the dying – derive some 70% of their collective annual income of about £1.4 billion from fundraising, and the rest from the state. When the first coronavirus lockdown began, much of their voluntary income disappeared overnight because of the temporary closure of their charity shops and the cancellation of fundraising events. The government knew, however, that hospices were too important to be allowed to close, because it needed their help to take pressure off the NHS. Hospice UK, the umbrella organisation for hospices, distributed the £200 million from the government in March 2020 among hospices in England; the devolved governments in Scotland, Wales and Northern Ireland received another £30 million to allocate to hospices in those countries. The £200 million absorbed the lion's share of the £750 million the government made available to charities.

This initiative meant that the NHS was able to move patients into available beds in hospices, which have proper facilities for infection control and intensive care. Patients known or suspected to have contracted coronavirus were moved into 'red' zones in the hospices, while others were cared for in 'green' zones. By the autumn of 2020 Hospice UK had not yet calculated how many people had been successfully cared for or died in hospices while suffering from the virus, but two nursing staff in hospices had died after being infected. Many hospices also offered help to nearby care homes, which were short of personal protective equipment in the early phase of the crisis and did not have as much expertise in infection control. "Hospices were very much in the front line and there was some amazing innovation to meet patient needs," says Sarah West of Hospice UK. "It was a story that didn't always come across."

In April 2020, Hospice UK also joined other charities, including the mental health charity Mind and Samaritans, in launching Our Frontline, designed to offer support and counselling to NHS staff, emergency services personnel and other key workers under stress from dealing with the deaths and distress caused by the virus. Hospice staff and volunteers trained to deal with bereavement and trauma were among those who were available to respond to calls or texts from front-line staff, who were also offered online advice on looking after their mental health. The service was supported by the Royal Foundation, the charity of the Duke and Duchess of Cambridge, which in July donated £1.8 million to Hospice UK and nine other charities to meet rising demand for helpline and chat services. "It was an example of charities pulling together as a coalition," says West. "Because there was a need, they threw all they had at it."

In the 50 years since 1970 hospices have opened in the UK at an average rate of four per year, and by 2020 there were more than 220 of them, supporting 225,000 people a year with terminal and life–limiting conditions, according to Hospice UK.[3] This equates to more than four in ten people among those deemed to need expert end-of-life care. There was steady growth in the number of hospices for adults in the 1970s and 1980s, and in the number of hospices specifically for children after 1982, when the first of these, Helen and Douglas House in Oxford, was opened. In recent years hospices have moved away from providing 24–hour residential care and towards more day care, home care support and other community services: 90% of hospice care was delivered as day care or at home by 2020. In that year about 125,000 people were volunteering for the hospices in a variety of ways – serving as trustees, working in charity shops and helping in the hospices themselves with ordinary tasks such as making tea or befriending patients. The value of volunteers was estimated at £200 million.

Since the welfare state was created following the Second World War, advocates have argued that if charities can demonstrate the need for a particular service, the state should adopt it, make it generally available and finance it out of taxation. The value of hospices and the need for them appears beyond dispute: for more than 50 years they have relieved pressure on hospital beds and community services and helped make death less painful and traumatic for hundreds of thousands of people and their families. A survey of bereaved people in 2015 found that 79% of respondents rated hospice care as good, excellent or outstanding, while only 69% gave the same rating to hospitals.[4]

Despite their proven value, hospices have not been taken over by the state and have remained as charities. They do receive some state funding, however: adult hospices receive 33% of their costs from the state in England, 38% in Scotland, 28% in Wales and 34% in Northern Ireland.[5] Children's hospices receive 15%, reflecting the fact that people donate more readily to help children. In 2016/17, state funding of hospices totalled £350 million; of the £1.4 billion they spent in that year, £954 million went on services and £476 million on fundraising activities. The logic of these figures is that the state would have to provide about another £600 million a year to run the hospices entirely by itself. Altogether, hospices need to raise more than £1 billion a year (amounting to £2.7 million a day) from local communities, using methods such as charity shops and lotteries. Hospices have pushed for more state funding and protested when the funding is cut, but few want to relinquish their charitable status and become part of a state system.

Why is that? "It's because you would end up with a Ford Focus rather than a Rolls Royce," says Martin Edwards, chief executive of Julia's House, a children's hospice that has two sites in Dorset and Wiltshire:

> "Funding could be raided in lean times, and respite family support would be particularly vulnerable. If you work alongside the NHS rather than being part of it, you can still be master and be run locally. Charitable services have also been shown to have higher standards than those run by the state or the private sector: a quarter of hospices are graded as outstanding by the Care Quality Commission, compared with 2 to 3% in the other sectors. So there's something special about being not-for-profit and locally responsive: people like the local link, and many communities are very attached and committed to their local hospice."

Julia's House normally receives only 5% of its income from the state, and Edwards thinks that hospices begin to lose their independence if they receive more than about a third of their funding from the NHS or local authorities. With public money come tighter service specifications and requirements for more detailed reporting of its use, he says, along with greater dependency on health service decisions about securing or continuing the funding. He prefers to rely on what he calls robust and entrepreneurial fundraising:

> "It appears anomalous, but in hospices you get better services if they're not provided by the state, especially in what you might call pastoral or community support, which is much more vulnerable in a state system. The voluntary sector ethos means that quality is top of the agenda – we have more staff per patient, and we have time to care. We've had nurses who leave us to go and work in the NHS, but have then come back saying they found they were discouraged from talking to patients and families and wanted to be back in a hospice."

One family helped by Julia's House is Hannah and Mike Jolliff and their sons Kieran and Ollie. When Kieran was born at Poole Hospital in Dorset in 2006, he was rushed by air ambulance to Great Ormond Street Hospital in London, suffering from a condition which meant that his liver was unable to process protein. He was deemed ineligible for a liver transplant because he was also suffering from epilepsy and cerebral palsy, and received an injection of liver cells instead, but eventually died in 2011 at the age of four-and-a-half. During his life, Julia's House helped with his needs: nurses and carers would spend time with him when he was in hospital and come to the family's home so his parents could have some time to themselves. Hannah says it would have been hard to manage without Julia's House:

> "They were able to give us some sanity by giving us some time. When Kieran passed away at King's College Hospital in London, we brought him back to Julia's House. It was comforting to see him there in his bedding that we brought from home, with his favourite books, not all wired up to machinery any

more, asleep like a normal little child. The nurses and carers had decorated the walls with pictures of him and put on the music he loved, and they helped to get him ready on the day of the funeral."

When their second son, Ollie, was born in 2015, he suffered from the same condition and received the same kind of help from Julia's House as Kieran. But after a liver transplant he began to thrive, and by 2018 he was a normal two-and-a-half-year-old, preparing to go to school. Martin Edwards says the support the Jolliffs received is typical of children's hospices:

"We can't do the job of specialist hospitals and they don't do the kind of holistic family support that we can provide. There's so much that's not available on the state, and so the two services are complementary. Hospices have rigorous quality standards but are small enough not to be dominated by bureaucracy and to get to know families as individual people."

How hospices develop in the wake of coronavirus remains to be seen. Questions about the future first came into sharp focus in 2019 when St Clare's Hospice in Jarrow on Tyneside became the first hospice to close: the previous year it had been rated 'inadequate' by the Care Quality Commission (CQC).[6] Acorns Children's Hospice in Walsall in the West Midlands averted closure with an emergency appeal for £2 million in 2019, combined with its share of the £200 million coronavirus-related government subvention in 2020. David Clark, professor of medical sociology at the University of Glasgow and a vice-president of Hospice UK, warned that another 50 hospices were potentially at risk.[7]

Jonathan Ellis, director of policy and advocacy at Hospice UK, says that 2019 produced a "perfect storm": NHS support for hospices had been static for several years, while fundraising had become more difficult, costs had risen – mainly because pay is linked to NHS rates – and demand had grown. This had left hospices short of £30 million, which was only partly offset by an extra subsidy of £25 million from the government. "It was a helpful contribution, but only a token recognition of the rising pressure on costs," he says. "What's significant, though, is that the government agreed to look again at how the country addresses end-of-life needs."

The coronavirus crisis added a new urgency to questions about the fragility of the funding model: by August 2020, the £200 million injection was running out, and in October some hospices were facing redundancies. It was also far from clear when and if charitable donations would return to accustomed levels. Some hospice charity shops reopened in the summer with social-distancing measures, but had to close again during further lockdowns; some were likely to close for good. Edwards predicts "a long, slow recovery" in fundraising income, with more effort going into online methods. Whatever the eventual outcome, Ellis thinks the state's contribution may have to increase, but should not go above the 50% that would confer control:

> "There is a huge range of opinion about the best balance between state and charitable funding, which varies significantly from place to place. Hospices really value and benefit from the freedom to innovate, which is often easier outside rather than inside the NHS, and they have a very strong sense of community ownership because of the funds they raise locally. There is no easy answer about what the balance should be. Most hospices I speak to would not be in favour of a majority of statutory funding because it would take away some of what they might see as their essential qualities. But demand is also growing because of the ageing population and other factors, so more investment will be necessary in hospices and community care across the board."

The air ambulances

As long ago as the 1930s aircraft were occasionally used to transfer seriously ill patients to hospital from remote locations such as the Orkney Islands, or between hospitals. But it was not until the 1980s that the first helicopter air ambulance was set up, after a review of ambulance provision in Cornwall concluded that it would help to rescue people from beaches, cliffs and moorland. Air ambulances were by then operating widely in many other countries, including Germany and the US, but health authorities in the UK were not convinced that such a service would be cost-effective.

Eventually Geoff Newman, a local freelance pilot, persuaded Stephen Bond, proprietor of the private company Bond Helicopters, to supply an aircraft free of charge for three months. The experimental service began in April 1987, with the medical staff provided by the Cornwall ambulance service. In his book about the genesis of the service, Newman described the tortuous negotiations with the NHS as 'a little like wandering around a huge beached whale, trying to find the correct orifice through which an intelligent conversation may be had'.[8] He also recalled the first callout, to a young woman climber who had fallen off a coastal cliff and injured her spine. When she was being unloaded at the hospital in Treliske, she told the paramedic what a wonderful service the helicopter was and asked how long it had been going. "Since about eight-thirty this morning, actually," came the reply.

The results of the trial were encouraging, but the health service still felt unable to provide the necessary long-term finance to run the aircraft, and Bond Helicopters could not provide its services indefinitely for nothing. The result was the establishment of a charity to finance the service, and the Cornwall Air Ambulance celebrated 30 years of operation in 2017. During that time, it flew more than 26,000 missions and saved many lives.[9] It takes off 700 times a year, on average, and can reach any part of Cornwall in 12 minutes, and the Isles of Scilly in 30 minutes.

Before long the charity-based service in Cornwall was being replicated in other areas, but without any coordinated planning or a standard funding system: London and Kent started operations in 1989, Devon in 1992, the North-West in 1999, Yorkshire in 2000 and Northern Ireland in 2017. The fragmentation and variation of the services around the country has led to some pressure for a fully funded national service, including a petition to the government in 2019 that attracted

134,000 signatures, qualifying it for a parliamentary debate. Only Scotland has an air ambulance service that is entirely funded by the state; it runs two helicopters and two fixed-wing aircraft, supported by a charity that has one helicopter. According to Air Ambulances UK, there were 21 air ambulance charities covering most of the UK in 2020, raising donations totalling more than £160 million a year which were used to run their 39 aircraft, which are mostly hired, along with their pilots, from private companies. The paramedics and doctors who take to the air are provided and funded by the local statutory ambulance service, with the exception of one service in the Midlands.

Despite the occasional conflicts, and doubts about cost-effectiveness, most of the UK is covered by air ambulance services that operate with increasing consistency and are starting to work at night as well as in the daytime. Ed Pajak, administrator of the Association of Air Ambulances in 2018, says that there is little pressure for creating a state-funded national service: "The 19 charities in our membership are very happy as they are, raising funds for their own operations, with the clinical governance done by the relevant ambulance service." As in the case of the hospices and lifeboats, he says, there is considerable pride in each region about its own air ambulance and the fact that it is supported by local fundraising rather than being entirely publicly funded. When the 2019 petition for a fully funded service was launched, Devon Air Ambulance appealed for supporters not to sign it.[10] 'Subject to the same constraints as our other essential services, we would face a stark choice between cutting services or cutting quality,' it said. 'Our service is run by and for the people of Devon who fund it.'

Like the hospices, then, air ambulance services are hybrids, financed partly by charitable donations and partly by state funding, with some commercial sponsorship and occasional extra contributions by the state. In 2019, for example, nine of them shared £10 million provided by the Department of Health and Social Care to upgrade facilities and equipment, and in 2020, as mentioned above, they received £6 million from the £750 million emergency fund for charities to help them cope with the coronavirus pandemic. The way they operate varies: in London, for example, helicopters are reserved for incidents involving major trauma, while services in other parts of the country will go out to less serious cases, especially in remote locations. Their activities also have to be coordinated with the search and rescue helicopters operated by the Maritime and Coastguard Agency – larger machines that have winching facilities that can be vital in mountain and maritime missions, but do not generally carry medical or paramedical staff. The decision whether to deploy an air ambulance or call on a search and rescue helicopter is always taken by the local ambulance service, but in the majority of incidents occurring on land rather than at sea, air ambulances are used. In all, they are despatched to about 20,000 incidents annually and about 70 patients are helped every day, according to the Association of Air Ambulances. There is little doubt that the service saves lives and results in quicker treatment and less suffering for hundreds of patients every year.

Rescued by helicopter

A case in point is that of Talan Carter from Cornwall, who was being driven home by his grandmother on a sunny July afternoon in 2017, when he was two-and-a-half years old. When their Peugeot 205 emerged from a roundabout near Liskeard, it collided head-on with a van. Witnesses reported the car being thrown into the air and pieces of it landing all over the road. Talan's grandmother managed to get out, despite her injuries, but he was stuck in his car seat with a wound across his forehead that exposed his skull. Fortunately, bystanders, including a trained nurse, managed to get him out and give him first aid while waiting for an ambulance to arrive.

Talan's father, Robin, who worked nearby, was on the scene within ten minutes, and shortly after that the Cornwall air ambulance arrived from its base more than 30 miles away in Newquay and landed on some open ground nearby with a paramedic on board. By the time Talan's mother, Kelly, arrived, the decision had been made to take him in the air ambulance to Derriford hospital in Plymouth, 20 miles away, rather than to use the road ambulance that also attended. "A policewoman kept me away from him to avoid either of us getting too distressed," says Kelly:

> "And then he went off in the helicopter by himself and Robin and I were rushed to the hospital by police car. When we got there the doctors had done a scan and discovered there was some blood on his brain and they weren't happy with his responses. The helicopter pilot and paramedic were still there, and it was decided the best option was to transfer him to the children's hospital in Bristol, which was at least two hours away on the road. But the helicopter could get him there in half an hour, so that's what they did. Again we followed by police car, and by the time we got there a neurosurgeon was looking after Talan and he was on his way into the operating theatre."

Two hours later, Talan emerged with 39 stitches in his head and spent three days in intensive care, two of them under sedation. After a further two days in the children's ward, the stitches were removed and he was on his way home with his parents by train, already recovered enough to insist that they buy him a pasty at the station. His scar has healed well, Kelly says, some mobility problems with his arm resolved themselves and nine months later he was attending pre-school and enjoying rugby tots. His grandmother's injuries – a broken collarbone and extensive bruising – have also healed, and Kelly has been left feeling that the role of the air ambulance was crucial in facilitating Talan's rapid recovery from an extremely serious accident:

> "In Cornwall in summer, the main roads are crazily busy and there are no real alternative routes. Transporting him by air saved so much time, and the paramedic was able to sedate him really quickly so his brain was resting and starting to recover. It also meant he had the same team with him all the way, with the same faces and voices. They even gave him a teddy to fly with. You see the helicopters quite a lot around here, but it's only when you get personally

involved like this that you really understand how important they are."

Charity worth a billion pounds

Given what modern public services are expected to include, the services described in this chapter would almost certainly have to be provided by the state if charities did not supply them. If state services were to function at standards comparable to those of the charities, it would cost the state the best part of £1 billion a year at 2018 prices: £200 million for the lifeboats, an additional £600 million for the hospices and an extra £160 million for the air ambulances. That total of nearly £1 billion is roughly what it costs to provide all the public services in Newcastle upon Tyne, one of the country's main conurbations, which featured as a case study in Chapter 12. The sum is small when set against the total annual UK public spending in 2018 of nearly £800 billion; it might also be smaller if the government decided to lower the standard of the services, or to reduce the number of them. But it is nonetheless a substantial amount, contributed for the public good out of the pockets of individual citizens, and a salient example of charitable activity. It also falls within the centuries-old tradition of charities, starting with the hospices of mediaeval times and continuing with the spirit of the preamble to the 1601 Statute of Elizabeth, which enumerated the wide variety of public service that the state expected from charities.

14

Charities as pioneers

Decisions about which services the state should provide, and whether it can afford to do so, lie at the heart of politics and depend on ideology and the level of taxation that governments deem appropriate. Politicians of all stripes accept that the public purse is not bottomless, and that hard decisions must be made about how to allocate resources. Once the decisions are made, however, some social needs are inevitably left out and some publicly funded services are usually capable of improvement. This is the home territory of many charities; they try, with varying success, to fill in the gaps in provision, and they pioneer improvement in delivery methods and press for increases in funding.

Many well-known organisations fall into this bracket, including, for example, Macmillan Cancer Support, the MS Society, Missing People and Crisis; behind them stand hundreds of smaller charities, few of them household names, that provide help for the homeless or refugees, run foodbanks or provide supplementary health services. They receive little or no public funding, and if they did not exist it is arguable whether the state would consider their services so essential that it would step in and provide them instead. But many such charities are a lifeline to those who use them, and this chapter looks at the work of four of them. Some of the case study charities presented in this chapter were winners or shortlisted in the Charity Awards run by Civil Society Media.

The question of supplementary services was addressed by Lord Beveridge in the middle of the 20th century:[1]

Even after the extension of social insurance in 1946, many urgent needs of many citizens will remain ... and can be met only or best by voluntary action ... Voluntary action is needed to do things which the state should not do, in the giving of advice, or in organising the use of leisure. It is needed to do things which the state is most unlikely to do. It is needed to pioneer ahead of the state and make experiments. It is needed to get services rendered which cannot be got by paying for them ...

Hope for Tomorrow

When Christine Mills' husband, David, was diagnosed with cancer in 2002, the couple found that the stress of making the 56-mile round trip from their home in Tetbury, Gloucestershire, to the hospital in Cheltenham for him to receive chemotherapy added extra pressure to the trauma of his illness. After David died the following year, Christine wanted to help people in a similar situation, living miles away from cancer treatment services. She mentioned this to the medical director at Gloucestershire Royal Hospital, Dr Sean Elyan, who said he had also been pondering how to bring chemotherapy closer to his patients. "It was a light-bulb moment for me," said Christine, speaking before she also died in 2018. "I knew we had to do it."

Four years after David's death, the newly registered charity Hope for Tomorrow launched the world's first mobile chemotherapy unit in Gloucester. In 2017, its tenth anniversary year, the charity opened its 12th mobile cancer care unit, with improved treatment facilities. It owns and maintains the mobile units, which are specially built on a Mercedes chassis for £250,000 each and are furnished with comfortable leather chairs, a lift, a toilet and home comforts such as kettle, toaster and microwave. By 2020 it had a total of 14 vehicles, each of which costs more than £70,000 a year to run.

The medical and nursing staff are supplied and paid by the NHS, and most units visit up to five locations each week, with up to 20 adult patients benefiting each day. The locations are chosen by the respective NHS trust, and the charity aims to provide 15% of all the oncology department activity of each trust. In 2018 more than 14,000 treatments were delivered at 34 locations.[2] More than 20 types of cancer are treated on board, including breast, bowel, prostate and pancreatic. As well as chemotherapy, the units do blood tests, blood transfusions and flushing of peripherally inserted central catheter (PICC) lines – the tubes that convey drugs from an entry point in an arm to a large vein in the chest. Even some experimental biological immunisation therapies are done on the buses, and a couple of units are trialling cooling caps, which help to prevent chemotherapy patients' hair from falling out.

During the coronavirus pandemic, Hope for Tomorrow was an outstanding example of Lord Beveridge's assertion that voluntary action is needed 'to pioneer ahead of the state'. With hospitals under huge pressure and many cancer patients instructed to shield, its mobile units were suddenly in huge demand. In June 2020, BBC News interviewed the chief executive of NHS England, Sir Simon Stevens, on one of the buses, but, to the charity's chagrin, he did not mention its name. Nikki Budding, its fundraising manager, says:

> "The message that came across was that the NHS has adapted well to COVID, they've got these mobile cancer units – but there was no mention of Hope for Tomorrow and the fact that we design, build and maintain the units, and give them to the NHS for free. This was a bit frustrating – I think the problem is that we're just not that well known."

Much of the increased demand came from NHS trusts that already worked with the charity. The one covering Airedale in Yorkshire, for instance, was given the use of one of the charity's two reserve vehicles. Some trusts requested longer hours or use of the buses at weekends; others commandeered the charity's nurse support vehicles to deliver oral chemotherapy to patients who were shielding. "Basically, we adapted to whatever was required," says Budding. But other NHS trusts also became aware of the benefits of the charity's service:

"After lockdown on 23 March, we had 22 more NHS trusts contact us, wanting units. Before that we were in talks with a couple of trusts, but then COVID hit and suddenly everyone was on the phone asking if we could just pop over and drop off a bus to them. They've all woken up to the value of our mobile service."

As with many charities, the increased demand came at a time of shrinking resources. Hope for Tomorrow's income, which comes entirely from voluntary sources such as legacies, corporate partners and charitable trusts, topped £1.5 million in 2015 but fell back to £732,000 by 2019.[3] It normally gets about a sixth of its income from fundraising events, and when all events were cancelled because of the pandemic it launched a three-month emergency fundraising appeal. This brought in 96% of its target, but in mid-2020 Budding was still worried about the future:

"We're doing well so far in comparison to some other charities, especially when you consider the other things we're up against. For example, a couple of years ago we were told by HM Revenue and Customs that we were no longer VAT-exempt, because we don't offer 'ambulatory care'. Apparently, that's because our wheels aren't turning at the time the patient is receiving treatment. And we can't benefit from any of the government's coronavirus grant schemes because we don't meet their criteria. We fall between all the cracks."

One woman's story

Rachel Stokes is a payroll administrator and mother of two from Sudbury in Suffolk who was diagnosed with breast cancer in July 2016 and had a mastectomy and reconstruction, followed by six doses of chemotherapy over 18 weeks. Her nearest hospital is a 30-mile round trip from her home, so when she learned that Hope for Tomorrow's mobile cancer care unit regularly parked outside the local community health centre, just a mile from her house, she says she was thrilled:

"I had a PICC line fitted so that meant I had to go to the hospital or the unit every week and have it flushed. For me, the unit was an absolute godsend. I didn't want to give everything to cancer. I wanted to retain as much of my normal life as I could, so having the unit just around the corner was a massive thing for me. I'd just leave work, go and have the flushes and injections done, and go straight back to work. If I'd had to go to the hospital each time, it would have meant taking almost half a day off work. All the staff are just so nice – they help you out, make a cup of tea for you and your visitors and just sit and chat. In the hospital you're in a bay with maybe six or seven others, and the nurses are running around between all of you, whereas on the bus you've got almost one-to-one attention. It was also nice to meet people in a similar position to me – I met people who live local to me who were also going through treatment."

After Rachel finished the chemotherapy, she required Herceptin injections every three weeks for a further period, so all in all she used the mobile unit for just over a year. "I saved a massive amount of time and angst, not to mention money in fuel and hospital car parking charges," she says.

Blood bikes

Few people who receive blood transfusions, either in a Hope for Tomorrow mobile cancer care unit or in a hospital, will be aware that the blood they receive may well have been transported by a leather-clad volunteer motorcyclist.

The concept of motorcycle-based volunteer medical courier services is not new; many motorcycle clubs began offering services as long ago as the 1960s.[4] But this was unstructured, and for many years the image of bikers did not appeal to the medical profession. In 2009 there were only six blood bike groups in the UK, mainly in the south of England, responding to around 4,000 requests from hospitals each year.

But demand from hospitals for a reliable service to transport blood and blood products was soaring, particularly after a reduction in the number of local blood testing laboratories.[5] Four of the five existing groups met in 2008 and concluded that the blood bike service needed to be extended across the UK. A five-year plan was drawn up; they knew they needed not only to recruit hundreds of volunteers, but also to win over the hospitals and authorities such as the police, the Department for Transport, the Medicines and Healthcare products Regulatory Agency and HM Revenue and Customs. They decided they could do this only by improving the image of the bikers and achieving a professional level of service.

Various proposals were adopted: all riders were required to wear a uniform, the bikes had to have standard branding, and the boxes used to carry the blood had to be capable of maintaining the correct temperature. The bikers also realised that they needed an umbrella body to set standards and share good practice, and the Nationwide Association of Blood Bikes (NABB) was established as a charity in 2011.

It typically takes between six and nine months to recruit and train volunteers, register a new group as an independent charity, establish a service-level agreement with the local hospital, find funding and buy the bikes. But the service has grown steadily: by 2020 there were 32 blood bike groups, with well over 3,000 volunteers responding to more than 100,000 requests from hospitals and laboratories each year. Most trips are made overnight on weekdays or at weekends and bank holidays, partly because most volunteers work full time. As well as blood, the bikers carry surgical tools, human milk, spinal fluid and even faecal transplant material, used in the event of complications following antibiotic treatment for bowel infections.

Thanks to lobbying by the NABB, all blood bike groups can now recover VAT on the supplies they need, and riders have the same speeding exemptions as the emergency services. There are also six blood bike groups operating in Ireland, and the NABB has consulted with groups in Canada, Australia, Belgium and Cameroon about setting up similar services. In 2016 its chair, John Stepney, estimated that its work saves the NHS between £2 million and £3 million a year.[6]

Demand for blood bikers' services increased markedly during the coronavirus pandemic, and many groups extended their hours to respond to requests 24 hours a day, seven days a week. At the same time, their fundraising events had to be called off but the NABB provided some relief when it convinced the oil company BP to include blood bikes in its pandemic-response free fuel initiative for police, fire and ambulance services. For ten weeks in the spring of 2020 all blood bike charities across the UK were supplied with free fuel.

Foodbanks: from garden shed to national network

Few examples of charitable activity expose the inadequacies of state welfare provision as foodbanks do. Research carried out in 2018 suggested that one in fifteen adults had claimed emergency food parcels for themselves or their families from a foodbank.[7] In 2018/19 the number of three-day food parcels handed out topped 1.6 million.[8] As the coronavirus crisis took hold in April 2020, the Trussell Trust – the UK's biggest foodbank network – reported an 89% increase in demand for help.

Feeding the hungry is one of the oldest charitable undertakings, but in the modern world this does not enjoy unqualified support. Critics say foodbanks are used by the Left and anti-poverty campaigners to attack the Conservative government's welfare reforms, and that vouchers issued by agencies for use at foodbanks are not always given to the most deserving people. When he was the secretary of state for work and pensions, Iain Duncan Smith MP told the Trussell Trust to stop "scaremongering".[9] Other opponents say that the rising popularity of foodbanks is driven by the existence of the service – if there are more foodbanks around, the argument goes, it stands to reason that more people will use them.

But there's no doubt that foodbanks have become part of the social fabric of the UK, and they are known to have been used by a wide assortment of people, among them lone parents, ex-services personnel, the self-employed and people with disabilities. The Trussell Trust's first foodbank was set up in Salisbury by the charity's founders, Paddy and Carol Henderson, in 2000.[10] The Hendersons had been shocked by the response of a local mother to a fundraising appeal they were involved in to feed street children in Bulgaria. The mother told them that her own children were going to bed hungry each night and that they ought to do something about that before helping children overseas. After local care professionals in the city confirmed that they regularly saw some clients going hungry, the Hendersons set up a foodbank in the shed at the bottom of their garden. They were determined that the project would be run by the community, for the community, and they set out core principles that have endured – all food should be donated, volunteers should be recruited to distribute it, and support to clients should be non-judgemental.

After three years, the Hendersons collated a foodbank manual, which became the foundation of the social franchise model that enabled the concept to expand beyond the garden shed. The first associated foodbank was launched in Gloucester in 2004, and in its first year distributed 16 tonnes of emergency food to 1,746 people.[11] The Trust's marketing manager, Samantha Lane, said:

> "Our target was to encourage a foodbank in every town in the UK. We decided to use the church as our primary launch platform because there is a church in most UK towns, they are well connected in the community and they are motivated by their faith to feed the hungry."

The network in 2019 comprised 426 foodbanks operating more than 1,200 food distribution centres, supported by more than 40,000 trained volunteers. Each foodbank either is a charity in its own right or is run by a charitable organisation, such as a church. The service works through a voucher system; specified agencies such as GPs, schools, churches, social services, Citizens Advice Bureaux and JobCentres are authorised to decide whether people need a food parcel and issue them with a voucher.

The Trust realised early on that its network gave it unprecedented access to information about the extent of food poverty in the UK, and it knew it ought to capitalise on that.

It developed data-collection systems to record the activities of each foodbank, including beneficiaries' age group, ethnicity and primary reason for referral, and produced comprehensive national data on food poverty. In 2015/16 the main reasons for referral were delays in the payment of state benefits (30%), low incomes (22%) and benefit changes (14%).[12] Once the Trust had this data, it began using it to lobby government for changes to benefits and other policies.[13] In 2019 it was still using its evidence to campaign against the roll-out of Universal Credit, the new benefits system that merged six previous benefits into one and reportedly caused delays for thousands of claimants.[14] It was also running More Than Food, a programme launched in 2014 that enables clients in its cafe-style foodbanks to receive advice on budgeting, benefits, housing and other legal matters.[15]

Support for veterans

One of the groups that has been known to use foodbanks are ex-military personnel, many of whom fall on hard times because of experiencing problems such as debt, mental ill-health, homelessness and loneliness. The government recognised that statutory provision for ex-servicemen and women was not as extensive as it might be and in April 2018 it announced the first UK Veterans Strategy, appointing a taskforce of officials from departments across Whitehall to consult with veterans and determine how best to tackle the issues they faced. The new strategy was published in November 2018.[16]

Fortunately, former servicemen and women have not had to rely solely on the state to support them in times of need. The earliest example of modern charitable provision to former members of the armed forces was the Lloyd's Patriotic Fund, founded in 1803 to help those who served in the Napoleonic Wars.[17] SSAFA, the Armed Forces charity, started life in 1885 as the Soldiers' and Sailors' Families Association.[18] Between 1916 and 1920, 11,407 First World War-related charities were registered with local authorities, with another 6,492 exempted from registration, including many of today's best-known charities.[19] During that war, the massive increase in fundraising for wartime causes had created fertile ground for fraud and corruption, and legitimate charities lobbied for compulsory licensing for war-relief charities. The War Charities Act 1916 prohibited charities from raising money unless they had been registered, and gave local authorities the power to decide which organisations would be registered or exempt.[20] Today, the sector has a few high-profile organisations, such as the Royal British Legion, Combat Stress and, more recently, Help for Heroes, but fewer charities in total than a century ago. An analysis of the sector in 2020 found there were 1,843 such charities across the UK, serving an armed forces community of around 6.3 million, including nearly 192,000 serving personnel and 2.5 million ex-servicemen and women.[21] Some 479 of those charities provide welfare support and most of these offer grants to individuals. The sector's total annual income in the year to 1 April 2019 was £1.1 billion, but nearly three-quarters of the charities had incomes of less than £100,000. Only 43 charities in this sector have incomes over £5 million.

Revenues from this sector's best-known fundraising campaign, the Royal British Legion's Poppy Appeal for Remembrance Day in November, were expected to fall millions of pounds short of the target in 2020 as the second coronavirus lockdown cancelled public collections. The appeal usually raises about £55 million, getting on for a third of the Legion's income, and the charity urged people to donate online instead.

As it developed its Veterans Strategy, the government acknowledged the value of charities; in a 2018 report summarising the charitable provision to the forces community, it wrote: 'Recognising the vital role played by these organisations to support the Armed Forces community, the Ministry of Defence along with the UK Government and Devolved Administrations should continue to work with these charities and support their efforts as much as possible.'[22]

Combat Stress: meeting changing needs

After the First World War, thousands of servicemen returned home with severe mental health problems. There was little understanding of or sympathy for their conditions, and many were simply consigned to mental hospitals. But a few far-sighted people believed that the men could be rehabilitated if they had the right support, and in May 1919 the Ex-Servicemen's Welfare Society was born, offering occupational therapies such as basket weaving.[23] Its first 'recuperative home' was opened in 1920 on Putney Hill in London. Over the past century, the charity that was to become Combat Stress has helped former servicemen and women deal with conditions such as anxiety, depression and post-traumatic stress disorder (PTSD) by providing clinical treatment and welfare support.

After the start of military operations in Afghanistan in 2001 and Iraq in 2003 the number of veterans seeking help from or being referred to Combat Stress began to increase rapidly. In the year to March 2001 the charity received 710 new referrals; over the next 15 years this annual number more than trebled, and in 2016 more than 2,400 veterans were referred for treatment.[24]

Before 2011, Combat Stress mainly provided low-level residential respite care, with a few group therapy sessions and little individual treatment. But a series of clinical audits of veterans with mental illness, carried out between 2005 and 2009, found very high rates of PTSD, for which existing treatment programmes were not very effective. The charity realised that the most severe cases became revolving-door patients, funded through a war pensions system that kept them registered as 'sick'. They would be admitted for two-week sessions three times a year, and improvements in their mental health were not seen for at least two years.

Combat Stress's medical director, Dr Walter Busuttil, had previously worked in the Royal Air Force, where he had designed a new clinical model for people with the severest cases of PTSD.[25] At Combat Stress he used this as the basis for a new, evidence-based, intensive treatment programme for veterans with complex combinations of PTSD and depression.[26] The six-week residential programme combines group skills training and group psychotherapy with individual cognitive behaviour therapy. Some veterans require specific interventions before being stable enough to embark on the programme, such as anger-management counselling or detoxification, and these elements are also provided by Combat Stress.

The intensive treatment programme was launched at the charity's main centre in Leatherhead, Surrey, in 2011 and rolled out at the other two centres in Ayrshire and Shropshire in 2012. All three centres had to be modified to accommodate the therapies provided, at a cost of £4.9 million. At the end of the first two years a review was published in the *British Medical Journal* of the 401 veterans who had completed the programme.[27] The results revealed 'significant reductions in PTSD severity 12 months after completing treatment', with a third of the veterans no longer meeting the criteria for PTSD.

Nicola Hudson, press officer at Combat Stress, says that the introduction of the intensive treatment programme marked a big turning point for the charity, in that it became more clinical: "Prior to 2007 we were much more occupational-therapy based, with short-term treatment programmes. Since then we've become a lot more clinical and it's changed a lot of the services we deliver." The programme has since been awarded NHS National Specialised Commissioning Status and approved by the National Institute for Health and Care Excellence (NICE), which means it receives funding for each patient. These service-delivery contracts are supplemented by charitable donations, corporate partnerships and support from other military charities. In 2017 Combat Stress announced a new five-year strategic plan to improve the recovery of its beneficiaries, whose average age was dropping fast.[28] In January 2018 triage nurses began to work alongside the 24-hour helpline team, so veterans have a quicker start to their recovery.[29] The charity also designed non-residential programmes in the community that fit around veterans' work or family life. The intensive residential treatment programmes are now concentrated at the Surrey and Ayrshire centres, while Shropshire has been adapted to focus on outpatient services. The charity is also exploring digital methods, such as using Skype to improve access to therapy.

★ ★ ★

Apart from the benefits provided to individuals, all the case studies in this chapter illustrate the ability of charities to be agile and responsive to changing times and needs. By introducing cooling caps to mobile cancer units so that patients worried about losing their hair can still receive treatment, expanding the patchy provision of blood bike services across the nation or dialling up the intensity of therapy for ex-soldiers when it was clear that existing programmes weren't adequate, these charities were not only pioneering ahead of the state but continually innovating and adapting when they saw the need. Many thousands of people rely on their work, and without their efforts and commitment the sum of human misery would undoubtedly be higher. Some charities of this kind have a high profile and will continue, like the foodbanks, to attract controversy, while others will struggle to make themselves better known and attract more support. But they are all part of the fabric of Lord Beveridge's good society, where 'the many urgent needs of many citizens' are provided for by voluntary organisations when the state falls short.

PART V

Preserving the past, preparing for the future

15

Castles, canals and stately homes

Environment and heritage charities provide some of the clearest examples of the benefits charities have provided for the citizens of the UK. Pre-eminent among them is the National Trust, founded in 1895, which has preserved huge stretches of the country's most spectacular landscapes and coastlines, including parts of the Lake District, protected them from development and kept them open for public use. The National Trust for Scotland was created in 1931, and since 1998 the government has transferred several more heritage organisations to the care of charities: Historic Royal Palaces, the Canal and River Trust, English Heritage and the Royal Parks. The creation of the modern welfare state in 1945 meant that many charities, particularly hospitals and schools, were taken over by the state; in the case of these four heritage entities, however, the traffic has gone the other way.

As well as having charitable status in legal terms, the countryside owned by the National Trust, the towpaths of the Canal and River Trust and the green spaces of the Royal Parks are also charitable in the sense that access to them, and their scope for health, recreation and contact with nature, costs nothing. By contrast, the stately homes owned by the National Trust and most of the historic sites run by English Heritage charge for access, through membership or a fee for each admission. The public benefit they provide is therefore not universally available. One consequence of this was that the charities that charge admission were drastically affected by the coronavirus pandemic, which closed them during successive lockdowns from 2020 and provided only limited access in part of the summer: Historic Royal Palaces, for example, predicted a devastating fall in income of 85% in 2020 because of the collapse of tourism. This chapter looks at the origins of these five major organisations and other smaller heritage charities, how they work and the challenges that face them in the future.

Early heritage charities, and the National Trust

Well before the 20th century, the role of charities in the country's heritage began through the classic charitable route of voluntary initiative. An early milestone was the foundation in 1707 of the Society of Antiquaries, a charity that is still active, with many archaeologists among its 3,000 fellows. In 1877 William Morris, the designer and luminary of the Arts and Crafts movement, was so concerned by what he considered to be inappropriate restoration work on Tewkesbury Abbey in Gloucestershire that he founded the Society for the Protection of Ancient Buildings, also still going strong. Another example of the involvement of charities in the heritage sector was the purchase in 1847 by the Shakespeare Birthplace Trust, also still active, of the house in Stratford-on-Avon where the playwright was born. Yet another early heritage charity was the Commons Preservation Society, now called the Open Spaces Society; the year after its formation in 1865, 120 supporters dismantled overnight two miles of railings that had been put up around Berkhamsted Common in Hertfordshire.[1]

But perhaps the most significant of all the long-established heritage charities is the National Trust for Places of Historical Interest and Natural Beauty, founded in 1895 by the social-housing pioneer Octavia Hill and two associates, Sir Robert Hunter and Canon Hardwicke Rawnsley. The National Trust was initially concerned mainly with preserving what Hill described as 'a few acres where the hill top enables the Londoner to rise above the smoke, to feel a refreshing air for a little time, and to see the sun setting in coloured glory'.[2] Since then, empowered by six Acts of Parliament which prevent its property being bought, sold, mortgaged or even compulsorily purchased by the government without the permission of Parliament, the Trust has come to own 1.5% of the land area of England, Wales and Northern Ireland.[3] It has 500 heritage sites ranging from 200 grand historic houses to 35 pubs, several entire villages, gardens, industrial monuments and the childhood homes of John Lennon and Paul McCartney. The portfolio includes a quarter of the Lake District, including its third-highest mountain, Great Gable, gifted to it in memory of climbers killed in the First World War. The Trust also owns or protects 775 miles (one fifth) of the coastline of those three countries of the UK (the separate National Trust for Scotland owns coastlines including 400 islands and islets).

Until the 1930s, the Trust remained a small organisation focused on protecting open countryside and a small number of buildings. But from its inception it had pressed for property left to the nation to be exempted from 'death duties' – the forerunner of the modern inheritance tax – which were taking a heavy toll on the houses and estates of the landed gentry. Eventually Parliament legislated in 1937 to permit owners to give property to the National Trust in lieu of death duties, provided the houses were open to the public for at least 30 days a year. Over the following two decades this enabled the Trust to acquire dozens of estates. Critics felt that throwing a lifeline to the aristocracy was not what the Trust had been set up for, but the post-war Labour government favoured the scheme as socialism in action – making beautiful historic houses and parks accessible to the people. The pace of acquisition slowed in the 1960s, when the Trust began Enterprise Neptune to acquire and protect more coastline, but increased again after 1975, when taxes were introduced on transfers of property made in an owner's lifetime as well as on death.

Controversy over the Trust's policies and activities has rarely been absent. Against the wishes of the countryside lobby, it banned hunting with dogs on its land in 1997, but since 2004, when hunting was made illegal, it has incurred the anger of another charity, the League Against Cruel Sports (see Chapter 7), for permitting trail hunts, where riders and dogs follow an artificial scent.[4] As a large landowner, it has been caught up in heated debates about the reform of farm subsidies, the rewilding of some of its land in the Lake District and fracking.[5,6] Not everyone has favoured its move towards highlighting life below as well as above stairs in its grand houses, illustrated by the acquisition of former homes of the poor as well as the rich, including the Birmingham Back to Backs, a terrace of former slums. In 2017 it ran a programme highlighting the connection of its properties with people who were lesbian, gay, bisexual and transgender or involved in LGBT issues, and was obliged to backtrack on requiring its volunteers to wear rainbow badges.[7] None of this prevented its membership increasing from 226,000 in 1970 to more than 5.2 million in 2019 – more than the membership of all UK political parties put together, as the Trust's website points out.

The biggest threat to the seemingly unstoppable rise of the National Trust has been the coronavirus pandemic. The closure of its houses, cafes and shops for several months meant that the Trust expected to lose £200 million of its income in 2020 – almost of third of the previous year's total of £634 million. It consulted staff about 1,200 redundancies, including many curatorial posts, among its 9,500 workforce, and was simultaneously involved in a row over an internal policy document proposing 'a revolution' in the way its houses were used.[8] *The Art Newspaper* commented: 'Many staff feel senior management are using the crisis as an excuse to finally transform the National Trust from an organisation whose primary purpose is preservation to one that prefers to deal in entertainment and experiences.'[9]

Then another row broke out: in September 2020 the Trust published a meticulously researched report that showed that a third of its properties had links to colonialism and slavery.[10] A group of 20 MPs and peers calling itself Common Sense then wrote to *The Daily Telegraph* in protest: 'Part of our mission is to ensure that institutional custodians of history and heritage, tasked with safeguarding and celebrating British values, are not coloured by cultural Marxist dogma, colloquially known as the "woke agenda".'[11] The Charity Commission also became involved, saying: 'We have written to the National Trust to understand how the trustees consider its report helps further the charity's specific purpose to preserve places of beauty or historic interest, and what consideration the trustees gave to the risk that the report might generate controversy.'[12] The culmination was a debate in Parliament in which Nigel Huddleston MP, a junior minister at the DCMS, said the report was 'unfortunate ... for many people, it did cause offence. The trust must reflect on that and learn from it.'[13]

The Common Sense Group, which by the end of 2020 had expanded to 59 MPs and 7 peers, also criticised the National Maritime Museum, a charity, after an article in *The Daily Telegraph* on 10 October that year suggested that the museum was planning to review the 'heroic status' of Lord Nelson, victor of the Battle of Trafalgar in 1805.[14] The director of the museum denied there were any such plans.[15] Shortly afterwards the group also took issue with the children's charity Barnardo's for a blog about how parents could talk to their children about the concept of White privilege.[16] The charity argued that it had a responsibility to raise awareness of all issues affecting children.[17]

These episodes were salient examples of how charities can become involved in so-called 'culture wars'.

Converting public bodies to charities

The conversion of public bodies into charities had its origins in the drive by the Conservative government led by Margaret Thatcher to set up executive agencies to carry out many of the functions of government departments. Historic Royal Palaces was one of the first of these, and within a decade it was working so well that the Labour government in 1998 decided to go a step further. Tom Clarke, a minister in the then Department for Culture, Media and Sport, told Parliament that the agency had been an outstanding success: in nine years, turnover had increased from £15 million to £50 million, taxpayer support had decreased from £12 million to £4 million, and visits were no longer "a forbidding experience ... one now feels welcomed to the palaces; there is more to see, more to learn and, indeed, more to buy".[18]

The palaces were duly turned into a non-departmental public body (NDPB) that was also a charity and had a Royal Charter. An NDPB, also known as a quasi-autonomous non-governmental organisation, or quango, is not under the direct control of ministers and can make long-term financial plans, unlike other public bodies, which are subject to annual budgets. "As a charity," said Clarke, "the new body will have greater independence and should be more attractive to sponsors and grant-giving bodies." There were warnings about excessive commercialism, but no real resistance, and the new charitable trust took over the running of the Tower of London, Hampton Court Palace, Kensington Palace state apartments, the Banqueting House in Whitehall, Kew Palace and Hillsborough Castle in Northern Ireland.

Public subsidy ceased, and by 2019/20 income had risen to £102 million, of which £66 million came from admission charges from about five million visitors and £26 million from shops and other trading.[19] But the success story was brought to a sudden halt in 2020 when the coronavirus pandemic first closed venues and then reduced tourism to a trickle. As mentioned above, the charity was predicting a shortfall of £98 million in August of that year, some 85% of its projected annual income, and was not expecting 2021 to be substantially better. Whatever happens, however, the palaces are likely to endure: they are all still owned by the Queen on behalf of the monarchy and cannot be leased, sold or otherwise disposed of, and the government remains ultimately responsible for their care.

Other major heritage charities, along with most smaller ones, have also suffered from the effects of the pandemic. Among those that have suffered least, principally because they do not rely on admission charges, is the second major national body to be converted to charitable status: the Canal and River Trust.

'A waterways and well-being trust'

In their golden age between 1760 and 1830, Britain's canals transported the coal, raw materials and finished goods that fuelled the Industrial Revolution. Factory owners, investors and speculators built more than 4,000 miles of waterways, which featured engineering masterpieces such as the flight of 19 locks at Caen Hill on the Kennet and Avon Canal in Wiltshire, completed in 1810, and the dramatic, 300-yard-long Pontcysyllte Aqueduct, built by Thomas Telford in 1805 to carry the Llangollen Canal on 19 stone arches over the river Dee in north Wales. The aqueduct is one of five UNESCO World Heritage Sites on the British canal system.

The decline of the canals began with the coming of the railways from 1830: most narrowboats could transport only 30 tons at the pace of the horses that drew them, but trains were soon carrying many times that weight at many times the speed, and by 1850 water-borne traffic had dropped by some two-thirds. Nevertheless, the canals survived, partly by filling the gaps in the growing network of railways or by concentrating on local supply routes that were more convenient than rail. Even after the expansion of motorised road traffic following the First World War, they continued to carry cargoes on a small scale until the 1950s.

After the Second World War, attempts to make the canals commercially viable failed, and in 1963 they were handed to a new body, the British Waterways Board, that was tasked, roughly speaking, with preventing the canals from becoming a public nuisance. Many were becoming derelict, sometimes filling up with rubbish and the discarded supermarket trolleys that for a while became their hallmark in the public mind. It was a low point in their 200-year history.

Fortunately, a new age of leisure was gathering momentum and the Inland Waterways Association, a charity formed in 1946, was campaigning to save and restore canals and promote their use for narrowboat cruising and fishing. From 1968, British Waterways began to respond, and by the end of the 20th century many canals had been reopened and leisure traffic was expanding. Many projects benefited from grants from the National Lottery-funded Millennium Commission, notably the Falkirk Wheel – a massive boat lift connecting the Union Canal and the Forth and Clyde Canal in Scotland, which cost £78 million and opened in 2002. But British Waterways never had enough money to keep the system in optimum condition.

In the 1950s the idea had been floated that the canals should be taken over by the National Trust or a similar charitable body, but was not taken up until Gordon Brown became prime minister of the Labour government in 2007. He was optimistic about the role of charities in social and economic regeneration generally, and his administration's last budget, in March 2010, contained a firm proposal to turn British Waterways into a charity. The Coalition government that came to power five weeks later took the proposal forward with enthusiasm, not least because one of its first programmes was the so-called 'bonfire of the quangos' – an attempt, as austerity took hold after the global financial crisis of 2008, to shed or abolish as many government agencies and arms-length bodies as possible.

One of the government's motivations for setting up the Canal and River Trust in 2012 was no doubt to reduce, over time, the cost to the taxpayer; another was simply to free itself from a headache. But some six years after the transfer, the chief executive of the Trust, Richard Parry, was confident that it was well on the way to providing the public benefit that is the defining feature of charities.

His summary of the change is that British Waterways had essentially been a big, inward-looking state machine, focused primarily on the engineering challenge of keeping the canal system in working order and inhibited by governmental control of its resources. The charity continues to meet the imperatives of maintenance and reconstruction, Parry argues, but is becoming "a waterways and well-being trust", more focused on communities and people:

> "We used to be more insular – now we're facing the outside world. Charities are about causes and the difference you can make to people's lives, not clinical engineering. My predecessors spent a lot of time managing upwards – dealing with Whitehall, with the minister of the day, with changes in government policy, with the news halfway through the year that they're going to take money back because they're a bit short somewhere else, or that they're giving us more money because they can't spend it somewhere. Now I spend hardly any time on all that and we can be single-minded about what we're here for, thinking about our beneficiaries and the users of the waterways."

It costs more than £200 million a year to look after the canals, and the government has pledged to supply about a quarter of that until at least 2027. Other income includes boat licences and mooring fees, dividends from the charity's £800 million-worth of investments, admission to the two canal museums and collaborations with utility firms for activities such as small hydro-electric projects, water-based heat transfer schemes and the use of towpaths as routes for fibre-optic cables. Charitable status also means the Trust can benefit from tax breaks, take out loans and apply to grant-making bodies that would never have funded a public agency. Partnerships have also been set up with other charities, commercial organisations and local councils for projects such as improving access to towpaths. The coronavirus pandemic caused relatively little disruption to the canals and was expected to reduce income for the year 2020/21 by only £10 million.

Will the government eventually be able to cease its subsidy, as it did with the Historic Royal Palaces? Access on foot to the canal network remains free, so there is little scope for membership and admission charges. Parry says a realistic ambition for donations from the public is about £10 million a year – no more than a fifth of the government grant. So, when negotiations begin for extending the grant beyond 2027, the charity's case will centre on the high level of charitable public benefit derived from a relatively low level of public funding. The advantages it will emphasise, according to Parry, are the growth in volunteering and community involvement, the increased use of the canals for leisure and recreation and their general contribution to well-being:

> "When you're part of the public sector, people say, when are you going to fix things? But when you're a charity, people seem to think, 'I'm going to help fix this myself, because it's a charity now'. We certainly didn't invent volunteering, because there have been canal societies and the Inland Waterways Association has been restoring canals for 50 or 60 years. But we're now able to do it at scale – communities getting involved in keeping the towpath clean, helping boats

through locks and so on. Suddenly you're not just a professional, staff-based body – you've got an army of people who affect the way you do things."

The year after the charity was created, it had around 1,800 volunteers; by 2020 it had 3,600.[20] More than 180 community groups had adopted a stretch of their local canal, maintaining it and sometimes running wildlife projects as well. Parry asserts that volunteers are happy because they are able to put something back: "We have a structure, we give them uniforms, we pay their expenses, we give them training, we commit to them and we reap the benefits. People feel better because they can get involved."

Parry says this "release of authority" creates a demand for new initiatives, including access for paddle boarders and collecting plastic debris. Canoeists can now navigate from Goole on the Humber estuary to Liverpool, which involves passing through the Foulridge tunnel near Colne in Lancashire, which Parry says British Waterways would probably have prohibited. He also doubts it would have become involved in gay pride events in Manchester, where Canal Street runs through the area known as the gay village.

Surveys show signs that canals are becoming more like linear national parks where walking, cycling and angling are on the increase. The charity has calculated that 9.2 million adults use the canals in an average two-week period.[21] Parry says there's hard evidence that time on the towpath makes people happier and healthier:

> "Our recent surveys showed that some 250,000 people would not take the exercise they do take if they didn't have an accessible waterway on their doorstep. We've had some nice examples of GPs prescribing walking by the canal – we're not going to give you any pills, they say, and instead you do three miles a day. You can't get lost, there aren't too many hills, and it's on your doorstep. In the Midlands, most of the population lives within a mile of a canal."

English Heritage: 'this is what you get from being a charity'

Just south of Telford in Shropshire, the world's first iron bridge, some 40 yards long, spans the gorge of the river Severn. It's a single, elegant arch, built between 1777 and 1781 by Abraham Darby to connect two expanding industrial villages. Over 150 years, the bridge survived floods, an earthquake and constant use before the government declared it to be an ancient monument in 1934 and closed it to traffic. It's now a UNESCO World Heritage Site, visited by thousands of people each year, and is looked after by English Heritage – a charity.

By the second decade of the 21st century the engineers concluded that the bridge required complete renovation. It was a complex and expensive project, and the charity used online crowdfunding that raised £70,000 from 900 people. BBC television also made a documentary, interviewing the conservation staff and filming the divers examining the foundations. Kate Mavor, the chief executive of English Heritage, takes up the story:

> "The next thing was, blow me down, this chap in Germany, who was picking up BBC programmes, saw this item about the bridge. He was on the board of the Hermann Reemtsma Foundation, which funds social and cultural projects, and he knew his director was about to retire and was looking for a final project. Long story short is that Jochen, the retiring director, comes over to Shropshire, gets out of the car, has never seen the Iron Bridge before, is awed at the sight of it and spends 40 minutes with our conservation manager in a love-in about load bearing and cast-iron cracking and earthquakes. We then went to the cafe and he said in fluent English, 'Ms Mavor, it is with enormous pleasure that I would like to give you this cheque for a million euros towards your project'. It was amazing, and for me the Iron Bridge project is one reason why we're a charity: that million euros wouldn't have come to us otherwise. It's not the kind

of thing that happens to a non-departmental public body, which is what we used to be – it's what you get from being a charity and shouting about what you do."

Mavor had led the National Trust for Scotland before being recruited as chief executive of English Heritage when it became a charity in 2015. Her job involves looking after some 420 historic sites, ranging from Iron Age hill forts to mediaeval castles and stately homes of various periods that have been acquired by the government over the last 150 years. Among the jewels in its crown are the stone circle of Stonehenge and Tintagel, the ruined castle in Cornwall linked with the legend of King Arthur, where the charity opened a dramatic new access bridge in 2019.

The campaign to protect such sites was led by charities in the 19th century as more ancient structures were damaged by careless owners and the number of visitors increased, inspired in part by the historical novels of Sir Walter Scott and transported on the growing railway network. In 1882 Parliament passed the Ancient Monuments Act, and the government gradually acquired 'a sparkling and growing portfolio of historic sites', according to Simon Thurley, a former chief executive of English Heritage.[22] By the Second World War, he writes, the Ancient Monuments Department was administering 'by far the largest visitor attraction business in the country', reformulated as English Heritage in 1983. The job of running the sites was given to the charity in 2015, while ownership and archaeological direction were retained in a government agency, Historic England. Mavor thinks this brought great opportunities:

"English Heritage of old was subject to continual cuts from the Treasury. Yes, the new model is partly about saving public money and an ideological motivation to get things off the government's books. But it was also created to see if the organisation could be a successful master of its own destiny. What is different now is that we've got to earn our own keep. That means we've got to be relevant to the people whose money we solicit to deliver our charitable purpose.

We have to work much harder to persuade people that looking after these sites is worthwhile, relevant, something they would like to be involved in. That doesn't mean diluting what we're trying to do – it means working more creatively, imaginatively and entrepreneurially to present the stories in a way that people find appealing.

The world is moving much faster now and people will not sit and read a huge panel on the wall to find out what happened at the Battle of Hastings. They want an audio version, or to be able to look it up on their smartphone before they visit the site. Things have to be packaged up in a way that people who are used to getting things in bite-sized chunks can digest. Now that doesn't mean you dumb down – on the contrary, there's a real skill in taking the same content and presenting it in a way that allows people to go down through the layers rather than getting that huge wodge of text that they find difficult to focus on."

This attempt to engage with a wider public has included a big expansion in digital material, including 65 online resources for teachers, linked to key stages of the national curriculum. Other projects include a series of videos that attracted 15 million views in which an actor plays Mrs Croakham, the cook in Victorian times at the stately home Audley End in Hertfordshire, making dishes from the recipe book she left behind. A collaboration with Google Arts and Culture also involves displaying images of English Heritage sites, including a high-resolution video of the magnificent painted ceiling at Kenwood House in north London.

Another example of the new approach was at Framlingham Castle in Suffolk, where a major restoration programme removed vegetation and restored the stonework; visitors were given access to the work and could then return to ground level in an unconventional way, says Mavor:

"It just occurred to us that it would be fun for them to be able to slide down, so we installed a temporary slide. And you can be all po-faced and say, oh, that's like a theme park, or you could say, what a good idea. And it attracted a lot more people to go up and find out more about the stonework, so I strongly refute any suggestion that we just did it to bring the punters in. Also, fun is good for the soul – you learn better when you're happy, and people who are relaxed are more disposed to take in what they're hearing about."

Like the Canal and River Trust, English Heritage began making more use of volunteers, such as the local people who were recruited and trained as guides to explain to visitors what was being done to restore the Iron Bridge: the charity's annual report for 2017/18 calculated that 3,000 volunteers gave a total of 153,000 hours. The entrepreneurial aspect mentioned by Mavor is found in the sale of things in visitor shops that relate to the sites – mead and drinking horns, for example, are sold in most of the shops at mediaeval castles and became bestsellers as the TV show *Game of Thrones* gained popularity. Deals were done with commercial partners such as Craghoppers, which supplies staff uniforms carrying the company's branding. Mavor bristles at the suggestion that such things are at odds with being a charity.

"Commercial is sometimes seen as the antithesis of charitable, which I don't really accept. Say you go to Bolsover Castle, and you have a fabulous day out, the kids watch the jousting, and afterwards you go to the cafe and the whole day is a fantastic success. Oh dear, no, hot chocolate and cake, that's commercial! [She imitates the sound of a siren]. But commercial is all part of it and the cake is all part of a quality visitor experience. You can buy sweatshirts in the Stonehenge shop, people like them and buy them, and that money is then invested in looking after the lonely little abbey in a field in Cumbria that you can't charge anyone to see, but which has a fantastic history. So I think the commercial income is benign."

When English Heritage became a charity it was given two streams of government grant: £80 million to be used gradually for conservation and new visitor facilities, and £89 million for a tapering annual subsidy – £13.7 million in 2018/19 – until projected self-sufficiency in 2023. Things were going to plan until everything was thrown into the air by the coronavirus pandemic lockdowns from 2020. Revenue from admissions, shops, cafes and venue rental – some 55% of total income of £121 million in 2019 – disappeared for several months and was expected to come back only slowly. The charity feared its income for 2020 would be down by £70 million, and was relieved to hear that it qualified for a share of £100 million earmarked for national cultural institutions in the government's £1.57 billion rescue package for arts, culture and heritage.[23]

In the longer term, Mavor is counting mainly on increased income from membership, admission and retail sales to bring the charity eventually to self-sufficiency. Membership topped one million in 2018, a 21% increase on the final year as a government agency, and visitor numbers exceeded six million, a 15% rise. Mavor says the increases show the charity has "a real clarity of purpose":

> "Our charitable cause is inspiring people through human ingenuity, whether it's in building beautiful abbeys or castles or in mediaeval church wall paintings. We bring history to life – we can tell you what's been happening for six millennia in this land and illustrate it with sites where things actually happened."

Heritage charities 'at a pivotal stage'

Besides the National Trust and the four charities more recently created by the government, there are legions of smaller charities in the sector: a search for 'heritage' on the register of the Charity Commission for England and Wales produces 324 results, ranging from the East Kent Nostalgic Bus and Coach Trust to the Friends of Friendless Churches. Sources of funding for restoration and development include the National Lottery Heritage Fund, which gives grants to the tune of £300 million a year, and the much smaller Historic Houses Foundation, which in 2018 gave £576,000 to projects in rural historic buildings.

But the heritage sector, including its charitable component, is at a pivotal stage, according to Dr Oliver Cox, heritage engagement fellow at the Oxford Centre for Research into the Humanities at Oxford University. His work includes coordinating research projects between the university and heritage bodies, and he is a trustee of the charity that runs Compton Verney Art Gallery and Park, an 18th-century mansion in Warwickshire.

Since 2010, Cox says, the policies of austerity have meant a steady withdrawal of public funds from most heritage bodies. This has left them more reliant on entry charges, donations and fundraising at a time when they are potentially less attractive to visitors, he says; in addition, the coronavirus pandemic has sharpened all these issues, which will have to be faced with fewer staff:

> "The challenge for charitable organisations is that we now have a large number of them going after the same pots of money with very similar business models, and that's ultimately unsustainable. The result is a growing crisis about the financial underpinnings of the range of charities that now look after an increasing percentage of the nation's heritage. The great confidence trick the aristocracy managed to pull off is convincing us that their houses are the national heritage. In the next 50 years people are going to question that a lot more."

Like Kate Mavor of English Heritage, Cox thinks the challenge for heritage bodies is to become more commercially astute and to research and draw more deeply on their own history:

> "They can respond by broadening the focus beyond the material culture – the shiny things – towards thinking about the way archives of the family or the place interact with a broader range of society past and present. Just being the houses of the elite won't work any more. It's partly about how to be

more entrepreneurial about running a charity, which sounds rather contradictory, but shouldn't be. You have to hold the charitable objectives together with the commercial reality of how you deliver those objectives. I think the key to marrying the two is to improve the visitor experience by having richer, deeper, more nuanced stories to tell. It improves the bottom line because people stay longer, have a second coffee, probably buy something in the gift shop, and at the same time you are nurturing the charitable aims of access, education and so on. It's also really important to balance culture and commerce along with new drivers of inclusion and diversity."

He cites recent National Trust initiatives as examples of the richer stories he thinks heritage charities will need to offer. In 2019 it marked the 200th anniversary of the Peterloo Massacre – the bloody repression of a demonstration in Manchester calling for parliamentary reform – with a programme called People's Landscapes, which included exhibitions, art installations and podcasts.

Another example was Women and Power in 2018, which included We Are Bess, a programme based on research by some of Cox's Oxford colleagues that compared the limits to power faced in Elizabethan times by Bess of Hardwick, who built Hardwick Hall in Derbyshire, now owned by the Trust, and the experience of women today:

"Colleagues have said that dynamic programming about the theme increased visitor numbers, so the explicit attempt to tell a wider range of narratives is not just messianic or altruistic – it does have a commercial return. This kind of active recovery of histories, presented in an engaging and appealing way, actually hits both charitable and commercial aims square on."

Cox thinks the state will start increasing its funding of heritage again only if the sector can sell itself differently, by demonstrating its value to health and well-being, for example, as the Canal and River Trust is trying to do, or showing it can enhance community cohesion and a shared sense of history:

> "Far too often it can appear, especially at the cash-strapped local council level, as a bottomless pit. They can't see much return from it – why have we got all this old stuff, what value does it bring? At the moment the sector is mostly still seen as a begging bowl rather than an untapped asset, and I think we just need to get on with the business of making it more sustainable."

16

Museums and the perils
of charitable status

At the last count in 2015 there were 2,635 museums in England; the majority of them are charities, and those that operate as businesses or are run by local authorities usually benefit indirectly from charitable status through a friends or supporters group that is registered as a charity.[1] There are a huge variety of museums, ranging from 40 national institutions such as the world-famous British Museum, the National Gallery and the Natural History Museum, to 245 museums run by local authorities, 145 armed forces museums, 55 university museums and 1,640 independent museums covering subjects ranging from transport to industrial heritage, local history and the lives of famous individuals. The numbers have expanded considerably since the Second World War.

Most museums, however, are financially insecure. More than half of them charge for entry, if only to special exhibitions rather than their permanent collections, but this is rarely sufficient to keep them afloat. Many regional and local institutions rely on grants from local councils, which were whittled back in the years of austerity after the global financial crisis, or on hard-won awards from the Arts Council. Even flagship national institutions that receive about half of their income from the state do not always find it easy to earn the rest or raise it from philanthropists and the public. This endemic insecurity was compounded in 2020 by the collapse in visitor numbers caused by the coronavirus pandemic. As a result, many museums face an uncertain future, and a unique institution in County Durham is a case in point.

'The Victoria and Albert of the North'

On a slope above the river Tees on the edge of Barnard Castle stands a building that would look more at home in the Loire valley: the Bowes Museum, built in the style of a 17th-century French chateau, with a grand parterre garden, an elaborate façade and an imposing entrance hall and staircase. It was purpose designed, with high galleries lit by glazed roofs, and it houses a high-quality collection of European fine and decorative arts, including paintings by Canaletto, El Greco, Goya and van Dyck. Its special attraction – used in the museum's logo – is the Silver Swan, a glittering, life-sized automaton built more than 200 years ago. Accompanied by tinkling music, the swan moves its head one way, then the other, then bends forward to pick a tiny fish out of the water, simulated by rotating glass rods.

The museum was a remarkable act of philanthropy by the wealthy local Victorian landowner John Bowes and his French wife, Joséphine. Bowes was the illegitimate son of the 10th Earl of Strathmore, whose wealth was derived from rent, coal mines and shipping, and Joséphine was an actor he met while living in Paris. They were unable to have children, and decided to build a museum in the north of England: perhaps it was a way of giving something back to the region that had provided the family's wealth. The French architect they used was inspired by the Tuileries palace in Paris; the architecture critic Nikolaus Pevsner, in his 46-volume work *The Buildings of England*, called the result 'gloriously inappropriate for the town to which it belongs'.

The couple filled the museum with about 15,000 items, including paintings, sculpture, tapestries, ceramics, furniture, textiles, clocks and watches. They set it up as a charity with an endowment of £125,000, and in the year after it opened in 1892 it attracted 63,000 visitors. "The collection is outstanding in the breadth of its artefacts and paintings," says Jane Whittaker, head of collections at the museum. "That's why it's been called the Victoria and Albert of the North, although it's not a term we use ourselves. The galleries have these huge lofty ceilings, and there is the wow factor of this huge edifice on a hill – the sense of awe as soon as you turn the corner and see it."

The museum was rarely free of financial problems, however, and in 1956 Durham County Council took over as the sole trustee of the charity. It ran the museum with free admission, staging a successful show of contemporary artists in 1996 which featured Damian Hirst. But expenses were rising, and rather than close the museum during the winter the council transferred control back to a full board of charity trustees, whose first task was to raise money to repair the roof, refurbish the tired-looking galleries and give the place fresh life. The declining subsidy from the county council was bolstered by grants from charitable trusts and National Lottery funds, and admission charges were introduced. Freedom from council control enabled the museum to be more enterprising and fleet of foot, according to Whittaker: "no tortuous committees to go through". Family activities and links with the local community were increased, including a Christmas market. A high point came in 2016, when the exhibition 'Yves Saint-Laurent, Style is Eternal' was a great success, bringing in a record 140,000 visitors.

But numbers have declined and admission charges have increased since then, and the museum's special challenge remains its location in an agricultural area with a small, undiverse population, far from big towns and cities. It is close to the A66 arterial road to the Lake District, but the nearest station, at Darlington, is 40 minutes by bus or a £30 taxi ride away. The latest attempt to put the museum on a firmer financial footing began in 2018, when a new chair was appointed and the governance was restructured. The first success under the new regime was persuading Durham County Council to add a total of £700,000 over five years to its annual grant of £244,000.

One new trustee, Steve Howell, a former director of sport and tourism at Durham County Council, says the new funding reflects confidence that governance is now more robust and "no longer about sitting back and attending a few openings. The extra money gives us a solid foundation over a reasonable period to work on transformation and a strategy for attracting more visitors." He thinks the museum needs to present itself less as a national arts institution and more as a tourist attraction, making use of its extensive grounds and appealing to people on holiday in the area: "That's not to say we won't do blockbusters like Yves Saint-Laurent that put County Durham on the map. But we can't play that game all the time." The coronavirus pandemic put extra stress on the museum's finances, but the government's furlough scheme helped it through the lockdown periods, and it was open in the summer of 2020 with limited admission and social distancing.

'Greater freedom, greater insecurity'

The Bowes Museum is far from being the only one to transfer from local council control to charitable status: by 2005, 27 had made the move, and by 2014 the figure was 38.[2] They include the museums of cities including Birmingham, York, Derby and Sheffield in England, and Glasgow in Scotland. Alistair Brown is policy officer for the Museums Association, members of which run nearly 1,800 museum sites. He says many, like Bowes, experience the charitable model as a breath of fresh air:

> "We hear stories about local authority museums where they don't have any control over their own communications strategies, where they're only allowed to use the council Twitter account a limited number of times in between tweets about bins being collected, and so on. They also have to do their procurement through internal systems and it's not as competitive as it could be. So things like this are being pitched as the benefits of moving to trust status. You can take control, and museums that have made the move tend to be a bit more vibrant, and certainly better at communications."

Brown adds, however, that the price of greater freedom and flexibility is often greater insecurity, especially over raising fresh funds to replace local authority subvention:

"There is only a handful of big trusts and foundations that give as a matter of course to cultural organisations, and our members say it has become a lot more competitive in recent years, which is partly down to austerity and partly to the fact that more players are competing for the same or diminishing amounts of funding."

This means that entry charges have been introduced and increased at many charitable museums. The Labour government led by Tony Blair set the gold standard in 2001 by implementing free admission to the permanent collections of the big national museums, but 52% of all museums in the UK still charge for entry, although they often have a wide range of concessions, including for school visits.[3] People might expect that charitable status should entail free entry, but there is no automatic link between the two, according to Brown:

"In fact, I would say it's probably a weakening link as more museums move out of local authority control into charitable status. You end up with a larger independent charitable sector, and over time, as local authority funding for those charitable museum trusts continues to come under extreme pressure, they will, as trusts, have the freedom to choose charging more easily than a local authority museum might. At the same time those trusts may still in reality be viewed as the civic museum, the big museum in town, so it can still become a political issue. Charging is a patchwork, and there are different policies for different museums, depending on the governance and the political lie of the land locally. Charging is always a hot political potato."

On other fronts, museums that are charities enjoy the usual advantages of charitable status, including exemption from most taxation, Gift Aid, a variety of potential sources of income and the reputational boost that comes with the word 'charity'. One of the biggest tax breaks is the statutory exemption from

80% of business rates on their buildings; the remaining 20% is waived at the discretion of the local authority, and in the years of austerity some councils have ceased to waive it for some charities. After the York Museums Trust argued successfully in a tribunal in 2017 that net surplus income rather than rental or replacement value should be used to calculate the rateable value of old or unusual buildings that are an attraction in themselves, many museums are paying much less: the New Art Gallery in Walsall in the West Midlands, for example, had its rateable value reduced from £25,000 to £1, while that of Chatham Historic Dockyard in Kent was cut from £470,000 to £66,000.[4]

Museums and public benefit

The public benefit provided by museums can be partly illustrated by the number and frequency of visits. For the year 2017/18, a survey called *Taking Part*, conducted by the DCMS, found that 50% of the population over the age of 16 in England – roughly the same proportion as in the previous few years – reported having visited a museum or gallery in the previous 12 months.[5] The figure had been below 40% before 2001, when free entry to the permanent collections of the DCMS-funded national museums began.

Brown says another indicator of public benefit is the way museums increasingly try to collaborate with other public services:

> "They think a lot about their social impact – how they contribute to health and well-being, place-making and education. A huge part of what they do is based on working in partnership with other charitable organisations, schools, the NHS and other public services, to offer something those organisations can't deliver by themselves. That might be use of museum venues, access to collections or a combination of those things. Having said that, I think that museums find it hard to measure their impact scientifically. There have been good academic studies of individual projects, but the sector struggles when

it's asked to demonstrate impact, outcomes and so on. That's because you have different organisations with different ideas and different collections trying out different things in different areas – it's not like service delivery in some charities that are trying to deliver one thing well across the whole country. So, in a way, their own diversity is a challenge for museums."

Looking at it from a less technical point of view, the public benefit of museums seems undeniable. The millions who visit the Victoria and Albert Museum in London, for example, have their eyes opened to the best decorative arts and design down the centuries. Children who spend a day at the Beamish Open Air Museum in County Durham are unlikely to leave without learning something about mining or tramcars that will stick in their mind. This is perhaps why it's rare for the charitable status and activities of arts organisations and museums to attract criticism in the same way as, for example, independent schools, overseas aid charities or campaigning bodies occasionally do.

The bigger picture

Museums form a significant chunk of the charity world: the register of the Charity Commission for England and Wales includes nearly 3,000 charities – nearly 2% of the total – that have the word 'museum' in their title. In England about 1,700 of them are accredited by the Arts Council, which means they conform to prescribed standards in managing their collections and attracting audiences. The total income of English museums in 2015 – comprising entry charges if they have them, sales in their shops, fundraising, donations and grants from national or local government – was £2.64 billion; for comparison, the sales of the retail chain Boots totalled £2.3 billion in 2018. Their economic output – paying staff, any surplus earned before tax and expenditure on buildings and other assets – was £1.45 billion.[6] They employed some 38,000 people in 2015.

The biggest museums and galleries enjoy an international reputation, and in normal years tourists from abroad form nearly half of admissions to 15 institutions in England that have free admission and are funded by the DCMS, according to official statistics.[7] The tourist authority Visit Britain lists seven of these museums and galleries in its table of the top ten free visitor attractions in the UK, led by Tate Modern and the British Museum, which both had nearly six million visitors in 2018.[8] On display in museums are not only sublime works of art but also fascinating stories and bizarre oddments: in Eyam in Derbyshire, for example, there is a small museum, run by volunteers, that deals with the years 1665 and 1666, when bubonic plague killed 260 inhabitants in the village, which chose to isolate itself in order to prevent the spread of the infection. The holdings of smaller museums in London alone include a stuffed walrus, one of Madonna's old credit cards and a set of Sir Winston Churchill's dentures.

The future shape of this valuable segment of the charitable world was thrown into doubt by the coronavirus pandemic. The reopening of many museums in the summer of 2020 did not necessarily mean recovery, not least because a second and third lockdown followed: several months of admission and sales income had been lost, and many were operating at only 20% or 30% of capacity because of social distancing and reduced demand from the public. National museums and others that are heavily reliant on tourists from overseas, or located in city centres, were said to be doing less well between lockdowns than those situated in the countryside or attracting more domestic tourism, such as the Weald and Downland Museum or the Black Country Living Museum.

Alistair Brown of the Museums Association says that the £1.5 billion Cultural Recovery Fund announced by the DCMS "sounds like a lot, but scratch the surface and it increasingly looks like quite a small pot". Museums could apply to the Arts Council for a share of the first round of £500 million, but the maximum grant was £3 million which, given the scale of the losses, was "a drop in the ocean" for many organisations:

> "The big question is what on earth will happen in 2021. Local authority budgets are in tatters, civic museums have had a decade of spending cuts and there will be more to come. At the start of the crisis

there was a wave of independents saying they had up to four months of reserves and after that would have to close. The phasing out of the government's furlough scheme, the arrival of a second outbreak of the virus and future decisions by local authorities and the Arts Council about funding in the future are going to be crucial."

17

The minefield of charitable education

Education, along with the relief of poverty, is one of the oldest charitable purposes. In the statute that laid the foundations of charity law in 1601, education was one of the main charitable activities the state wanted to encourage. Centuries later, when Parliament produced an updated list of 13 charitable purposes in the Charities Act 2006, 'the advancement of education' was in second place after 'the prevention or relief of poverty'.

Few would object to education as a charitable activity in itself. What could possibly be wrong with charitable status, including tax breaks and the respect and confidence conferred by the word 'charity', for helping young people to realise their potential, contribute to society and thus provide public benefit? In practice, however, the charitable status of education has become a social and political minefield.

Schools in England are a complex mosaic (the other parts of the UK have different systems, not examined here). The 13,254 English schools in 2019 that are free, publicly funded and run by local authorities do not have charitable status.[1] But the 8,398 academy schools, also free and publicly funded but run by central government, are exempt charities (see Chapter 1); this means that the secretary of state for education is their principal regulator, but they have governing bodies required to comply with charity law.

English universities are also exempt charities, with the Office for Students as their principal regulator, while universities in Wales and Scotland are registered charities, regulated directly by the Charity Commission for England and Wales and the Office of the Scottish Charity Regulator, respectively. Meanwhile, about 1,300 of some 2,300 independent schools in England were also registered charities in 2016 – the rest are businesses.[2]

In the case of academy schools and universities, the controversy about charitable status is relatively mild and mainly concerns effective governance, including actual or potential conflicts of interest for trustees. But in the case of independent schools, the controversy is incendiary: just mention the word 'Eton'. How, critics ask, can a school that charges more than £40,000 a year – nearly one and a half times the median UK income of £29,400 in 2019 – be a charity? Among more than 1,300 independent schools in the UK that are members of the Independent Schools Council (ISC), about 1,000 of which were charities, the average annual fees for senior school pupils in 2019 were more than £15,000 a year for day schools and nearly £34,000 a year for boarding schools.[3,4]

There are regular calls for these schools to be deprived of charitable status. During debates on the Charities Bill in 2006, for example, the veteran Labour politician Lord (Dale) Campbell-Savours declared that charitable status for fee-charging schools was "an embarrassment to the whole charity sector" and the notion that they provided benefit to the community was "absolute tripe".[5,6] But the government – led by Tony Blair, who was educated at the independent school Fettes College in Scotland – side-stepped the formidable political and legal task of removing independent schools from the charity envelope. Instead, it compromised by requiring charitable schools, which had enjoyed a presumption that they provided public benefit, to actually demonstrate, like all charities, that they provided such benefit.

The knotty task of testing the public benefit of charitable independent schools was handed to the Charity Commission, a move compared afterwards to a 'hospital pass' in rugby.[7,8] The chair of the Commission was Dame Suzi Leather, a Labour Party member, and the Commission's approach to drawing up guidance for schools was criticised as politically biased, even though she did not take a direct part in it because one of her own children was at a fee-charging school. Soon after two schools visited by the Commission were deemed to be providing insufficient public benefit, the matter landed in the courts on an initiative by the ISC in tandem with the Attorney General.

A lengthy judgment in the Upper Tribunal in 2011 concluded that the public benefit requirement did indeed mean that charitable schools had a legal duty to provide opportunities for people unable to afford the fees, but it was up to the trustees of each charity, not the Commission, to decide what the school should provide in the form of bursaries, use of facilities by the local community, teaching help to state schools and so on.[9] Independent schools breathed more easily and the Commission revised its guidance.

The controversy still lurks, however, and erupts with increasing frequency. A year after the Upper Tribunal judgment, for example, *The Times* columnist and former Conservative MP Matthew Parris wrote a scathing article headlined 'Schools that sell privilege can't be charities'.[10] In 2017 the cabinet minister Michael Gove MP, a former secretary of state for education, said that independent school fees should attract VAT.[11] At the Labour Party's annual conference in 2019, delegates voted to integrate private schools into the state sector.[12] *Posh Boys: How the English Public Schools Ruin Britain*, by the journalist Robert Verkaik, argued that 'the public schools were founded to educate the poor and ended up serving the interests of the rich'.[13] *Engines of Privilege*, by the academics Francis Green and David Kynaston, commented that 'the conjunction of charitable status and privilege jars the moral compass, provoking an understandable sense of outrage'.[14]

It seems clear that the charitable status of independent schools is kicked around more often, and with stronger feelings, than most political footballs. Meanwhile, what is actually happening at Eton?

The playing fields of Eton

In the middle of Eton village, not far from Windsor Castle, stand the ancient red-brick buildings of Eton College, complete with a statue of Henry VI, who founded it in 1440 to educate 70 poor boys and send them to the King's other great educational foundation, King's College, Cambridge. There is the tall chapel, and a staircase to the Blue Corridor, lined with portraits of famous old Etonians, among them 19 prime ministers, such as Harold Macmillan and David Cameron, and the left-wing writer George Orwell.

The rest of the College is a jigsaw of more recent buildings, and beyond are the playing fields, called Agar's Plough, where the Duke of Wellington, another Old Etonian, is said to have remarked, while watching cricket after his most famous victory of 1815, that "the Battle of Waterloo was won here". Two hundred years on, Eton is at the centre of another battle – the one to demonstrate that such schools can improve educational opportunity and achievement for more than just the few who can afford the fees.

In 2016 the school appointed Tom Arbuthnott, himself an Old Etonian, as director of outreach and partnership. He started his teaching career in a state secondary school in the Midlands where "you couldn't cross the playground without being told to eff off five times by a bunch of 16-year-olds – it was feral". He moved back to the independent sector so he could continue to teach the International Baccalaureat rather than A levels, and became involved in outreach work that brought him back to Eton.

Arbuthnott estimates that in 2019 the College was spending about £7.3 million of its £70 million income on helping those unable to afford the fees – a combination of 90 free places and bursaries averaging 33% of fees for a quarter of the 1,300 pupils – and on partnerships with state schools. Bursaries used to be on the basis of academic excellence, he says, which meant they often went to boys from wealthy families. But since the mid-1990s they have been awarded in such a way that more of them go to boys from less well-off families:

> "For example, giving a free place to a boy who's already in a grammar school in Kent is all very well, but we feel that the distance travelled by that boy to top grades at A levels, which is where we hope to get him, is much less than taking a boy from a south London comprehensive, where he's had average grades at GCSE, and seeing him go on to get a place at Cambridge or Oxford. Ten years ago, it was more about the former boy than the latter – academically

selective rather than transformatively selective. Now we are trying to spot the boys with potential for whom spending two years or five years at Eton is going to totally change their life chances."

Eton's partnerships include seconding one teacher to the London Academy of Excellence (LAE) in east London – a selective state sixth-form 'free school' (a newly founded academy school, as opposed to a converted local authority school) in a deprived, multi-ethnic area, set up by Eton and five other independent schools in 2012. In 2019, 25 pupils at the LAE were offered places at either Oxford or Cambridge university.[15] Eton also sponsors Holyport College in nearby Maidenhead, the first boarding school in the free schools scheme, set up in 2014: staff have been seconded to teach Latin and art, Holyport pupils use Eton's sports facilities, and donations have included furniture, a minibus and two pianos.[16] The coronavirus crisis also prompted Eton to give state schools access to some of its online courses, and to pledge £100 million over five years 'to programmes that assist in addressing educational inequality both at Eton and in the nation'.[17]

To what extent were such initiatives influenced by the requirement in the Charities Act 2006 to demonstrate public benefit, and by the latent threat to remove charitable status from independent schools or levy a tax on school fees?

"I don't think the two big things – the foundation of the LAE and Holyport College – were done because the government was putting us under pressure. They were done because the sector was moving in that direction – the concept of what an independent school does was changing and Eton wanted to provide leadership. The reason we do charitable things is because we're a charity, not because we're subject to pressure from government."

Eton could cope financially with loss of the tax advantages of charitable status, Arbuthnott says, but it would hurt many smaller private schools: "The threat of removing charitable status has certainly focused governors' minds and they are asking questions that they didn't ask even five years ago: what are we doing for public benefit, for school partnership?" In 2017 Arbuthnott was involved in founding Schools Together, a project of the ISC which brings together nearly 400 independent and state schools:

> "It's a really exciting exercise – how we move partnerships on from being fragmented and small to being strategic, important and reciprocal. The more we can combine the extractive, bursary model with partnership with the community more broadly, the more effective we will be as what I call a social mobility charity. The independent sector has an enormously important role in modelling excellence and learning. Britain's educational commonwealth would be so much worse off without it. I don't think the debate will ever go away, because it's about privilege and social mobility, and is really important to us as a country. But I would hope very much it doesn't end up in a reductive, unintelligent rule of 'ban all independent schools, kick them in the bin'."

Defending independent charitable schools

Critics of independent schools have a tenacious adversary in the ISC, which runs an annual census of members that produces statistics on charitable public benefit. The 2019 edition, for example, reported that 1,142 of the ISC's 1,300 member schools had partnerships with state schools involving teaching, sport, music and drama.[18] A 2018 report commissioned by the ISC concluded that by educating more than 600,000 pupils, independent schools saved the taxpayer £3.52 billion a year, which would pay the salaries of 108,000 nurses.[19] The report added that discounts, bursaries and free places deprived the schools of £800 million of fees, or 9.6% of their total income of £8.3 billion. Green and Kynaston commented in *Engines of Privilege*, on the other hand, that the savings to the taxpayer 'could be promoted as a small efficiency gain in defence of private schooling', but it would 'strain credulity' to suggest that the partnerships such as those enumerated in the ISC census 'even begin to surmount the huge resource gap between the two sectors, or engineer any meaningful social mixing between the children of the different educational sectors'.[20]

The chairman of the ISC is Barnaby Lenon, a former headmaster of the prestigious Harrow School. He says schools have responded "incredibly well", but in proportion to their resources, to the Upper Tribunal judgment that they must be accessible in some form to what the Charity Commission called 'the poor':

> "The wealthy ones have responded very fulsomely –
> Eton and Winchester College, for example – but the
> number that are really wealthy is quite small. Eton
> is not typical. The whole group is not very wealthy,
> particularly the former direct grant schools, which
> before 1976 had very large numbers of free places
> – Manchester Grammar School, for example.[21] A
> typical ISC day school has an average of 400 children
> aged 5 to 13, paying about £13,500 a year, and would
> make a small surplus or deficit of about £50,000 a
> year. They would love to offer more bursaries because
> they believe in it, but are never going to be able to
> do it on the scale of the big foundations. Apart from
> raising money from alumni, the only other option
> is putting fees up, and it's beyond doubt that if they
> did that they would have to close."

The ISC could have "relaxed a bit" after the 2011 judgment, says Lenon, but what actually happened was "an acceleration of bursaries and partnerships ... driven mainly by a sense of moral purpose – which our opponents would probably regard with cynicism – and by individuals, and by the zeitgeist". Former direct grant schools raise money for bursaries because they want to attract pupils from low-income families, he says, not to satisfy the Charity Commission.

And how appropriate is charitable status for fee-charging schools? Lenon says it is partly a matter of law, and shedding charitable status is not always easy:

"But the high fees of some schools make our charitable status appear to be a misnomer. There are plenty of schools that would rather not be called charities because it is politically uncomfortable, and the financial benefits are relatively small. Charitable status is sometimes used by politicians as a stick to beat us with, and some of us think it would be better to reclassify us into a category similar to community amateur sports clubs [CASCs], which would be a kind of middle road."

As mentioned in Chapter 1, CASCs receive tax advantages and cannot distribute profits, but register with HM Revenue and Customs rather than the Charity Commission for England and Wales and are not subject to charity law.

State schools and charitable status

Many independent schools have been charities for centuries; the question of state schools becoming charities became an issue in 2000, after the Labour government under Tony Blair allowed state-funded schools to opt out of the control of local education authorities and become academies. Blair's education advisor, Andrew (later Lord) Adonis, thought academy status would enable state schools to be more independent and entrepreneurial, and David (later Lord) Blunkett, at the time the secretary of state for education, said it would "improve pupil performance and break the cycle of low expectations".[22]

By 2010 some 200 local authority schools had converted to academies. All were registered charities, regulated directly by the Charity Commission, but pressure was building up to change their governance: Labour's then secretary of state for education, Ed Balls said that "deregulation and reduction of bureaucracy" would make them run better, and proposed that they should become exempt charities – still subject to charity law, but with a principal regulator other than the Charity Commission.

The Conservative shadow education minister at the time, Michael Gove MP, agreed, but the Charity Commission briefed all MPs that the move would be 'a retrograde step, at odds with the direction of government policy on exempt charities', and would pose a 'serious risk of damaging public trust and confidence both in academies and in charity more widely'.[23] The government thought again, and announced that academies would continue to be registered charities after all, but with a simplified registration process.[24]

Now Gove objected, saying the government was "relentlessly undermining the independence of academies" and "piling on more and more red tape";[25] so, when the 2010 general election brought the Coalition government of Conservatives and Liberal Democrats to power and Gove took over at the Department for Education, he performed a U-turn on Labour's U-turn: from 2011, academies were going to be exempt charities after all, and he, as secretary of state for education, would be the principal regulator.[26] The Commission acquiesced, saying it had received reassurances that it would be consulted on any changes in academies' governing documents that were 'key to charitable status'. Day-to-day oversight of academies was given to the Education and Skills Funding Agency (ESFA), and from 2014 many decisions were devolved to eight regional schools commissioners, who are civil servants. Giving academy schools exempt charity status remains what one charity lawyer described to the authors as "a funny one – it seems odd to create more exempt charities when they had otherwise been moving away from them".

From 2010 there was a rapid increase in the conversion of local authority schools to academies, and a steady growth in newly established free schools on the academy model. By 2018, a report from the NAO said 35% of the 21,538 state-funded schools in England were academies, of which 6,996 had converted and 476 were free schools.[27] This expansion was accompanied by controversy not only on educational matters, such as selective entry and the freedom of academies not to follow the national curriculum, but also on governance, including the lack of transparency in the appointment of trustees of the exempt charities that own and run the academies, a shortage of information about how decisions are taken and money spent, and the freedom of academies to set their own pay and conditions for teachers.[28]

This raised concern in other education charities about the independence of trustees, which is a key aspect of charities. In 2012 Neil McIntosh, who was chief executive of the Centre for British Teachers for 22 years, said that academies potentially compromised "the distinctiveness of the third sector" because they were funded by the government and subject to a regulatory regime overseen by a politician: "They are, at their weakest, agencies that are independent in name only." He pointed out that academy trustee boards, unlike those of most charities, included two employees – the head teacher and a representative of the teaching staff. This put staff in too powerful a position, especially in setting salaries, he said.[29] The Academies Commission – an independent body made up of senior education professionals backed by the Royal Society of Arts and the Pearson think-tank – also warned in 2013 that the presence of head teachers on academy boards was too 'cosy' and potentially compromised the ability of trustees to hold head teachers to account.[30] It said of academy governors that 'there needs to be a radical shift in their capacity, knowledge and attitude if they are to take on both the leadership role expected in an academised system and fulfil their legal responsibilities as directors of charitable companies'.

There was also concern over the increase in multi-academy trusts, on the grounds that the individual schools in such trusts lose, in effect, much of the freedom and autonomy that the government intended academy status to confer on them. By 2019 there were 1,170 multi-academy trusts in England managing at least two schools each, 29 with 26 or more schools, 85 with between 12 and 25 schools and 259 with between 6 and 11 schools.[31]

Some aspects of the governance of academies that came in for criticism initially were quickly changed – a power of the minister to remove trustees was abolished, for example. But the criticism didn't go away: two experienced charity lawyers, interviewed by the authors in 2019 on condition of anonymity, describe as "horrific" their firm's involvement in an early conversion of a local authority school to an academy:

> "What shocked us was the attitude of the board, the lack of commitment to good governance, and the

apparent conflicts of interest that they just seemed to shrug their shoulders at. Our impression is that a lot of academy conversions happened on the basis of 'here's a pre-printed form, fill in the boxes and sign' – no real due diligence on whether there were hidden charitable trusts, whether conflicts of interest were a major issue. We just don't see how it's a sustainable model. Isn't it meant to be about having governance closer to the school? Well, if you're in a multi-academy trust you haven't even got a governing body at the level of each school any more.

The trouble with having an elected politician as principal regulator is that everything is looked at through a political lens, which is very different from how the Charity Commission operates. We also think there's a certain possessiveness in the Department for Education – 'the money comes from us, we're in charge and we do what we think fit'. I'm sure there are pockets of excellence, but most of the professionals we speak to can give examples of these organisations being run by self-serving, self-interested people. If a school suddenly happens to be buying services from a company owned by their head or a related company, who actually monitors that? The body responsible for the funding is clearly not capable of it. The rationale was that academies were going to be more business-like, but businesses will invest in getting things right, and they aren't doing that."

'A catastrophic failure of governance'

These questions of governance, conflicts of interest and pay were thrown into sharp relief in 2015 by the case of Durand Academy, a primary school in south London where Greg Martin became head teacher in 1986. In the following decade a swimming pool, sports facilities and living quarters were built on the spacious Victorian site and were available for hire when not in use by the school. In 1997 a private trading company, London Horizons Ltd, was set up as a tax-efficient way of transferring the profits to the school, and in 2001 a company controlled – and initially wholly owned – by Martin was awarded a ten-year contract to run London Horizons Ltd.

In 2010 the school became an academy and was planning to open a boarding school in Sussex. Durand's success attracted the attention of Michael Gove MP, who visited the school as secretary of state for education in 2011. It also brought benefits for Martin, whose salary in 2012/13 rose by 56.5% to £229,000; the contract to run London Horizons Ltd for another five years was awarded to another service company wholly owned by him in 2012; and he received a knighthood in 2013.[32]

But when the ESFA, regulating exempt educational charities on behalf of the secretary of state, reviewed the academy's financial statements for 2012/13 it became concerned. The House of Commons PAC was alerted, and the NAO published a report in 2014 into the ESFA's oversight of 'related party transactions' at Durand Academy – in essence, the contract between the academy and the head teacher's company.[33] The report noted that the Durand Academy Trust 'had a large number of conflicts of interests in the way that it managed its academy and its assets'. This led to a lively hearing of the PAC in which the chair, Margaret Hodge MP, declared that Martin's combined income of £420,000 from his salary and his service company was "pretty gob-smacking stuff".[34]

The Charity Commission began a formal statutory inquiry into the Durand Education Trust, the registered charity that owned the land and property used by the Durand Academy Trust which, like all academies, was an exempt charity with the secretary of state for education as its principal regulator. The inquiry resulted a year later (by which time Martin had resigned) in a report that said there had been no proper leases, tenancy or rental agreements, and insufficient recognition of the separate legal status of the different entities supporting the academy and of their roles.[35] Most crucially, the payments to Martin's company agreed in the 2012 contract 'were not reasonable in all the circumstances'.

Over the five years of the 2012 contract, the report concluded, Martin's company would have been paid a total of £840,000, plus a payment on termination of the contract of £1.8 million.

The total the company was going to earn from the contract was therefore at least £2.6 million. During the inquiry, however, a cap of £850,000 on the severance payment was negotiated, thus making nearly an extra £1 million available to the Durand Education Trust to use for its charitable educational purpose. But the PAC, which published a report about academy schools generally in January 2019, was not mollified:[36]

> There has been a succession of high-profile academy failures that have been costly to the taxpayer and damaging to children's education. Some academy trusts have misused public money through related-party transactions and paying excessive salaries ... This cannot be allowed to happen again – governance at academy trusts needs to be stronger and the Department for Education's oversight and intervention needs to be more rigorous. The Education and Skills Funding Agency is taking steps to control executive pay and related party transactions, but these actions are as yet unproven and in isolation will not prevent abuse. We expect to return to these issues in future ... Despite a catastrophic failure of governance, the previous executive head teacher at Durand Academy Trust is apparently entitled to a lump sum payment which, even after a statutory inquiry by the Charity Commission, totals £850,000. This is a shocking reward for failure ...

There had been 'serious failures of governance and oversight' not only at Durand but also at Bright Tribe Trust, a multi-academy trust in the north-west of England, the PAC concluded. The City of London Police fraud squad was asked by the local police fraud to investigate allegations by the BBC *Panorama* programme that Bright Tribe Trust had claimed money for work that had not been completed, but concluded in September 2020, by which time the Trust was being wound up, that there was insufficient evidence for a prosecution.[37]

The government agreed with all but one of the PAC's recommendations, including one to strengthen sanctions against academy trustees and leaders responsible for serious failings.[38] Durand and Bright Tribe may be extreme examples of governance failures at academies, but they illustrate the difficulties that can arise in the regulation of exempt charities.

Oxbridge colleges: a law unto themselves?

While academy schools were being permitted to become exempt charities rather than registered charities, the opposite was happening in other, highly prestigious educational institutions. *Private Action, Public Benefit*, the review of charities and voluntary organisations by the prime minister's strategy unit in 2002, had concluded that some exempt charities were unaware of the requirements of charity law regarding, for example, governance and stewardship of funds, which laid them open to challenge.[39] The report recommended that larger exempt charities without a principal regulator should be registered with the Charity Commission.

The government decided that the Higher Education Funding Council (now the Office for Students) would remain the principal regulator for English universities, but concluded that there was no suitable principal regulator for the independent, self-governing colleges of the universities of Oxford, Cambridge and Durham, and for the universities in Wales. The decision that these bodies would therefore have to become registered charities came as something of a shock to the colleges of Oxford and Cambridge, many of which had been set up by Royal Charter centuries earlier.

They were also accustomed to minimal oversight of their use of funds. In 2006, for example, New College, Oxford, almost doubled the value of its endowment by selling for £55 million some land that had been given to it in 1386 by the Bishop of Winchester.[40] Controversially, it decided to use some of the money to increase the salaries of its 39 fellows (the senior academic and administrative staff) for the following three years, a move that David Palfreyman, bursar of the College, described as "putting some jam on the college scone". It was emphasised that the College was not acting unlawfully, but some academics disapproved: one was quoted as saying that the College was a charity and shouldn't behave like a company giving out a dividend. Charitable funds were, in effect, being used for private benefit.

The charity lawyers quoted above, who are familiar with the Cambridge colleges, say the process of becoming registered from 2010 was regarded as very burdensome:

> "They didn't want to do it. They had been self-governing communities of academics where, as exempt charities, they were subject to charity law, but only if the Attorney General, who is not the most active enforcer, stepped in. Now they were being required to send in annual reports to a regulator, describing their public benefit, making serious incident reports if anything went wrong and so on. It was a fundamental change – and quite a change in psychology."

The colleges, which formerly had a variety of governance structures, have set up boards of trustees, drawn from among their fellows. One of each board's functions is managing the private benefits that fellows typically receive, including not only their salaries, pension schemes and childcare in some cases, but also free meals, with silver on the table in the mediaeval halls of the older colleges and wine from the cellars. This is part of the attraction of Oxbridge colleges to the best academics, say the lawyers: the difficulty the trustees face is that they personally enjoy some of the benefits that they sanction – on the face of it, a classic conflict of interest:

> "Were the requirements of charity law to be followed to the letter, it would upset what in some colleges is hundreds of years of tradition, and if benefits that were part of someone's employment package were summarily withdrawn, other risks and liabilities would be created. We think the Charity Commission took the view that when you've got something that has a set of unique hallmarks, you don't dismantle it without justification. I think they felt that as long

as the right balances were being struck, they would be prepared to live without strict compliance with absolutely every principle under charity legislation."

The lawyers say that, ten years after becoming registered charities, colleges are more attuned to good governance and managing conflicts of interest, partly because students have become more like consumers: "The colleges don't want to be seen as overly generous with the charitable assets, living high on the hog, when students are paying high tuition fees and incurring large amounts of debt." Colleges are being run more professionally, they add, with more leaders appointed from outside, such as former civil servants and journalists: "Twenty years ago it would be Buggins' turn, and the master would be promoted from within the fellowship."

The negotiations with the Charity Commission on behalf of the Cambridge colleges were led by Dr George Reid, former bursar of St John's College, who says a model conflicts of interest policy was agreed with the Commission and adapted by the 31 colleges:

> "Getting them all into the same mindset and carrying them along was no mean task, I can tell you. The gain is that it has removed a source of friction or comment – 'Oh, those Oxbridge colleges, they're a law unto themselves, they're exempt charities'. Well, you just cannot say that any more now that we have the benefit of being registered charities like any other."

Professor David Yates, warden of Robinson College, who was also involved in the negotiations, says benefits to fellows are "pretty marginal" in the context of the total cost of charitable education provided by the colleges: "It's not a lot of people with their hands in a big sack of goodies – that isn't how it works ... I don't think we're in a position where we're somehow flouting charity law." Has the change been a good thing, overall? "It hasn't been a bad thing – put it like that."

The Charity Commission concluded a review in 2016 of how registered charity status was bedding in at the Oxford and Cambridge colleges. In response to a request under the Freedom of Information Act, it declined to release the review on the grounds that it 'may lead charities to be less candid with the Commission in the future'. But it did confirm that it had 'received a complaint about a particular college which, amongst other things, included allegations about unmanaged conflicts'.

Defusing the controversies

It is clear that the entanglement of education with charitable status, overlaid by the legal uncertainties over the term 'public benefit', has become controversial and problematic, particularly in schools. The twists and turns over the kind of charities academy schools should be were almost farcical: making them exempt charities looked like a matter of political convenience, and there are fears that weaknesses of governance, exemplified in the case of Durand Academy, threaten to undermine the integrity of charitable status generally.

Efforts are undoubtedly being made to extend the privileges of charitable private schools more widely through bursaries and partnership schemes, developed partly because of the requirement to demonstrate public benefit and partly because of a sense of mission and social responsibility at a time of growing social inequality. At the elite colleges of Oxford and Cambridge, efforts have also increased to attract applications from a wider range of students and make college bursaries available to them.

Whether such efforts to strengthen governance and spread the benefits of elite institutions are sufficient to defuse the controversies, especially over independent charitable schools, remains to be seen. The ideal is to secure an excellent education for everyone. The partnerships, bursaries and free places offered by independent schools benefit a few talented and fortunate students who are in the right place at the right time, but hardly seem like a formula for a wholesale righting of the inequalities between private and state education.

18

Pushing the boundaries of medicine and science

One of the charitable causes most favoured by the British public is medical research. In its annual survey of giving, CAF found in 2018 that 25% of people who said they had given to charity in the previous four weeks had chosen medical research, beaten only by animals at 26% and children and young people, also at 26%. Of the total amount people said they had donated, medical research received 10%, behind only overseas aid at 11% and religious organisations at 19%.[1]

These donations, combined with grants from charitable trusts and foundations, meant that in 2019 the 142 charities that are members of the Association of Medical Research Charities (AMRC) invested just over £3 billion in research – almost half of all publicly funded medical research in the UK.[2,3] The record income for the biggest cancer charity in the country, CRUK, was £647 million in 2016/17, most of which went to support research in universities and hospitals.[4] Collective scientific knowledge would undoubtedly be much poorer if it weren't for charities in this sector.

Charities were also at the forefront of efforts to find treatments and a vaccine for COVID-19. Wellcome Trust, a charitable foundation with huge investments, had already given $100 million (£78 million) in 2017 to help set up the Coalition for Epidemic Preparedness Innovations, which finances research into vaccines for emerging infectious diseases prioritised by the WHO. In early 2020 the charity provided a further $50 million (£39 million) to establish the COVID-19 Therapeutics Accelerator, a joint venture with the Bill and Melinda Gates

Foundation and Mastercard to speed up the development of treatments. Wellcome Trust, now known as simply 'Wellcome', also allocated £10 million to support urgent coronavirus research in poorer countries and pledged its continuing support for scientists around the world who were switching their focus to COVID-19.[5]

Within three weeks of the virus taking hold, and without any government support, the Francis Crick Institute, a leading biomedical research centre in London supported by both CRUK and Wellcome, had set up an accredited virus-testing facility for front-line NHS workers. It also started several COVID-related research projects, including investigations into how the coronavirus is transferred from animals to humans, how it replicates in human cells, why it affects some people more severely than others and how the treatment of cancer patients is affected by the virus.[6]

But much of the vital work that was already under way in the biomedical research field before the pandemic struck found itself suddenly under threat in 2020. Individuals taking part in clinical trials of new drugs were told to stop, because the outbreak made it too dangerous for them to visit hospitals. The financial impact on the sector was enormous – because so many research charities rely heavily on fundraising events and charity shops, the lockdowns and social distancing measures devastated their budgets. CRUK cut its spending on research by £44 million in 2020 and warned that it was facing a hole in its fundraised income of £150 million a year for the next three years – the amount it would normally spend on ten years of clinical trials.[7] Breast Cancer Now expected to lose a third of its income – about £16 million – over the first year, and was planning to reduce its staff by about a fifth.[8] Baroness Morgan, chief executive of Breast Cancer Now, described COVID-19 as "the greatest threat the cancer charity sector has ever faced".[9]

Research into other diseases was similarly curtailed: the BHF said it would slash its spending on research from £100 million to £50 million in 2020.[10] The Stroke Association suspended almost three-quarters of its research projects in reaction to an expected funding shortfall of £1.5 million.[11] On average, members of the AMRC predicted a reduction in research spending over the year from April 2020 of 41% – a shortfall of £310 million.[12] The Institute for Public Policy Research warned that in a reasonable worst-case scenario, scientific research stood to lose nearly £8 billion of investment between 2020 and 2027.[13] In June the AMRC coordinated a call from 60 of the country's top scientists, 151 of its member charities and 30 pharmaceutical and health tech companies for the government to invest urgently in a 'Life Sciences–Charity Partnership Fund' to protect biomedical research and the life-sciences industry.[14] They proposed that the government should match-fund all donations raised by charities from the public for medical research over three years. Sir Paul Nurse, executive director of the Francis Crick Institute, told the BBC that the sector was facing an "existential crisis", with large numbers of scientists at risk of losing their funding:[15]

"The UK is a world leader in biomedical research and innovation. It saves lives, it improves the quality of life, but it also drives the economy…. but this cut we're seeing could lead to very significant numbers of scientists and researchers losing their support and losing their positions. It puts all of this work at risk. The aim is to close this £300 million a year funding gap. That's a very significant sum, but not so big when you look at the money the government is spending to deal with other problems associated with the pandemic."

Wellcome: a giant of scientific research

As mentioned above, one of the biggest donors to coronavirus research is Wellcome, which is endowed by the proceeds of the sale of a pharmaceutical company founded in the late 19th century. Sir Henry Wellcome studied pharmacy in the US before coming to England in 1880 to join fellow American Silas Burroughs in his new pharmaceutical distribution business. They built Burroughs Wellcome & Co into a multinational powerhouse, and after Burroughs died of pneumonia, Wellcome added research laboratories that developed various antitoxins, standardised insulin and isolated histamine. He also assembled a vast collection of books, medical instruments and artefacts from all over the world, many of which are in the Wellcome museum and library on London's Euston Road.[16]

When Wellcome died in 1936, his will vested the entire shareholding of the Wellcome Foundation Ltd in a medical research charity, Wellcome Trust. After some difficult times, the company's fortunes improved in the 1950s and the blockbuster drugs it produced included the best-selling Zovirax, which is used to treat cold sores, shingles and chicken-pox. But eventually the Trust sold all the company's shares and invested the proceeds more widely to fund its grant making.

Today Wellcome is an immense charitable undertaking. Its investments are worth nearly £27 billion, producing income that in 2018/19 allowed it to distribute £1.1 billion in grants; it supports biomedical science, population health, product development and applied research, humanities and social science, public engagement and the creative industries.[17] Its funding has contributed to the sequencing of the human genome, the invention of insecticide-treated bed nets for malaria, the development of Ebola treatments and a longer life of better quality for people with AIDS. In his biography of Henry Wellcome, Robert Rhodes James described the charity as 'the greatest single private contributor in Britain alone to medical science and research and the history of medicine'.[18]

In the devastating Ebola outbreak in the Democratic Republic of Congo from 2014 to 2016, which killed more than 1,800 people in its first year – two-thirds of all those who contracted the disease – the charity played a pivotal role in improving survival rates. It invested £4 million in research, rolled out a vaccine developed by the pharmaceutical company Merck to 200,000 people and developed two new treatments that have been proven to save lives.[19] Sir Jeremy Farrar, director of Wellcome, described the results of the treatment trials as "an amazing breakthrough". He told the BBC in August 2019:

> "It was a trial of four drugs; two have now been dropped as not effective but the other two will continue. If people are treated early with one of these drugs, about 6% will die, compared with 70

or 80% who don't have it. You can never eradicate Ebola because it exists in populations of animals across large swathes of sub-Saharan Africa, but now with vaccines, public health and treatment, we can turn what was a terrifying epidemic and disease into something preventable and, if you do get it, treatable."

Researchers funded by Wellcome say that it gives them greater continuity and freedom than they would have under some other funders. One of the 12,000 UK-based researchers is Professor Helen McShane, who leads a team at the University of Oxford trying to develop a vaccine for tuberculosis (TB), the lung disease that is still rife in the developing world, claiming 1.4 million lives each year.[20] The work of McShane and her team laid the foundation for the giant pharmaceutical company GlaxoSmithKline to produce a new TB vaccine known as M72 that was shown in a clinical study in 2018 to have some degree of efficacy.[21] McShane says:

"I've had continuous Wellcome funding since 2001, which has been fantastic. Unlike most other funding, it doesn't come with narrowly defined milestones and deliverables. The point of science is that you're working at the edges of what's known, and as you progress you can end up going in a completely different direction to that which you anticipated. The Wellcome Trust gets that and has always got that. They treat you like a grown-up – of course you must stay within the scope of your scientific interests and competence, but they trust you within that context. That scientific freedom is absolutely critical. Over the last 20 years, TB research has been gaining a real momentum, not just in vaccine research but in drug research and diagnostics. Wellcome has been pivotal in leading this effort."

On the face of it, Wellcome, with its vast assets, could single-handedly plug the UK's £310 million research funding gap identified by the AMRC in the wake of the coronavirus pandemic. But the charity points out that it is a global foundation, with a mission far beyond the UK, and its investment portfolio is structured to exist in perpetuity. A statement by Wellcome said:

> The unplanned dispersal of assets can be damaging. Diverting Wellcome funds to plug a funding gap elsewhere would also severely undermine our ability to advance our charitable mission. Our governance requires us to look at each funding application individually and support only those that fit our strategic goals. This is the same for any other research charity, with their own mission and strategies that do not – and should not – align with ours.

Breast Cancer Now: giving voice to patients

CRUK is easily the largest cancer charity, but there are many more that are searching for a cure, experimenting with treatments to prolong and improve life, or providing care and support. Breast Cancer Now is the UK's biggest breast cancer charity, formed in 2015 by the merger of the long-established Breakthrough Breast Cancer and Breast Cancer Campaign.

Breakthrough is an example of how the charitable impulses of individuals can result in the development of major organisations. It was the brainchild of Bill Freedman, the widower of the actor Toby Robins, who died from breast cancer in 1986. Freedman wanted to establish a centre of excellence for research and enlisted the support of the Institute of Cancer Research. When the businesswoman Mary-Jean Mitchell Green also died from the disease in 1990, her husband, Peter Green, donated £1.6 million to the project; the charity Breakthrough Breast Cancer was then registered in the following year to fundraise for more.[22] By the time the Toby Robins Research Centre opened in 1999 in the Mary-Jean Mitchell Green Building at the Institute of Cancer Research, the charity had accumulated more than £15 million.[23]

When Breakthrough joined forces with Breast Cancer Campaign in 2015, it was one of the biggest charity sector mergers to date. Mergers are comparatively rare in the charity world; in 2015 there were 560 mergers and acquisitions involving commercial companies in the UK, and only 54 in the charity sector.[24,25] The new organisation, Breast Cancer Now, was headed by Delyth Morgan, Baroness Morgan of Drefelin, who had been chief executive of both the original charities at different times. In 2019, Breast Cancer Now merged with another charity, Breast Cancer Care, creating an even more powerful voice for those affected by the disease.[26] The charity's vision, agreed when the first merger took place, is that 'by 2050, everybody with breast cancer will live, and live well'.

In the 20 years before that first merger, Breakthrough had raised more than £100 million and Breast Cancer Campaign more than £60 million to invest in breast cancer studies.[27] They had different approaches: Breakthrough conducted most of its work through its Toby Robins Centre, whereas Campaign funded scientists at universities across the country. But they were both highly successful, and between them had moved breast cancer knowledge forward significantly. By 2019, two-thirds of all breast cancer research going on in UK universities was paid for by charities, according to Fiona Hazell, director of communications and influencing at Breast Cancer Now. But the role charities play is much broader than funding laboratory research, she says:

> "If I look back and think of what breast cancer charities have achieved, the shift from the idea that 'doctor knows best' to patient advocacy and a situation where informed patients have choices is one of the most fundamental changes in public health. In our field, patients have been at the forefront of that, but charities have really worked with it and championed it."

Charities also work to ensure that government policy and NHS practice are driven by research and the needs of patients. One example of this was the move to ensure that patients with primary breast cancer are always treated by a multidisciplinary team, which was included in the first national cancer strategy.

"That was one of the first policy changes that really led to improvements in survival, along with screening, better detection and greater awareness," Hazell says.[28] Most lobbying now is about access to drugs, such as Kadcyla:

> "Kadcyla is a critical drug for women with secondary breast cancer who essentially have limited treatment options. At the moment, once you get secondary breast cancer it's incurable, so the question is how long you can stay alive. At the time of our merger there hadn't been a secondary breast cancer drug approved by NICE for about a decade. It was clear we needed to do much more for women with secondary breast cancer, because while there has been a lot of progress in treatment of primary breast cancer and more women are surviving, there are still 11,000 women a year who die. So we publicly lobbied the pharma company, Roche, to bring down the price of the drug, as well as lobbying NICE. We believed there was a way to get Kadcyla onto the NHS at a price the NHS could afford. We brought all parties together and said they had to find a way, because this was a real example of research progress that was not reaching patients because of the system.
>
> "Ultimately it was a negotiation between the pharma and NICE, but we made sure the views of patients were considered in that discussion. Within a few weeks of launching the campaign we had 115,000 signatories, and the strength of feeling became clear to NICE and Roche that this was an issue that really mattered to patients and they had to try harder. They did, and Kadcyla is now available on the NHS, keeping a lot of women alive for longer and giving them precious time with their families and friends that they otherwise wouldn't have had."

In parallel with the rise in patient advocacy has come a shift in the attitudes of charity supporters, according to Dr Simon Vincent, Breast Cancer Now's director of research:

"That slightly paternalistic model of charity which goes 'You can trust us – if you give us lots of money we know how to spend it' is becoming outdated. We're moving much more towards a model of needing to report impact, with donors being savvier about where their money goes and treating it more like an investment. That's having a major impact on charities and causing a lot to rethink the way they fund research. It's a good thing – it forces charities which might have become a little complacent to go back to their founding principles and remember the passion and vision of those individuals who wanted to make a difference."

The charity revolution in hearing aids

Charities are adept at spotting and harnessing new technologies. SolarAid, for example, works to increase the use of solar lights in Africa, replacing kerosene and paraffin lamps, which are highly polluting and a fire risk. The BHF has supplied defibrillators to all Asda stores in the UK and trained the company's staff in how to use them. The RSPB is deploying drones to photograph, map and monitor bird habitats, providing enhanced detail of its reserves and enabling the creation of 3D digital surface models. But few organisations can claim the level of success that the Royal National Institute for Deaf People (RNID) achieved at the turn of the century with its campaign for mass access to digital hearing aids.

In the late 1990s, audiology had a low priority in the NHS. Audiology departments were run down and under-resourced and staff morale was at rock bottom. Yet the problem of hearing loss in the UK population was significant: 55% of people over 60 suffered some form of hearing loss.[29] The condition brought serious disadvantages: sufferers were around four times more likely to be unemployed than those with good hearing, and poor hearing was known to contribute to the loss of social networks and depression.[30] The average age of patients when fitted with their first NHS hearing aid was 75, but most had put up with some degree of deafness for at least ten years.[31] Two million people had been prescribed clunky, analogue NHS hearing aids, but these tended to amplify all types of sound, often making things worse for the wearer. It was estimated that more than a third of the aids supplied were not actually being worn.[32]

Meanwhile, new digital hearing aids were not only much lighter and less visible than analogue ones, but also worked better. The problem was cost – digital aids cost up to £2,500 on the high street.[33] The charity RNID was sure that the new technology presented a huge opportunity for economies of scale that could bring down the costs. In an article written for *Social Enterprise Journal*, Brian Lamb, then the charity's executive director of advocacy and policy, and Alex Murdock, professor of not-for-profit management at London Southbank University, wrote that there was 'no better opportunity in the NHS to change so many lives, so radically, at such low cost per capita'.[34]

The charity put together a business plan and took it to the secretary of state for health. Lamb and the chief executive at the time, John Low (later Sir John), proposed that the charity should manage the modernisation of a first wave of 20 NHS audiology departments – the first time a charity had ever asked to manage the modernisation of a public service. In the article for *Social Enterprise Journal*, Murdock and Lamb wrote:[35]

> RNID knew that there was a significant hill to climb to convince a government that investment on such a scale was needed. After all, hearing loss was not in itself a life-threatening illness like cancer, and though the analogue hearing aids were outpaced by the new technology, they were both well-established and reasonably straightforward. It was somewhat akin to the difference between a Zimmer walking frame and an electric disability scooter in respect of a disabled person. Both were functional, but one was far more effective and expensive than the other.

The charity worked hard to convince ministers, parliamentarians, civil servants and senior NHS officials that its proposals were sound, and at the same time mobilised its 300,000 supporters, who sent thousands of e-mails, letters and postcards to their

MPs, succeeded in getting questions asked in Parliament and attracted plenty of attention from the national media. In the end the government agreed, and in the first month of the new millennium the Department of Health announced it would allocate £10.7 million to modernise 20 sites that provided hearing aid services. The RNID put together a team to manage the programme, and by March 2002 all 20 were offering digital aids and delivering an efficient, modern service. The cost for each aid had plummeted from £2,500 to £165, and some 20,000 people had been fitted with them. After further lobbying, the government was persuaded that scaling up the programme would deliver value for money – proof that it was committed to NHS modernisation and a better quality of life for hundreds of thousands of people.

In the end, the government allocated a total of £125 million to modernise NHS hearing aid services and retained the RNID to deliver the national roll-out.[36] By the time the modernisation process ended in April 2005 and the charity handed management of the service back to the NHS, more than 350 audiology clinics had been created or upgraded and 1.5 million people had been fitted with digital hearing aids. In an evaluation in 2004 the ministers in charge, MPs Paul Boateng and Fiona Mactaggart, said: 'The RNID has proved that it is possible to combine a campaigning role – that of achieving better quality of life for deaf and hard-of-hearing people – with a service delivery role.'[37] In the article that Murdock and Lamb co-authored they said the episode demonstrated how charities could add real value to public services: they spoke with authority because they were close to their beneficiaries; they were nimble and flexible because they could think and act 'outside the tramlines of government'; and they could offer personalised services. They also, they said, had passion and continuity of commitment, and were still there long after ministers and officials had moved on.

Mapping for good

The final case study in this chapter is another example of the combination of compassion and technical ingenuity that characterises many modern charitable initiatives. When a humanitarian emergency strikes, the collection of accurate information about which areas are worst affected and who needs help the most is key to an effective response. Members of the charity MapAction's team of 70 highly trained volunteers are often on the scene of a disaster within a day or two, gathering data on where the most vulnerable people are, what has happened to transport routes and communication networks and where supplies are needed most. As well as gathering the data, the volunteers portray it visually in the form of maps that can be used by governments, aid agencies and local non-governmental bodies.

The idea for MapAction came initially from Rupert Douglas-Bate when he was working as an emergency water engineer in Bosnia in 1994.[38] The first staff member was hired in 2002 and by the end of 2003, 29 volunteers were on board. The charity's first deployment was in 2003, in response to a food-security crisis in Lesotho. The next year, its rapid-response capacity was tested for the first time when a massive tsunami hit the Indian Ocean on Boxing Day in 2004. Sixteen volunteers travelled to Sri Lanka to help with that emergency. By 2018 the Oxfordshire-based charity was employing 15 staff, mostly part time, and had 70 volunteers. It was operating on an income of around £900,000 a year, a fifth of which came from DfID.

Since its launch, MapAction has sent teams to support relief and development efforts in more than 80 humanitarian crises, including earthquakes in Nepal, hurricanes Irma and Maria in the Caribbean, the outbreak of Ebola in West Africa in 2016 and the influx of Rohingya refugees into Bangladesh from Myanmar in 2017. In 2020 it created an online dashboard of different governments' measures to combat the coronavirus, such as where borders were closed and which areas were in lockdown, so that partner agencies could adapt their provision of aid. It also sent a team to Beirut in the aftermath of the devastating explosion in the city's port in August 2020.

In the Ebola crisis, its first deployment in West Africa was to Liberia, but there were also subsequent operations in Sierra Leone, Mali and Ghana at the request of humanitarian partners. The charity produced more than 320 maps that conveyed critical information about the crisis and were used to brief the authorities, including the President of Sierra Leone.

In Liberia, volunteers trained civil servants to use the mapping functions they set up. In Sierra Leone, mapping was combined with infographics to provide a day-by-day picture of bed spaces in treatment centres, alongside the changing prevalence of the disease. In Mali, where there were only a handful of Ebola cases, MapAction helped the authorities to put systems in place to manage and contain any future outbreaks so that the situation would not escalate as it had in neighbouring countries.

According to the Centers for Disease Control and Prevention in the US, the Ebola virus infected 28,600 people across the region, a number which would undoubtedly have been higher without MapAction's staff and volunteers.[39] Emma Mumford, the charity's operations director, says:

> "It's not possible to put a figure on the number of ultimate beneficiaries, but when you consider the scale of the emergency and the populations of the affected countries – 10 million in Liberia and Sierra Leone alone – we can be confident that MapAction's work in the affected region has made an important contribution to saving the lives of thousands of people as well as strengthening national information management structures in the event that they might have to respond to a similar emergency in the future. Our partners told us that our mapped analysis was particularly useful in identifying transmission routes and understanding where to locate treatment centres – two key components of the response."

★ ★ ★

In summary, UK-based medical research funded by charities during more than a century has benefited millions of people worldwide by financing the discovery of vaccines and treatments that underpin key aspects of modern public health services. Charities have also acted as advocates, drawing on the close contact they have with patients and their families to influence medical attitudes and practice and to press for key drugs to be made available. The examples provided in this chapter also illustrate how charities have devised ways of making breakthroughs in other branches of science and technology available for public as well as private benefit, both in the UK and abroad.

Much of the income of medical charities derives from public fundraising, which to a great extent went on hold in 2020, causing projects to be cut back or paused: there was a certain irony in the way medical research was impeded by a viral pandemic, and it was not clear by the end of that year when or if the funding gap would be filled by government subvention or by the restoration of usual fundraising activities. The best hope was that the emergence in late 2020 of several promising vaccines for COVID-19 would bring back some form of normality by Easter 2021.

PART VI

The way ahead

19

Reviews and strategies

It has become clear in earlier chapters which kinds of charities are most likely to spark controversy. Education is a battleground and is likely to remain so because of the charitable status of most fee-charging schools and the perceived inadequacies of the governance of academies. Public service delivery is full of uncertainties and hazards for charities, linked to the perennial wider tensions between the sector and government. Overseas development is also hedged about with risks, ranging from the diversion of funds for improper purposes to the safeguarding of beneficiaries and changes in the political climate: at the start of 2020, for example, Anne-Marie Trevelyan MP, who had earlier tweeted 'Charity begins at home', was appointed as the secretary of state for international development, and DfID was, controversially, later merged into the Foreign and Commonwealth Office. Charitable think-tanks, as was seen in Chapter 3, can find it hard to comply with regulatory requirements for party political independence and are frequently the subject of dispute and controversy. The environmental campaigner George Monbiot, for example, considers it 'remarkable' that the think-tank Policy Exchange, which has influenced many Conservative policies and does not reveal all its funders, can remain a registered charity.[1]

Although not dealt with specifically in this book, religion – one of the earliest charitable purposes – has also been highly controversial. The Church of England and the Roman Catholic Church have both been caught up in well-publicised scandals about child abuse. The Independent Inquiry into Child Sexual Abuse reported in October 2020 that 390 members of the

Church of England clergy had been convicted of offences against children between the 1940s and 2018 – an average of more than five a year.[2] Professor Alexis Jay, chair of the inquiry, said: 'Over many decades, the Church of England failed to protect children and young people from sexual abusers, instead facilitating a culture where perpetrators could hide and victims faced barriers to disclosure that many could not overcome.' Earlier, Catholic Care (Diocese of Leeds) spent three years trying to overturn the Charity Commission's refusal to allow it to change its objects so that it could discriminate against gay couples in its adoption service.[3] Churches outside the mainstream have also been problematical: the Commission had a long dispute with the Plymouth Brethren, for example, before persuading its congregations in 2014 to commit themselves to 'Christian compassion' when disciplining their members and to make their meetings more open to the public.[4] The regulator also had a long court battle with Jehovah's Witnesses and found 'serious' failings in the safeguarding of young people in one of its congregations.[5]

But it's also become clear in recent years that all charities, whatever their cause areas, have become increasingly vulnerable to potential risks and criticism on a number of fronts. Two of these are fundraising and campaigning, which were examined in Chapters 2 and 3. Three more – governance, transparency and the all-important question of independence – will be discussed in the final three chapters. This chapter, however, looks first at two major reviews of the state of the voluntary sector, and at the content of government policy towards it, at the start of the third decade of the 21st century.

In the first two decades there was rapid change, expansion and diversification of the sector, accompanied by much controversy and criticism. There were the creation of new legal forms, changes in legislation and regulation, a growth of social enterprise and the expansion of public service delivery by charities. Many of the changes stemmed from the way a sympathetic Labour government between 1997 and 2010 took forward much of the agenda of the seminal 1996 report of the Commission on the Future of the Voluntary Sector, entitled *Meeting the Challenge of Change: Voluntary Action into the 21st Century*.[6] When the Coalition and Conservative governments after 2010 backed away from such close engagement during the years of austerity after the financial crash, and the sector stumbled into a number of scandals, the feeling grew among sector organisations and concerned politicians that it was time to take stock again: not one but three major inquiries were set up.

The first of these was conducted by a committee of the House of Lords, chaired by the experienced voluntary sector specialist Baroness (Jill) Pitkeathley, and produced a report in March 2017 entitled *Stronger Charities for a Stronger Society*.[7] Like all reports from cross-party committees, it was constrained by the need to find common political ground, but it nonetheless reached 100 conclusions and made 43 recommendations. It welcomed the updating of the *Charity Governance Code* and its endorsement by the Charity Commission; it said more should be done on trustee training and diversity; payment of trustees should remain exceptional; allowing time off work for trusteeship should be considered; impact reporting should be boosted; payroll giving and volunteering should be promoted; and most charities needed to raise their digital game.

The report was at its most robust in its warning of the damage to charities if the Charity Commission went ahead with a plan to charge them for regulation; in its recommendation that trustees should serve no longer than nine years; and in its strictures on the commissioning of public services from charities. It said public bodies that commissioned services from charities should be sure to provide for their core running costs; that contracts should run for periods long enough for charities to plan properly; and that commissioners should have to 'account for' rather than just 'consider' social value in their decisions. It also said the government should soften the Lobbying Act (see Chapter 3) and argued that government support for social impact bonds – an attempt to attract more private finance into service delivery by charities – was 'disproportionate to their potential impact'.

The Lords committee also struck a blow for campaigning by charities:

> ... advocacy is a central part of their work and a sign of a healthy democracy. Whilst charities are quite

properly regulated in their campaigning activities, particularly at election times, any new regulation or guidance should clearly recognise that advocacy is an important and legitimate part of their role and be set out in clear and unambiguous language.

Civil Society Futures

The second inquiry was conducted by a varied group of researchers and experts, funded by a number of charitable grant makers.[8] Civil Society Futures took a different approach from that of the Lords committee, concentrating less on what the government might do and more on the changes that civil society might make to itself. It gathered evidence from usual sources, such as the government, regulators, umbrella groups and large charities, but its main focus was on the information gained by taking what it called 'deep dives' into nine places around the country. 'Some inquiries end with a list of specific recommendations, usually addressed to other people,' the inquiry's chair, Dame Julia Unwin, wrote in the foreword. 'This one ends with an urgent call for us all to behave differently in order to meet the challenges of the next decade.'

The report, published in November 2018, presented a comprehensive analysis of the context for civil society in the second decade of the 21st century: inequality of income and wealth, the economic gap between regions, the rise of the gig economy, the retreat of the state, cuts in local authority funding, declining wealth and opportunity for young people, a rise in loneliness, changes in religious and secular practice, the decline of traditional media, the growth of online activism, populism and political polarisation, and increasing environmental stress, including climate change.

To this formidable tally the report added its research findings on the questions that concern people involved in civil society organisations: power and powerlessness; the importance of place, identity and belonging; the conflict between work and volunteering; and deficiencies in the way civil society is currently organised. 'The big message from the many hundreds of discussions we have held and submissions we have received,' it concluded, 'is that the big role for civil society in the coming years is to generate a radical and creative shift that puts power in the hands of people and communities, preventing an "us and them" future, connecting us better and humanising the way we do things'.

The report also asserted that 'civil society is political: we will challenge those in power – even if they fund us – and work with others to fundamentally change systems of inequality and powerlessness'. But its main thrust was for a comprehensive culture change across civil society itself, exhorting everyone to improve by following an agenda led by idealistic, high-level principles. Its demands of government were relatively few, which is perhaps encouraging for those who think that the less the sector has to do with the government, the better, not least for the sake of the sector's independence.

What was the response to these two inquiries? The government took nine months to respond to the Lords committee's report, playing a dead bat to nearly all the recommendations, which Pitkeathley described as 'disappointing'. On the Unwin report there was no published comment from ministers, but at least one aspect of it found favour with the chair of the Charity Commission, Baroness Stowell, who said its findings 'echo the Commission's: namely that change is needed if civil society is to reach its potential and counter the forces of division and disaffection'.[9] Andrew Purkis, a former board member of the Charity Commission and former charity chief executive, called the Unwin report 'a polemic – passionate, interesting, but flawed': he took issue with its description of itself as 'an urgent call for us all to behave differently' and criticised an 'untenable level of generalisation'.[10]

The third inquiry, the Law Family Commission on Civil Society, was launched at the end of 2020 to spend two years conducting research into 'how best to unleash the full potential of the UK's civil society'.[11] Chaired by the former cabinet secretary Lord (Gus) O'Donnell, financed by the Law Family Charitable Foundation and run by the charity Pro Bono Economics, it had 17 members with a wide range of experience. Using one of the government's three-word slogans, O'Donnell said: "It is essential all parts of society are involved in the conversation and working as one if the UK is to build back better from the COVID crisis. If we leave even one sector out, attempts to create inclusive growth will fail."

Government strategies

In August 2018 – 18 months after the Lords committee report, but three months before the Unwin report – the civil society minister Tracey Crouch MP (the sports minister upon whom this extra brief had been loaded in 2017) launched a fresh strategy under a title that reflected the language of the then prime minister, Theresa May MP: *Building a Future that Works for Everyone.*[12] Perhaps the most definite part of the document concerned the Lords committee's recommendation for all public sector commissioners to 'account for' social value when awarding contracts to the voluntary sector, as opposed to just 'considering' it; government departments would be expected to do this, said the strategy (while making no mention of what local authorities should do). It also pledged £90 million for an initiative to get disadvantaged young people into work, said the government was trying to release £20 million from inactive charitable trusts for use by community organisations, and endorsed a number of existing commitments, including the training of 3,500 community organisers by 2020 (see Chapter 8).

On the thorny question of campaigning, the document contained no proposal to tone down the Lobbying Act or gagging clauses in contracts. Instead it asserted that 'the government is determined that charities and social enterprises should be fully confident in their right to speak in public debates and to have a strong role in shaping policy and speaking up on behalf of those they support'. The word 'determined' reads oddly in the context, in the sense that it implies that the confidence of charities is somehow in the gift of the government: otherwise, few would find fault with the statement and its apparent support for the advocacy role of charities.

The strategy went on, however, to draw a distinction between campaigning generally and campaigning by charities that receive public money. 'It is right that we have government grant standards which prevent taxpayers' money being spent on political lobbying,' the strategy said. 'However, simply being in receipt of taxpayers' money should not inhibit charities from making their voices heard on matters of policy and practice.' This formulation appears to draw a distinction between two activities that might in practice be difficult to separate: 'political lobbying' on the one hand, and 'making their voices heard on policy and practice' on the other. Alternatively, the wording may have been intended to mean that funded organisations *can* make their voices heard, provided that they demonstrably avoid using any of the funding in the process.

Commenting on the strategy, Unwin chose a positive interpretation of this section, writing that 'it – rightly – defends the role of civil society groups in campaigning and raising concerns, including when they receive government funds: which is key if citizens are to have a voice'.[13] She also welcomed the strategy's recognition of the sense of alienation in local communities that her own inquiry uncovered, and of the role civil society would have to play in social renewal. Giving people greater control over their lives through the kind of 'deliberative democracy' mooted by the strategy would involve Whitehall giving up some real power, she wrote, but she added that the feelings of alienation in the country could not be blamed entirely on the government: 'If government decisions have felt far too remote for most people, Britain's leading charity and voluntary sector organisations have almost all been almost entirely absent from the communities we've spoken to.'

Others were less positive about Crouch's new strategy. Steve Reed MP, then the Labour Party's civil society spokesman, called it "little more than a tick-box exercise to cover up the government's total neglect of the sector".[14] Some in the charity world were equally dismissive, while others were unsure, including Vicky Browning, chief executive of Acevo. She blogged that the document touched on a lot of relevant questions but was not particularly inspiring and contained few commitments: 'The crucial question, and the one that we don't yet have an answer to, is whether the strategy is just warm words designed to placate, or the beginning of a real shift in the relationship between civil society and government. I am cautious.'[15]

Progress was inhibited by ministerial changes and the general political turmoil involved in Brexit. Three months after launching her strategy, Crouch resigned as a minister in a dispute over gambling, which was another part of her extensive brief. Her resignation was a protest at the delay in implementing a decision to reduce the maximum stake in fixed-odds gaming machines from £100 to £2. She was replaced by Mims Davies MP, who was replaced in turn in July 2019 by Diana Barran, made a life peer the previous year as Baroness Barran, who stood out from most of her predecessors because of her extensive experience in the charity world. After an early career in investment banking, she worked for the research body New Philanthropy Capital before founding SafeLives, a domestic abuse charity, in 2004. She was its chief executive until 2017 and served as a trustee of Comic Relief and the grant-making Henry Smith Charity.

In an interview soon after her appointment she said she had three priorities: building more resilient communities by engaging civil society organisations in healing divisions "whether those are Brexit-shaped divisions or religious, ethnic, generational, class or whatever they might be"; refreshing the government's approach to young people; and improving the commissioning process, using the Social Value Act to best effect.[16] She said she was developing a forward plan that would "give local people a sense of agency in what is delivered in their communities".

Barran's priorities picked up the theme of social value in commissioning from the 2018 strategy and reflected the emphasis in the strategy and the Civil Society Futures report on empowering local communities. But her remit, although not as wide as that of Crouch, extended beyond civil society to youth and social action, loneliness, all DCMS business in the House of Lords and the Government Inclusive Economy Unit. In her first months, loneliness appeared to be a priority, including the launch of a £2 million fund for measures to alleviate it. Early in 2020 she also launched a consultation on the prospects of extending an unclaimed assets scheme that benefits charities to insurance, pension schemes and investment funds. But at the time of her appointment there was already disappointment in the sector about the lack of progress with the strategy, and at the start of 2020 few people familiar with the affairs of charities and voluntary organisations thought that the 'real shift' mentioned by Browning was in the offing, despite Barran's evident suitability for the charities job.[17]

A call for more localism

When Boris Johnson became prime minister in July 2019 his initial preoccupation with Brexit seemed to preclude any significant change in the government's relationship with the sector. After the coronavirus crisis struck and the government responded to the charity sector's estimated income shortfall of £4 billion with a fund of only £750 million – more than a quarter of it earmarked for hospices – one commentator, Joe Saxton of the research consultancy nfpSynergy, took it as fresh evidence of the political powerlessness of charities: 'This powerlessness stems partly from a lack of awareness of the indispensable and ubiquitous role that charities play in society by those in power.'[18] But in June 2020 the Prime Minister set up yet another inquiry, this time by Danny Kruger MP, who had won the constituency of Devizes for the Conservatives the previous December.[19] He is the co-founder and former chief executive of the criminal justice charity Only Connect, and his brief was to work with Barran on how volunteers, community organisations, faith groups, charities and social enterprises could contribute to the recovery from coronavirus and to the government's 'levelling up' agenda.

When the report, *Levelling Up Our Communities: Proposals for a new Social Covenant*, was published in September 2020, it appeared only on Kruger's own website, not on the government portal gov.uk.[20] It was accompanied by a letter from Prime Minister Johnson thanking Kruger for his 'comprehensive and hugely ambitious report' containing 'many exciting ideas which are actively being considered by DCMS'.[21] But there was no official response to it from the government and the general sector reaction was muted: Jay Kennedy, director of policy and research at the publishing and research charity the Directory of Social Change, said it inspired a sense of 'meta-policy-deja-vu'.[22] Propositions that had been made before included an enhanced role for charities in designing public services, reforming how public services are commissioned, more match-funding from the Treasury for private philanthropy, and the revival of councils for voluntary service to support local charities. Even the policy proposals that Kennedy considered the most interesting – two new multi-million-pound funds to help communities recover from the impacts of the coronavirus restrictions – were to be drawn partly from dormant insurance accounts in the same way that £1.2 billion from dormant bank accounts was released to certain charitable causes in 2008.[23]

However, more original ideas included a volunteer passport system, a 'probation' period for new charities and a more local distribution model for the National Lottery Community Fund. Kruger summed up:[24]

> Britain's social model suffers from centralisation and silos. Too many services delivered in communities answer not to local people or their representatives, but to hierarchies centred in Whitehall … Like all the recommendations in this report, the intention is to allow a greater diversity of local practice, with more freedom for communities to innovate.

But therein lay the most likely reason for the apparent absence of overt political support for the document: the Johnson administration had demonstrated its preference for centralised rather than local power, and the likelihood was that most of Kruger's recommendations would remain ambitions. In the foreseeable future, the relationship between the voluntary sector and the government was likely to continue to be problematic and restrictive, both generally because of the Lobbying Act and specifically through restrictive clauses in the often underfunded contracts with charities that deliver public services. In this context, the continuing challenge for charities in their relations with government was likely to be continued protection of their independence, which is considered in the final chapter.

Charities reforming themselves

Perhaps the most positive developments for the sector between 2015 and 2020 were in the way it started to reform itself, both under pressure from government and the Charity Commission as a result of scandals over fundraising and Oxfam, and on its own initiative in response to other concerns and controversies. The government tightened the law and stood ready to impose statutory regulation on fundraising after the Olive Cooke fundraising affair, but the new Fundraising Regulator was instead set up in 2016 on the basis of self-regulation, working with the co-operation of the sector. The creation of the regulator, combined with the effect of the EU's General Data Protection Regulation which came into effect in May 2018, meant that charities that used to overstep the boundaries of good fundraising practice became more respectful towards donors and more careful about their use of data. In 2016 and 2017 the Information Commissioner's Office (ICO) had fined 13 charities a total of £181,000 for data security breaches, but early in 2020 Elizabeth Denham, UK Information Commissioner, said she thought charities had improved significantly.[25] She told a conference:

> "What I see in the charitable sector and what I hear from my colleagues at the Fundraising Regulator and the Charity Commission, is that the sector takes data protection seriously, and that you've moved forward in putting in place practices that are as much ethical as they are legal to ensure that your donors' data is accounted for and is used in a fair way."

There was also progress on the question of ethics more generally. After the Oxfam and Save the Children scandals in 2018, the NCVO asked Dame Mary Marsh, former chief executive of the NSPCC, to produce a code of ethics for the sector generally. She formed an advisory group of charities of various sizes, produced a draft for consultation and in 2019 published *Charity Ethical Principles*, a succinct six-page document with four key headings – putting beneficiaries first, integrity, openness, and the right to be safe.[26] Compliance is voluntary, and Marsh said that the code was an overarching framework to guide decision making, good judgement and conduct: 'Trustees in particular will find it helpful to make reference to the principles when faced with difficult decisions. The principles could also be useful to review the application of the *Charity Governance Code*, and of the specific code of conduct that any charity has.'

The *Charity Governance Code* that Marsh mentions began life in 2005 but was revised extensively after some of the governance controversies mentioned in Chapter 2, including the Cup Trust affair and the collapse of Kids Company. A steering group of seven organisations, chaired by Rosie Chapman, a former senior official at the Charity Commission, came up in 2017 with a number of significant changes to earlier versions of the Code.[27] For example, the Code now says that charities are expected to review the performance of the board and individual trustees annually, and that in larger charities this process should be conducted by an outside evaluator every three years; that arrangements with trading subsidiaries should be reviewed regularly; that trustees should not serve more than nine years unless there is good reason; and that charities should consider questions of experience and diversity when recruiting trustees.

The Charity Commission endorsed the Code – which, like the code of ethics, is voluntary – and withdrew its own document titled *The Hallmarks of an Effective Charity*. 'The bottom line is, good governance is no longer an optional extra,' blogged Sarah Atkinson, then director of strategy, policy and communications at the Commission. 'It's essential to charities' effectiveness and probably their survival too. Charities need to be able to demonstrate that they take it seriously, allowing it to change the way they operate.'[28] After a consultation, the Code was 'refreshed' in 2020 to spell out that policies on equality, diversity and inclusion should include agreeing plans, setting targets and monitoring progress; and that charities should make clear how anyone in contact with them could raise safeguarding concerns.[29]

The next chapter goes further into questions of governance, including whether a system of unpaid volunteer trusteeship is fit for purpose in larger charities, whether the increasing responsibilities of trusteeship are making recruitment more difficult, and the vexed question of board diversity.

20

Charity governance:
fit for purpose?

People rarely seemed to worry much about the details of charity governance until well into the present century. *Taken on Trust*, a report by the NCVO and the Charity Commission in 1992, indicated that up to a third of charity trustees did not understand their legal responsibilities, or even know that they were trustees.[1] Then, as now, the vast majority of charities had no paid staff and were both governed and run by their trustee board, so the demarcation between governance and management was virtually non-existent in most of the sector. Even in larger charities with voluntary boards of trustees governing paid executive teams, many boards were collectives of retired White men with a relaxed approach to governance. Important functions such as strategic planning, stewardship, performance monitoring, managing stakeholder relationships and ensuring legal compliance were seldom on the agenda.

Diversity was and remains a particular problem. There is growing acceptance that diverse boards make better decisions, but research has consistently shown that charity boards generally are short of women, the young, people from minority groups and those with disabilities. In 2017, 86% of the UK population was White, but 92% of charity trustees were White, as were 99% of trustees of grant-making foundations.[2,3] One study by a recruitment agency found that 34 of the 100 biggest UK charities had entirely White boards and senior leadership teams.[4] Charity boards clearly have some way to go in reflecting the proportion of the population that identifies as being from a

BAME background. Various proposals have been made to improve recruitment from minority groups, such as an end to word-of-mouth recruiting, targeted advertising of vacancies and payment of board members. Progress has been slow, however, despite commitments to action by a number of individual charities and some of the sector's representative bodies.

A turning point in charities' approach to governance was the collapse of Kids Company in 2015. The question of checks and balances exerted by its board over its chief executive, Camila Batmanghelidjh, meant that governance was thrust into the spotlight, and suddenly trustees all over the land were searching out *The Essential Trustee*, the Charity Commission's key guidance: the evidence of the chief executive of Nucleus Arts (see Chapter 11) bears out this point. Politicians and the media were suddenly very interested in how charities ran themselves. Questions were also asked about the supervisory role of trustees in fundraising charities after the death of the 92-year-old poppy seller Olive Cooke whose suicide sparked uncomfortable revelations about the extent to which many charities were swapping lists of supporters and chasing prospective donors for money (see Chapter 2).[5] With hindsight, these two major scandals in 2015 were wake-up calls for charity boards: as Margaret Casely-Hayford, then chair of ActionAid UK, wryly told the NCVO Trustee Conference in 2015, governance had become "the new black".[6]

Not long before, the Charity Commission itself had faced criticism from the NAO and MPs in the PAC over its woeful handling of the Cup Trust Gift Aid affair and its performance generally.[7,8] It responded with a flurry of new or updated guidance documents, with the result that trustees by 2020 were expected to have regard to 50 of them, mostly about governance, plus 140 'guidance notes'.[9] In the Charities Act 2016 the regulator was also given new legal powers allowing it to remove and disqualify trustees and to issue them with official warnings.

The dubious tactics employed by some fundraising organisations also led to a government review, an investigation by the ICO and a tightening up of the rules around fundraising, including the establishment of a new regulator, the Fundraising

Regulator.[10,11,12] Crucially for trustees, they were required by the 2016 Act to give a detailed account in their annual report of their charity's fundraising policies, which many in the past had left to the executives.

On top of these new regulatory requirements, from 2017 trustee boards were also, as described in the previous chapter, encouraged to benchmark themselves against the updated *Charity Governance Code* – drawn up independently of the Charity Commission but endorsed by it; two years later, the NCVO published *Charity Ethical Principles*, cited in the previous chapter. Add to these the compliance requirements from other regulators, such as the CQC, Ofsted and the Health and Safety Executive, not to mention HM Revenue and Customs, and it's hard to see how charity boards have time to focus on anything but compliance. When a bid by the Official Receiver failed in the High Court early in 2021 to disqualify the trustees of Kids Company as company directors, the judge said: 'It is vital that the actions of public bodies do not have the effect of dissuading able and experienced individuals from becoming or remaining charity trustees.'[13]

As more regulation and guidance has been heaped upon trustees, their role has become correspondingly more onerous, with seemingly little regard for the fact that they are almost always unpaid and usually meet monthly at most, and more likely every two or even three months. The Commission's *Essential Trustee* seeks to reassure charities that regulation rests on voluntarism, and implies that leeway will be given to erring trustees who can show they have done their best to understand and act on their responsibilities; nevertheless, the rush of new material remains a formidable prospect for trustee boards.

Many boards assume they are on top of matters, but this is not always the case. Research by the Commission in 2017 found that 82% of trustees questioned said they recognised their legal obligations – a huge improvement on the responses from their counterparts back in 1992.[14] But, when asked about specific duties, many turned out to be much less knowledgeable than they thought they were.[15] Separately, the Fundraising Regulator found that only 40% of charities were fully compliant with the fundraising reporting requirements of the Charities Act

2016, and published new guidance early in 2020 to help them improve.[16]

Failings of governance continued, despite the renewed focus. In June 2020, for example, the Charity Commission published a statutory inquiry report into a school and children's home run by the blindness charity RNIB.[17] Part of the RNIB Pears Centre for Specialist Learning provided care for children with complex needs and was therefore registered with the CQC. In 2017 and 2018, serious issues were identified by Ofsted and the CQC and various reviews were instigated. These found that the Centre operated with too much independence from the main charity, was resistant to criticism, provided poor staff training and made frequent errors in medication.

The Commission report said that 'some beneficiaries suffered harm or distress and they and their families were badly let down by RNIB'. In part, it blamed the RNIB's 'broader corporate governance, which did not adequately address the complexity, scale, nature and associated risks of the charity's activities and disparate group structure'. At the time, half of the trustees were elected and the charity's constitution stated that 75% had to have a sight impairment. One independent review recommended simplifying the charity's governance and making it easier to recruit trustees on the basis of their skills. Helen Stephenson, chief executive of the Commission, said:[18]

> "This is one of the worst examples we have uncovered of poor governance and oversight having a direct impact on vulnerable people. A catalogue of serious failings were allowed to occur, because the charity's governance was simply too weak for the trustees in charge of the charity to do the job that beneficiaries needed them to do."

RNIB has since recruited new trustees, including a safeguarding lead, as well as several new executive directors. In 2018 the charity had already announced plans to shut the Pears Centre, and since then it has also committed to transfer of all its regulated care services to other providers.

The existing governance model

Charities come in all shapes and sizes, and yet a single model of governance continues to prevail. The feeling has grown, however, that this model is no longer fit for purpose in large, complex organisations. One of the main criticisms is that legal responsibility for what the charity does is taken by a board of volunteers who can never be as close to the day-to-day operation as the executive team, and so can never entirely assure themselves that the organisation is complying with all the rules and regulations. The senior executives can be excluded from the ultimate decision making, despite their much deeper knowledge of the organisation and its activities – which can feel highly disempowering for those executives. Alternatively, the executive leaders may do all the decision making outside the boardroom and then bring their plans to the trustees, who don't have the capacity to challenge them and simply rubber-stamp their decisions.

Some governance experts believe that some of these frustrations can be eased by adopting a unitary board model, where one or more of the executives (usually the chief) joins the trustee board, acquiring voting rights and the same legal duties and responsibilities as the other trustees. Unitary boards are common in both the public and private sectors, where all members, whether executive or non-executive, are usually remunerated. In the charity sector, trustees are not usually paid for being a trustee, so if a charity does have a unitary board, volunteer board members generally serve alongside one or two trustees who are paid for their executive role but not their trustee role.

Charities can appoint an employee to the trustee board without obtaining consent from the Charity Commission, but as soon as they want to offer a pay rise to that staff member they must seek authorisation from the Commission, unless the power to do so is already in the charity's governing document. The regulator will want to be satisfied that having the employee on the trustee board is in the best interests of the charity and that the potential conflicts of interest, such as their pay, are properly managed.

Paying trustees for being trustees is debated from time to time. Under charity law, trustees cannot derive any private benefit from their trusteeship; they can claim reasonable expenses but can't be paid for being a trustee unless the charity's governing document specifies it, or the charity gets permission from the Charity Commission or the courts. The Commission's *Taken on Trust* research in 2017 found that only 1.6% of respondents said that their charity was permitted to pay trustees.[19] Some sector figures have argued that being allowed to pay trustees at will would improve the diversity of boards by opening up trusteeship to people from a broader range of socioeconomic backgrounds; others contend that it would be a further risk to public trust and confidence in the sector by adding fuel to the accusation that charities spend too much on 'overheads'. Also, remuneration provides no guarantee of effective governance: there is no shortage of commercial sector governance failures where the culprits were being paid handsomely.

Alternative models of governance

So what options are proposed by those who claim the current model is not working? One is put forward by Philip Kirkpatrick, a partner at the law firm Bates Wells. After scandals at Oxfam and Save the Children (described in the next chapter), he argues that the governance model for large charities needs radical reform.[20] "No one can look at what is demanded of part-time, unpaid, non-executive trustees of complex operational charities and say it is fair or appropriate that those trustees are held to account for everything the charity does," he says. "It is time to recognise realities and offer a new model."

Under his proposed 'assured unitary governance' structure, a charity above a specified size would have an entirely paid unitary trustee board, comprising its senior executive team – chief executive officer (CEO), finance director, director of fundraising and so on – plus an independent chair and one other non-executive member. The structure would be similar to that of most commercial companies, but with the addition of a secondary or 'assurance' board of around six people, comprising or drawn from the members of the charitable company or charitable incorporated organisation, depending on the constitution of the charity. (These would be the members in a company law sense – the owners of the corporate entity – rather than members in the sense of people who pay to join charities such as the National Trust or the RSPB and derive customer benefits.) Kirkpatrick outlines several options for how the assurance board could be chosen: appointment by the trustee board; appointment by a wider membership; appointment by the assurance board itself – or a combination of these.

This entirely unpaid assurance board would have certain powers and responsibilities, such as approving the appointment of the two non-executive trustees and their pay and benefits, but would not be legally responsible for the governance or management of the charity. It would be consulted on strategy, but would have only limited powers, and no legal responsibility if things should go wrong. The ultimate legal responsibility would rest with the paid trustee board.

If the assurance board comprised all the members of the charitable company they would have extra powers, including the power to remove and replace trustees, change the articles of association and wind up the charity. This balance of power, Kirkpatrick suggests, should convince the paid trustees to give due consideration to the views of the assurance board. "It would, at the very least, be wise to seek their views on the strategy," he says. "It could even be a requirement."

Kirkpatrick argues that such a system would keep voluntarism at the heart of the charity, in the form of the assurance board, without making volunteers legally liable. It would not be appropriate to all charities, but should be available to large, complex organisations.

Another alternative model featuring a separate volunteer body that advises the legally constituted board of trustees is favoured by Cliff Mills, a lawyer from Anthony Collins Solicitors who specialises in co-operatives.[21] He agrees with Kirkpatrick that the governance model of most large charities is under stress because the people with the greatest knowledge and understanding of the day-to-day operations are not part of the body that carries the legal and constitutional authority for it. But he contends that having a majority of executives on the board, as in Kirkpatrick's model, gives too much power to the executive team: "It is not their organisation, and they should always be located in a context of accountability where they have to take with them on any big decision a majority of other individuals who genuinely understand the issues at stake," he says.

Mills believes that the governance model for NHS Foundation Trusts provides a possible alternative template.[22] In essence, the governing board with legal responsibility for the organisation comprises the chief executive, one or two other executive directors and a majority of appointed non-executive board members, who may or may not be paid, depending on the sector, local culture and the needs of the organisation. The chair is always a non-executive director, and the non-executives have the power to appoint and dismiss the executive members of the board.

But significant power also resides with a separate, elected representative body, which consists of voluntary participants who have a keen interest in the organisation and how it is run, but may not have the requisite skills, experience or desire to run it.[23] It might be populated with members (in this case meaning those who have joined the organisation to derive some benefit), staff, service users or volunteers – anyone with a legitimate interest in the organisation. This body has real teeth – the power to appoint and remove the non-executive directors who form the majority of the board, to approve their remuneration and other terms and conditions and to approve forward plans. The board of trustees is also required to take into account the views of the representative body.

This separation of interested, motivated but generally unskilled people from the expertise-based, independent board has a number of advantages, Mills contends:

> "The reason you want people from a particular constituency, whether they be employees, tenants or members, is because you want their voice, their passion and their engagement. But you don't actually want them running the show, because they don't have the ability. And actually, most of them don't want to be running the show. If you try and do representativeness and competence in the same body,

it's either a bit of a fudge or it doesn't work. You can't elect competence – you have to appoint it. What you want on the board are non-executive people with equivalent experience and expertise to the executive – business people, legal people, finance people. They need to be on the same level professionally as the executive team, so they can really challenge them and hold them to account. Regulators are attracted to this approach, as it provides greater assurance."

A governance model based on this system has been operating for several years at two housing providers – Rochdale Boroughwide Housing and Merthyr Valleys Homes. These entities, according to Mills, are the UK's first tenant- and employee-owned housing associations, constituted as community benefit societies (bencoms, see Chapter 1; they are also recognised as charitable for tax purposes by HM Revenue and Customs, but have a regulator other than the Charity Commission). The model has also been introduced in a social care charity in Wales, Cartrefi Cymru, and a version of it is operating in youth services in Knowsley, Liverpool, in leisure services in Salford, at Learning Disability England and at the Active Wellbeing Society in Birmingham.

In defence of the status quo

Not everybody agrees that the existing charity governance model is outdated or inappropriate. John Williams is a former Charity Commission board member, former deputy chair of ChildLine and vice chair at the Association of Chairs, a membership body for chairs of trustee boards. He questions the need for a new model, arguing that the relatively rare scandals in the charity sector are a failure not of structure, but of culture, behaviour or simply poor compliance. "The rules and guidance are there – they just need to be followed," he says. Williams argues that charities are well aware that they no longer get a free pass from the media or society in general and are, in the main, stepping up to meet those greater expectations by addressing diversity, being values led and impact focused and improving their governance practices. He also refutes the suggestion that trustee boards are not sufficiently skilled or professional, pointing to CRUK's board as a good example: "Seven professors, past or present CEOs, a senior audit partner, a strategy director and a FTSE finance director – hardly well-meaning amateurs."

Williams contends that the lauded advantages of the CEO joining the trustee board – that they bring detailed knowledge, become directly accountable and feel more empowered – might sound beneficial but, in practice, should not be necessary.

> "They are already in the room at meetings, presenting and debating – if they have the support and respect of the board, as they should, there is no good reason for them to feel disempowered. The CEOs that I see in action know that the ultimate responsibility in practice lies with them, and their jobs and reputation are constantly on the line – the added motivation of legal liability seems a burden too far."

He also queries whether the representative board in Mills' model would ever use the powers it has to, say, remove board members. "In company law, shareholders as members have sanctions over board membership and pay, but they have generally proved pretty compliant about approving directors' plans. Would this really be a powerful tool in practice?" And he worries about the impact on board diversity, especially in Mills' model, where all trustees are recruited primarily for their functional skills and experience:

> "These new models would blur the centre of responsibility and the role of trustees to be guardians of the long-term well-being of their charity and its purpose, free from the conflicts of managing the day-to-day. Their detachment and distance are a strength, not a weakness. It's refreshing and heartening that thousands volunteer to do an unpaid yet hugely responsible role as part of their civic contribution, for the cause, not because it's an opportunity to be paid. Volunteering is still the bedrock of charitable

activity, and volunteer leadership symbolises and embeds it."

A view similar to that of Williams was vividly expressed in an advice column in 2016 by Peter Cardy, a former chief executive of Macmillan Cancer Relief.[24] Asked why the chief executive of a charity should not be on the board, he replied:

> "I explain my view to boards thus: 'If the s**t hits the fan, I lose my job; you go to prison.' It's crude, but the greatest value of a chief executive, responsible for performance, is giving detached advice and guidance to the trustees, who are responsible for governance. When the chief is also a director [trustee], roles are ambiguous and the chief executive's detachment is compromised."

★ ★ ★

No model of charity governance is likely to be perfect, and in such a heterogeneous sector one size is never going to fit all. But for large charities, particularly those with vital safeguarding responsibilities, those that bear the ultimate legal responsibility for an organisation really do need to have confidence that they know what it does. The example of the RNIB Pears Centre, as outlined earlier, was a case in point – making it mandatory for three-quarters of board members to have a sight impairment may have ticked all the boxes for service-user involvement in governance, but it proved to be inadequate for protecting vulnerable children. At the very least, there is a strong argument for greater flexibility to adopt alternative structures for charity governance, which could both provide greater assurance to regulators and give organisations a better chance of avoiding damaging mistakes and controversies.

21

Coming clean with the public

Charity Ethical Principles, the document published in 2019 by the NCVO and mentioned in Chapter 19, asserts that charities should create a culture where donors, supporters and the wider public can 'see and understand how they work, how they deal with problems when they arise, and how they spend their funds ... charities should be willing to share information about how they work, ensuring it is easily accessible'.[1]

This is often easier said than done. Charities live in fear of anything that will damage their reputation and pose a threat to their funding, and possibly to their very existence. They know that the word 'charity' arouses expectations in the public mind that they are somehow saintly and have higher standards of behaviour than the rest of society. Charities also know that donors generally don't want their contributions spent on salaries, pension contributions, comfortable offices and the cost of fundraising; they tend to want every penny to go to 'the cause' and every charity worker, metaphorically speaking, to wear a hair shirt.

The tendency therefore is for charities to keep an eye on these unrealistic public expectations in the way they present themselves to the world. This can mean disguising problems if possible, and being coy about salaries, overheads and fundraising costs. For example, some of the costs of direct mail, intended mainly to raise money, are often assigned in the accounts to education, which is more likely to meet approval than fundraising costs. This may be justifiable to a certain extent, but can be taken too far.

There is inevitably a tension between that tendency to control and massage information and the NCVO's exhortations to transparency. This chapter looks at two main channels through which charities communicate with their stakeholders and the public, assesses the extent to which they provide transparency and explores proposals and prospects for improvement. The two are interaction with the media and published accounts.

Partial stories: Oxfam and Save the Children

When a huge earthquake hit the impoverished country of Haiti in 2010, killing more than 220,000 people, one of the first charities to respond was Oxfam, the biggest and best-known UK aid organisation. It sent 100 people to the island, recruited 450 local staff and by the end of 2014 had spent almost £80 million providing food, water, shelter and sanitation. But Oxfam's involvement in Haiti is likely to be remembered not so much for its relief work as for a scandal that emerged seven years later, indicating that it had been less than frank with donors and regulators, and leaving it vulnerable to accusations of a cover-up. It was the sharpest controversy to strike the charity since its foundation, casting a shadow over the work of other UK charities involved in overseas aid or disaster relief.

The saga began when the charity was told in July 2011 that some staff were bringing sex workers into their accommodation.[2] A team was sent out from the UK to investigate, and the first employee to admit to paying for sex was the Haiti country director, Roland van Hauwermeiren, a Belgian. The charity informed DfID – a major UK funder of Oxfam's work – that an internal inquiry was under way.

Neither the report to DfID nor a brief media release mentioned prostitution, although Oxfam told the Charity Commission several weeks later that nine members of staff had been disciplined or dismissed for 'inappropriate sexual behaviour, bullying, harassment and intimidation of employees'.[3] The Commission responded that 'as Oxfam has taken appropriate action following the incident we have no regulatory concerns'; a second Oxfam press statement said six staff in Haiti had been involved in 'a number of instances of misconduct', but gave no detail.[4] The charity refused to answer any questions about this statement.[5]

At this point, the affair appeared, from the charity's point of view, to have been successfully dealt with. Offenders had been weeded out; DfID and other donors had been informed (albeit in non-specific terms); the Charity Commission had been told a bit more (including 'inappropriate sexual behaviour') but was content with the action taken; and the media had been kept in the dark about prostitution, which would inevitably have led to extensive publicity and all the damage that could do to Oxfam's reputation and donations.

Things were afoot, however, that led to the full details coming out later and enveloping the charity in scandal. Since a report in 2002, concern had been growing about sexual exploitation by aid staff, and agencies including Oxfam had drawn up stronger safeguarding policies.[6] But when *The Times* published a story in 2017 about allegations of sexual harassment within the charity, the Commission investigated and reported that Oxfam had 'more to do' on safeguarding.[7,8] Two months later, matters came to a head when the same newspaper published full details of what had gone on in Haiti in 2011.[9] The House of Commons select committee on international development launched an inquiry which, among many other matters, elicited evidence that Oxfam's decision to conceal the full nature of events in 2011 had been taken on legal advice.

Evidence to the inquiry from Dame Barbara Stocking, chief executive of the charity in 2011, shows that it considered whether to give full details to the regulator, donors and possibly the media, but followed advice that it should not.[10] She submitted an extract from a letter from an employment law specialist at the big London firm of solicitors Lewis Silkin, which said: 'we do have some concerns about some of the information that you are considering sharing externally. I think your option of taking a more "vague" approach is likely to be a safer way of handling this...'[11] Naming names 'would not be prudent. I think that there is a risk in relation to potential privacy/human rights claims that could arise if we name employees in the press in this way.' As for details of the allegations:

> Ideally, this would again be limited – perhaps simply refer to the fact that there have been various

allegations of 'wrongdoing' or some equally generic word ... On a wider note, I think that there are potentially privacy and defamation risks here, depending on the level of information that you give out and the fact that information may be put together in a way which results in a misleading impression.

Stocking made it clear to the parliamentary committee that she thought the decision to follow the lawyers' advice was justified because it averted the risk of criticism or legal challenge. But Caroline Thompson, chair of the charity's trustees from 2017 and a former BBC executive, took a different view.[12] She told the committee that in 2011 the charity should have said the allegations were about the use of prostitutes: "That should have been made clear in the report to the Charity Commission, the report to DfID and in the press release. It should, essentially, just have been more explicit." The committee highlighted accusations that Oxfam had failed to report in clear terms what had happened for fear of damage to its reputation and potential loss of funding.[13] The Charity Commission's inquiry report, published in June 2019, also said Oxfam should have been more full and frank in its reporting; it concluded there had been mismanagement and gave the charity an official warning.[14]

It seems clear that Oxfam could have decided in 2011 to prioritise its commitment to transparency over the cautious advice of its lawyers and give a more explicit account to the regulator, to DfID and to the public. Had it done so, it could have gone on the front foot, taken control of the story, emphasised the decisive action it had taken, minimised the damage and taken credit for transparency. This could have been done without naming names, thus obviating the risk cited by the lawyers that the people involved might launch a libel action, complain to an employment tribunal or claim infringement of their human rights.

By following the advice of its lawyers – which offered the less painful way forward, at least in the short term – the charity instead made itself a hostage to fortune, and when the story did come out it was the media and the charity's critics who took control of it, putting Oxfam on the back foot. With hindsight, it was an object lesson for charities in how not to handle the transparency and public relations aspects of a crisis.

The underlying issue was, of course, the serious question of the safeguarding of beneficiaries, deemed after some debate to include all Haiti citizens, rather than just those it was helping. But greater transparency can mean better safeguarding, as events indicated. Before Haiti, Oxfam was logging and reporting safeguarding incidents; in 2012, after Haiti, it appointed Helen Evans to the post of head of global safeguarding. She resigned three years later when the charity turned down her request for more resources, despite an internal survey showing instances of Oxfam staff being accused of sexual harassment and even rape.[15] It was only after the full story came out in 2018 that the charity embarked on 'a deeper transformation', tripling its safeguarding resources, setting up a confidential whistleblowing hotline and changing the way it dealt with references for staff.[16] Nonetheless, a follow-up inquiry by the international development committee of MPs in January 2021 said 'sexual exploitation and abuse continues to be a scourge on the sector'; and the committee chair, Sarah Champion MP, remarked that the sector had 'effectively become the last safe haven for perpetrators'.[17,18]

Coincidentally, the UK's other top aid charity, Save the Children, was caught up in scandal over safeguarding and transparency at the same time as Oxfam. The chief executive, Justin Forsyth, and the head of policy and advocacy, Brendan Cox, had left the charity in 2015 and 2016, respectively, but the full reasons only came out in 2018 in *The Daily Mail* and on BBC radio.[19] They had both been involved in the sexual harassment of women at Save the Children's London headquarters. An inquiry report by the Charity Commission concluded in 2020 that there had been mismanagement at the charity, which had also been 'unduly defensive' in response to media inquiries and had made statements that were 'not wholly correct'.[20] But the Commission gave it credit for overhauling its safeguarding and whistleblowing policies.

Events at both charities were grist to the mill of the anti-aid lobby. It was significant that the key stories were broken by right-of-centre newspapers, and the scandals formed part of the background to the decision by the government led by Boris Johnson in 2020 to merge DfID with the Foreign and Commonwealth Office, examined in Chapter 10.

How charities deal with the media

Only a small proportion of charities are big enough to employ anyone at all, let alone fund a media or public relations officer. But larger charities do have public and media relations departments, geared mainly to seeking good publicity for their successes. Some are effective at responding to criticism and controversy: a good example of this came towards the end of 2019, when *The Times* and *The Daily Mail* ran stories about the RNLI training lifeguards overseas and providing 'burkinis' for female Muslim trainees.[21] The charity stood its ground, pointing out that only 2% of its spending went overseas and helped to save many lives, mostly of children. It faced down a storm on Twitter, attracted the support of celebrities such as Gary Lineker and Stephen Fry and enjoyed a rise in donations.

But charities are sometimes ill prepared to cope when coverage turns sour, according to Becky Slack, an experienced journalist and public relations consultant specialising in the charity sector:[22]

> Many charities lack understanding as to what makes a good news story; are unable to provide strong, interesting and relevant case studies; and operate with slow and bureaucratic internal processes that result in missed deadlines. Most frustratingly of all, when the going gets tough, many have a tendency to stick their heads in the sand and hope it will all just go away (it won't).

Charities have sometimes seemed to believe that negative publicity stems from an information deficit – that the media and the public do not know enough about how charities work and the good they contribute to society, and that if they were better informed the negative stories would not see the light of day. The information deficit theory is not universally embraced, however: William Shawcross, the author who was chair of the Charity Commission of England and Wales from 2012 to 2018, said he thought the public had "a pretty good understanding of things that really do matter in charities" and that a lack of understanding by the public was "too often wheeled out as a convenient defence mechanism when charities are challenged".[23] Similarly, Polly Neate, chief executive of Shelter, told a conference in 2017 that charities did have some communications problems, but these were a symptom rather than a cause of the loss of trust.[24] "I do not think that people are losing trust in charities because they do not understand how charities work," she said.

To address the perceived deficit, however, the Understanding Charities Group was formed in 2014 and developed by a range of membership and umbrella bodies in the voluntary sector. One resulting initiative is Constructive Voices, a unit in the NCVO that acts as a link between charities that want to publicise their work and journalists on the lookout for subjects to write about or for experts to help with stories.[25] The unit attempts to promote a type of journalism that goes beyond problems to consider solutions. It also liaises with AskCharity, a website that has a large searchable database of charities and allows journalists to put in requests for case studies on a given subject: charities can respond if they fit the bill.[26]

Both organisations have had a measure of success. Constructive Voices, for example, lists on its web page more than 100 instances between 2016 and the end of 2019 of the media – national newspapers and the BBC as well as smaller, lesser-known organisations – picking up stories from it. Both media initiatives appear to be helping to make coverage of charity activity more normal than exceptional. There are also pages on the NCVO website intended to give the public more and better information about subjects including fundraising and accountability, and to help charities deal with the media. The page called 'Communications Toolkit', for example, advises charities to acknowledge concerns about senior pay, the amount of donations reaching the front line, fundraising costs and effectiveness. 'It's important that concerns are acknowledged and addressed before trying to engage audiences with a narrative about the positive role charities play,' it advises. 'You need to show that you "get it". Adopting a defensive tone or failing to acknowledge concerns will turn audiences off.'

All these initiatives may help to widen appreciation of the work of charities; but it's open to question how much they help with dealing with substantial controversies such as the Olive Cooke affair or the Oxfam scandal. The media, despite pressure for constructive journalism, is by nature and purpose more focused on things going wrong, and will invest more effort in that: journalists tend to want stories they can characterise as revelation and disclosure. This can engender a feeling among charities that the media is unrelentingly and unfairly negative, which can then result in a tendency to dismiss media reports as ill-informed, misguided or malicious.

When the media does discover wrongdoing or scandal in a charity, the painful truth is that each charity is usually on its own when facing questions about the details of the case. There are various sector and sub-sector membership and umbrella groups that might be able to help by explaining the wider background, such as the NCVO, Acevo, the Chartered Institute of Fundraising, the Charity Finance Group or the AMRC. But mistakes or misdeeds are often very specific to the charities in question: only they know the answers, and they usually have to face the music alone.

There has been some success in improving relations between the media and charities in respect of routine, positive or uncontroversial coverage, as the data from Constructive Voices indicates. There is less evidence that there has been an improvement in the way charities handle controversial or critical stories, when anxiety, defensiveness and lack of preparation and experience are more likely to dominate their response. Examples other than Oxfam include the NSPCC in 2019, which initially declined to comment, and then apologised, after it controversially cut ties with a transgender activist shortly after appointing her as an ambassador.[27] Charities under pressure can sometimes act as if their admirable motives and good work should excuse them from scrutiny or criticism when mistakes are made or things go wrong. This mindset can result in a refusal to answer questions, or in answers that conceal part of the story, or in an unwillingness to admit mistakes.

Conversely, charities should have the confidence to resist unfair or untrue criticism or smears, as in the case of the RNLI cited at the beginning of this section. As mentioned at the start of this book, there was a kind of open season on charities during the 2010s. And when the media gets it wrong, charities should make full use of the opportunities for redress, including complaints to the media organisation concerned and the Independent Press Standards Organisation.

What charities should never do, according to Becky Slack, is say 'no comment', in the hope that this will mean there will be no story.[28] Her advice is that charities should plan how to respond to a crisis and make sure they react quickly and decisively:

> There is a lot to be said for the phrase 'honesty is the best policy'. The truth will out eventually and will only come back to haunt you, which will make the situation much worse and possibly do irreparable damage to your brand and its reputation. Stick to the facts. Don't deliberately miss out certain information if it doesn't work in your favour, as this can be damaging … A lack of communication is a sure-fire way to build mistrust, suspicion and rumour.

A similar point was made by the Charity Commission in its report on sexual harassment at Save the Children UK, related above: 'A charity's reputation will usually be best served by being open, giving full and complete explanations and not making any statement which is open to criticism as being partial or incomplete.'[29]

The mysteries of charity accounting

A key part of transparency concerns finance: people are less likely to trust a charity and donate to it if they can't easily find and understand the key figures, or if the figures disguise matters that can be controversial, such as staff pay and fundraising costs. Improvements in charity accounting standards have been credited with helping trustees and funders, making it easier for charities to attract donations and enabling regulators to identify failings more easily.[30] But questions have been raised about whether charity accounts meet modern expectations, make sense to non-specialists and are sufficiently rigorous. The collapse of Kids Company was a factor in the change of mood: the charity's auditors had certified that it was a 'going concern' 11 months before it folded.[31]

Charities with income above £250,000 are required to follow the *Statement of Recommended Practice* (Sorp) for charities when they prepare their annual accounts.[32] The Sorp is issued jointly by the three charity regulators in England and Wales, Scotland and Northern Ireland, and follows *Financial Reporting Standard 102*, which applies to 'public benefit entities', issued by the Financial Reporting Council, the body that regulates auditors, accountants and actuaries in the UK. The Sorp is monitored by a committee, consisting mainly of finance and accountancy experts, whose principal function is to identify potential changes to the Sorp and advise the Sorp-making body (the three charity regulators).

It's a complex set-up, and the version of the Sorp that took effect in January 2019 runs to 216 pages and contains detailed instructions on how to record items ranging from staff remuneration to putting a price on historic buildings. Sorp-compliant accounts begin with the Statement of Financial Activities (Sofa), intended as 'a single accounting statement … prepared with the needs of the charity's stakeholders in mind'.[33] The Sofa often fits on a single page, but the full accounts can extend to 50 or 60 pages in a large charity, couched in terminology that the layperson might not easily understand.

A prominent critic of charity accounting is Joe Saxton, head of the research consultancy nfpSynergy and a member of the Sorp committee from 2014 to 2017. After he left, his company published *Sorped Out*, arguing that 'the public want clearer, more transparent and more accessible financial results from charities, and the current approach doesn't provide them'.[34] The consultancy's own research showed that the public were concerned about what happened to their donations, would never normally look at a 60-page annual report and wanted simpler, summary information.[35] The Charity Commission's research *Trust in Charities 2018* also found the most important factor, rated at 8.5 out of 10, was being 'transparent about where the money goes'.[36]

The Sorp-making body commissioned a review from Gareth Morgan, emeritus professor of charity studies at Sheffield Hallam University. His report in 2019 concluded that it was 'essential that the focus of the Sorp and the way it is developed are significantly changed to have stronger emphasis on public interest ... profound changes are now needed ... if the Sorp is to continue to be fit for purpose'.[37] The Sorp should take greater account of the needs of small charities, engage wider interest groups in its development, and produce 'an easy read for proxy users and those interested in the work of charities'; non-statutory or informal financial reporting in documents other than the formal accounts should be consistent with the main accounts, it added.

The report did not receive full backing from the Sorp committee at its meeting in July 2019: some members had 'significant reservations' and questioned 'the realism of the ideal that everyone should be able to understand "simple" annual reports and accounts produced by charities while at the same time requiring consistent and high quality finance reporting'; there was also opposition to 'the radical nature and appropriateness of some of the recommendations'.[38]

Nevertheless, the Sorp-making body responded with a plan to reduce the number on the Sorp committee and include four representatives of small charities, two from funders or donors, and two from 'sector commentators'.[39] It also decided to recruit seven 'engagement partners' to be continually consulted by the committee, including trustees, donors, academics and 'proxies for the public interest'. The aim was to create 'a framework that ensures that the accounts are not simply "true and fair" but that they are meaningful to users of charity reports and accounts, providing the information needed to underpin decision making by donors, funders and others interested in the work of the sector'. Early in 2020, the 14 members of the new committee were appointed, and the stakeholder groups recruited, with the aim of producing a new Sorp by 2022.

In the same year, nfpSynergy published *Show Me the Money*, which looked at 22 varied charities and found that in ten of them key figures were published only in the formal accounts.[40] Where key figures were reported on websites or in other publications, it found 'many examples of discrepancies between the formal accounts and the informal presentation of accounts'. Administration costs and staff pay, known to be a key concern of the public, could usually be found in the formal accounts, but were rarely among summary figures in other places.

The main focus of the research was fundraising costs, where comparisons can be complex because charities use a variety of fundraising methods, some of which are more expensive than others. The report argued that charities could be required to 'consistently unpack' the contents of the 'raising funds' expenditure line in the Sofa, using the headings of seeking donations and legacies, trading and retail, fundraising events and membership schemes: 'If these categories were then systematically used in summary figures outside of the accounts, this would mean a clearer definition ... and consistency in presenting it.' It was 'misleading and potentially confusing' to leave the costs of fundraising out of informal summaries of expenditure, and support costs and pay 'could be relatively easily extracted and summarised'.

The Morgan review and the ensuing proposals for change do not satisfy Saxton, who had pressed for the Sorp committee to be part of a new charity financial reporting board that would have strong representation of the public and donors and be modelled on the Fundraising Regulator:

> "I think the Morgan review has lots of good stuff in it. My problem is that the process has been handed back to the same team that managed it before. It needs drive and energy from a senior figure or figures to shake things up. At the moment financial regulation is completely in bed with the financial community. The Sorp members all have two hats on, which is a conflict of interest. When there's talk of changing something, they say, 'this would be hard for our clients or members', and so it doesn't happen. Everywhere else, the regulator and regulated are different: the Sorp acts in response to consultations

of the regulated. There's a strong parallel with fundraising. You might get change if something hits the headlines along the lines of the Olive Cooke incident. But the charity sector is not good at acting in anticipation of possible problems. It tends to change only when something goes hideously wrong."

Accountants focus more on conformity to international accounting standards. "When people squeal about the Sorp committee, they should really be squealing about the standards underlying the Sorp," says Don Bawtree, special adviser and former head of charities at the global accountancy firm BDO, and co-author of the 1,000-page *Charity Administration Handbook.* "The argument is about whether the Sorp is an accounting standard that fits in with this big panoply of standards that apply across the globe, or whether it is some kind of cottage industry for charities." Bawtree is sceptical about the extent of public pressure for simpler financial information:

> "I just don't think this interest exists that Joe Saxton is concerned about. It only comes out when people are presented with a list of choices by researchers and have to tick a box. Someone who gives £10 to Oxfam doesn't ask to see the accounts or read them. They're responding to the brand or to the child in the advert. When I give to a charity I do it because I know roughly what they do and I trust the people who are running it. And the bigger, more sophisticated donor *will* engage with the accounts."

Bawtree does think there are aspects of the Sorp that need reform. For example, the category of 'designated funds' could be abolished, he says, because it allows trustees to reduce the amount shown in a charity's free reserves by earmarking large sums for distant future expenditure, such as maintenance of buildings: this makes the charity appear less wealthy than it actually is and sharpens its fundraising call. More information could also be required about senior pay, he says, as recommended by the NCVO in 2014.[41] "Things like this could reduce the scope for window-dressing accounts, but they're not necessarily the kind of things Joe Saxton is going on about," says Bawtree.

At the time of writing, it remained to be seen what changes would be made by the restructured Sorp committee, with its new engagement partners. Bawtree fears that the changes might prove cosmetic and little will result, although he thinks the Sorp could become less onerous for smaller charities. More generally, he thinks that the pressure to simplify charity accounting contrasts with the corporate world, where events such as the collapse of the giant outsourcing company Carillion in 2018 prompted a more rigorous assessment of whether an organisation is viable.

Overall, it seems unlikely that a form of simple, standardised summary reporting could be devised that would permit meaningful comparisons across the sector: there are too many different types of charity, with widely varying business models and sources of finance. But that does not entirely invalidate the proposition – the form of summary reporting required could differ for various sub-sectors, for example. Nor does it weaken the case for charities to include figures on pay and fundraising in their informal summaries so that people do not have to decipher the formal accounts. Some accountancy professionals are scathing about proposals to make financial information about charities more accessible, but the final word rests with the regulatory bodies; and in 2020 larger charities remained vulnerable to the contention that they do not show a sufficiently clear and simple picture of their finances to the public whose support and donations they solicit.

22

The pursuit of independence

Concern about voluntary organisations' independence from government in the age of the welfare state was flagged up by Lord Beveridge in 1948.[1] 'The independence of Voluntary Action does not mean lack of co-operation between it and public action,' he wrote. 'Co-operation between public and voluntary agencies ... is one of the special features of British public life. But the term Voluntary Action does imply that the agency undertaking it has a will and a life of its own.'

As examined earlier in this book, restrictions on charity campaigning and the growth of public service delivery by the voluntary sector over more than half a century since Beveridge's remarks have contributed to a growing, if sometimes fluctuating, threat to that 'will and a life of its own'. In 2011 the Baring Foundation, a charitable grant-maker set up by Barings Bank years before it collapsed in the 1990s, funded a panel to monitor the independence of the sector, and its four annual reports made uncomfortable reading. The final report, in 2015, concluded that things had got worse year by year.[2]

> The voluntary sector's independent voice, freedom of purpose and action are being undermined by a negative climate. This includes the lobbying act, 'gagging clauses' in public service contracts, new restrictions on the ability of voluntary organisations to use the courts to overturn poor government decisions, truncated government consultations, commissioning and procurement for public services that does not support independence and diversity

in the voluntary sector; and weakened safeguards to protect the sector's independence. Some of these problems could be quite easily reversed but underlying attitudes also need to change – a more challenging task. It is becoming more common for government ministers and MPs to attack campaigning by the sector. Reports of self-censorship by voluntary organisations may be understandable but are no less worrying ... At the root of these threats to independence, we believe, is an implicit and growing view that the voluntary sector should be at the service of the state, rather than of its own independent mission.

In 2007, research by the Charity Commission had also concluded that the independence of charities involved in public services was compromised. Its report *Stand and Deliver* found that only 26% of charities that delivered public services agreed that they were free to make decisions without pressure to conform to the wishes of funders.[3] This is hardly surprising: national and local politicians often find it difficult not to try to control whatever they fund, or to tolerate much dissent from those that are funded: he who pays the piper calls the tune, in effect.

But the Charity Commission's research also looked at the independence from their funders of charities that are not involved in public services and found that it also was compromised, although not to the same extent. These are charities that decide for themselves what they would like to do and, unless they can raise sufficient funds from the public, seek funding from trusts, foundations and philanthropists. Fifty-five per cent of charities in this position felt free to make decisions without pressure to conform to the wishes of funders – a much higher figure than in the case of those delivering public services; put another way, however, nearly half of these charities evidently did feel pressure to align their priorities to those of non-statutory funders.

What this means in practice, and whether it is necessarily a bad thing, was addressed by one charity chief executive shortly after the Commission published its research and its then chair, Dame Suzi Leather, made a speech warning about loss of independence. Jeremy Swain, then chief executive of Thames Reach, a charity for the homeless, said that it was dangerous for charities not to respond to stakeholders:[4]

> "The danger of what she is saying is that it suggests you have all the answers and no one can challenge that. But funders have some very good ideas. The sector often starts with the assumption, which we know in our hearts is wrong, that we always know what is best for our beneficiaries. Of course the board should take the final decision. But it has to make sure the organisation is financially viable, and it has to do that with funders ... Let's ask funders some simple questions – 'what do you like about what we are doing? What can we do differently?' We do not have to use that, but we think the people that fund us have a pretty good idea of how to meet the needs of those people we are supporting."

Seventy per cent of the funding of Thames Reach came from statutory sources, and Swain later became deputy director of rough sleeping at the Ministry for Housing, Communities and Local Government.[5] This does not invalidate his point that charities should listen to others with relevant expertise, which they might not do if their funding was either raised from the public without strings attached or given by certain charitable trusts that are relatively unprescriptive about the use of grants. However, a funder's familiarity with a charity's cause area will vary from case to case, and, as a general rule, charities are much closer than funders to the needs of their beneficiaries.

The political independence of the Charity Commission

Another potential constraint on the independence of charities comes from the Charity Commission for England and Wales. The Commission regulates charities according to the law, as do its counterparts in Scotland and Northern Ireland; but it also issues guidance and policy documents, and makes pronouncements which are determined in part by leaders whose political impartiality has come into question. The report of the independence panel quoted above asserted that 'the political independence of the regulator is critical to an independent sector'.[6]

This question of the political independence of the Commission has become more pointed since the Charities Act 2006. Before then, it was run by a chief commissioner and up to four other commissioners – all civil servants, and two of them lawyers. But the Labour government at the time concluded that the Commission was insufficiently accountable to the public and other stakeholders, including charities themselves, and the Act brought in a new structure with a chair, a chief executive and a board of nine. The chair is chosen by the public appointments process, in which the final decision is made by a government minister.

The first occupant was Geraldine Peacock, formerly chief executive of Guide Dogs and the National Autistic Society, who was appointed without apparent controversy by the then home secretary, David Blunkett. When she stood down after 18 months, for personal reasons, she was succeeded by Dame Suzi Leather, whose experience in regulation included four years as chair of the Human Fertilisation and Embryology Authority. Leather did not relinquish her membership of the Labour Party, however, which led to accusations that she was a 'Labour career quangocrat' and the leadership of the Commission was becoming politicised.[7]

That impression was strengthened by the appointment of the author William Shawcross as Leather's successor in 2012 by the Coalition government of 2010–15. When the House of Commons Public Administration Committee narrowly backed his appointment by four votes to three, the dissenting members drew attention to his political views, including an article he had written before the 2010 election in which he had said 'only a vote for the Conservatives offers any hope of drawing back from the abyss'.[8]

This prompted concern in some quarters. The respected charity lawyer Stephen Lloyd came to the conclusion that 'the commission is being dragged into the political arena, which is completely inappropriate for a quasi-judicial body'.[9]

The NCVO put forward a variety of options for increasing the involvement of Parliament in appointing the chair of the Commission in order to 'distance the appointment process from party political influences and expand the power of parliament'.[10]

These concerns apparently fell on deaf ears, for in 2018 the government announced that the successor to Shawcross was Baroness Stowell of Beeston, who had briefly been leader of the House of Lords and a member of David Cameron's Conservative cabinet. This time the House of Commons Public Administration and Constitutional Affairs Committee voted unanimously against confirming her appointment, but they were brushed aside by the relevant minister at the time, Matt Hancock MP, "because I have known and worked with her, I knew she would do a brilliant job".[11] Stowell resigned the Conservative whip and became a cross-bench peer, but this did not mollify the critics. Perhaps the most telling intervention came from Andrew Hind, who had been chief executive of the Commission from 2004 to 2010:[12]

> Slowly but surely, over a series of four appointments, we have moved from the chair of the Charity Commission being selected on merit, to a situation where the job appears to be little more than a party political appointment in the gift of the prime minister.

The Commission and the independence of charities

What effect has all this had on the way charities are regulated and, crucially, on their independence? Some of the Commission's guidance emphasises how important it is for trustees to act independently of funders and stakeholders. On public service delivery, for example, it says: 'You and the other trustees should be able to decide for yourselves how to deliver the service. You should not be unreasonably influenced or directed by the public authorities you are working with. Charities must be independent, even if they receive all or most of their funding from government.'[13] The Commission also steps in when charities stray into party politics, as described in Chapter 3. In many ways, the Commission acts as a bulwark of charity independence.

There have been cases, however, when the courts have ruled that the Commission itself was infringing the independence of charities. As mentioned in Chapter 17, the Upper Tribunal found that the Commission, in effect, was usurping the role of trustees of charitable schools by prescribing too closely how they should provide public benefit. Another case came up in 2015, when the Commission chair was William Shawcross, in which he and some members of his board extracted an undertaking from the Joseph Rowntree Charitable Trust that they would never repeat their funding of a controversial campaigning organisation called Cage.[14] But in a judicial review before the Lord Chief Justice, the Commission was obliged to concede that it had no legal power to fetter the discretion of charity trustees in this way.[15] The case prompted a detailed revision of Commission guidance to charities about funding non-charities such as Cage.

But the effects of this case rumbled on. The Commission issued a statement during the Cage affair saying it expected trustees to use all funding 'in the way the public would expect'.[16] Shawcross added:[17]

> "Some people have questioned whether it is for the Commission to decide what is in the public interest, or what might damage public trust and confidence in charities. Of course it is. As regulator, we exist to regulate charities on behalf of the giving and volunteering public. Public trust is vital to charities. If this is under threat in any way, we must act."

Charities were left in some confusion about the meaning of 'in the way the public would expect', and how it was being related to the public interest, which is a complex legal concept, and public benefit, which is a fundamental principle of charity law. Duncan Shrubsole, director of policy at the Lloyds Bank Foundation, which has funded less popular causes such as sex workers and refugees, commented:[18]

> "Who is to deem what the public should expect? Foundations have got to be able to fund difficult

causes without thinking that the Commission is hovering over their shoulder, about to pronounce them as funding not what the public would expect. It's a potential big brother in the funding world."

Sir Stephen Bubb, at the time chief executive of Acevo, said it was worrying if the Commission thought its job was interpreting the public interest:[19]

> "That's not the job of a regulator. There's a big difference between ensuring that charities work for the public benefit and stretching that to interpret what's in the public interest. We could end up with a situation where the only causes that attract support are those that find favour with *The Daily Mail*."

Shawcross's successor, Baroness Stowell, continued the theme of "legitimate public expectation of charity" and how the Commission would "speak out more strongly to encourage the behaviour that people expect".[20] Eventually Jay Kennedy, director of policy and research at the Directory of Social Change, entered a protest: the first objective of the Commission in charity law was to 'increase public trust and confidence in charities', he wrote, but the Commission's interpretation of this had moved ever closer to following 'public opinion about charity' and was delivered in 'an insufferably patronising, moralising, hectoring, lecturing tone':[21]

> This mission drift has perhaps been most confused around public benefit, an historically contested (and confusing) but real concept in charity law. The commission's leadership now seems to be conflating it in practice with public opinion and public expectations, neither of which have any legal basis at all ... in fact the very existence of certain charities, their beneficiaries, their views and work may well be in conflict with public opinion – and that's OK. Charities are an instrument to yield public benefit, which may be unpopular but still charitable.

How much does all this matter in practice? One experienced advisor to charities says that the Commission leadership's talk about public expectations is mainly "PR spin and a sound bite", often in the context of criticism of charities in the media:

> "Commission case workers apply the public benefit test – you would never hear them talking about public expectations. And most charities just get on with what they're doing – unless, of course, they get caught in the crossfire. But the political aspect of appointing the chair makes charities vulnerable – it doesn't necessarily affect them, but it could."

Another charity expert says 'public expectation' is an idea manufactured in an age of populist politics from "a few surveys and focus groups. Whether charities brush it off or take it to heart will vary in different cases. I don't think most of them take much notice, but it does pile yet more stress on trustees."

Unlike her two predecessors, Stowell did not seek a second three-year term, from 2021, and at the time of writing her successor had not been announced. But her theme of regulation by public expectation is clearly a worrying notion for charities, some of which have been set up to take issue with conventional public expectations in their cause areas. It might also have some surprising results – defending asylum seekers might be seen as uncharitable by this yardstick, but so might Eton College. It is clearly more of a spectre than a reality, but the mood music from the Commission, like the Lobbying Act and the no-lobbying clauses examined in Chapter 3, has a potentially chilling effect nonetheless, particularly on charities and grant-makers working in controversial areas. The message from the top of the Commission has appeared to be that Lady Bountiful is looked on more favourably than the rebellious suffragette.

★ ★ ★

In summary, the strongest threat to independence comes when government or statutory agencies see charities that they fund as 'in service to the state', as expressed by the Baring panel and quoted at the start of this chapter. A crucial characteristic of charities is that they are not part of government or any other vested interest, and are often at odds with them. For this reason some charities decline to take any money from government. Public sector contracts are inevitably prescriptive, top-down and often influenced by politics, and charities that take them on inevitably risk a distortion of their mission. Examples include some of those that took part in the Work Programme and Transforming Rehabilitation, as related in Chapter 12.

Trusts, foundations or philanthropists that fund charities usually have particular themes or causes that they want to advance and will therefore impose conditions and restrictions. These may include stipulations about the scope of the project and how the money is used, and the nature and frequency of accounting and reporting. Charities have to consider whether those conditions and restrictions affect their independence to an unacceptable extent and drive them too far from their mission. The risk is that charities may sometimes drift away from their true purpose in the search for funding.

As for the Charity Commission, its leaders' political independence from the government may be called into question occasionally, and exceptional cases may come up from time to time, but in its guidance and day-to-day regulatory work it is in the main a guarantor of the independence of charities. The extent to which the pronouncements of its appointed leaders inhibit the independence of charities is hard to pin down, but they will probably pass most charities by.

Overall, the independence of charities is inevitably constrained to some extent by what government or charitable foundations will fund and what the public is prepared to give money to. This means that, in practice, independence is perhaps more an attitude of mind than an achievable reality. The difficulty comes in applying judgement and managing trade-offs to find the right balance, and the pitfall for charities is in making too many compromises and moving away from their mission. The biggest danger lies in looking upwards to government or funders for direction, or even inwards to staff, rather than outwards to their beneficiaries.

The challenge involved in protecting the independence of charities was summarised by the Conservative peer

Lord Hodgson in his review in 2012 of the workings of the Charities Act 2006, and his conclusion was just as relevant at the end of the decade:[22]

> Although it is part of the existing common law that charities must be, and be seen to be, free from the influence of Government or any other group, no more formal protection of that status exists. The sector must continue to be seen as more than an outlier to local or national government. How independence can best be promoted and safeguarded must be an important feature of any debate on the future of the sector.

Postscript

This book was all but finished when the COVID-19 pandemic landed in the UK. After March 2020 we watched with dismay as successive lockdowns and ensuing restrictions wreaked havoc on charities, cutting off fundraising revenues while also driving up demand for help and support. Charities suffered one body blow after another. The big organisations announced redundancies at an alarming rate: the BHF shed 300 jobs, the National Trust 1,200, Oxfam 200, the RSPCA 300, CRUK 500 – a quarter of its workforce. Less publicised cuts at charities with smaller workforces were inevitably a greater threat to their survival. Small charities with no workforce were either asking more of their volunteers or going into hibernation.

By the end of 2020 the total loss of jobs was expected to top 60,000 – more than 6% of the total charity workforce, or 1 in every 15 jobs. In June 2020, Pro Bono Economics predicted that the sector would suffer a funding shortfall of £10.1 billion in the second half of the year – a hole in income of £6.7 billion plus a rise in demand for services totalling £3.4 billion. This crisis is unprecedented in nearly two decades we have spent observing the voluntary sector: nothing has come close to such a huge change in such a short time. The austerity imposed by the Coalition government after the 2008 global financial crash destabilised many charities, but the effects were more gradual and less extensive.

Revising our text to incorporate the impact of the pandemic on charities has been to follow a moving target, with new stories emerging almost daily of fresh challenges and difficult decisions facing charity leaders. We have included accounts of heroic responses, particularly in volunteering, alongside stories of cuts and warnings about sustainability. There were rays of light such as the distribution of £200 million of public funds to more than 8,000 small and medium-sized charities, and media excitement about the late Captain Sir Tom Moore completing 100 circuits of his garden before his 100th birthday, gaining a knighthood and raising £39 million for the NHS.

As we finalised the chapters, several promising vaccines against coronavirus were beginning to be distributed, but government borrowing had reached its highest-ever level in peacetime and the country was facing the worst recession for 300 years. The Chancellor of the Exchequer warned that the problems were only just beginning: the economy had shrunk by 11% in 2020 and was not expected to recover for at least two years. Unemployment was predicted to rise to 7.5% of the workforce.

Some charities may well emerge from this crisis leaner and stronger; the large ones may benefit from the opportunity to restructure themselves and take forward some of the efficiencies and the greater use of information technology that were forced upon them in lockdown. Some charities that close may not be missed. Perhaps the most positive aspect of the crisis is that the community spirit and impulse for mutual aid that underpin charitable activity have either revived or thrived in many places around the country.

But small-scale voluntary activity is unlikely by itself to meet the need that will result from the oncoming recession and surge in unemployment that seems inevitable. For charities to continue, in harder times, to do the things they do best, some of which have been described in this book, they will need significant support from the government as well as from donors and volunteers.

Notes

Chapter 1

1 British Red Cross, *Trustees' Report and Accounts 2018* (www.redcross.org.uk/ about-us/how-we-are-run/our-finances/annual-reports-and-accounts).

2 Charity Commission for England and Wales website, *Charities in England and Wales – 31 December 2019* (https://apps.charitycommission.gov.uk/ showcharity/registerofcharities/SectorData/SectorOverview.aspx).

3 British Council, *Annual Report and Accounts 2018/19*, p 81 (www. britishcouncil.org/sites/default/files/2018-19-annual-report-final.pdf).

4 Charity Commission for England and Wales, *Guidance, Public Benefit: The Public Benefit Requirement*, 16 September 2013 (www.gov.uk/government/ publications/public-benefit-the-public-benefit-requirement-pb1).

5 National Audit Office, *Regulating Charities: A Landscape Review*, Fact Sheet (https://www.nao.org.uk/wp-content/uploads/2012/07/Regulating_ charities_facts_sheet.pdf).

6 Charity Commission for England and Wales, *Charity Types: How to Choose a Structure (CC22a)* (www.gov.uk/guidance/charity-types-how-to-choose-a-structure).

7 HM Revenue and Customs, *UK Charity Tax Relief Statistics 1990–91 to 2018–19* (https://assets.publishing.service.gov.uk/government/uploads/ system/uploads/attachment_data/file/811710/UK_Charity_Tax_Relief_ Statistics_Commentary.pdf).

8 National Council for Voluntary Organisations, *UK Civil Society Almanac 2020* (https://ncvo-app-wagtail-mediaa721a567-uwkfinin077j. s3.amazonaws.com/documents/ncvo-uk-civil-society-almanac-2020.pdf).

9 Pro Bono Economics website, 'Charities facing £10.1 billion funding gap over the next six months', 10 June 2020 (www.probonoeconomics. com/News/pres-release-charities-facing-101-billion-funding-gap-over-the-next-six-months).

10 Chime website (www.chimehealth.co.uk/about-chime).

11 Regulator of Community Interest Companies, *Annual Report 2017/18*, p 11 (https://assets.publishing.service.gov.uk/government/uploads/ system/uploads/attachment_data/file/727053/cic-18-6-community-interest-companies-annual-report-2017-2018.pdf).

12 Department for Business, Innovation and Skills, *A Guide to Mutual Ownership Models*, November 2011 (www.gov.uk/government/ publications/mutual-ownership-models-a-guide).

13   Social Enterprise UK, *Hidden Revolution: Size and Scale of Social Enterprise in 2018* (www.socialenterprise.org.uk/the-hidden-revolution).

14   Divine Chocolate website (www.divinechocolate.com/).

15   Community Dental Services website (https://communitydentalservices.co.uk/).

16   Henry James, preface to *The Tragic Muse*, New York, 1890.

17   National Audit Office, *Regulating Charities: A Landscape Review*, July 2012 (www.nao.org.uk/wp-content/uploads/2012/07/Regulating_charities.pdf).

Chapter 2

1   Sir Stuart Etherington, Lord Leigh of Hurley, Baroness Pitkeathley and Lord Wallace of Saltaire, *Regulating Fundraising for the Future: Trust in Charities, Confidence in Fundraising Regulation*, September 2015 (www.ncvo.org.uk/images/documents/policy_and_research/giving_and_philanthropy/fundraising-review-report-2015.pdf).

2   Susannah Birkwood, 'The fundraising practices of big charities have harmed small ones', *Third Sector*, 24 February 2016 (www.thirdsector.co.uk/fundraising-practices-big-charities-harmed-small-ones-says-chief-executive-sane/fundraising/article/1384875).

3   Charities Aid Foundation, *UK Giving 2019* (www.cafonline.org/docs/default-source/about-us-publications/caf-uk-giving-2019-report-an-overview-of-charitable-giving-in-the-uk.pdf?sfvrsn=c4a29a40_4).

4   Charity Financials, *Income Spotlight Report*, 28 June 2019 (www.charityfinancials.com/insights/reports/income-spotlight-report-2019).

5   National Council for Voluntary Organisations, *Fact Sheet: Why Do Charities Have Paid Staff?* (www.ncvo.org.uk/2-content/1748-why-do-charities-have-paid-staff).

6   Christopher Hope, '30 charity chiefs paid more than £100,000', *Daily Telegraph*, 6 August 2013 (www.telegraph.co.uk/news/politics/10224104/30-charity-chiefs-paid-more-than-100000.html).

7   Andy Ricketts, 'Two Wellcome Trust investment experts shared more than £9 million in benefits last year as its portfolio value soared', *Third Sector*, 16 December 2020 (https://www.thirdsector.co.uk/two-wellcome-trust-investment-experts-shared-9m-benefits-last-year-its-portfolio-value-soared/finance/article/1702908?bulletin=third-sector).

8   Liam Kay, 'Regulator asks Marie Stopes International to explain salary package of £434,000', *Third Sector*, 27 August 2019 (www.thirdsector.co.uk/regulator-asks-marie-stopes-international-explain-salary-package-434000/management/article/1594919).

9   House of Commons Public Administration and Constitutional Affairs Committee, *The Collapse of Kids Company: Lessons for Charity Trustees, Professional Firms, the Charity Commission, and Whitehall*, HC433, 1 February 2016 (https://publications.parliament.uk/pa/cm201516/cmselect/cmpubadm/433/433.pdf).

10 Royal Courts of Justice, Case No: CR-2017-006113, 12 February 2021, paras 877 and 814 (https://www.judiciary.uk/wp-content/uploads/2021/02/Official-Receiver-v-Batmanghelidjh-judgment-120221.pdf).

11 Charity Commission for England and Wales, *Charity Inquiry: The Royal National Institute of Blind People (226227) and RNIB Charity (1156629)*, 25 June 2020 (www.gov.uk/government/publications/charity-inquiry-the-royal-national-institute-of-blind-people-and-rnib-charity).

12 HM Treasury and Cabinet Office, *The Future Role of the Third Sector in Social and Economic Regeneration: Final Report*, The Stationery Office, July 2007 (https://assets.publishing.service.gov.uk/government/uploads/system/uploads/attachment_data/file/228900/7189.pdf).

13 David Ainsworth, 'Analysis: the Office for Civil Society', *Third Sector*, 19 November 2013 (www.thirdsector.co.uk/analysis-office-civil-society/policy-and-politics/article/1221298).

14 Stephen Cook, 'A good choice, but is she overloaded?', *Third Sector*, 18 July 2017 (www.thirdsector.co.uk/good-choice-she-overloaded/policy-and-politics/article/1438963).

15 Parliament.uk, *Public Administration Select Committee – Minutes of Evidence*, HC 76, 30 October 2012 (https://publications.parliament.uk/pa/cm201314/cmselect/cmpubadm/76/121030.htm).

16 Stephen Cook, 'Interview: Trevor Morris', *Third Sector*, 27 January 2014 (www.thirdsector.co.uk/interview-trevor-morris/communications/article/1228493).

17 National Audit Office, *The Regulatory Effectiveness of the Charity Commission*, 4 December 2013 (www.nao.org.uk/report/regulatory-effectiveness-charity-commission-2/).

18 Charity Commission for England and Wales, *Tackling Abuse and Mismanagement 2014/15*, 17 December 2015 (www.gov.uk/government/publications/tackling-abuse-and-mismanagement-2014-15/).

19 Analysis: 'An emphasis on regulation and a move toward the right', *Third Sector*, 13 May 2013 (www.thirdsector.co.uk/analysis-an-emphasis-regulation-move-toward-right/governance/article/1182014).

20 Stephen Cook, 'Interview: Peter Clarke', *Third Sector*, 26 November 2013 (https://www.thirdsector.co.uk/interview-peter-clarke/governance/article/1222085).

21 Richard Kerbaj, '"Deadliest threat" to charities is extremism', *Sunday Times*, 20 April 2014 (www.thetimes.co.uk/article/deadliest-threat-to-charities-is-extremism-0tbp60vxf99).

22 Susannah Birkwood, 'Tory cancellation of event sponsored by Islamic group is attempt to demonise Muslims, says Sir Stephen Bubb', *Third Sector*, 5 October 2015 (www.thirdsector.co.uk/tory-cancellation-event-sponsored-islamic-group-attempt-demonise-muslims-says-sir-stephen-bubb/policy-and-politics/article/1367132).

23 Baroness Warsi, *Connections, not Coexistence: Building Bridges Between Communities*, Hinton Lecture 2017 (www.ncvo.org.uk/images/documents/training-events/hinton-lectures/Baroness_Warsi_Hinton_Speech_2017.pdf).

24 Andrew Cole, 'Charities and terrorism: "deadly threat" or a distraction from the real issues facing the sector?', *The Guardian*, 9 February 2016 (www.theguardian.com/voluntary-sector-network/2016/feb/09/charities-terrorism-deadly-threat-distraction-sector).

25 Charity Commission for England and Wales, *Tackling Abuse and Mismanagement, 2012/13*, and subsequent years (https://assets.publishing. service.gov.uk/government/uploads/system/uploads/attachment_data/file/455047/Tackling_abuse_and_mismanagement_2013_14.pdf).

26 Charity Commission for England and Wales, *Baroness Stowell: The Future of Charity*, 5 October 2018 (www.gov.uk/government/speeches/baroness-stowell-the-future-of-charity).

27 Tina Stowell, 'Oxfam is not the only charity that has damaged itself', *The Times*, 14 June 2019 (www.thetimes.co.uk/article/oxfam-is-not-the-only-charity-that-has-damaged-itself-rzk7vvwrc).

28 Kirsty Weakley, 'NCVO accuses Commission chair of presenting a "partial" message about charities', *Civil Society News*, 17 June 2019 (www. civilsociety.co.uk/news/ncvo-accuses-charity-commission-of-presenting-a-partial-message-about-the-sector.html).

29 Stephen Cook, 'Fundraising survey: giving is still strong, but what about trust?', *Third Sector*, 31 March 2015 (www.thirdsector.co.uk/fundraising-survey-giving-strong-trust/fundraising/article/1339736).

30 Charity Commission for England and Wales, *Trust in Charities 2018*, July 2018.

31 nfpSynergy, *Trust in Charities (Year 2017)* (https://nfpsynergy.net/free-report/trust-charities-2017).

32 David Owen, *English Philanthropy 1660–1960*, Oxford: Oxford University Press, 1965, p 331.

33 John Campbell, *Margaret Thatcher. Volume 2: The Iron Lady*, London: Jonathan Cape, 2003, p 390.

34 'From the Observer archive: this week in 1986', *The Guardian*, 29 November 2015 (www.theguardian.com/commentisfree/2015/nov/29/from-the-observer-archive-1986).

35 David Ainsworth, 'Former charity chief executive jailed for five years for £900,000 fraud', *Civil Society News*, 3 January 2018 (www.civilsociety. co.uk/news/former-charity-chief-executive-jailed-for-900-000-fraud. html#sthash.5ZqH0iBQ.dpuf).

36 Kirsty Weakley, 'Five jailed for Marie Curie collection scam', *Civil Society News*, 9 April 2013 (www.civilsociety.co.uk/news/five-jailed-for-marie-curie-collection-scam.html#sthash.elVX7joo.dpuf).

37 Croner, Charity Rewards Survey, 'Charity pay falls behind other sectors by up to 32 per cent', 5 October 2017 (https://croner.co.uk/resources/pay-benefits/charity-pay-falls-behind-sectors-32/).

38 Civil Society Futures, *Civil Society in England: Its Current State and Future Opportunity*, November 2018 (https://civilsocietyfutures.org/wp-content/uploads/sites/6/2018/11/Civil-Society-Futures__Civil-Society-in-England__small-1.pdf).

39 Charity Commission for England and Wales, *Trust in Charities 2018*, July 2018 (https://assets.publishing.service.gov.uk/government/uploads/system/uploads/attachment_data/file/723566/Charity_Commission_-_Trust_in_Charities_2018_-_Report.pdf).

40 nfpSynergy website, 'What are charities trusted to do?', 5 July 2017 (https://nfpsynergy.net/press-release/new-research-what-exactly-are-charities-trusted-do#downloads).

41 WWF International, *Living Planet Report 2018: Aiming Higher* (https://c402277.ssl.cf1.rackcdn.com/publications/1187/files/original/LPR2018_Full_Report_Spreads.pdf?1540487589).

42 Eleanor Busby, 'Excluded schoolchildren at "serious risk of becoming involved in knife crime", charity warns', *The Independent*, 30 October 2018 (www.independent.co.uk/news/education/education-news/school-exclusions-pupils-knife-crime-violence-pupil-referral-units-education-barnardos-a8609046.html).

Chapter 3

1 Stephen Cook, 'Interview: Gwythian Prins', *Third Sector*, 29 September 2013 (www.thirdsector.co.uk/interview-gwythian-prins/governance/article/1213800).

2 Stephen Lloyd, 'Back to the future', *Civil Society News*, 1 October 2014 (www.civilsociety.co.uk/finance/back-to-the-future.html).

3 W.K. Jordan, *Philanthropy in England, 1480–1660*, London: George Allen & Unwin, 1959, p 18.

4 'London lives 1690–1800: crime, poverty and social policy in the metropolis', *Associational Charities* (www.londonlives.org/static/Associational Charities.jsp).

5 M.G. Jones, *The Charity School Movement: A Study in Eighteenth Century Puritanism in Action*, Cambridge: Cambridge University Press, 1938, p 351.

6 *Bowman v Secular Society*, 1917 (www.uniset.ca/other/cs5/1917AC406.html).

7 *National Anti-Vivisection Society v Inland Revenue Commissioners*, 1948.

8 *McGovern and others v Attorney-General and others*, 1982.

9 Paul Jump, 'Shadow charities minister hits out at political campaigning', *Third Sector*, 27 November 2007 (www.thirdsector.co.uk/search/articles?keywords=%22minefield%20of%20confusion%22&headlinesOnly=False).

10 Helena Kennedy QC, *Report by the Advisory Group on Campaigning and the Voluntary Sector*, 2007 (https://bateswells.co.uk/wp-content/uploads/2020/12/advisory-group.pdf).

11 HM Treasury and Cabinet Office: *The Future Role of the Third Sector in Social and Economic Regeneration: Final Report*, The Stationery Office, July 2007 (https://assets.publishing.service.gov.uk/government/uploads/system/uploads/attachment_data/file/228900/7189.pdf).

12 Charity Commission for England and Wales, *Campaigning and Political Activity Guidance for Charities*, 1 March 2008 (www.gov.uk/government/

publications/speaking-out-guidance-on-campaigning-and-political-activity-by-charities-cc9).

13 *Third Sector*, 'Charity Commission acts on complaints in the run-up to the election', 28 May 2015 (www.thirdsector.co.uk/charity-commission-acts-complaints-run-up-election/article/1348574).

14 Liam Kay, 'Charity Commission in contact with 41 charities during election period', *Third Sector*, 17 July 2017 (www.thirdsector.co.uk/charity-commission-contact-41-charities-during-election-period/governance/article/1439625).

15 Charity Commission for England and Wales, *Regulatory Case Report: The Atlantic Bridge Education and Research Scheme*, 26 July 2010 (https://publications.parliament.uk/pa/cm201012/cmselect/cmstnprv/1887/188710.htm).

16 Charity Commission for England and Wales, *Operational Case Report: Oxfam*, 19 December 2014 (https://assets.publishing.service.gov.uk/government/uploads/system/uploads/attachment_data/file/431592/ocr_oxfam.pdf).

17 Charity Commission for England and Wales, *Inquiry Report: The Smith Institute*, 8 July 2008 (https://webarchive.nationalarchives.gov.uk/20080906031320/www.charity-commission.gov.uk/Library/investigations/pdfs/smithir.pdf).

18 Charity Commission for England and Wales, *Operational Case Report: The Institute for Public Policy Research*, 16 December 2014 (https://assets.publishing.service.gov.uk/government/uploads/system/uploads/attachment_data/file/431599/ocr_institute_for_public_policy_research.pdf).

19 Legislation.gov.uk, *Transparency of Lobbying, Non-party Campaigning and Trade Union Administration Act 2014* (www.legislation.gov.uk/ukpga/2014/4/contents/enacted).

20 Sam Burne James, 'Electoral Commission guidance on the lobbying act is "incomprehensible", says Sir Stephen Bubb of Acevo', *Third Sector*, 7 August 2014 (www.thirdsector.co.uk/electoral-commission-guidance-lobbying-act-incomprehensible-says-sir-stephen-bubb-acevo/policy-and-politics/article/1306994).

21 Sam Burne James, 'How can charities comply with the new lobbying act?', *Third Sector*, 4 September 2014 (www.thirdsector.co.uk/charities-comply-new-lobbying-act/communications/article/1309023).

22 Andy Ricketts, 'Lobbying act infringed "legitimate democratic engagement ahead of the election", says report', *Third Sector*, 9 September 2015 (www.thirdsector.co.uk/lobbying-act-infringed-legitimate-democratic-engagement-ahead-election-says-report/communications/article/1363360).

23 Lord Hodgson of Astley Abbotts, *Third Party Election Campaigning: Getting the Balance Right*, Cm 9205, March 2016 (https://assets.publishing.service.gov.uk/government/uploads/system/uploads/attachment_data/file/507954/2904969_Cm_9205_Accessible_v0.4.pdf).

24 House of Commons Hansard, 23 February 2015, col 2WS (https:// publications.parliament.uk/pa/cm201415/cmhansrd/cm150223/ wmstext/150223m0001.htm#1502232000003).

25 Cabinet Office press release, 'Government announces new clause to be inserted into grant agreements', 6 February 2016 (www.gov.uk/ government/news/government-announces-new-clause-to-be-inserted-into-grant-agreements).

26 House of Commons Hansard, 9 March 2016, col 264 (https:// publications.parliament.uk/pa/cm201516/cmhansrd/cm160309/ debtext/160309-0001.htm#16030943000007).

27 Third Sector, 'Chair of think tank gave money to minister', 25 February 2016 (www.thirdsector.co.uk/chair-think-tank-gave-money-minister/ article/1384613).

28 Rebecca Cooney, 'Anti-campaigning clause could be more damaging than lobbying act, says Sir Stuart Etherington', *Third Sector*, 17 February 2016 (www.thirdsector.co.uk/anti-campaigning-clause-damaging-lobbying-act-says-sir-stuart-etherington/policy-and-politics/article/1383890).

29 'Peter Holbrook: The government has listened to us on the anti-lobbying clause', *Third Sector*, 5 December 2016 (www.thirdsector.co.uk/peter-holbrook-government-listened-us-anti-lobbying-clause/communications/ article/1417725).

30 Cabinet Office, *Guidance for General Grants*, 30 June 2020, para 9 (https:// assets.publishing.service.gov.uk/government/uploads/system/uploads/ attachment_data/file/896341/Grants-Standard-SIX-Grant-Agreements. pdf).

31 Stuart Etherington, 'A resolution to the anti-lobbying clause', blog on NCVO website, 2 December 2016 (https://blogs.ncvo.org. uk/2016/12/02/a-resolution-to-the-anti-lobbying-clause/).

32 Stephen Bubb, *The History of British Charity*, lecture delivered at New College, Oxford, 3 July 2017, p 29 (http://charityfutures.org/wp-content/ uploads/2019/01/history-of-charity-lecture-online-copy-30-6.pdf).

Chapter 4

1 HM Treasury, 'Soft drinks industry levy comes into effect', 5 April 2018 (www.gov.uk/government/news/soft-drinks-industry-levy-comes-into-effect).

2 Public Health England press release, 'Excess weight can increase risk of serious illness and death from COVID-19', 25 July 2020 (www.gov.uk/ government/news/excess-weight-can-increase-risk-of-serious-illness-and-death-from-covid-19).

3 Department of Health and Social Care policy paper, *Tackling Obesity: Empowering Adults and Children to Live Healthier Lives*, 27 July 2020 (www.gov.uk/government/publications/tackling-obesity-government-strategy/).

4   Sustain website, 'Government confirms 9pm watershed for junk food adverts amongst raft of policies to tackle obesity', 27 July 2020 (www.sustainweb.org/news/jul20-government-confirms-9pm-watershed-for-junk-food-adverts/).

5   Office for Budget Responsibility, *Tobacco Duties* (https://obr.uk/forecasts-in-depth/tax-by-tax-spend-by-spend/tobacco-duties/).

6   Action on Smoking and Health website, 'Media briefing', 10 October 2005, para 21 (https://ash.org.uk/media-and-news/press-releases-media-and-news/ash-media-briefing-health-improvement-and-protection-bill-smoking-in-workplaces-and-enclosed-public-places/).

7   Action on Smoking and Health website, 'Media briefing', para 19.

8   Action on Smoking and Health, *Comprehensive Smoke-free Legislation in England: How Advocacy Won the Day* (www.researchgate.net/publication/5798645_Comprehensive_smoke-free_legislation_in_England_How_advocacy_won_the_day).

9   *Labour Party Manifesto 2005*, p 66 (http://news.bbc.co.uk/1/shared/bsp/hi/pdfs/13_04_05_labour_manifesto.pdf).

10 Patrick Wintour and Colin Blackstock, 'Let the poor smoke, says health secretary', *The Guardian*, 9 June 2004 (www.theguardian.com/uk/2004/jun/09/smoking.politics).

11 UK Parliament, *Transcript of Oral Evidence Given to the Commons Health Committee*, 24 November 2005, Q432-73 (https://publications.parliament.uk/pa/cm200506/cmselect/cmhealth/uc485-iii/uc48502.htm).

12 BBC news, 'Smoking ban in all pubs and clubs', 14 February 2006 (http://news.bbc.co.uk/1/hi/uk_politics/4709258.stm).

13 Action on Smoking and Health, *Comprehensive Smoke-free Legislation in England: How Advocacy Won the Day*, p 426.

14 Deborah Arnott and Ian Willmore, 'Smoke and Mirrors', *The Guardian*, 19 July 2006 (www.theguardian.com/society/2006/jul/19/health.healthandwellbeing).

15 Michael Rush and Philip Giddings (eds), *The Palgrave Review of British Politics 2006*, Basingstoke: Palgrave Macmillan 2007.

16 Action on Smoking and Health, *Beyond Smoking Kills* (https://ash.org.uk/information-and-resources/reports-submissions/reports/beyond-smoking-kills/).

17 Legislation.gov.uk, *The Standardised Packaging of Tobacco Products Regulations 2015* (www.legislation.gov.uk/uksi/2015/829/contents/made).

18 Clare Murphy, 'Heart attack admissions fall after smoking ban', BBC News, 9 June 2010 (www.bbc.co.uk/news/10266997).

19 Office for National Statistics, *Adult Smoking Habits in the UK: 2018* (www.ons.gov.uk/peoplepopulationandcommunity/healthandsocialcare/healthandlifeexpectancies/bulletins/adultsmokinghabitsingreatbritain/2018#main-points).

20 NHS Digital, *Statistics on Smoking, England, 2017* (https://digital.nhs.uk/data-and-information/publications/statistical/statistics-on-smoking/statistics-on-smoking-england-2017-pas).

21 Jennifer Whitehead, 'Dripping fat smoking ad leads to record site hits for BHF', *Campaign*, 3 February 2004 (www.campaignlive.co.uk/article/dripping-fat-smoking-ad-leads-record-site-hits-bhf/201331).

22 Office for National Statistics, *Retail Sales, Great Britain: March 2020* (www.ons.gov.uk/businessindustryandtrade/retailindustry/bulletins/retailsales/march2020#:~:text=Supermarket%20stores%20saw%20a%20strong,%2Don%2Dmonth%20growth%20rates.).

23 Arabella Mileham, 'UK's overall consumption of alcohol halved during lockdown, data finds', *The Drinks Business*, 7 September 2020 (www.thedrinksbusiness.com/2020/09/nielsen-uks-overall-consumption-of-alcohol-halved-during-lockdown/).

24 Alcohol Change UK press release, 'New research reveals how UK drinking habits have changed during lockdown', 16 April 2020 (https://s3.eu-west-2.amazonaws.com/files.alcoholchange.org.uk/images/Drinking-in-lockdown-press-release-final.pdf?mtime=20200415181333).

25 Alcohol Change UK press release, 'New research reveals that without action lockdown drinking habits may be here to stay', 3 July 2020 (https://s3.eu-west-2.amazonaws.com/files.alcoholchange.org.uk/images/Lockdown-easing-press-release-FINAL.pdf?mtime=20200702175422).

26 The Institute of Promotional Marketing, *Cancer Research Dryathlon 2016*, 17 December 2015 (www.promomarketing.info/cancer-research-dryathlon-2016/).

27 Katie O'Malley, 'British people get drunk more often than anyone else in the world, study reveals', *The Independent*, 15 May 2019 (www.independent.co.uk/life-style/health-and-families/alcohol-drinking-uk-survey-world-alcohol-consumption-a8915206.html).

28 Alcohol Change UK, *The Dry January Story* (https://alcoholchange.org.uk/get-involved/campaigns/dry-january/about-dry-january/the-dry-january-story).

29 John Naish, 'Abstinence after the boozing. Can you make it a dry January?', *The Times*, 31 December 2014 (www.thetimes.co.uk/article/abstinence-after-the-boozing-can-you-make-it-a-dry-january-0twp709lw35#).

30 James Hakner, 'Dry January leads to less drinking all year round', University of Sussex website, 14 November 2014 (www.sussex.ac.uk/broadcast/read/27612).

31 Jason Murugesu, 'Why science says doing dry January is good for you, even if you don't quite succeed', *New Statesman*, 15 January 2018 (www.newstatesman.com/politics/health/2018/01/why-science-says-doing-dry-january-good-you-even-if-you-don-t-quite-succeed).

32 Alcohol Change UK, *The Dry January Story* (https://alcoholchange.org.uk/get-involved/campaigns/dry-january/about-dry-january/the-dry-january-story).

33 Dr Graham Durcan, Nick O'Shea and Louis Allwood, 'Covid-19 and the nation's mental health', *Centre for Mental Health*, May 2020 (www.centreformentalhealth.org.uk/sites/default/files/2020-05/CentreforMentalHealth_COVID_MH_Forecasting_May20.pdf).

[34] Mind survey, *The Mental Health Emergency*, p 10, June 2020 (/www.mind.org.uk/media-a/5929/the-mental-health-emergency_a4_final.pdf).

[35] Rosie Waterhouse and Rhys Williams, 'The Clunis case', *The Independent*, 19 July 1993 (www.independent.co.uk/news/uk/the-clunis-case-passing-the-buck-carried-on-until-an-innocent-man-died-the-independents-own-1485772.html).

[36] Annabel Ferriman, 'The stigma of schizophrenia', *British Medical Journal*, 19 February 2000 (www.ncbi.nlm.nih.gov/pmc/articles/PMC1127555/).

[37] Mind, *Attitudes to Mental Illness 2014 Research Report* (www.time-to-change.org.uk/sites/default/files/Attitudes_to_mental_illness_2014_report_final_0.pdf).

[38] Jim Read and Sue Baker, *Not Just Sticks and Stones*, Centre for Disability Studies, University of Leeds, November 1996 (https://disability-studies.leeds.ac.uk/wp-content/uploads/sites/40/library/MIND-MIND.pdf).

[39] Claire Henderson and Ruth Stuart, *Time to Change Phase 2 Evaluation: Final Report*, 2015, Health Services and Population Research Department, King's College London Institute of Psychiatry, Psychology and Neuroscience.

[40] Time to Change, *Mind over Matter*, 13 November 2017 (www.time-to-change.org.uk/news/first-time-print-media-reporting-mental-health-significantly-more-balanced-and-responsible-more).

[41] Time to Change website, 'Time to Change to close after funding ends', 26 October 2020 (https://www.time-to-change.org.uk/news/time-to-change-to-close-after-funding-ends-statement).

[42] Katie Silver, 'Embarrassment makes women avoid smear tests, charity says', BBC News, 22 January 2018 (www.bbc.co.uk/news/health-42747892).

Chapter 5

[1] BUP/Policy Press house style is to use initial capitals for both 'Black' and 'White' as racial groups, so as to avoid the implication of 'white' as standard.

[2] Voice4Change England, 'Bridge the gap: what is known about the BME third sector in England?', October 2007 (https://voice4change-england.com/wp-content/uploads/2020/11/v4ce_bridge_the_gap_what_is_known_about_the_bme_third_sector_in_england_october_2007.pdf).

[3] Stand Against Racism and Inequality website, *SARI Statement re Black Lives Matter protest* (www.sariweb.org.uk/news-information/blm-protests/).

[4] Stand Against Racism and Inequality website, *Statement from the Chair of SARI (Stand Against Racism & Inequality), Irvin Campbell on behalf of our Board of Trustees re: The Black Lives Matter Protest, Sunday 7th June 2020* (www.sariweb.org.uk/news-information/sari-statement-re-bristol-black-lives-matter-protest/).

[5] UKBLM fund organiser, 'Fundraiser update', 7 August 2020 (www.gofundme.com/f/ukblm-fund).

[6] The full text of the speech was reproduced by *Daily Telegraph*, 6 November 2007 (www.telegraph.co.uk/comment/3643823/Enoch-Powells-Rivers-of-Blood-speech.html).

7   Gov.uk website, *The Stephen Lawrence Inquiry: Report of an Inquiry by Sir William Macpherson of Cluny*, Cm 4262-I, February 1999 (https://assets.publishing.service.gov.uk/government/uploads/system/uploads/attachment_data/file/277111/4262.pdf).

8   Cabinet Office, *Race Disparity Audit Summary Findings from the Ethnicity Facts and Figures website*, October 2017 (revised March 2018) pp 23, 26 (https://assets.publishing.service.gov.uk/government/uploads/system/uploads/attachment_data/file/686071/Revised_RDA_report_March_2018.pdf).

9   Ibid, p 37.

10   Ministry of Justice, *NOMS Offender Equalities Report 2015 to 2016: Supplementary Tables*, Ch1, table 1.1 (2016) (www.gov.uk/government/statistics/noms-annual-offender-equalities-report-2015-to-2016).

11   E.J.B. Rose and associates, *Colour and Citizenship: A Report on British Race Relations*, Oxford: Oxford University Press, 1969.

12   BBC News '"Right to rent" checks breach human rights – High Court', 1 March 2019 (www.bbc.co.uk/news/uk-47415383).

13   Amelia Gentleman, 'Right to rent rule "justified", finds UK appeal court', *The Guardian*, 21 April 2020 (https://www.theguardian.com/politics/2020/apr/21/right-to-rent-rule-justified-finds-uk-appeal-court).

14   JCWI website, 'We won! Home Office to stop using racist visa algorithm' (www.jcwi.org.uk/news/we-won-home-office-to-stop-using-racist-visa-algorithm).

15   Judith Barrett, 'Inclusiveness: finding diverse service users', *Third Sector*, 7 March 2007 (www.thirdsector.co.uk/inclusiveness-finding-diverse-service-users/management/article/637443).

16   National Council for Voluntary Organisations, *UK Civil Society Almanac 2019: Who Works for Voluntary Organisations?* (https://data.ncvo.org.uk/workforce/demographics/).

17   Thomas Lawson, 'Us white charity CEOs need to talk', *Governance & Leadership*, 5 January 2018 (www.civilsociety.co.uk/governance/us-white-charity-ceos-need-to-talk.html).

18   Dr Sanjiv Lingayah, Kristiana Wrixon and Maisie Hulbert, *Home Truths: Undoing Racism and Delivering Real Diversity in the Charity Sector*, Acevo, June 2020 (www.acevo.org.uk/publications/home-truths/).

19   Karl Wilding, *Equity, Diversity and Inclusion at NCVO: What We Need to Do Next*, NCVO website, 5 August 2020 (https://blogs.ncvo.org.uk/2020/08/05/equity-diversity-and-inclusion-at-ncvo-what-we-need-to-do-next/).

20   Rebecca Cooney, 'Bullying and harassment took place "with impunity" at all levels of the NCVO, report concludes', *Third Sector*, 5 February 2021 (www.thirdsector.co.uk/bullying-harassment-took-place-with-impunity-levels-ncvo-report-concludes/management/article/1706637).

21   Sarah Vibert, *NCVO's Equity, Diversity and Inclusion (EDI) Work Over the Last Year*, NCVO website, 8 February 2021 (https://blogs.ncvo.org.uk/2021/02/08/ncvos-equity-diversity-and-inclusion-edi-work-over-the-last-year/).

22 Aasma Day, 'Citizens Advice slammed for "horribly racist" guidance on BAME communities', *Huffington Post*, 14 August 2019 (www.huffingtonpost.co.uk/entry/citizens-advice-bame-communities_uk_5d54244ee4b05fa9df0870a9).

23 The 4F Group, *The Rubicon Review: Exposing the Impact of Ignoring Class–Race Intersectionality in the Charity Sector*, August 2020 (https://drive.google.com/file/d/1id0wvBkGim5-_fgguGbFOHKnKT-XAnnB/view).

24 See article 'Antislavery medallion' on website of National Museum of American History (https://americanhistory.si.edu/collections/search/object/nmah_596365).

25 Andrew Purkis, '"Our good old English fashion": England's history of campaigning for charitable causes', lecture at Cass Business School, City University, London, 4 September 2015 (https://cdn.baringfoundation.org.uk/wp-content/uploads/2015/09/Cass-Lecture-Latest.pdf).

26 Letter to the *Leeds Mercury* in 1830, quoted in Cecil Herbert Driver, *Tory Radical: The Life of Richard Oastler*, Oxford: Oxford University Press, 1946.

27 House of Commons Hansard, 21 April 1847, col 1143 (https://api.parliament.uk/historic-hansard/commons/1847/apr/21/factories-bill#S3V0091P0_18470421_HOC_47).

28 Mind website, 'PIP ruling "a victory for people with mental health problems", says Mind', 21 December 2017 (www.mind.org.uk/news-campaigns/news/pip-ruling-a-victory-for-people-with-mental-health-problems-says-mind/#.WmW5Zq5l_IV).

Chapter 6

1 Maya Oppenheim, 'Visits to national domestic abuse helpline website surge by 950 per cent during lockdown', *The Independent*, 27 May 2020 (www.independent.co.uk/news/uk/home-news/coronavirus-uk-domestic-abuse-helpline-calls-rise-refuge-a9534591.html).

2 Jamie Grierson, 'Labour urges emergency aid for domestic abuse services', *The Guardian*, 8 April 2020 (www.theguardian.com/society/2020/apr/08/labour-urges-emergency-aid-for-domestic-abuse-services).

3 Imkaan Position Paper, *The Impact of the Two Pandemics: VAWG and COVID-19 on Black and Minoritised Women and Girls*, 11 May 2020 (www.imkaan.org.uk/covid19-position-paper).

4 Gov.uk, 'Emergency funding to support most vulnerable in society during pandemic', 2 May (www.gov.uk/government/news/emergency-funding-to-support-most-vulnerable-in-society-during-pandemic).

5 Mark Townsend, 'Shock new figures fuel fears of more lockdown domestic abuse killings in UK', *The Observer*, 15 November 2020 (https://www.theguardian.com/society/2020/nov/15/shock-new-figures-fuel-fears-of-more-lockdown-domestic-abuse-killings-in-uk).

6 Southall Black Sisters website, *Kiranjit Ahluwahlia* (https://southallblacksisters.org.uk/campaigns/domestic-violence/kiranjit-ahluwalia/).

7   Haroon Siddique, 'John Worboys must stay in prison, says Parole Board', *The Guardian*, 19 November 2018 (www.theguardian.com/uk-news/2018/nov/19/john-worboys-must-stay-in-prison-says-parole-board).

8   BBC News, 'John Worboys case: Met Police loses "landmark" appeal', 21 February 2018 (www.bbc.co.uk/news/uk-43140827).

9   HM Government, *Transforming the Response to Domestic Abuse, 8 March–31 May 2018* (https://consult.justice.gov.uk/homeoffice-moj/domestic-abuse-consultation/supporting_documents/Transforming%20the%20response%20to%20domestic%20abuse.pdf).

10   Ministry of Justice, *Code of Practice for Victims of Crime*, October 2015 (https://assets.publishing.service.gov.uk/government/uploads/system/uploads/attachment_data/file/476900/code-of-practice-for-victims-of-crime.PDF).

11   Office for National Statistics, *Crime in England and Wales: Annual Supplementary Tables 2020*, Table S41b (www.ons.gov.uk/peoplepopulationandcommunity/crimeandjustice/datasets/crimeinenglandandwalesannualsupplementarytables).

12   Crown Prosecution Service, *Violence Against Women and Girls Crime Report 2016–17*, p 6 (www.cps.gov.uk/publication/cps-violence-against-women-and-girls-crime-report-2016-2017).

13   Office of the United Nations High Commissioner for Human Rights, *Convention on the Elimination of All Forms of Discrimination against Women*, New York, 18 December 1979 (www.ohchr.org/en/professionalinterest/pages/cedaw.aspx).

14   Women's Aid website, *An Historical Perspective on Legal and Cultural Attitudes to Domestic Abuse – Some Helpful Facts* (https://1q7dqy2unor827bqjls0c4rn-wpengine.netdna-ssl.com/wp-content/uploads/2016/02/23.-Supporting-Resources-An-Historical-Perspective.pdf).

15   Ibid.

16   Derek Heater, *Citizenship in Britain: A History*, Edinburgh: Edinburgh University Press, 2006, pp 107–36.

17   Karma Nirvana website, 'How many calls does the helpline receive?', 27 October 2017 (https://karmanirvana.org.uk/how-many-calls-does-the-helpline-receive/).

18   BBC News, 'Lack of awareness around forced marriage laws', 17 January 2019 (www.bbc.co.uk/news/uk-england-leeds-46895699).

19   Fawcett Society website, 'Sex discrimination law review', January 2018 (www.fawcettsociety.org.uk/Handlers/Download.ashx?IDMF=e473a103-28c1-4a6c-aa43-5099d34c0116).

20   Madison Marriage, 'Men only: inside the charity fundraiser where hostesses are put on show', *Financial Times*, 23 January 2018 (www.ft.com/content/075d679e-0033-11e8-9650-9c0ad2d7c5b5).

21   'Presidents Club to close after sexual harassment exposé', *Financial Times*, 24 January 2018 (www.ft.com/content/d00e9f82-012d-11e8-9650-9c0ad2d7c5b5).

22 Fawcett Society website, 'Fawcett Society and Young Women's Trust to begin merger talks', 11 November 2020 (https://www.fawcettsociety.org.uk/news/fawcett-society-and-young-womens-trust-to-begin-merger-talks).

23 Committee on Homosexual Offences and Prostitution, *Report of the Committee on Homosexual Offences and Prostitution*, London: Her Majesty's Stationery Office, 1957.

24 'No early vice law change: "further study of report needed"', Lord Chancellor's statement', *The Times*, 5 December 1957, p 10.

25 Local Government Act 1988, section 28 (www.legislation.gov.uk/ukpga/1988/9/section/28/enacted).

26 Andrew Reynolds, 'The UK's parliament is still the gayest in the world after 2019 election', *Pink News*, 13 December 2019 (www.pinknews.co.uk/2019/12/13/uk-gay-parliament-world-2019-general-election-snp-conservatives-labour-lgbt/).

Chapter 7

1   Kit Heren, 'Greta Thunberg back at school after year of environmental campaigning', *Evening Standard*, 25 August 2020 (www.standard.co.uk/news/world/greta-thunberg-school-year-environmental-campaigning-a4532551.html).

2   Olivia Rosane, 'UK parliament first in world to declare a climate emergency', *EcoWatch*, 2 May 2019 (www.ecowatch.com/uk-parliament-climate-emergency-2636090140.html?rebelltitem=1#rebelltitem1).

3   Matthew Smith, 'Concern for the environment at record highs', YouGov, 5 June 2019 (https://yougov.co.uk/topics/politics/articles-reports/2019/06/05/concern-environment-record-highs).

4   Union of Concerned Scientists, 'World Scientists' Warning to Humanity', April 1997 (https://www.ucsusa.org/sites/default/files/attach/2017/11/World%20Scientists%27%20Warning%20to%20Humanity%201992.pdf).

5   Civil Society Equity Review Reports (http://civilsocietyreview.org/).

6   Rising Up! website, 'Extinction Rebellion occupy Greenpeace offices', October 2018 (https://risingup.org.uk/extinction-rebellion-occupy-greenpeace-offices).

7   Rex Weyler, 'Extinction and rebellion', Greenpeace International website, 17 May 2019 (www.greenpeace.org/international/story/22058/extinction-and-rebellion/).

8   Extinction Rebellion website, 'About us' page (https://extinctionrebellion.uk/the-truth/about-us/)

9   Right Livelihood Award website, 'One million SEK to Greta Thunberg's new foundation', 20 February 2020 (www.rightlivelihoodaward.org/media/the-right-livelihood-award-one-million-sek-to-greta-thunbergs-new-foundation/).

10 Human Act website, 'Human Act Award goes to Greta Thunberg' (https://humanact.org/human-act-award-2020/).

Notes

11 ActionAid website, 'Greta Thunberg to donate 100,000 euros prize money to flood relief efforts in India and Bangladesh', 29 July 2020 (www.actionaidindia.org/press-release/greta-thunberg-donate-e100000-prize-money-flood-relief-efforts-india-bangladesh/).

12 BBC News, 'Climate change: Greta Thunberg gives 1m euros to climate charities', 21 July 2020 (www.bbc.co.uk/newsround/53483155).

13 Charities Aid Foundation, *UK Giving 2019* (www.cafonline.org/docs/default-source/about-us-publications/caf-uk-giving-2019-report-an-overview-of-charitable-giving-in-the-uk.pdf?sfvrsn=c4a29a40_4).

14 Kirsty Weakley, 'Projects to prevent ecological collapse are desperately underfunded warn scientists', *Civil Society News*, 23 May 2019 (www.civilsociety.co.uk/news/scientists-warn-philanthropists-that-projects-to-prevent-ecological-collapse-is-desperately-underfunded.html).

15 BBC News, 'Jeff Bezos: World's richest man pledges $10bn to fight climate change', 17 February 2020 (www.bbc.co.uk/news/business-51539321).

16 WWF-UK website, 'Delivering water-sensitive farming in East Anglia' (www.wwf.org.uk/updates/coca-cola-great-britain-and-wwf-renew-partnership-protect-precious-uk-river-habitats).

17 RSPB website, 'Our history' (www.rspb.org.uk/about-the-rspb/about-us/our-history/).

18 European Commission website, 'New rules for captive bird imports to protect animal health in the EU and improve the welfare of imported birds' (https://ec.europa.eu/commission/presscorner/detail/en/IP_07_40).

19 House of Commons Hansard, 18 November 2004, col 1487 (https://publications.parliament.uk/pa/cm200304/cmhansrd/vo041118/debtext/41118-11.htm).

20 European Commission website, 'Bathing water quality' (https://ec.europa.eu/environment/water/water-bathing/summary.html).

21 Rachael Thorn, 'Could Brexit affect beach water quality?', BBC News, 5 September 2016 (www.bbc.co.uk/news/uk-england-devon-37198688).

22 Department for Environment, Food and Rural Affairs, *Statistics on English Coastal and Inland Bathing Waters: A Summary of Compliance with the 2006 Bathing Water Directive*, 12 December 2018 (https://assets.publishing.service.gov.uk/government/uploads/system/uploads/attachment_data/file/763499/EMBARGOED_STATS_bathing-water-release-revised20182.pdf).

23 Roland Geyer, Jenna R. Jambeck and Kara Lavender Law, 'Production, use and fate of all plastics ever made, 2017', *Science Advances*, 1 July 2017 (www.researchgate.net/publication/318567844_Production_use_and_fate_of_all_plastics_ever_made).

24 Robert Day, David Shaw and Steven Ignell, *The Quantitative Distribution and Characteristics of Neuston Plastic in the North Pacific Ocean, 1985–88. Final Report to U.S. Department of Commerce, National Marine Fisheries Service, Auke Bay Laboratory*, Auke Bay, Alaska, pp 247–66 (https://swfsc.noaa.gov/publications/TM/SWFSC/NOAA-TM-NMFS-SWFSC-154_P247.PDF).

25 Richard A. Lovett, 'Huge garbage patch found in Atlantic too', *National Geographic*, 2 March 2010 (www.nationalgeographic.com/news/2010/3/100302-new-ocean-trash-garbage-patch/).

26 UNESCO website, *Facts and Figures on Marine Pollution*, 2017 (www.unesco.org/new/en/natural-sciences/ioc-oceans/focus-areas/rio-20-ocean/blueprint-for-the-future-we-want/marine-pollution/facts-and-figures-on-marine-pollution/).

27 Chantal Borciani, 'Biggest Spring Beach Clean ever sees over 35,500 volunteers clean 571 UK beaches', *Yachting & Boating World*, 24 April 2018 (www.ybw.com/news-from-yachting-boating-world/biggest-big-spring-beach-clean-66898).

28 Phoebe Taplin, 'Plastic-free coast: 10 seaside communities to visit in the British Isles', *The Guardian*, 7 June 2019 (www.theguardian.com/travel/2019/jun/07/plastic-free-coast-10-uk-seaside-towns-sustainable).

29 Surfers Against Sewage website, 'Plastic Free Communities goes global' (www.sas.org.uk/news/plastic-free-communities-goes-global/).

30 House of Commons Environmental Audit Committee, *Plastic Bottles: Turning Back the Plastic Tide*, 20 December 2017 (https://publications.parliament.uk/pa/cm201719/cmselect/cmenvaud/339/33905.htm).

31 Carly Cassella, 'Norway's insanely efficient scheme recycles 97% of all plastic bottles they use', *Science Alert*, 10 March 2019 (www.sciencealert.com/norway-s-recycling-scheme-is-so-effective-92-percent-of-plastic-bottles-can-be-reused).

32 Department for Environment, Food and Rural Affairs, *Consultation Outcome: Introducing a Deposit Return Scheme (DRS) for Drinks Containers (Bottles and Cans)*, 22 August 2019 (www.gov.uk/government/consultations/introducing-a-deposit-return-scheme-drs-for-drinks-containers-bottles-and-cans).

33 Sandra Laville, 'Surfers Against Sewage urge MPs to make parliament plastic-free', *The Guardian*, 1 February 2018 (www.theguardian.com/environment/2018/feb/01/surfers-against-sewage-urge-mps-to-make-parliament-plastic-free).

34 Thames 21 website, 'Break the bag habit' (www.thames21.org.uk/joinacampaign/breakthebaghabit/).

35 ITV website, 'Plastic bag charge: why was it introduced and what impact has it had?', 25 August 2018 (www.itv.com/news/2018-08-25/plastic-bag-charge-why-was-it-introduced-and-what-impact-has-it-had/).

36 Department for Environment, Food and Rural Affairs, 'Plastic bag sales in "big seven" supermarkets down 86% since 5p charge', 27 July 2018 (www.gov.uk/government/news/plastic-bag-sales-in-big-seven-supermarkets-down-86-since-5p-charge).

37 Church Commissioners, *Annual Report 2019*, p 7 (https://www.churchofengland.org/sites/default/files/2020-05/33295_CofE_AR19.pdf).

38 Tania Mason, 'High ideals: why the Church Commissioners invest ethically', *Governance & Leadership*, 13 November 2017 (www.civilsociety.co.uk/governance/high-ideals-church-invest-ethical.html).

39 BBC News, 'Wonga row: Archbishop of Canterbury "embarrassed" over Church funds', 26 July 2013 (www.bbc.co.uk/news/business-23459932).

40 Andrew Grice, 'War on Wonga: we're putting you out of business, Archbishop of Canterbury Justin Welby tells payday loans company', *The Independent*, 24 July 2013 (www.independent.co.uk/news/uk/home-news/war-on-wonga-were-putting-you-out-of-business-archbishop-of-canterbury-justin-welby-tells-payday-8730839.html).

41 Business and Human Rights Resource Centre website, 'Shareholder resolution calls on ExxonMobil to disclose climate risks for its business', 12 April 2016 (www.business-humanrights.org/en/shareholder-resolution-calls-on-exxonmobil-to-disclose-climate-risks-for-its-business).

42 Marianne Lavelle, 'Exxon shareholders approve climate resolution: 62% vote for disclosure', *Inside Climate News*, 31 May 2017 (https://insideclimatenews.org/news/31052017/exxon-shareholder-climate-change-disclosure-resolution-approved).

43 Church of England website, 'Success for shareholders as ExxonMobil confirms implementation of resolution on climate change disclosure', 12 December 2017 (www.churchofengland.org/more/media-centre/news/success-shareholders-exxonmobil-confirms-implementation-resolution-climate).

Chapter 8

1 David Robinson, *The Moment We Noticed*, The Relationships Project, July 2020, p 12 (https://relationshipsproject.org/content/uploads/2020/07/The-Moment-We-Noticed_RelationshipsProject_202.pdf).

2 COVID-19 Mutual Aid website (https://covidmutualaid.org).

3 NHS website, News, 'NHS army of volunteers to start protecting vulnerable from coronavirus in England', 7 April 2020 (www.england.nhs.uk/2020/04/nhs-volunteer-army-now-ready-to-support-even-more-people/).

4 Steve Wyler, *Community Responses in Times of Crisis*, Local Trust, April 2020 (https://localtrust.org.uk/wp-content/uploads/2020/05/22040_Community-responses-in-times-of-crisis_online_lr.pdf).

5 Steve Wyler, *In Our Hands: A History of Community Business*, CoVi Productions, 2017, p 188.

6 Lorraine Hart, *To Have and To Hold: The Development Trusts Association Guide to Asset Development for Community and Social Enterprises (Second Edition)*, Locality website (https://locality.org.uk/wp-content/uploads/2018/03/To-have-and-to-hold-210910-for-web-FINAL.pdf).

7 Plunkett Foundation website, 'Our story' (https://plunkett.co.uk/our-story/).

8 British Institute of Innkeeping, 'Coronavirus and reopening: results of our members survey', June 2020 (www.bii.org/fileadmin/partner-files/downloads/Coronavirus/BII_Members_Survey_Report_June_2020.pdf).

9 Office for National Statistics, 'Economies of ale: small pubs close as chains focus on big bars', 26 November 2018 (www.ons.gov.uk/

businessindustryandtrade/business/activitysizeandlocation/articles/economiesofalesmallpubscloseaschainsfocusonbigbars/2018-11-26).

10 Robinson, *The Moment We Noticed*, p 4.

11 Mathew Little, 'Analysis: why Alinsky's supporters lost out', *Third Sector*, 8 March 2011 (www.thirdsector.co.uk/analysis-why-alinskys-supporters-lost/infrastructure/article/1058293).

12 Andy Hillier, 'Analysis: Community organisers – how we set up a local town team', *Third Sector*, 29 January 2013 (www.thirdsector.co.uk/analysis-community-organisers-set-local-town-team/management/article/1168466).

13 Daniel Cameron, Kimberley Rennick, Rosemary Maguire and Alison Freeman, *Evaluation of the Community Organisers Programme*, Ipsos Mori Social Research Institute, December 2015 (https://assets.publishing.service.gov.uk/government/uploads/system/uploads/attachment_data/file/488520/Community_Organisers_Programme_Evaluation.pdf).

Chapter 9

1 Val Cipriani, 'Online donations to foodbanks showing signs of compassion fatigue, research finds', *Civil Society News*, 29 June 2020 (www.civilsociety.co.uk/news/online-donations-to-foodbanks-showing-signs-of-compassion-fatigue-research-finds.html).

2 Stephen Delahunty, 'FareShare receives record number of donations in response to Marcus Rashford's campaign', *Third Sector*, 23 October 2020 (https://www.thirdsector.co.uk/fareshare-receives-record-number-donations-response-marcus-rashfords-campaign/fundraising/article/1698181).

3 FareShare annual report 2018/19 (https://fareshare.org.uk/wp-content/uploads/2019/11/Annual-Report-2019-interactive-export.pdf).

4 Andrew Rogers, *Being Built Together: A Story of New Black Majority Churches in the London Borough of Southwark, Final Report*, University of Roehampton, Southwark for Jesus and Churches Together in South London, June 2013 (www.cte.org.uk/Publisher/File.aspx?ID=137246).

5 Trussell Trust website, 'Start a food bank' (www.trusselltrust.org/get-involved/start-a-food-bank/).

6 Harriet Sherwood, 'Grenfell Tower priest tells of community's anger and grief in poem', *The Guardian*, 10 September 2017 (www.theguardian.com/uk-news/2017/sep/10/grenfell-tower-priest-community-anger-grief-poem).

7 Andy Hillier, 'Analysis: How the floods are driving community involvement', *Third Sector*, 25 February 2014 (www.thirdsector.co.uk/search/articles?keywords=chertsey%20floods&headlinesOnly=False).

8 Roy Walmsley, *World Prison Population List, 12th edition*, Institute for Criminal Policy Research, 6 November 2018, pp 11–14 (www.prisonstudies.org/sites/default/files/resources/downloads/wppl_12.pdf).

9 Offender Management Statistics Bulletin, England and Wales, 2019 (https://assets.publishing.service.gov.uk/government/uploads/system/

uploads/attachment_data/file/882163/Offender_Management_Statistics_
Quarterly_Q4_2019.pdf).

10 Scottish Centre for Crime and Justice Research, University of Glasgow, *Scotland's Prison Population*, (https://www.sccjr.ac.uk/wp-content/uploads/2019/10/7-Scotlands-prison-population.pdf).

11 Prison Reform Trust website, 'Prison: the facts' (www.prisonreformtrust.org.uk/Portals/0/Documents/Bromley%20Briefings/Prison%20the%20facts%20Summer%202019.pdf).

12 Ministry of Justice, *Economic and Social Costs of Reoffending – Analytical Report, 2019* (https://assets.publishing.service.gov.uk/government/uploads/system/uploads/attachment_data/file/814650/economic-social-costs-reoffending.pdf).

13 Ministry of Justice, *Analysis of the Impact of Employment on Re-offending Following Release from Custody, Using Propensity Score Matching*, March 2013 (https://assets.publishing.service.gov.uk/government/uploads/system/uploads/attachment_data/file/217412/impact-employment-reoffending.pdf).

14 Prison Reform Trust website, 'Prison: the facts'.

15 Forward Trust website, 'Origins – "About Blue Sky"', *Pulse #6*, p 4 (https://www.forwardtrust.org.uk/media/1851/item-3-pulse-6-april-2019-final.pdf).

16 The Forward Trust website, 'The Forward Trust (formerly Blue Sky) wins major charity award for ground-breaking partnership', 21 April 2016 (www.forwardtrust.org.uk/news-and-updates/the-forward-trust-formerly-blue-sky-wins-major-charity-award-for-ground-breaking-partnership/).

17 Katie Allen, 'Ex-inmates find honest jobs courtesy of banker and colleague, the bank robber', *The Guardian*, 21 January 2015 (www.theguardian.com/society/2015/jan/21/ex-prisoner-jobs-social-entereprise-blue-sky).

18 Ministry of Justice, *Justice Data Lab Reoffending Analysis: Blue Sky* (https://assets.publishing.service.gov.uk/government/uploads/system/uploads/attachment_data/file/249228/blue-sky-sept-2013.pdf).

19 Deloitte website, 'Brighter prospects for Blue Sky' (https://www2.deloitte.com/uk/en/pages/about-deloitte-uk/articles/blue-sky.html).

20 Clinks, *Annual Report 2019*, p 8 (www.clinks.org/sites/default/files/2019-11/clinks_annual-report-2019_FINAL_0.pdf).

21 Clinks website, 'The voluntary sector working in the criminal justice system' (www.clinks.org/about/sector).

22 The Clink Charity website, 'The charity' (https://theclinkcharity.org/the-charity).

23 Barnardo's website, 'Children affected by parental imprisonment' (www.barnardos.org.uk/what_we_do/children_of_prisoners.htm).

24 Prison Reform Trust website, 'Keeping in touch' (www.prisonreformtrust.org.uk/uploads/documents/KEEPING_IN_TOUCH_book4.pdf).

25 NPC website, *Improving Prisoners' Family Ties*, 2008 (www.thinknpc.org/wp-content/uploads/2018/07/Improving-prisoners-family-ties.pdf).

26 Storybook Dads website, *Annual Review 2018* (www.storybookdads.org.
uk/annual-review-2018).

27 Storybook Dads website.

28 Tania Mason, 'Charities versus Covid: How different subsectors have
responded', *Governance & Leadership*, 15 July 2020 (www.civilsociety.co.uk/
governance/charities-versus-covid.html).

Chapter 10

1 Russell Hargrave, 'International aid charities face losing billions of
pounds', *Civil Society News*, 14 April 2020 (www.civilsociety.co.uk/news/
international-aid-charities-face-losing-billions.html).

2 Peter Beaumont, 'Oxfam to close in 18 countries and cut 1,500 staff amid
coronavirus pressures', *The Guardian*, 20 May 2020 (www.theguardian.
com/global-development/2020/may/20/oxfam-to-close-in-18-countries-
and-cut-1500-staff-amid-coronavirus-pressures).

3 Russell Hargrave, 'Oxfam GB places more than 200 jobs at risk', *Civil
Society News*, 4 June 2020 (www.civilsociety.co.uk/news/oxfam-gb-
announces-more-than-200-jobs-are-at-risk.html).

4 National Statistics, *National Statistics on International Development: Provisional
UK Aid Spend 2018*, 4 April 2020 (www.gov.uk/government/statistics/
statistics-on-international-development-provisional-uk-aid-spend-2019).

5 Bond website, 'UK aid cuts: what's being prioritised and what we still need
to know', 27 July 2020 (www.bond.org.uk/news/2020/07/uk-aid-cuts-
whats-being-prioritised-and-what-we-still-need-to-know).

6 Gov.uk website, 'Changes to the UK's aid budget in the Spending Review',
25 November 2020 (www.gov.uk/government/news/changes-to-the-uks-
aid-budget-in-the-spending-review).

7 Anna Mikhailova, 'Britain only one in five countries to meet UN
foreign aid target', *Daily Telegraph*, 9 April 2018 (www.telegraph.co.uk/
politics/2018/04/09/britain-one-five-countries-meet-un-foreign-aid-target/).

8 Bond website, 'Financial trends for UK-based INGOs', 8 October 2018
(www.bond.org.uk/resources/financial-trends-2018).

9 Organisation for Economic Co-operation and Development, 'Development
resource flows: Total official and private flows' (https://data.oecd.org/drf/
total-official-and-private-flows.htm).

10 Gates Foundation website, 'Who we are', 31 December 2018 (www.
gatesfoundation.org/who-we-are/general-information/foundation-
factsheet).

11 BRAC, *Annual Report 2018* (www.bracuk.net/wp-content/
uploads/2019/06/BRAC-UK-Annual-Report-2018-web.pdf).

12 Comic Relief website, 'History' (www.comicrelief.com/about-comic-
relief/history).

13 World Bank website, 'Poverty overview', 3 April 2019 (www.worldbank.
org/en/topic/poverty/overview).

14 World Bank website, 'Decline of global extreme poverty continues but has
slowed: World Bank', 19 September 2018 (www.worldbank.org/en/news/

press-release/2018/09/19/decline-of-global-extreme-poverty-continues-but-has-slowed-world-bank).

15 Ian Goldin, *Development: A Very Short Introduction*, Oxford: Oxford University Press 2018, p 36.

16 Homi Kharas and Kristofer Hamel, 'A global tipping point: half the world is now middle class or wealthier', Brookings Institute website, 27 September 2018 (www.brookings.edu/blog/future-development/2018/09/27/a-global-tipping-point-half-the-world-is-now-middle-class-or-wealthier/).

17 End Malaria website, 'New reports focus on malaria eradication goal', 23 August 2019 (https://endmalaria.org/news/new-reports-focus-malaria-eradication-goal).

18 World Health Organization website, *World Malaria Report 2018* (www.who.int/malaria/publications/world-malaria-report-2018/en/).

19 Unicef website, 'Malaria', June 2018 (https://data.unicef.org/topic/child-health/malaria/).

20 World Health Organization website, 'WHO commends the Roll Back Malaria Partnership's contribution to global progress as governing board disbands secretariat', 25 August 2015 (www.who.int/malaria/news/2015/governing-board-disbands-rbm-secretariat/en/).

21 Molly Anders and Christin Roby, 'Ghana eliminates trachoma', Devex website, 14 June 2018 (www.devex.com/news/ghana-eliminates-trachoma-92929).

22 World Health Organisation, Fact Sheets: Trachoma, 11 August 2020 (https://www.who.int/news-room/fact-sheets/detail/trachoma)

23 Unicef website, 'Under-five mortality', September 2019 (https://data.unicef.org/topic/child-survival/under-five-mortality/).

24 Jessica van Haaften, 'Bangladesh has reduced child mortality rates by 78 per cent', Kinder website, 30 October 2018 (https://kinder.world/articles/solutions/bangladesh-has-reduced-child-mortality-rates-by-78-percent-19673).

25 Jared Ferrie, 'Afghan province declared landmine-free after 10-year clearance drive', Reuters, 15 February 2018 (www.reuters.com/article/us-afghanistan-conflict-landmines/afghan-province-declared-landmine-free-after-10-year-clearance-drive-idUSKCN1FZ1NY).

26 Larry Elliott and Ashley Seager, '£30bn debts write-off agreed', *The Guardian*, 11 June 2005 (www.theguardian.com/politics/2005/jun/11/uk.g8).

27 Linda Yueh, 'Is it possible to end global poverty?', BBC News, 27 March 2015 (www.bbc.co.uk/news/business-32082968).

28 Goldin, *Development: A Very Short Introduction*.

29 Tania Mason, 'International NGOs are "not just charities", says Mercy Corps Europe chief', *Civil Society News*, 22 March 2019 (www.civilsociety.co.uk/news/international-ngos-are-not-just-charities-says-mercy-corps-europe-chief.html#sthash.uEWDXtBn.dpuf).

30 M&G Investments, *Charity Financials Top 100 Fundraisers Spotlight*, April 2019 (https://spotlight.wilmingtononline.co.uk/docs/papers/charity-top-100-fundraisers-spotlight-report-april-2019.pdf_754.pdf).

31 Emma Graham-Harrison, 'Muslim charity's board steps down over antisemitism row', *The Guardian*, 23 August 2020 (www.theguardian.com/news/2020/aug/23/islamic-relief-worldwide-entire-board-steps-down-over-antisemitism-row).

32 Stephen Delahunty, 'Third senior figure at Islamic Relief steps down after making antisemitic comments', *Third Sector*, 16 November 2020 (www.thirdsector.co.uk/third-senior-figure-islamic-relief-worldwide-steps-down-making-antisemitic-comments/management/article/1699971).

33 Harriet Whitehead, 'Islamic Relief Worldwide chief executive to leave after 27 years at the charity', *Civil Society News*, 17 November 2020 (www.civilsociety.co.uk/news/islamic-relief-worldwide-chief-executive-to-leave-after-27-years-at-the-charity.html).

34 Gov.UK press release, 'Regulator oversees governance improvements after senior figures in development charity post anti-Semitic and offensive social media comments', 20 January 2021 (https://www.gov.uk/government/news/regulator-oversees-governance-improvements-after-senior-figures-in-development-charity-post-anti-semitic-and-offensive-social-media-comments).

35 Dominic Grieve QC, *Independent Commission into Governance and Vetting at Islamic Relief*, 14 January 2021 (https://www.islamic-relief.org.uk/wp-content/uploads/2020/09/Independent-Commission-Report-29.01.2021.pdf).

36 David Ainsworth, 'Muslim donors give more on average than other religious groups in the UK', *Third Sector*, 26 July 2013 (www.thirdsector.co.uk/muslim-donors-give-average-religious-groups-uk/fundraising/article/1192969).

37 UNHCR News, 'Uganda launches new education response plan for Africa's biggest refugee crisis', 17 September 2018 (www.unhcr.org/afr/news/press/2018/9/5b9fabe84/uganda-launches-new-education-response-plan-for-africas-biggest-refugee.html).

38 Hope Health Action website, 'How we're making a difference' (https://www.hopehealthaction.org/).

39 Charity Commission Register, Hope Health Action financial history (https://register-of-charities.charitycommission.gov.uk/charity-search/-/charity-details/5061301/financial-history).

40 Development in Action website, 'DiA blogger Joe Corry-Roake comments on the dangers of voluntourism' (www.developmentinaction.org/volontourism-the-dangers/).

Chapter 11

1 House of Commons Public Administration and Constitutional Affairs Committee, *The Collapse of Kids Company: Lessons for Charity Trustees, Professional Firms, the Charity Commission, and Whitehall*, HC433, 1 February 2016 (https://publications.parliament.uk/pa/cm201516/cmselect/cmpubadm/433/433.pdf).

2   Voluntary Arts website, 'Big Conversation 2017 results' (www.
    voluntaryarts.org/news/big-conversation-2017-results).

Chapter 12

1   Kate Ogden and David Phillips, *COVID-19 and English Council Funding:
    How Are Budgets Being Hit in 2020–21?*, Institute of Fiscal Studies,
    19 August 2020 (www.ifs.org.uk/publications/14977).

2   W.K. Jordan, *Philanthropy in England, 1480–1660*, London: George Allen
    & Unwin, 1959, p 140.

3   Ibid, p 149.

4   Blake Bromley, *The 1601 Preamble: The State's Agenda for Charity*, presented
    at Charity Law in the Pacific Rim Conference, Brisbane, 2001 (https://
    www.studocu.com/en-gb/document/university-of-london/equity-and-
    trusts/lecture-notes/charity-states-agenda/2173572/view).

5   David Owen, *English Philanthropy 1660–1960*, Oxford: Oxford University
    Press, 1964, p 6.

6   Frank Prochaska, *Women and Philanthropy in Nineteenth Century England*,
    Oxford: Clarendon Press, 1980, quoted in Justin Davis Smith, Colin
    Rochester and Rodney Hedley (eds), *An Introduction to the Voluntary Sector*,
    London: Routledge, 1990, p 20.

7   Constance Braithwaite, *The Voluntary Citizen*, London: Methuen, 1938, p 121.

8   Owen, *English Philanthropy 1660–1960*, p 530.

9   Justin Davis Smith, *100 Years of NCVO and Voluntary Action: Idealists and
    Realists*, Basingstoke: Palgrave Macmillan, 2019, p 61.

10 William Beveridge, *Voluntary Action: A Report on Methods of Social Advance*,
    Abingdon: Routledge, 2015 (first published 1948), p 74.

11 Ibid, p 304.

12 Cabinet Office, *Partnership in Public Services: An Action Plan for Third Sector
    Involvement*, December 2006 (not available online).

13 National Council for Voluntary Organisations, *UK Civil Society
    Almanac 2020: What Is the State of the Sector's Finances?* (https://almanac.
    fc.production.ncvocloud.net/financials/).

14 Ibid.

15 Nick Davies et al, *Government Procurement: The Scale and Nature of
    Contracting in the UK*, Institute for Government, December 2018, p 5
    (www.instituteforgovernment.org.uk/sites/default/files/publications/
    IfG_procurement_WEB_4.pdf).

16 Pete Alcock, 'The history of third sector service delivery in the UK',
    chapter 2 in James Rees and David Mullins (eds) *The Third Sector Delivering
    Public Services: Developments, Innovations and Challenges*, Bristol: Policy Press,
    2017.

17 James Rees, Adam Whitworth and Eleanor Carter, *Support for All in the UK
    Work Programme? Differential Payments, Same Old Problem …*, Third Sector
    Research Centre Working Paper 115, December 2013 (www.birmingham.
    ac.uk/Documents/college-social-sciences/social-policy/tsrc/working-
    papers/working-paper-115.pdf).

18 Kirsty Weakley, 'Employment charity Tomorrow's People collapsed owing £1.63m', *Civil Society News*, 24 May 2019 (www.civilsociety.co.uk/news/tomorrow-s-people-collapsed-owing-1-63m.html#sthash.ThI9igWz.dpuf).

19 Vibeka Mair, 'Charities highlight financial risk of Work Programme to MPs', *Civil Society News*, 9 February 2012 (https://www.civilsociety.co.uk/news/charities-highlight-financial-risk-of-work-programme-to-mps.html).

20 House of Commons Committee of Public Accounts, *Government Contracts for Community Rehabilitation Companies*, 14 March 2018, p 9 (https://publications.parliament.uk/pa/cm201719/cmselect/cmpubacc/897/897.pdf).

21 Ibid, pp 5–7.

22 House of Commons Justice Committee, *Transforming Rehabilitation*, 19 June 2018, p 37 (https://publications.parliament.uk/pa/cm201719/cmselect/cmjust/482/482.pdf).

23 National Audit Office, *Transforming Rehabilitation: Progress Review*, 1 March 2019, p 7 (www.nao.org.uk/wp-content/uploads/2019/02/Transforming-Rehabilitation-Progress-review.pdf).

24 Clinks, *Under Represented, Under Pressure, Under Resourced: The Voluntary Sector in Transforming Rehabilitation*, April 2018 (https://www.clinks.org/publication/under-represented-under-pressure-under-resourced).

25 National Audit Office, *Transforming Rehabilitation: Progress Review*.

26 National Council for Voluntary Organisations, *UK Civil Society Almanac 2020*.

27 Mary O'Hara, 'The Society Interview: 4Children spearheads early years initiative', *The Guardian*, 31 May 2011 (www.theguardian.com/society/2011/may/31/anne-longfield-4children-spearheads-early-years-initiative).

28 Katy Morton, '4Children and NCB chosen to deliver strategic support', *Nursery World*, 24 May 2013 (www.nurseryworld.co.uk/nursery-world/news/1107075/4children-ncb-chosen-deliver-strategic-support).

29 Social Finance website, 'Social Finance raises £1.7m for 4Children to expand its UK children's centres and nurseries operations', 13 October 2014 (www.socialfinance.org.uk/sites/default/files/news/4children-final-press-release.pdf).

30 House of Commons Library, *Briefing Paper, Sure Start (England)*, 9 June 2017 (https://commonslibrary.parliament.uk/research-briefings/cbp-7257/).

31 Emily Corfe, 'All senior staff at 4Children among redundancies', *Civil Society News*, 5 September 2016 (www.civilsociety.co.uk/news/all-senior-staff-at-4children-among-redundancies.html).

32 Newcastle City Council Voluntary Sector Liaison Group, *VCS investment 2017/18*, 13 December 2018 (https://democracy.newcastle.gov.uk/documents/s138668/10.%20VSLG%20VCS%20Investment%20-%20Dec%202018.pdf).

33 Ibid, Appendix 1.

34 Newcastle City Council, 'The Newcastle Fund' (www.newcastle.gov.uk/services/communities-and-neighbourhoods/newcastle-fund).

35 Newcastle Council for Voluntary Service, 'Do we need to talk? Public sector procurement and contracts: a thought piece', June 2018 (www.bl.uk/collection-items/do-we-need-to-talk-public-sector-procurement-and-contracts-a-thought-piece).

36 National Council for Voluntary Organisations, *Ten Procurement Barriers Affecting Charities and Social Enterprises* (www.ncvo.org.uk/images/documents/policy_and_research/public_services/ten-procurement-barriers-affecting-charities-and-social-enterprises.pdf).

37 NPC website, 'Charities taking charge: transforming to face a changing world', May 2017 (www.thinknpc.org/resource-hub/charities-taking-charge/).

38 Charity Commission for England and Wales, *Accounts Monitoring Review: Charities with Audit Reports Identifying that They May Be in Financial Difficulty*, September 2016 (https://assets.publishing.service.gov.uk/government/uploads/system/uploads/attachment_data/file/554358/amr_charities_with_audit_reports_identifying_that_they_may_be_in_financial_difficulty.pdf).

39 Hft website, 'New report "a red flag for the future of social care", as providers warn cuts could soon be felt by vulnerable adults', 12 February 2019 (www.hft.org.uk/blog/sector-pulse-check-2018/).

40 Charity Commission for England and Wales, *Guidance: Charities and Public Service Delivery: An Introduction and Overview*, 1 March 2012 (www.gov.uk/government/publications/charities-and-public-service-delivery-an-introduction-cc37/).

41 Third Sector, 'Anti-lobbying clause put on hold for a review', 26 May 2016 (www.thirdsector.co.uk/anti-lobbying-clause-put-hold-review/article/1396088).

42 Paul Morgan-Bentley, 'Charities gagged by ministers over Universal Credit', *The Times*, 12 October 2018 (www.thetimes.co.uk/article/charities-gagged-by-ministers-over-universal-credit-rcq6b8g72).

43 Charity Commission for England and Wales, 'Acevo Annual Conference 2012: William Shawcross's speech', 2 November 2012 (www.gov.uk/government/speeches/acevo-annual-conference-2012-william-shawcrosss-speech).

44 Kirsty Weakley, 'You're not a charity if you're funded by government, charity leader tells Tory Party Conference', *Civil Society News*, 6 October 2015 (www.civilsociety.co.uk/news/you-re-not-a-charity-if-you-re-funded-by-government--charity-leader-tells-tory-party-conference.html#sthash.aLYXsWW8.dpuf).

45 David Walker and John Tizard, *Out of Contract: Time to Move on from the 'love in' with Outsourcing and PFI*, The Smith Institute, January 2018 (www.smith-institute.org.uk/wp-content/uploads/2018/01/Out-of-contract-Time-to-move-on-from-the-%E2%80%98love-in%E2%80%99-with-outsourcing-and-PFI.pdf).

46 John Tizard and David Walker, 'Charities have a role in public services, but not as surrogate businesses', *Third Sector*, 22 January 2018 (www.thirdsector.co.uk/charities-role-public-services-not-surrogate-businesses/management/article/1455038).

47 Institute of Fiscal Studies, *Recent Cuts to Public Spending*, October 2015 (www.ifs.org.uk/tools_and_resources/fiscal_facts/cuts_to_public_ spending).

48 NPC website, 'Charities taking charge: transforming to face a changing world'.

Chapter 13

1 nfpSynergy website, 'Facts and figures: volunteering', 3 November 2016 (https://nfpsynergy.net/free-report/facts-and-figures-volunteering# downloads).

2 RNLI website, 'RNLI Chief Executive, Mark Dowie, writes open letter during pandemic', 26 May 2020 (https://rnli.org/news-and-media/2020/ may/26/rnli-chief-executive-mark-dowie-writes-open-letter-during- pandemic).

3 Hospice UK website, 'Facts and figures' (www.hospiceuk.org/about- hospice-care/media-centre/facts-and-figures).

4 Office for National Statistics, *National Survey of Bereaved People (VOICES): England, 2015* (www.ons.gov.uk/peoplepopulationandcommunity/health andsocialcare/healthcaresystem/bulletins/nationalsurveyofbereaved peoplevoices/england2015).

5 Hospice UK website, 'Facts and figures'.

6 Care Quality Commission, *St Clare's Hospice*, December 2018 (www.cqc. org.uk/location/1-106196515/reports).

7 David Clark, 'Hospices are facing financial ruin – here's how we can sustain end-of-life care', *The Independent*, 19 February 2019 (www.independent. co.uk/news/health/hospice-end-life-care-medicine-hospital-doctor- treatment-a8773831.html).

8 Geoff Newman, *The Genesis of the Cornwall Air Ambulance Service*, Lulu Publishing Services, 2017.

9 Cornwall Air Ambulance Service website, 'Our story' (https:// cornwallairambulancetrust.org/about-us/).

10 Devon Air Ambulance website, 'Why we are asking our supporters not to sign the petition for government to fund air ambulances' (www.daat. org/news/why-we-are-asking-our-supporters-not-to-sign-the-petition- for-government-to-fund-air-ambulances).

Chapter 14

1 William Beveridge, *Voluntary Action: A Report on Methods of Social Advance*, Abingdon: Routledge, 2015 (first published 1948), p 116 and pp 301-2.

2 Hope for Tomorrow website, 'About us' (https://hopefortomorrow.org. uk/about/).

3 Hope for Tomorrow website, *Annual Report 2019* (https://apps. charitycommission.gov.uk/Showcharity/RegisterOfCharities/ FinancialHistory.aspx?RegisteredCharityNumber=1094677&Subsidiary Number=0).

4   BBC News, 'Blood bikers: the volunteer motorcyclists who help the NHS', 18 December 2016 (www.bbc.co.uk/news/magazine-38330814).

5   John Carvel, 'NHS faces new strike threat over blood service closures', *The Guardian*, 3 October 2006 (www.theguardian.com/society/2006/oct/03/health.politics).

6   NABB's entry to the Charity Awards 2016, not available online.

7   May Bulman, 'Nearly 4 million adults forced to use food banks, figures reveal', *The Independent*, 7 June 2018 (www.independent.co.uk/news/uk/home-news/food-banks-uk-how-many-people-adults-poverty-a8386811.html).

8   Trussell Trust website, 'End of year stats' (www.trusselltrust.org/news-and-blog/latest-stats/end-year-stats/).

9   Toby Helm, 'Charities condemn Iain Duncan Smith for food bank snub', *The Observer*, 21 December 2013 (www.theguardian.com/politics/2013/dec/21/iain-duncan-smith-food-banks-charities).

10 Trussell Trust website, 'Our story' (www.trusselltrust.org/about/our-story/).

11 Charity Awards 2016 website, 'The Trussell Trust' (https://charityawards.co.uk/past-awards/2016-2/the-trussell-trust/).

12 Trussell Trust website, 'Foodbank use remains at record high, as new data mapping tool gives fresh insights into UK hunger', 15 April 2016 (www.trusselltrust.org/wp-content/uploads/sites/2/2015/06/Foodbank-use-remains-at-record-high.pdf).

13 Trussell Trust website, 'Universal Credit and food banks' (www.trusselltrust.org/what-we-do/research-advocacy/universal-credit-and-foodbank-use/).

14 Ben Glaze, 'Universal Credit "fuels foodbank use", suggests new Trussell Trust study', *The Mirror*, 19 September 2019 (www.mirror.co.uk/news/politics/universal-credit-fuels-foodbank-use-20090526).

15 Trussell Trust website, 'More than food' (www.trusselltrust.org/what-we-do/more-than-food/).

16 Ministry of Defence and Cabinet Office, 'Strategy for Our Veterans', 14 November 2018 (www.gov.uk/government/publications/strategy-for-our-veterans).

17 Lloyd's website, 'Lloyd's Patriotic Fund' (www.lloyds.com/about-lloyds/responsible-business/community-involvement/lloyds-patriotic-fund).

18 SSAFA website, 'Our history' (www.ssafa.org.uk/about-us/our-history).

19 HM Government, *The UK Armed Forces Charity Sector: A Summary of Provision*, November 2018 (https://assets.publishing.service.gov.uk/government/uploads/system/uploads/attachment_data/file/759046/6.5046_MOD_Military_Charity_Report_v3_webNH.PDF).

20 Carol Harris, '1914–1918: how charities helped to win WW1', *Third Sector*, 27 June 2014 (www.thirdsector.co.uk/1914-1918-charities-helped-win-ww1/volunteering/article/1299786).

21 Directory of Social Change, *Sector Insight: Armed Forces Charities – an Overview and Analysis*, 2020, p xiv (https://www.armedforcescharities.org.uk/Public/Research/Reports/Sector-Insight-2020/Public/Research_

Tab/Sector%20Insight%202020.aspx?hkey=373c6464-2919-43cf-9d25-5b125b928ba9).

22 Ministry of Defence and Cabinet Office, *Strategy for Our Veterans*, 14 November 2018 (www.gov.uk/government/publications/strategy-for-our-veterans).

23 Combat Stress website, 'Our history' (www.combatstress.org.uk/about-us/our-history).

24 Combat Stress's entry to the Charity Awards 2016, not available online.

25 Expert in Mind website, 'Dr Walter Busuttil' (www.expertinmind.co.uk/experts/profile/dr-walter-busuttil).

26 Charity Awards website, 'Combat Stress', 2016 (https://charityawards.co.uk/past-awards/2016-2/combat-stress/).

27 *British Medical Journal*, 'Long-term responses to treatment in UK veterans with military-related PTSD: an observational study', 2016 (https://bmjopen.bmj.com/content/6/9/e011667.abstract).

28 Combat Stress website, 'Our strategy' (www.combatstress.org.uk/strategy).

29 Combat Stress website, 'Press release: Our new five-year strategy' (www.combatstress.org.uk/about-us/press/combat-stress-announces-new-five-year-strategy-improve-veterans%E2%80%99-access-mental-health).

Chapter 15

1 Hertfordshire Life, 'Herts history: The battle of Berkhamsted', 14 March 2016 (www.hertfordshirelife.co.uk/home/herts-history-the-battle-of-berkhamsted-1-4455536).

2 Tristram Hunt, 'Octavia Hill: her life and legacy', National Trust website (www.nationaltrust.org.uk/features/octavia-hill---her-life-and-legacy).

3 National Trust, 'Information for journalists' (www.nationaltrust.org.uk/features/information-to-journalists).

4 Tom Wall, 'A year on from National Trust row, activists keep watch on trail hunts', *The Observer*, 16 December 2018 (www.theguardian.com/uk-news/2018/dec/16/national-trust-trail-hunting-row-one-year-on).

5 Patrick Barkham, '"It is strange to see the British struggling with the beaver": why is rewilding so controversial?', *The Observer*, 3 July 2017 (www.theguardian.com/environment/2017/jul/01/rewilding-conservation-ecology-national-trust).

6 Alan Jones, 'Ineos threatens to sue National Trust so it can carry out fracking survey on its land', *The Independent*, 20 July 2017 (www.independent.co.uk/news/business/news/ineos-national-trust-fracking-lawsuit-energy-firm-legal-action-clumber-park-nottinghamshire-seismic-a7851581.html).

7 David Rankin, 'National Trust back down in volunteers gay rainbow badge row', *The Times*, 5 August 2017 (www.thetimes.co.uk/article/national-trust-backs-down-in-volunteers-gay-rainbow-badge-row-2vvcjfpll).

8 National Trust website, 'Our spending cut plans in response to coronavirus losses', 29 July 2020 (www.nationaltrust.org.uk/news/our-spending-cut-plans-in-response-to-coronavirus-losses).

9   Bendor Grosvenor, 'National Trust restructuring plans are "one of the most damaging assaults on art historical expertise ever seen in the UK"', *The Art Newspaper*, 21 August 2020 (www.theartnewspaper.com/comment/national-trust-restructuring-plan-job-cuts).

10   National Trust, *Interim Report on the Connections between Colonialism and Properties now in the Care of the National Trust, Including Links with Historic Slavery*, September 2020 (https://nt.global.ssl.fastly.net/documents/colionialism-and-historic-slavery-report.pdf).

11   Stephen Delahunty, 'Regulator received just three complaints about National Trust slavery report', *Third Sector*, 23 November 2020 (https://www.thirdsector.co.uk/regulator-received-just-three-complaints-national-trust-slavery-links-report/governance/article/1700842?bulletin=third-sector-pm&utm_medium=EMAIL&utm_campaign=eNews).

12   Stephen Delahunty, 'Charities criticise regulator over National Trust remarks', *Third Sector*, 26 October 2020 (https://www.thirdsector.co.uk/charities-criticise-regulator-national-trust-remarks/governance/article/1698332).

13   House of Commons Hansard, 'Future of the National Trust', 11 November 2020, cols 436WH and 442WH (https://hansard.parliament.uk/commons/2020-11-11/debates/14F2215E-66AC-4A16-B4E2-4937E24BAC26/FutureOfTheNationalTrust).

14   Craig Simpson, 'Lord Nelson's "heroic status" to be reviewed by National Maritime Museum', *Daily Telegraph*, 10 October 2020 (https://www.telegraph.co.uk/news/2020/10/10/lord-nelsons-heroic-status-reviewed-national-maritime-museum/).

15   Royal Museums Greenwich website, Update from Paddy Rodgers, Director, about the Museum and its commentary on Nelson (https://www.rmg.co.uk/join-support/nelson-update).

16   *Mail Online*, 6 December 2020 (https://www.dailymail.co.uk/news/article-9022461/Barnardos-sparks-row-suggesting-parents-teach-children-white-privilege.html).

17   Barnardo's website, Barnardo's response to MPs' letter about white privilege, 6 December 2020 (https://www.barnardos.org.uk/news/barnardos-response-mps-letter-about-white-privilege).

18   House of Commons, First Standing Committee on Delegated Legislation, 3 February 1998 (https://publications.parliament.uk/pa/cm199798/cmstand/deleg1/st980203/80203s01.htm).

19   Historic Royal Palaces, *Trustees' Report and Financial Statements as at 31 March 2020* (www.hrp.org.uk/media/2597/201920_hrpfinancialstatementscertified.pdf).

20   Canal and River Trust, *Annual Report and Accounts 2019/20*, p 27. (https://canalrivertrust.org.uk/media/original/42580-annual-report-and-accounts-2019-20.pdf).

21   Ibid, p 68.

22   Simon Thurley, *Men from the Ministry: How Britain Saved Its Heritage*, New Haven, CT: Yale University Press, 2013, pp 65 and 148.

23 Esther Addley, 'Stonehenge with no crowds? Big changes planned for reopening', *The Guardian*, 29 May 2020 (www.theguardian.com/uk-news/2020/may/29/stonehenge-with-no-crowds-big-changes-planned-for-reopening).

Chapter 16

1 Arts Council England, *The Economic Impact of Museums in England*, 2 March 2015 (www.artscouncil.org.uk/sites/default/files/download-file/The_Economic_Impact_of_Museums_in_England.pdf).

2 Association of Independent Museums website, 'About independent museums' (www.aim-museums.co.uk/about-independent-museums/).

3 Museums Association, *Museums in the UK 2018 Report*, February 2018 (www.museumsassociation.org/download?id=1244881).

4 Geraldine Kendall Adams, 'More museums appeal business rates after York Museums Trust ruling', *Museums Journal*, 18 July 2018 (www.museumsassociation.org/museums-journal/news/18072018-more-museums-appeal-business-rates).

5 Department of Digital, Culture, Media and Sport, *Taking Part Survey: England Adult Report 2017/18* (https://assets.publishing.service.gov.uk/government/uploads/system/uploads/attachment_data/file/740242/180911_Taking_Part_Adult_Annual_Report_-_Revised.pdf).

6 Ibid.

7 Department for Digital, Culture, Media and Sport, *Sponsored Museums Annual Performance Indicators 2016/17* (https://assets.publishing.service.gov.uk/government/uploads/system/uploads/attachment_data/file/657464/Sponsored_Museums_Performance_Indicators_2016_17.pdf).

8 Visit Britain, *Visitor Attraction Trends in England 2018*, August 2019 (www.visitbritain.org/sites/default/files/vb-corporate/Documents-Library/documents/England-documents/annual_attractions_survey_2018_trends_report.pdf).

Chapter 17

1 Department for Education, *Schools, Pupils and Their Characteristics 2019*, 27 June 2019 (https://assets.publishing.service.gov.uk/government/uploads/system/uploads/attachment_data/file/812539/Schools_Pupils_and_their_Characteristics_2019_Main_Text.pdf).

2 Catherine Fairbairn, *House of Commons Library Briefing Paper 05222, 17 October 2019: Charitable Status and Independent Schools*, p 7 (https://researchbriefings.parliament.uk/ResearchBriefing/Summary/SN05222).

3 Independent Schools Council, *Census and Annual Report 2019*, p 18 (www.isc.co.uk/media/5479/isc_census_2019_report.pdf).

4 About 1,000 independent schools, of which some 300 are charities, are not members of the ISC.

5 House of Lords Hansard, *Official Report of the Grand Committee on the Charities Bill*, 9 February 2005, col GC112 (https://api.parliament.uk/

historic-hansard/grand-committee-report/2005/feb/09/official-report-of-the-grand-committee#S5LV0669P0_20050209_GCR_6).

6 Annie Kelly, 'News in focus: tripe and barbarism on school menu', *Third Sector*, 9 February 2005 (www.thirdsector.co.uk/news-focus-tripe-barbarism-school-menu/article/610825).

7 House of Commons Public Administration Select Committee, *The Role of the Charity Commission and 'Public Benefit': Post-legislative Scrutiny of the Charities Act 2006*, 21 May 2013, p 24 (https://publications.parliament.uk/pa/cm201314/cmselect/cmpubadm/76/76.pdf).

8 A hospital pass is when a player receives the ball an instant before being tackled by a large opponent.

9 Upper Tribunal, Tax and Chancery Chamber, 13 October 2011 (http://taxandchancery_ut.decisions.tribunals.gov.uk/Documents/decisions/1_TheISC_v_TheCharityCommission_forEnglandWales.pdf).

10 Matthew Parris, 'Schools that sell privilege can't be charities', *The Times*, 9 June 2012 (www.thetimes.co.uk/article/schools-that-sell-privilege-cant-be-charities-0swsz5mshsd).

11 Michael Gove, 'Put VAT on school fees and soak the rich', *The Times*, 24 February 2017 (www.thetimes.co.uk/article/put-vat-on-school-fees-and-soak-the-rich-fmpjv2zd9).

12 BBC News online, 'Labour members call to "redistribute" private schools' assets', 23 September 2019 (www.bbc.co.uk/news/uk-politics-49786645).

13 Robert Verkaik, *Posh Boys: How the English Public Schools Ruin Britain*, Oxford: Oneworld Publications, 2018.

14 Francis Green and David Kynaston, *Engines of Privilege: Britain's Private School Problem*, London: Bloomsbury, 2019, p 209.

15 Headmasters' and Headmistresses' Conference website, 'London Academy of Excellence' (www.hmc.org.uk/about-hmc/partnerships/london-academy-excellence/).

16 Eton College website, 'Holyport College' (www.etoncollege.com/HolyportCollege.aspx).

17 Eton College website, *Eton2020 – A New Social Vision* (www.etoncollege.com/support-us/areas-for-support/eton-2020-a-new-social-vision/).

18 Independent Schools Council, *Census and Annual Report 2019*.

19 Oxford Economics, *The Impact of Independent Schools on the UK Economy*, October 2018, p 21 (www.oxfordeconomics.com/recent-releases/cc1e1bbc-4a9d-4bb7-bdc3-88add90e704a).

20 Green and Kynaston, *Engines of Privilege: Britain's Private School Problem*, 2019, p 189.

21 Until 1976 there were 174 direct grant schools, many of them long-established charitable foundations, admitting pupils on academic merit; a quarter of places were funded directly by the government, the rest by fees. When comprehensive education was introduced and direct grants abolished, a few of the schools closed, 45 joined the state system, and the rest joined the independent sector. From 1980, the Conservative government funded 'assisted places' that replicated the direct grant system

to some extent, but these were abolished by Labour in 1997 and the money was diverted to primary schools.

22 John Carvel, 'Blunkett plans network of city academies', *The Guardian*, 15 March 2000 (www.theguardian.com/uk/2000/mar/15/schools.news).

23 Paul Jump, 'Government rejects Charity Commission plea to halt exemption of academy schools', *Third Sector*, 12 January 2010 (www.thirdsector.co.uk/government-rejects-charity-commission-plea-halt-exemption-academy-schools/governance/article/977078).

24 Lauren Higgs, 'Government does U-turn on charitable status of academies', *Children and Young People Now*, 3 February 2010 (www.cypnow.co.uk/cyp/news/1049370/government-does-u-turn-on-charitable-status-of-academies).

25 Andy Ricketts, 'Tories would give academies "exempt charity" status, says Michael Gove', *Third Sector*, 2 February 2010 (https://www.thirdsector.co.uk/tories-give-academy-schools-exempt-charity-status-says-michael-gove/governance/article/981337).

26 Kaye Wiggins, 'Charity Commission will retain role in governance of academy schools', *Third Sector*, 7 September 2010 (www.thirdsector.co.uk/charity-commission-will-retain-role-governance-academy-schools/governance/article/1026250).

27 National Audit Office, *Converting Maintained Schools to Academies*, 22 January 2018 (www.nao.org.uk/wp-content/uploads/2018/02/Converting-maintained-schools-to-academies.pdf).

28 See, for example, Anne West and David Wolfe, *Academies, the School System in England and a Vision for the Future*, Education Research Group, Department of Social Policy, London School of Economics and Political Science, June 2018 (www.lse.ac.uk/social-policy/Assets/Documents/PDF/Research-reports/Academies-Vision-Report.pdf).

29 Andy Hillier, 'Analysis: Academy schools – charities, but not as we know them', *Third Sector*, 5 February 2013 (www.thirdsector.co.uk/analysis-academy-schools-charities-not-know/governance/article/1169415).

30 Academies Commission, *Unleashing Greatness: Getting the Best from an Academized System*, p 106, Pearson Think Tank and RSA, January 2013 (www.educationengland.org.uk/documents/pdfs/2013-academies-commission.pdf).

31 British Educational Suppliers Association website, 'Key UK educational statistics' (www.besa.org.uk/key-uk-education-statistics/).

32 National Audit Office, *Investigation into the Education Funding Agency's Oversight of Related Party Transactions at Durand Academy*, 13 November 2014, p 17 (www.nao.org.uk/wp-content/uploads/2014/11/Investigation-into-the-Education-Funding-Agencys-oversight-of-related-party-transactions-at-Durand-Academy.pdf).

33 Ibid, p 5.

34 Freddie Whittaker, 'Head who earned more than £400,000 grilled over private companies including dating agency', *Schoolsweek*, 26 January 2015 (https://schoolsweek.co.uk/durand-head-greg-martin-grilled-over-dating-agency-and-other-companies/).

35 Charity Commission for England and Wales, *Inquiry Report: Durand Education Trust*, 21 October 2016 (https://assets.publishing.service.gov. uk/government/uploads/system/uploads/attachment_data/file/561696/ durand_education_trust.pdf).

36 House of Commons Public Accounts Committee, *Academies Accounts and Performance Inquiry*, 23 January 2019, p 6 (https://publications.parliament. uk/pa/cm201719/cmselect/cmpubacc/1597/1597.pdf).

37 John Dickens, 'Fraud police drop Bright Tribe investigation', *Schools Week*, 25 September 2020 (https://schoolsweek.co.uk/fraud-police-drop-bright-tribe-investigation/).

38 HM Treasury, *Government Response to the Committee of Public Accounts on the 72nd to 77th Reports from Session 2017–19* (https://assets.publishing. service.gov.uk/government/uploads/system/uploads/attachment_data/ file/791269/CCS207_CCS0319925300-001_HMT_Government_ Response_Web.pdf).

39 Cabinet Office Strategy Unit, *Private Action, Public Benefit*, September 2002, p 87 (https://webarchive.nationalarchives.gov.uk/+/http:/www. cabinetoffice.gov.uk/media/cabinetoffice/strategy/assets/strat%20data.pdf).

40 Jessica Shepherd, 'Fellows share land sale bonus', *Times Higher Education*, 26 May 2006 (www.timeshighereducation.com/news/fellows-share-land-sale-bonus/203337.article#survey-answer).

Chapter 18

1 Charities Aid Foundation, *UK Giving 2019*, pp 12–14 (www.cafonline.org/ docs/default-source/about-us-publications/caf-uk-giving-2019-report-an-overview-of-charitable-giving-in-the-uk.pdf?sfvrsn=c4a29a40_4).

2 AMRC research expenditure dashboard (https://datastudio.google.com/re porting/1rjJpBX6RrXrPWjfmH0Iqso9ZCKuHp69i/page/RgHw).

3 AMRC website, 'Completing the puzzle' (www.amrc.org.uk/completing-the-puzzle).

4 CRUK *Annual Report and Accounts 2016/17*, p 1 (www.cancerresearchuk. org/sites/default/files/cruk_annual_report_2016-17.pdf).

5 Wellcome Trust website, 'Wellcome statements on novel coronavirus', 4 May 2020 (https://wellcome.ac.uk/press-release/wellcome-statements-novel-coronavirus-covid-19).

6 Paul Nurse, 'Coronavirus means science is suddenly being done differently – and so is politics', *The Guardian*, 2 May 2020 (www.theguardian.com/ commentisfree/2020/may/02/coronavirus-means-science-is-suddenly-being-done-differently-and-so-is-politics).

7 Adam Bennett and Ben Leo, 'Cancer Research to cut 500 jobs after taking £150m coronavirus funding hit', *The Sun*, 15 July 2020 (www. thesun.co.uk/news/12132429/cancer-research-cut-500-jobs-coronavirus-funding-hit/).

8 Harriet Whitehead, 'Breast Cancer Now to make approximately 60 redundancies', *Civil Society News*, 10 June 2020 (www.civilsociety.co.uk/ news/breast-cancer-now-to-make-approximately-60-redundancies.html).

9 Breast Cancer Now, 'Coronavirus is the greatest threat the cancer charity sector has ever faced', 1 June 2020 (https://breastcancernow.org/about-us/news-personal-stories/coronavirus-greatest-threat-cancer-charity-sector-has-ever-faced).

10 Lisa Jones, 'MPs urge Chancellor to support charity funded research', British Heart Foundation, 20 July 2020 (www.bhf.org.uk/what-we-do/news-from-the-bhf/news-archive/2020/july/mps-urge-chancellor-to-support-charity-funded-research).

11 Sarah Sarsby, 'UK's leading stroke charity warns research faces long-term threat due to coronavirus pandemic', *AT Today*, 15 July 2020 (http://attoday.co.uk/uks-leading-stroke-charity-warns-research-faces-long-term-threat-due-to-coronavirus-pandemic/).

12 AMRC website, 'Industry urge prime minister to protect charity research', 1 September 2020 (www.amrc.org.uk/news/industry-urge-prime-minister-to-protect-charity-research).

13 Harriet Whitehead, 'Covid-19 puts billions of medical research funding at risk due to lost fundraising', *Civil Society News*, 22 October 2020 (https://www.civilsociety.co.uk/news/covid-19-could-mean-7-8bn-less-for-medical-research-by-2027.html).

14 AMRC website, 'Life Sciences-Charity Partnership Fund', 3 June 2020 (www.amrc.org.uk/Handlers/Download.ashx?IDMF=1cf57b61-5794-46ff-b3a6-0814bc6e9127).

15 BBC, Today, 27 August 2020 (no longer available online).

16 Robert Rhodes James, *Henry Wellcome*, London: Hodder & Stoughton, 1994.

17 Wellcome Trust 'Annual Report 2019: highlights' (https://wellcome.ac.uk/reports/wellcome-annual-report-2019).

18 Robert Rhodes James, *Henry Wellcome*, p 385.

19 Kai Kupferschmidt, 'Finally, some good news about Ebola: two new treatments dramatically lower the death rate in a trial', *Science*, 12 August 2019 (www.sciencemag.org/news/2019/08/finally-some-good-news-about-ebola-two-new-treatments-dramatically-lower-death-rate).

20 TB Alliance website, 'The pandemic – a global threat' (www.tballiance.org/why-new-tb-drugs/global-pandemic).

21 GlaxoSmithKline website, 'GSK candidate vaccine helps prevent active pulmonary tuberculosis in HIV negative adults in phase II study', 25 September 2018 (www.gsk.com/en-gb/media/press-releases/gsk-candidate-vaccine-helps-prevent-active-pulmonary-tuberculosis-in-hiv-negative-adults-in-phase-ii-study/).

22 Breast Cancer Now website, 'Our research centre' (https://breastcancernow.org/breast-cancer-research/our-research-centre/our-research-centre).

23 Rand Corporation website, 'Examining the future outlook for breast cancer' (www.rand.org/randeurope/research/projects/breakthrough-breast-cancer.html).

24 Office for National Statistics, *The Number of Mergers and Acquisitions Involving UK Companies, 2010 to 2016*, Figure 2 (www.ons.gov.uk/

businessindustryandtrade/changestobusiness/mergersandacquisitions/
articles/ukmergersandacquisitionsactivityincontext/2016).

25 Eastside Primetimers, *The Good Merger Index, A Review of Not-for-Profit Mergers for 2015/16*, p 6 (https://ep-uk.org/wp-content/uploads/2017/05/good.merger.index_.2015-16.pdf).

26 Breast Cancer Now website, 'Becoming Breast Cancer Now' (https://breastcancernow.org/about-us/becoming-breast-cancer-now).

27 Tania Mason, 'Reducing the pink fog: how Breast Cancer Now made a go of merger', *Governance & Leadership*, 5 January 2018 (www.civilsociety.co.uk/governance/reducing-the-pink-fog.html).

28 eCancer website, 'Multidisciplinary teams improve survival rates', 19 June 2012 (https://ecancer.org/en/news/3178-multidisciplinary-teams-improve-survival-rates).

29 Alex Murdock and Brian Lamb, 'SERC 2008: The impact of a third sector organisation on public services – the case of audiology services', Powerpoint presentation.

30 Bridget Shield, *Hearing Loss – Number and Costs: A Report for Hear-It AISBL*, Brunel University, London, 2018, p 115 (www.hear-it.org/sites/default/files/BS%20-%20report%20files/HearitReportHearing LossNumbersandCosts.pdf).

31 Murdock and Lamb, 'SERC 2008'.

32 Alex Murdock and Brian Lamb, 'The impact of the RNID on auditory services in England: Borrowing lawnmowers and the price of salt', *Social Enterprise Journal*, 5(2), 2009: pp 141–53 (www.emerald.com/insight/content/doi/10.1108/17508610910981725/full/html).

33 Ibid, p 143.

34 Ibid, p 144.

35 Ibid, p 143.

36 Ibid, p 145.

37 Paul Boateng MP and Fiona MacTaggart MP, *Adding Value to Public Services*, RNID, 2004 (not available online).

38 MapAction website, 'Our history' (https://mapaction.org/about-us/our-history/).

39 Centers for Disease Control and Prevention website, '2014–16 Ebola outbreak in West Africa' (www.cdc.gov/vhf/ebola/history/2014-2016-outbreak/index.html).

Chapter 19

1 George Monbiot, 'No 10 and the secretly funded lobby groups intent on undermining democracy', *The Guardian*, 1 September 2020 (www.theguardian.com/commentisfree/2020/sep/01/no-10-lobby-groups-democracy-policy-exchange).

2 BBC News, 'Church of England failures "allowed child sex offenders to hide"', 6 October 2020 (www.bbc.co.uk/news/uk-54433295).

3   Tania Mason, 'Catholic Care goes back to court over gay adoption', *Civil Society News*, 12 September 2012 (www.civilsociety.co.uk/news/catholic-care-goes-back-to-court-over-gay-adoption.html).

4   Charity Commission for England and Wales, *Application for Registration of the Preston Down Trust, Decision of the Commission*, 3 January 2014, pp 4 and 20 (https://assets.publishing.service.gov.uk/government/uploads/system/uploads/attachment_data/file/336112/preston_down_trust_full_decision.pdf).

5   Charity Commission inquiry report into Manchester New Moston Congregation of Jehovah's Witnesses, 26 July 2017 (www.gov.uk/government/publications/manchester-new-moston-congregation-of-jehovahs-witnesses-inquiry-report/manchester-new-moston-congregation-of-jehovahs-witnesses#conclusions).

6   Nicholas Deakin et al, *Meeting the Challenge of Change: Voluntary Action into the 21st Century – The Report of the Commission on the Future of the Voluntary Sector*, National Council for Voluntary Organisations, 1 January 1996, ISBN-10: 071991499X (not available online).

7   House of Lords Select Committee on Charities, *Stronger Charities for a Stronger Society*, 26 March 2017 (https://publications.parliament.uk/pa/ld201617/ldselect/ldchar/133/133.pdf).

8   Civil Society Futures, *Civil Society in England: Its Current State and Future Opportunity*, November 2018 (https://civilsocietyfutures.org/wp-content/uploads/sites/6/2018/11/Civil-Society-Futures__Civil-Society-in-England__small-1.pdf).

9   Gov.uk, Baroness Stowell's speech at the Navca annual conference, 7 December 2018 (https://www.gov.uk/government/speeches/baroness-stowells-speech-at-the-nacva-annual-conference-2018).

10 Andrew Purkis, 'Strengths and weaknesses of the Civil Society Futures report', *Civil Society*, 13 March 2019 (www.civilsociety.co.uk/voices/andrew-purkis-strengths-and-weaknesses-of-the-civil-society-futures-report.html).

11 Pro Bono Economics, Press release: 17 commissioners appointed to lead new Commission on Civil Society, 9 October 2020 (www.probonoeconomics.com/news/17-commissioners-assembled-to-lead-new-commission-on-civil-society).

12 Department for Digital, Culture, Media and Sport, *Civil Society Strategy: Building a Future that Works for Everyone*, 29 August 2018 (www.gov.uk/government/publications/civil-society-strategy-building-a-future-that-works-for-everyone).

13 Julia Unwin, 'Government and charities don't do enough to give people power', *Civil Society News*, 14 August 2018 (www.civilsociety.co.uk/voices/julia-unwin-charity-and-voluntary-organisations-don-t-do-enough-to-give-people-power.html).

14 Rebecca Cooney, 'Civil society plans "a timid, tick-box exercise", says shadow charities minister', *Third Sector*, 20 November 2017 (www.thirdsector.co.uk/civil-society-plans-a-timid-tick-box-exercise-says-shadow-charities-minister/policy-and-politics/article/1450413).

15 Vicky Browning, 'We've got the style: now what about the substance?', Blog post, 19 September 2018 (https://acevoblogs.wordpress.com/2018/09/19/weve-got-the-style-now-what-about-the-substance/).

16 Kirsty Weakley, 'Baroness Barran: "Job number one as minister for civil society is to listen to charities"', *Civil Society News*, 16 September 2019 (www.civilsociety.co.uk/news/baroness-barran-job-number-one-as-minister-for-civil-society-is-to-listen-to-charities.html).

17 Lloyds Bank Foundation, 'Lloyds Bank Foundation for England and Wales comment on the implementation of the Civil Society Strategy', 8 August 2019 (www.lloydsbankfoundation.org.uk/our-impact/news-and-blogs/lloyds-bank-foundation-for-england-and-wales-comment-on-the-implementation-of-the-civil-society-strategy).

18 Joe Saxton, 'Eight flaws that the coronavirus crisis reveals about the charity sector', *nfpSynergy* blog, 14 May 2020 (https://nfpsynergy.net/blog/eight-flaws-coronavirus-crisis-reveals-about-charity-sector).

19 Orianna Rosa Royle, 'Prime minister asks MP Danny Kruger to review sector's role in Covid-19 recovery', *Third Sector*, 26 June 2020 (www.thirdsector.co.uk/prime-minister-asks-mp-danny-kruger-review-sectors-role-covid-19-recovery/policy-and-politics/article/1687907).

20 Danny Kruger MP, *Levelling Up Our Communities: Proposals for a New Social Covenant*, September 2020 (www.dannykruger.org.uk/sites/www.dannykruger.org.uk/files/2020-09/Levelling%20Up%20Our%20Communities-Danny%20Kruger.pdf).

21 Letter from Boris Johnson to Danny Kruger MP, 24 September 2020 (www.dannykruger.org.uk/sites/www.dannykruger.org.uk/files/2020-09/0239_001.pdf).

22 Jay Kennedy, 'Danny Kruger's review inspires a sense of meta-policy-deja-vu', Directory of Social Change website, 24 September 2020 (www.dsc.org.uk/content/danny-krugers-report-inspires-a-sense-of-meta-policy-deja-vu/?dm_i=6S7,71XVY,2MS0M3,SGYT8,1).

23 Legislation.gov.uk, *Dormant Bank and Building Society Accounts Act 2008* (www.legislation.gov.uk/ukpga/2008/31/contents).

24 Kruger, *Levelling Up*, p 41.

25 Rebecca Cooney, 'Charities have become more ethical in the use of donors' data, says Information Commissioner', *Third Sector*, 15 January 2020 (www.thirdsector.co.uk/charities-become-ethical-use-donors-data-says-information-commissioner/fundraising/article/1670949).

26 National Council for Voluntary Organisations, 'Charity ethical principles', 18 January 2019 (www.ncvo.org.uk/policy-and-research/ethics/ethical-principles).

27 *Charity Governance Code* (www.charitygovernancecode.org/en/front-page).

28 Sarah Atkinson, *The New Charity Governance Code: Essential Reading for All Trustees*, Charity Commission blog, 13 July 2017 (https://charitycommission.blog.gov.uk/tag/governance-code/).

29 'Charity Governance Code: Updating the Code' (www.charitygovernancecode.org/en/about-the-code-1/improving-the-code).

Chapter 20

1 Charity Commission for England and Wales, *Taken on Trust – The Awareness and Effectiveness of Charity Trustees in England and Wales*, January 2017, p 31 (https://assets.publishing.service.gov.uk/government/uploads/system/uploads/attachment_data/file/658766/20171113_Taken_on_Trust_awareness_and_effectiveness_of_charity_trustees.pdf).

2 Ibid, p 17.

3 Association of Charitable Foundations, *Foundation Giving Trends 2019*, p 16 (www.acf.org.uk/downloads/publications/ACF_Foundation_Giving_Trends_2019.pdf).

4 Green Park, *Third Sector Leadership 2000*, June 2018 (www.green-park.co.uk/insights/third-sector-leadership-2-000/).

5 Steven Morris, 'Poppy seller who killed herself got 3,000 charity requests for donations a year', *The Guardian*, 20 January 2016 (www.theguardian.com/society/2016/jan/20/poppy-seller-who-killed-herself-got-up-to-3000-charity-mailings-a-year).

6 Tania Mason, 'Donors must realise that good governance must be paid for, ActionAid chair says', *Civil Society News*, 4 November 2015 (www.civilsociety.co.uk/news/donors-must-realise-that-good-governance-must-be-paid-for--actionaid-chair-says.html).

7 UK Parliament, 'Charity Commission not fit for purpose', 5 February 2014 (www.parliament.uk/business/committees/committees-a-z/commons-select/public-accounts-committee/news/publication-of-report-tax-reliefs-on-charitable-donations/).

8 National Audit Office, *Regulatory Effectiveness of the Charity Commission*, 4 December 2013 (www.nao.org.uk/report/regulatory-effectiveness-charity-commission-2/).

9 Gov.uk, *List of Charity Commission 'CC' Guidance Publications*, 11 September 2019 (www.gov.uk/government/collections/list-of-charity-commission-cc-guidance-publications).

10 BBC News, 'Charities given "last chance" on fundraising', 25 January 2016 (www.bbc.co.uk/news/uk-35395456).

11 Information Commissioner's Office, 'Charity fundraising practices' (https://ico.org.uk/your-data-matters/charity-fundraising-practices/).

12 Sir Stuart Etherington, Lord Leigh of Hurley, Baroness Pitkeathley and Lord Wallace of Saltaire, *Regulating Fundraising for the Future: Trust in Charities, Confidence in Fundraising Regulation*, September 2015 (www.ncvo.org.uk/images/documents/policy_and_research/giving_and_philanthropy/fundraising-review-report-2015.pdf).

13 Royal Courts of Justice, Case No: CR-2017-006113, 12 February 2021, para 911 (https://www.judiciary.uk/wp-content/uploads/2021/02/Official-Receiver-v-Batmanghelidjh-judgment-120221.pdf).

14 Charity Commission for England and Wales, *Taken on Trust*, p 31.

15 Ibid, p 8.

16 Fundraising Regulator, *The Charities (Protection and Social Investment) Act 2016: Good Practice Guidance on Reporting Your Fundraising*, 15 January 2020

(www.fundraisingregulator.org.uk/more-from-us/resources/charities-protection-and-social-investment-act-2016-good-practice-guidance).

17 Charity Commission, *The Royal National Institute of Blind People and RNIB Charity*, statutory inquiry report, 25 June 2020 (www.gov.uk/government/publications/charity-inquiry-the-royal-national-institute-of-blind-people-and-rnib-charity/).

18 Kirsty Weakley, 'RNIB's governance failures led to young people being harmed, inquiry finds', *Civil Society News*, 25 June 2020 (https://www.civilsociety.co.uk/news/rnib-s-governance-failures-led-to-young-people-being-harmed-inquiry-finds.html).

19 Charity Commission for England and Wales, *Taken on Trust*, p 22.

20 Kirsty Weakley, '"Broken" governance model for large charities needs radical reform, says lawyer', *Civil Society News*, 22 February 2019 (www.civilsociety.co.uk/news/broken-governance-model-for-large-charities-needs-radical-reform-says-lawyer.html).

21 Cliff Mills, *Co-operative Governance Fit to Build Resilience in the Face of Complexity*, International Co-operative Alliance, 2015, pp 104–16 (www.ica-ap.coop/sites/ica-ap.coop/files/ICA%20GOVERNANCE%20PAPER%20-%20EN.pdf).

22 Legislation.gov.uk, *The Health and Social Care (Community Health and Standards) Act 2003* (www.legislation.gov.uk/ukpga/2003/43/pdfs/ukpga_20030043_en.pdf) and the *Health and Social Care Act 2012, Part 4, NHS Foundation Trusts and NHS Trusts* (www.legislation.gov.uk/ukpga/2012/7/part/4/enacted).

23 It is called the 'Council of Governors' in NHS Foundation Trusts.

24 Peter Cardy, 'Doing four jobs? You need treatment', *Third Sector*, 15 December 2016 (www.thirdsector.co.uk/peter-cardy-doing-four-jobs-need-treatment/article/1418672).

Chapter 21

1 National Council for Voluntary Organisations, *Charity Ethical Principles*, January 2019 (www.ncvo.org.uk/images/documents/policy_and_research/ethics/Charity-Ethical-Principles.pdf).

2 Parliament.uk, *Oxfam Great Britain: Written evidence to International Development Select Committee on Sexual Exploitation in the Aid Sector*, 20 February 2018 (http://data.parliament.uk/writtenevidence/committeeevidence.svc/evidencedocument/international-development-committee/sexual-exploitation-and-abuse-in-the-aid-sector/written/79130.pdf).

3 Charity Commission for England and Wales, *Statement of the Results of an Inquiry: Oxfam*, 11 June 2019, p 71 (https://assets.publishing.service.gov.uk/government/uploads/system/uploads/attachment_data/file/807945/Statement_of_the_Results_of_an_Inquiry_Oxfam.pdf).

4 Parliament.uk, *Oxfam Great Britain: Written evidence*.

5   David Ainsworth, 'Six Oxfam staff in Haiti found guilty of misconduct', *Third Sector*, 7 September 2011 (www.thirdsector.co.uk/six-oxfam-staff-haiti-found-guilty-misconduct/management/article/1089610).

6   Parliament.uk, *Sexual Violence and Exploitation: The Experience of Refugee Children in Liberia, Guinea and Sierra Leone*, February 2002 (www.parliament.uk/documents/commons-committees/international-development/2002-Report-of-sexual-exploitation-and-abuse-Save%20the%20Children.pdf).

7   Sean O'Neill, 'Oxfam workers claim bosses harassed them', *The Times*, 28 October 2017 (www.thetimes.co.uk/article/oxfam-workers-claim-bosses-harassed-them-grtbmwssq).

8   Charity Commission for England and Wales, *Oxfam: Case Report*, 19 December 2017 (www.gov.uk/government/publications/charity-case-report-oxfam/).

9   Sean O'Neill, 'Oxfam in Haiti: "It was like a Caligula orgy with prostitutes in Oxfam T-shirts"', *The Times*, 9 February 2018 (www.thetimes.co.uk/article/oxfam-in-haiti-it-was-like-a-caligula-orgy-with-prostitutes-in-oxfam-t-shirts-p32wlk0rp).

10   Parliament.uk, *Written evidence submitted by Dame Barbara Stocking*, 22 June 2018 (http://data.parliament.uk/writtenevidence/committeeevidence.svc/evidencedocument/international-development-committee/sexual-exploitation-and-abuse-in-the-aid-sector/written/86097.pdf).

11   House of Commons International Development Committee, *Sexual Exploitation and Abuse in the International Aid Sector, Annex 2: Exchanges of Correspondence Arising from Oral Evidence Given*, 23 July 2018, pp 104, 105 (https://publications.parliament.uk/pa/cm201719/cmselect/cmintdev/840/840.pdf).

12   House of Commons International Development Committee, *Oral Evidence: Sexual Exploitation in the Aid Sector*, 20 February 2018, HC 840, Q81 (http://data.parliament.uk/writtenevidence/committeeevidence.svc/evidencedocument/international-development-committee/sexual-exploitation-and-abuse-in-the-aid-sector/oral/78764.pdf).

13   House of Commons International Development Committee, *Sexual Exploitation and Abuse in the International Aid Sector*, p 8.

14   Charity Commission for England and Wales, 'Statement of the results of an inquiry: Oxfam', 11 June 2019, p 135 (https://assets.publishing.service.gov.uk/government/uploads/system/uploads/attachment_data/file/807945/Statement_of_the_Results_of_an_Inquiry_Oxfam.pdf).

15   Parliament.uk, *Written evidence from Helen Evans, former head of safeguarding at Oxfam GB from 2012 to 2015* (http://data.parliament.uk/writtenevidence/committeeevidence.svc/evidencedocument/international-development-committee/sexual-exploitation-and-abuse-in-the-aid-sector/written/81153.pdf).

16   Mark Goldring, 'The challenges of Haiti 2011 and lessons for how we approach safeguarding', *Oxfam Annual Review 2018* (www.oxfam.

org.uk/what-we-do/about-us/plans-reports-and-policies/living-our-values).

17 House of Commons International Development Committee, *Progress on Tackling the Sexual Exploitation and Abuse of Aid Beneficiaries*, 14 January 2021, p 5 (https://committees.parliament.uk/publications/4275/documents/43423/default/).

18 Andy Ricketts, 'Sexual exploitation of aid recipients remains "a scourge", group of MPs conclude', *Third Sector*, 14 January 2021 (www.thirdsector.co.uk/sexual-exploitation-aid-recipients-remains-a-scourge-group-mps-conclude).

19 Simon Walters, 'He grabbed her hips, pulled her hair and forced his thumb into her mouth in a sexual way', *Daily Mail*, 10 February 2018 (www.dailymail.co.uk/news/article-5376593/Jo-Coxs-husband-grope-claim.html).

20 Charity Commission for England and Wales, *Charity Inquiry: The Save the Children Fund (Save the Children UK)*, 4 March 2020, pp 32 and 22 (https://assets.publishing.service.gov.uk/government/uploads/system/uploads/attachment_data/file/870390/The_Save_the_Children_Fund__Save_the_Children_UK__Inquiry_report.pdf).

21 Rebecca Cooney, 'How the RNLI turned the tide on a national media storm', *Third Sector*, 14 November 2019 (www.thirdsector.co.uk/search/articles?KeyWords=RNLI&HeadlinesOnly=false&SortOrder=2&Date=2019).

22 Becky Slack, *Effective Media Relations for Charities*, Social Partnership Marketing LLP, 2016, p 6.

23 Sam Burne James, 'Charities often have a defensive mindset when criticised, says William Shawcross', *Third Sector*, 17 September 2014 (www.thirdsector.co.uk/charities-often-defensive-mindset-when-criticised-william-shawcross-says/governance/article/1312460).

24 Andy Ricketts, 'Larger charities must "give up some power", says Shelter head', *Third Sector*, 12 October 2017 (www.thirdsector.co.uk/larger-charities-give-power-says-shelter-head/management/article/1447235).

25 National Council for Voluntary Organisations, 'Constructive voices: helping charities tell their story' (www.ncvo.org.uk/about-us/media-centre/constructive-voices/for-charities).

26 CharityComms, 'AskCharity' (https://askcharity.charitycomms.org.uk/askcharity).

27 Cooney, 'How the RNLI turned the tide'.

28 Slack, *Effective Media Relations for Charities*, p 89.

29 Charity Commission for England and Wales, *Charity Inquiry: The Save the Children Fund*, p 22.

30 Independent Oversight Panel, *Guiding the Development of the Charities Sorp*, June 2019 (https://assets.publishing.service.gov.uk/government/uploads/system/uploads/attachment_data/file/806670/Guiding_the_Development_of_the_Charities_SORP.pdf).

31 Liam Kay, 'Kids Company puts the limits of audits under scrutiny', *Third Sector*, 21 January 2016 (www.thirdsector.co.uk/kids-company-puts-limitations-audits-scrutiny/finance/article/1379718).

32 The Charity Commission for Northern Ireland, the Charity Commission for England and Wales, and the Office of the Scottish Charity Regulator, *Charities Sorp (FRS102)*, January 2019 (www.charitysorp.org/media/647945/charities-sorp-frs102-2019a.pdf).

33 Ibid, p 37.

34 nfpSynergy, *Sorped Out: Why Financial Reporting for Charities Should Be Reformed*, March 2018 (https://nfpsynergy.net/free-report/sorped-out-why-financial-reporting-charities-should-be-reformed).

35 nfpSynergy, 'Public irritation with fundraising declines', October 2016 (https://nfpsynergy.net/press-release/public-irritation-fundraisers-declines#downloads).

36 Charity Commission for England and Wales, *Trust in Charities 2018* (https://assets.publishing.service.gov.uk/government/uploads/system/uploads/attachment_data/file/723566/Charity_Commission_-_Trust_in_Charities_2018_-_Report.pdf).

37 Independent Oversight Panel, *Guiding the Development of the Charities Sorp*, June 2019, p 6 (https://assets.publishing.service.gov.uk/government/uploads/system/uploads/attachment_data/file/806670/Guiding_the_Development_of_the_Charities_SORP.pdf)

38 Chartered Institute of Public Finance and Accountancy, *Charities Sorp Committee Minutes*, 17 July 2019 (www.charitysorp.org/media/647963/minutes170719.pdf).

39 The Charities Sorp-making Body, *The New SORP Development Process, What Is Changing, How You Can Get Involved, and the Impact We Hope to Make*, September 2019 (www.charitysorp.org/media/647696/the-new-sorp-development-process.pdf).

40 nfpSynergy, *Show Me the Money! The Challenges in How Charities Present Financial Information to the Public*, 12 March 2020 (https://nfpsynergy.net/free-report/show-me-money-report).

41 National Council for Voluntary Organisations, *Report of the Inquiry into Charity Senior Executive Pay and Guidance for Trustees on Setting Remuneration*, April 2014 (www.ncvo.org.uk/images/documents/about_us/our-finances-and-pay/Executive_Pay_Report.pdf).

Chapter 22

1 William Beveridge, *Voluntary Action: A Report on Methods of Social Advance*, Abingdon: Routledge, 2015 (originally published 1948), p 8.

2 Panel on the Independence of the Voluntary Sector, *An Independent Mission: The Voluntary Sector in 2015*, The Baring Foundation, 11 February 2015 (https://cdn.baringfoundation.org.uk/wp-content/uploads/2015/02/IP-Mission.pdf).

3 Charity Commission for England and Wales, *Stand and Deliver: The Future of Charities Providing Public Services*, February 2007, p 8 (https://

assets.publishing.service.gov.uk/government/uploads/system/uploads/attachment_data/file/284716/RS15text.pdf).

4   Andy Ricketts, 'Funders' friend', *Third Sector*, 14 March 2007 (www.thirdsector.co.uk/funders-friend/management/article/643412).

5   Ministry of Housing, Communities and Local Government website: 'News story: My 38 years in the world of rough sleeping by Jeremy Swain, Deputy Director for the Rough Sleeping Initiative', 4 October 2018 (www.gov.uk/government/news/my-38-years-in-the-world-of-rough-sleeping-by-jeremy-swain-deputy-director-for-the-rough-sleeping-initiative).

6   Panel on the Independence of the Voluntary Sector, *An Independent Mission*, p 53.

7   Melanie Phillips, 'Charities are being hijacked and turned into pawns in Labour's class war', *Daily Mail*, 20 July 2009 (www.dailymail.co.uk/debate/article-1200801/MELANIE-PHILLIPS-Charities-hijacked-turned-pawns-Labours-class-war.html).

8   William Shawcross, 'Britain's humiliation', *National Review* online, 29 April 2010 (www.nationalreview.com/corner/britains-humiliation-william-shawcross/).

9   Stephen Lloyd, 'Back to the future', *Civil Society News*, 1 October 2014 (www.civilsociety.co.uk/finance/back-to-the-future.html).

10 National Council for Voluntary Organisations, *Charity Commission Independence: NCVO Discussion Paper*, April 2015 (www.ncvo.org.uk/images/documents/policy_and_research/independence_and_values/charity-commission-independence-ncvo-discussion-paper-april-2015.pdf).

11 Liam Kay, 'Minister denies cronyism in appointment of Baroness Stowell', *Third Sector*, 15 March 2018 (www.thirdsector.co.uk/minister-denies-cronyism-appointment-baroness-stowell/policy-and-politics/article/1459590).

12 Andrew Hind, 'Where now for the political independence of the commission?', *Civil Society News*, 7 February 2018 (www.civilsociety.co.uk/voices/andrew-hind-where-now-for-the-political-independence-of-the-charity-commission.html#sthash.IH2F13Wr.dpuf).

13 Charity Commission for England and Wales, *Guidance, Public Service Delivery: Rules for Charities*, 23 May 2013 (www.gov.uk/guidance/public-service-delivery-rules-for-charities).

14 The Joseph Rowntree Charitable Trust is a grant-maker set up in 1904 by the Quaker founder of the Rowntree chocolate-making company in York. It had funded a group called Cage that had been set up to advocate for what it called the victims of the war on terror. Cage had in the past supported Mohammed Emwazi, nicknamed Jihadi John, who later fought for the so-called Islamic State in Syria and beheaded several Western hostages.

15 Order in the High Court of Justice, Queen's Bench Division, the Administrative Court, before the Lord Chief Justice and Mr Justice Ouseley, 21 October 2015 (https://assets.publishing.service.gov.uk/government/uploads/system/uploads/attachment_data/file/479701/court_order.pdf).

16 Gov.uk, Government response: *Charity Commission Statement: Charities Funding Cage*, 6 March 2015 (www.gov.uk/government/news/charity-commission-statement-charities-funding-cage).

17 Gov.uk, Speech: *Upholding Public Trust and Confidence*, Charity Commission Chairman William Shawcross speaking at Paris Smith's Charity Conference, 24 March 2015 (www.gov.uk/government/speeches/upholding-public-trust-and-confidence).

18 Susannah Birkwood and Stephen Cook, 'Analysis: the Joseph Rowntree Charitable Foundation vs the Charity Commission', *Third Sector*, 23 April 2015 (www.thirdsector.co.uk/analysis-joseph-rowntree-charitable-trust-vs-charity-commission/governance/article/1343596).

19 Ibid.

20 Gov.uk, Speech: *Baroness Stowell's Speech at the Navca Annual Conference 2018*, 7 December 2018 (www.gov.uk/government/speeches/baroness-stowells-speech-at-the-nacva-annual-conference-2018).

21 Jay Kennedy, 'The Charity Commission is losing the "trust and confidence" of charities', *Directory of Social Change*, blog post, 9 October 2019 (www.dsc.org.uk/content/the-charity-commission-is-losing-the-trust-and-confidence-of-charities/).

22 Lord Hodgson of Astley Abbotts, *Trusted and Independent: Giving Charity Back to Charities. Review of the Charities Act 2006*, London: The Stationery Office, July 2012 (https://assets.publishing.service.gov.uk/government/uploads/system/uploads/attachment_data/file/79275/Charities-Act-Review-2006-report-Hodgson.pdf).

Index

Page references for notes are followed by n